SAMS
Teach Yourself

Networking

in 24 Hours

Joe Habraken
Matt Hayden

THIRD EDITION

SAMS 800 East 96th Street, Indianapolis, Indiana, 46240 USA

Sams Teach Yourself Networking in 24 Hours, Third Edition

International Standard Book Number: 0-672-32608-6

Library of Congress Catalog Card Number: 2003094095

Printed in the United States of America

First Printing: May 2004

07   06   05   04   4   3   2   1

Trademarks

Warning and Disclaimer

Bulk Sales

Sams Publishing offers excellent discounts on this book when ordered in quantity for bulk purchases or special sales. For more information, please contact

U.S. Corporate and Government Sales
1-800-382-3419
corpsales@pearsontechgroup.com

For sales outside of the U.S., please contact

International Sales
1-317-428-3341
international@pearsontechgroup.com

Acquisitions Editor
Jenny Watson

Development Editor
Jonathan Steever

Managing Editor
Charlotte Clapp

Senior Project Editor
George Nedeff

Copy Editor
Rhonda Tinch-Mize

Indexer
Rebecca Salemo

Proofreader
Linda Seifert

Technical Editor
Marc Charney

Publishing Coordinator
Vanessa Evans

Interior Designer
Gary Adair

Cover Designer
Alan Clements

Page Layout
Kelly Maish

Contents at a Glance

Part V: Introduction to Network Administration

Part VI: The Future of Networking

Table of Contents

About the Authors

Matt Hayden is a systems engineer for a Silicon Valley technical firm. His primary expertise is operating systems and networking, and his background includes a stint as a technologist for a merchant banking firm. Matt holds a bachelor's degree in History and a master's degree in English. When he's not networking or traveling, he spends his time playing music, reading, and cycling.

Joe Habraken is a best-selling author, information technology professional, and educator. Joe has more than 15 years of experience as a network administrator, consultant, and IT professional. He is currently an assistant professor at the University of New England where he teaches a variety of information technology classes, introducing undergraduate students to computer basics, software applications, Web design, and the use of personal computers in business settings. His books include *Microsoft Office 2003 All in One*, *Practical Cisco Routers*, and *Sams Teach Yourself Microsoft Server 2003 in 24 Hours*.

Dedication

To all the computer professionals out there who try to make some sense out of the chaos that is information technology.

Acknowledgments

It really does take a team to create a book that covers a subject that seems to change on a daily basis.

First of all, I would like to thank Jenny Watson, our acquisitions editor. She worked hard to get the book through the approval process and assembled the team who worked on this book. She is truly a joy to work with.

I would also like to thank Jon Steever, the development editor, who burned the midnight oil to make sure that this was the best book possible. He also made many useful suggestions related to the subject matter included in the book. Another big thanks goes out to our technical editor, Marc Charney, who verified the technical aspects of the text and provided expert advice on the material we covered.

I would also like to thank Rhonda Tinch-Mize, our copy editor, for diligently cleaning up the text and making a number of great suggestions; finally, a big thanks to the project editor, George Nedeff, who ran the last leg of the race and made sure that this book got into print (and into your local bookstore). Thank you all very much!

We Want to Hear from You!

As the reader of this book, *you* are our most important critic and commentator. We value your opinion and want to know what we're doing right, what we could do better, what areas you'd like to see us publish in, and any other words of wisdom you're willing to pass our way.

You can email or write me directly to let me know what you did or didn't like about this book—as well as what we can do to make our books stronger.

Please note that I cannot help you with technical problems related to the topic of this book, and that due to the high volume of mail I receive, I might not be able to reply to every message.

When you write, please be sure to include this book's title and author as well as your name and phone or email address. I will carefully review your comments and share them with the author and editors who worked on the book.

Email: networking@samspublishing.com

Mail: Mark Taber
           Associate Publisher
           Sams Publishing
           800 East 96th Street
           Indianapolis, IN 46240 USA

Reader Services

For more information about this book or others from Sams Publishing, visit our Web site at www.samspublishing.com. Type the ISBN (excluding hyphens) or the title of the book in the Search box to find the book you're looking for.

Introduction

There is no doubt that computer technology continues to evolve at a rapid pace. And although the basic client/server model that we embrace for most networking services has remained a constant, computer hardware, software, and connectivity options still continue to change and grow, making the body of knowledge necessary to be a network administrator a constantly moving target.

Although it has always been a business necessity for medium and large companies to network their computer services, the options for networking make it possible for even the smallest companies to deploy networks. This means that people with the knowledge of how networks operate and how to deploy networks remain in demand even though recent years have seen a somewhat depressed computer technology job market.

This book provides a basic resource for someone who wants to get up to speed on networking theory and networking technologies. Because each piece of computer and networking hardware has its own particular idiosyncrasies and would require a book the size of the New York City white pages, this book concentrates on fundamental concepts and information shared across the different networking hardware and software options. Emphasis is placed on solid planning and the best practices for deploying and administrating networks that remain operational and secure.

Conventions Used in This Book

Certain conventions have been followed in this book to help you digest all the material. For example, new terms appear in **bold**. These terms can also be found in the Glossary, which supplies a short definition for each term.

At the beginning of each hour, you'll find a list of the major topics that will be covered. The end of each hour provides a Q&A Workshop, which provides a list of questions that have been posed from what we consider the reader's perspective. The answers will help you better understand the practical applications of the material covered in the hour.

You will also find special notes used throughout this book. These notes are accompanied by additional information on a subject, supply asides that provide useful insight and tips, or give warnings that can help you steer clear of problem areas related to a certain subject or technology. These notes are as follows:

These sidebars include additional information related to the current topic, but they do not have to be read in order for you to have complete understanding of the information provided in the regular text.

These sidebars contain higher-level information and tips related to a topic that expands on the material provided in a part of the hour.

Watch Out!

These note boxes attempt to provide you with warnings related to certain processes and practices. They attempt to keep you on track so that you can avoid pitfalls related to a particular hardware or software issue.

How This Book Is Organized

This book has been completely updated for its third edition. New coverage has been added related to Microsoft Windows Server 2003, the latest version of Microsoft's powerful network operating system. Expanded coverage of the Linux platform and the basics of wireless networking have also been provided in this latest edition.

The book is divided into five parts. Each part provides you a body of information that covers a particular area related to computer networking.

Part I of this book, "What Exactly Is Networking?," provides an introduction to networking that includes an overview of what networking is. The section provides you with a firm grasp of the broader issues related to how hardware and software work together to provide the basic platform that allows us to network computers and other devices.

Part II of the book, "The Basics," is dedicated to the concepts underlying data networking. We take a hard look at how packet-switched networking operates and look at how LAN and WAN technologies work. This section includes a discussion of networking protocols and the theoretical model that we use to discuss how network data is transformed as it moves from a sending computer to a receiving computer.

Part III, "Building Networks," walks you through the process of planning and building a network from conception to implementation. Issues related to capacity planning, building the network, and then connecting to the Internet are included as part of the discussion.

Part IV, "Network Operating Systems and Providing Network-Wide Services," provides an overview of network operating systems such as Microsoft Windows Server 2003 and Red Hat Linux. This section of the book also takes a look at issues related to the TCP/IP protocol and how you provide services on your network.

Part V, "Introduction to Network Administration," looks at the issues related to actually administering a running network. This section includes discussion on both troubleshooting and administrative tips and discusses issues related to security. Implementing new technologies such as wireless networking is also discussed.

Part VI, "The Future of Networking" looks at current and future implementation of wireless technology and networking. This section discusses the issues related to securing WiFi technology, as well as projects the future implementation of Linux, the Internet and the evolution of IPv6 and wireless networking.

Exploring the world of computer networking and acquiring the skills to be a network administrator is a truly exciting endeavor. This book should be viewed as your first stepping stone on your technical and personal journey.

PART I

What Exactly Is Networking?

HOUR 1

An Overview of Networking

In this hour, you'll have the opportunity to learn about the following topics:

▶ How we define a network

▶ Why you might need a network

▶ How networks are put together

▶ The different types of computer networks

▶ How Internet connectivity relates to your network

Computer networks are everywhere. You get your cash from the ATM (a computer), and computers are used by telemarketers to call you on the phone. Each of these instances of computer use requires a network. We all rely on the largest network in the world, the Internet, whenever we send email or browse the Web. Even your digital cable television is served to your home via a network. You really can't escape computers or the networks that enable the various computers that populate the networks to share data.

Although data networks have become an integral part of our lives (as have computers), most people consider networking too complex of a subject matter to even consider tackling the possibility of setting up their own computer network.

But I will share a secret: *Networking isn't really all that complicated.* It doesn't require a membership in any secret societies nor years and years of study.

Gaining the ability to create a computer network really only requires an understanding of some fundamental concepts and then the nuts and bolts common sense required to implement the software and the hardware aspects of the network's infrastructure.

Although there's a lot of technical terminology in this book. Don't let it scare you away. Computer networking, like any other technical discipline, has its own vernacular. Try to familiarize yourself with as many of the concepts and terms presented here as possible; the more jargon and acronyms you recognize, the easier it will be to learn. (The glossary at the end of this book can help if you forget a term or two.) A good knowledge base is one of your best assets for successful networking.

Did you Know?

Reading Is Fundamental!

The more you read about networking concepts and issues related to computer connectivity, the easier it will be to implement and maintain your own network. Check out www.informit.com for a variety of articles related to networking, software, and other computer-related topics.

What Is a Network?

In simplest terms, a computer network is two or more connected computers. The actual physical connection between the computers can take a number of forms, which include physical cabling and wireless connectivity strategies; we discuss the software and hardware required to make the "physical" connection in Hour 10, " Selecting Network Hardware and Software"

There is more to networking computers, however, than just supplying a connection between the computers. There are also some basic rules related to the actual communication that must take place between the computers if they are going to be capable of exchanging data. A very general set of requirements related to the computer networking and data communication would look something like the following:

▶ All hosts on a network must use the same standards for sending and receiving data.

▶ Information must be delivered without any corruption of data.

▶ There must be a method for ensuring that a destination computer acknowledges receipt of some data, and not of other data, as required.

▶ Computers (hosts) on a network must be capable of determining the origin and destination of a piece of information.

▶ There must be a standardized and scalable method for assigning network addresses.

▶ Computers (hosts) on a network must be capable of identifying each other across the network.

▶ For security and management, there must be a standard method for identifying and verifying devices connected to the network.

▶ The network should have so little effect on users that they need not know what applications run locally and what run across a network.

This certainly isn't an exhaustive list of the requirements that must be met for computers to communicate over the network. However, they do give you an idea of some of the issues that had to be faced when computer and networking gurus first tackled the overall concept of sharing data between computers. Obviously for computer networks to function, there must be software that provides for data communication; this software will have to follow a set of rules so that the data moves from source to destination and is actually readable and usable upon arrival.

Networks can be as simple as a file transfer protocol that enables two computers connected with a serial cable to communicate. Networks can also be as complex as the high-end banking systems that transfer data on pulses of light in fiber-optic cables. Despite the fact that these two examples operate at opposite ends of the data communication spectrum (as far as complexity is concerned), each has to follow the same fundamental rules that allow users to communicate over a network. We will explore both simple and complex networks in this book.

However, before we dive into the subject matter that provides for basic understanding of a network, we probably need to answer a nagging question related to computer networks. Why would you want to build a network?

Why Build a Network?

There are many reasons for building networks, whether they're computer networks or car-dealer networks. However diverse the reasons, they can ultimately be reduced to a few key points:

▶ They enable communications in ways that fundamentally change the way we view and interact with the world around us.

▶ They can, in a healthy organization, increase efficiency.

▶ They can help propagate standards, policies, procedures, and practices within an organization because of the ease of sharing information with members of the organization related to the organizational structure and its reason for being.

▶ Networks can help ensure that information is redundant—in other words, that it exists in more than one mind (or computer) at a time.

▶ They can offer access to resources that would otherwise be prohibitively expensive, unwieldy, unavailable, or all these things.

There are as many different reasons for building computer networks as the people and organizations building them. One person might have a bunch of computers at home—one for her, one for her kids, another for her husband. She wants to hook all the computers together so that they can have a common calendar and email—which (trust me) kids will read much more readily than they will a note on the fridge. Another person might have a small office with a couple of computers and a business DSL or cable connection, and wants to provide Internet access to all users. And then we have computer hobbyists who want to join together computers just because they can be joined together.

If you have a need to communicate or to share data, applications, Internet access, network games, or whatever and want to avoid running from machine to machine with disks and CD-ROMs, networking is the solution.

How Networks Are Put Together

If you were to break a network down into its simplest components, you'd have two pieces. One is the physical network—the wiring (or a wireless medium), network cards, computers, and other equipment the network uses to transmit data. The other is the logical arrangement of these physical pieces—the rules (which are software) that allow the physical pieces to work together. We will look at both of these broad categories in turn in this hour. Remember—all this is covered in more detail in the coming hours.

The Physical Network

The **physical network** is fairly easy to understand because it's easy to see—it's hardware! It's the wiring, network cards, computers, hubs, switches, printers, and all the other devices that enables the network to function.

While progress in wireless networking makes the physical connections between the various devices on the network seem a little more ethereal (wireless strategies such as wireless Ethernet are becoming more commonplace; wireless networking is discussed in Hour 23, "Security and Useablility"), how we describe the overall layout of the network is no different between those networks that use copper wire cables and those networks that use wireless strategies such as radio waves.

So, wireless connectivity aside, the physical network is all the equipment that you can actually hold in your hand. And although there are rules for how physical connections are established, physically connecting computers and other networking devices is a fairly straightforward endeavor.

Physical Layout—Network Topologies

As already mentioned, the physical side of the network is the various components that enable an actual physical connection between the computers. And whether you are using wires or a wireless strategy for connecting the computers, the connection point on the computer for the network medium is the **network interface card**, or **NIC**. The NIC handles a computer's interaction with the rest of the devices on the network.

When you connect computers together into a network, the type of connection medium (the actual type of physical cabling or wireless strategy) and network architecture that you use (such as Ethernet or IBM Token Ring; we discuss network architectures in Hour 10, "Selecting Network Hardware and Software") will dictate the overall layout or topology of the network. From a copper-wire medium perspective, only two topologies are still implemented today: star and ring.

The **star topology** uses a central connection point, usually a hub or a switch, and the computers on the network radiate out from this central connection point. A **ring topology** connects the computers so that the data moves from computer to computer via a ring. Although we differentiate between stars and rings, physically they pretty much look the same. Even ring networks have a central connection point that the computers connect to. It is actually how the logical network functions that really differentiates a star topology from a ring topology (see Chapter 10 for more about network architectures and their physical topologies).

So, in simplest terms, a **physical topology** is the arrangement of the connective medium (such as wires) on a network. Although stars and rings dominate new network installations, a third topology, the bus, still exists in older network implementations. A **bus** network is (essentially) a long cable with taps along its length to which computers connect. If any of the links between computers are broken, the network goes down.

Bus Architectures Are Fading Fast!

Ethernet 10BASE2 and 10BASE5 (early forms of the now ubiquitous Ethernet that used a bus topology) have more or less died out. We will, however, discuss these Ethernet topologies briefly in Chapter 10.

Let's take a closer look at the three different network topologies: bus, star, ring. We can then discuss some of the devices that would populate these physical topologies.

Physical Bus Topologies

The advantage of a bus-topology network is its simplicity—networking doesn't get much simpler than this (refer to Figure 1.1). Once the computers are physically connected to the wire, all you have to do is install the network software on each computer. In general, all the computers will be capable of seeing each other without difficulty. The downside of a bus network is that it has a lot of points of failure. If one of the links between any of the computers is broken, the network is down. And as of this writing (third edition, mid-2003), it would be difficult for you to actually purchase the cabling and devices that would allow you to configure a network with a bus topology. Bus topologies are a dead technology—with one of the many reason being that a bus network is very difficult to expand.

FIGURE 1.1
A diagram of a simple bus-topology network, showing how computers are connected together. Note that this is essentially a single wire punctuated by computers. One break in the wire causes the network to fail.

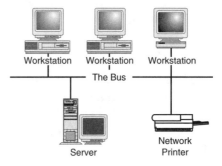

Physical Star Topologies

More complex networks are built on a physical star topology because this design is more robust and less prone to interruptions than a physical bus topology. In contrast to the bus topology in which the wire runs serially from computer to computer, star-topology networks use a junction box called a **hub** to connect computers to one another.

By the
Way

Switches Are Rapidly Replacing the Hub Switches

This provides for greater control of network bandwidth and provides a faster connection between computers that are rapidly replacing hubs as the central connecting point between networked computers.

All the computers connect to the hub using an individual cable. A computer architecture that uses the star topology is Ethernet 100BASE-T. Many readers might be familiar with this; if you have a cable or DSL Internet connection with a router/switch, it almost certainly uses 100BT Ethernet. Most current networks use some variation on this model.

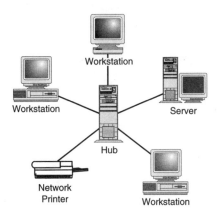

FIGURE 1.2
A simple star topology network.

Networks built on physical star topologies have a couple advantages over bus topologies. First and foremost is reliability. In a bus-topology network, disconnecting one computer is enough to crash the whole network; in a star-topology network, you can connect computers on-the-fly without causing network failures.

By the
Way

Other Network Architectures Embrace the Star Topology

Copper wire Ethernet or 10BaseT is not the only network architecture that embraces the star topology. Architectures using fiber-optic cable can also be arranged in a star topology. Examples are Gigabit Ethernet and Asynchronous Transfer Mode, also known as ATM. We'll discuss these later in the book. The key point is that these types of networking use a star layout for their wiring (or fiber).

Physical Ring Topologies

The physical layout of ring topologies (that use network architectures such as Token Ring and FDDI) actually will be arranged in the same physical star that we find in Ethernet star topology networks. The actual ring, which enables the data to circulate in a ring around the network (it's as if the computers are daisy-chained together in a circle) is a logical ring. This logical ring is provided by the connectivity device that is the central connection point for all the computers.

On an IBM Token Ring network, the central connection point is a Token Ring **MAU (Multistation Access Unit)**. The MAU is similar to a hub or switch in that it provides ports for physically connecting the computers on the network. However, as shown in Figure 1.3, the MAU moves the data from computer to computer in a path that duplicates a ring. (That's why it's called Token "Ring.")

Did you Know?

How Ethernet and Token Ring Are Different

We will discuss how different network architectures, such as Ethernet, Token Ring, and FDDI, move data on the computer and provide computers access to that data in Hour 3, "Getting Data From Here to There: How Computers Share Data."

FIGURE 1.3
A diagram of a simple Token Ring network.

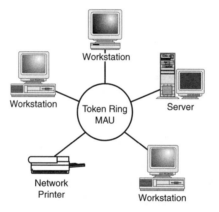

Another network architecture that uses a logical ring topology is **FDDI (Fiber Distributed Data Interface)**. FDDI networks run on optical fiber cables instead of copper cabling. FDDI's topology is very similar to that of Token Ring with one exception: A single computer can be connected to two concentrators/MAUs so that if one network connection fails, the other can automatically pick up the slack. Systems connected to more than one concentrator are called **dual homed** (see Figure 1.4), and are effectively connected to two rings simultaneously. FDDI is very fast. However, it is also very expensive to install and operate, so it is normally used only for high-end applications such as stock traders' terminals and other applications that demand the capability to push a lot of data over a wire.

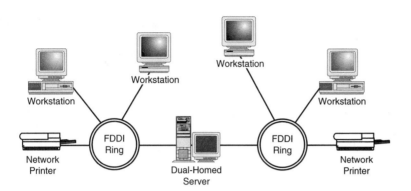

FIGURE 1.4
A diagram of a FDDI network, showing how dual-homed computers can be connected to multiple concentrators.

Network Devices

Earlier in this hour, we mentioned some of the reasons why you'd want a computer network. To get this functionality from your network, you need a host of **network devices** to connect to each other in specific ways. Without getting into the specifics of how to hook these things together, let's take a look at the basic network devices you'll encounter throughout this book. The first devices are computers and printers, neither of which require a network to function.

- A **workstation** is the computer on which a user does his work—hence workstation.

- A **server** is a computer whose resources are shared with other computers.

- A **network printer** is a printer connected to the network so that more than one user can print to it.

- An **Internet router** is a device that acts as a junction box that enables multiple computers to access the Internet through it. Internet routers can actually take the form of DSL routers and cable modems that enable broadband connections via a cable provider.

Figures 1.5, and 1.6, found later in this chapter, are schematic representations of these different types of devices connected to network wires.

Other devices that can be connected to a network were mentioned in the sections on physical topologies. They're absolutely central to the process of networking:

- **Routers** are devices that move data between networks to create larger networks. You'll learn more about them later in this hour and in Hours 3–5.

▶ Although **wiring and cabling** don't strictly sound like devices, they actually are pretty important to the process. Wire has to meet very stringent standards for networking to work properly, so it's included in the list of devices, although only peripherally.

By the way, if the number of terms you've encountered so far has been daunting, don't worry. To make certain that you're familiar with the jargon of networking, we'll revisit all these terms in much greater depth in the hours ahead.

The Varieties of Networks

The hardware and topologies that networks run on are only the beginning of networking. Once you understand the basic technical concepts, it's time to become familiar with the basic organizational concepts of networking: LAN (local area network) and WAN (wide area network).

It is important to remember that all the networks mentioned in this chapter are private networks. That is, they are used by one organization, even though the networks might be in more than one location. This is an important distinction, as detailed in the section on the Internet, later in this hour.

LANs

A **local area network**, or **LAN**, is the least complex organizational distinction of computer networks. A LAN is nothing more than a group of computers linked through a network—all located at a single site. LANs often come very close to fitting the descriptions shown in Figures 1.1 through 1.4, earlier in this chapter. LANs have the following parameters:

▶ They occupy one physical location, and one physical location only—hence the word local in the title.

▶ They have high-speed data transfer rates, typically 100 or 1,000 megabits per second.

▶ All data travels on the local network wiring.

Part of what makes a LAN a LAN is high-speed data transfer. Ethernet LANs usually transmit data at 100 megabits per second. For comparison, Token Ring operates at 4 and 16 megabits per second. FDDI and Fast Ethernet operate at a blistering 100 megabits per second or more. The fastest LANs run gigabit Ethernet.

Since about 2001, there's been a tremendous rise in the amount of wireless LANs (802.11b, 802.11g and 802.11a). Wireless LANs are in many ways simpler than wired LANs. Despite some ongoing security concerns, wireless LANs offer surprisingly good performance (up to 54Mbps) and ease of installation.

Did you Know?

What Are All Those Numbers?

Different connectivity strategies for networking are defined by the Institute of Electrical and Electronics Engineers, or IEEE. The specifications for wireless LANs include the IEEE specifications 802.11b, 802.11.g, and 802.11a. See Hour 23, "Security and Usability" for more information.

Although LANs are the simplest networks, it does not mean that they are either necessarily small or simple. LANs can become quite large and complex; it is not uncommon in trade press magazines to read about LANs with hundreds or thousands of users.

WANs

When geography (meaning the distance between company offices) requires that a series of LANs be connected, , it's time to build a **wide area network**, or **WAN**. Wide area networks are geographically scattered LANs joined together using high-speed interconnections and routers. A **router** is a device that manages data flows between networks.

How do you know how to get where you're going when you're driving in unfamiliar country? Chances are that you'll stop and ask for directions from the locals who know how to get *thay-uh* from *heah*, as we say in New England.

In a network, a router functions like the direction providing people you find along your route. Routers know the best ways for data to travel to get from point A to B—and they're always learning new routes.

Access to resources across a WAN is often limited by the speed of the phone line (some of the most popular digital phone lines have speeds of only 56 kilobits per second). Even full-blown phone company trunk lines, called *T-1s*, can carry only 1.5 megabits per second, and they can be very expensive. Although T-1 prices have come down with the rise of the Internet, it still isn't unusual to pay several thousand dollars a month to a phone company to use a T-1. When you contrast the speed of a 56-kilobits-per-second phone line or a 1.5-megabits-per-second T-1 with the speed of a local LAN or MAN running at 100 megabits per second, the slowness of digital phone lines is readily apparent. These speed restrictions are also called bandwidth issues. Of course, if you've got deep pockets, it's possible to run data over a T-3 (also called a DS3) line, which provides 45 megabits per second...faster than many networks.

Bandwidth is a term used to describe the maximum speed at which a given device (such as a network card or modem) can transfer data. In other words, measuring bandwidth is like measuring how much air a fan can move: A fan that can move 100 cubic feet of air per minute has a lower bandwidth than a fan that can move 1,000 cubic feet of air per minute. Bandwidth is measured in kilobits per second (Kbps) or megabits per second. Comparing megabits per second with kilobits per second is a lot like comparing a running person and a fast car: The car (which compares to megabits-per-second data speeds) is much faster than the runner (who compares to kilobits-per-second speeds).

WANs are often built when it is important that all users have the ability to access a common pool of information such as product databases or Automatic Teller Machine bank records. As long as the purpose of the WAN is well defined and limited, the speed restrictions imposed by phone lines are not an issue for network designers. If the quantity of data to be transmitted is less than or equal to the capacity of the line, the WAN works fine. Exceed the maximum bandwidth of the lines connecting the WAN, however, and your users will complain.

Unlike LANs, WANs always require routers. Because most of the traffic in a WAN takes place inside the LANs that make up the WAN, routers provide an important function—traffic control. Routers must be set up with information called routes (more on that in Chapter 14, "TCP/IP") that tell the router how to send data between networks. It's not very difficult to set up a router to do this; Cisco System's IOS (Internetworking Operating System) requires about a week of training, and you might not even need that if you can read a manual and know a bit about TCP/IP (more on that later).

Figure 1.5 shows a WAN configuration. Note that the main difference between a LAN and a WAN is that a WAN is essentially a series of LANs connected by routers.

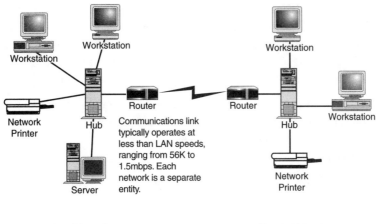

FIGURE 1.5
A typical WAN configuration.

How the Internet Relates to Your Network

The last ten years have seen an explosion of publicity for the Internet. Unless you've been in a cave somewhere, you've seen the proliferation of Web addresses, email addresses, and references to cyberspace that have pervaded the public consciousness. Dot-com mania invaded and was quickly followed by the "Dot bomb." Many Internet companies went belly up. This still has not cooled the public's desire to connect on the Internet nor has it changed the fact that the Internet provides a unique worldwide communication platform.

The goal of this section is to explain in very basic terms what the Internet is and what ramifications the Internet has for your local network. Ultimately, this section exists as a foil to the preceding material because it helps you understand how your network exists *vis-à-vis* the Internet, which is sort of the original network from which all other networks have descended.

What Is the Internet?

The standard answer to this question has been the following pithy quote:

> "The Internet is a network of networks."

Although no one really knows who first said this, it is probably fair to note that the speaker hadn't thought too much about his audience's level of familiarity with technology. A network of networks is a useful definition only if your audience already has some idea what a network is. Needless to say, most people don't have more than a terribly limited understanding of what a network is.

That definition is also somewhat inexact. The phrase "a network of networks" implies that all networks are open to all others, and that's not strictly true. There are public and private spaces on the Internet, and they interact in relatively specific, rules-based ways.

With that in mind, here's a less recursive, more accurate description of the Internet:

> The Internet is a series of private computer networks (LANs and WANs) connected to each other through larger networks run by **Internet service providers (ISPs)**—many of whom are in some way related by business ties to the telephone business.
>
> Each individual private network (called an Autonomous System in networking-ese) is composed of a series of connected computers within an organization. Each organization takes responsibility for only the computers in its sphere of influence.
>
> Typically, the individual networks are connected by special devices called *routers* and *firewalls* that are responsible for figuring out what data should stay inside the local network and what data should be passed on to other networks.
>
> Each private network also takes on the responsibility of telling the rest of the world which systems they have on their network (but only if they want the rest of the world to be able to find them—more on that in Hour 19, "Security").

What does this have to do with your network? Quite a bit, actually. If you build a small network, you have a private network. If you connect a router to your network and you're connected through an ISP, you can connect some systems on your network to the Internet.

Figure 1.6 shows how local networks connect to each other to make up the Internet.

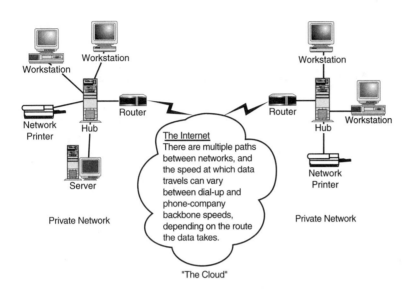

Understanding Bandwidth

As an astute reader, you're probably looking at Figure 1.6 and wondering what makes it different from the WAN in Figure 1.5. The two figures are almost the same. The important distinction is that in Figure 1.5, the WAN is all part of a single network and is under one organization's control. By contrast, the only parts of the Internet that can be identified as *strictly dedicated to the Internet* are the extremely fast (also called **high-bandwidth**) phone lines that make up what's called the backbone of the Internet.

The **backbone** is a series of very high-speed phone lines (ranging from 155 to 1.5 gigabits per second, or even more—*really* fast) that phone companies use to transmit high volumes of traffic. Compare this speed to the speed of your LAN (where data moves at 100 megabits per second, probably), and you begin to see why it's called the backbone.

Understanding Different Kinds of Internet Connections

A number of different possible onramps are provided to computer users who want to connect to the Internet. At the low end, in terms of access speed and the amount of bandwidth made available to the user, is the dial-up connection. Dial-up connections use a modem, which enables a maximum connection of 57,600bps (bits per second).

For many home and small business users, the next step is either a cable or DSL connection to the Internet. Cable and DSL provide much more bandwidth than an analog modem; cable modems and DSL connections can provide 500Kbps or greater, and business class connections providing even greater bandwidth can be leased by medium to larger size companies.

Even faster connections to the Internet can be procured by larger business and institutions by leasing trunk connections—T1s, E1s, and T3s. (These lines might also be called OS1s, DS1s, DS3s, and other names, depending on which phone company you're dealing with.) T1s are the most commonly used high speed lines and can provide bandwidth of 1.544Mbps. Connecting to the T-carrier system requires network connectivity devices that enable the company network to tie into the phone company's switched network.

Why Does the Internet Matter for Your Network?

As the Internet has increased in visibility, it's become a beacon for network designers everywhere. The Internet, unlike many smaller networks, is based on standards established by committee and common consent. These standards all exist in the public domain; none of the standards are proprietary, or the sole property of any single manufacturer. The result is that Internet-standards–based software is easy for software manufacturers to write because Internet standards are very well defined. Specifications for Internet standards are covered in exhaustive detail in a series of documents called **RFCs**, or **Requests for Comments**, which are readily available on the Internet. Because these standards are in the public domain, software developed using these standards is also cheaper to manufacture—there's no need for software manufacturers to pay royalties on patented or copyrighted ideas.

The best thing about Internet standards, however, is just that—they are *standards*. If you use Internet-standard software on your network, it will be much easier to ensure that your computers and applications will be able to interact. In fact, many products from wholly different manufacturers can work with one another if they're standards-compliant. When software products adhere to Internet standards, the resulting application cooperation is called interoperability, which essentially means that part A works with part B without undue difficulty. And interoperability means a local network that functions more smoothly and less expensively than one whose parts don't interoperate.

Intranets, Extranets, VPN, and the Internet

Typically, if you build a LAN or WAN—that is, a private network—using Internet standards, you've created an internal Internet, or an **intranet**. Intranets offer a great deal of promise for simplifying the networking of different manufacturers' components; used properly, intranets can reduce costs and simplify life for your end users as well. An example might be a company Web site that distributes company news—it's much cheaper and environmentally responsible to put the newsletter on a company intranet than to create a separate paper copy for each reader.

If you connect your intranet to the Internet and make provisions for your customers and business partners to use pieces of your intranet to do business with you, you've gone a step beyond an intranet and created an **extranet**. Extranets, which fall under the current rubric "B2B," for Business to Business, are essentially intranets that use the Internet as a vehicle to interact with their customers, suppliers, and business partners. With the proper security precautions, extranets offer tremendous value; they reduce the costs of tying your computer systems to your various business partners' systems and potentially expose your products to a huge audience.

Typically, an extranet needs to be secured so that your business dealings can be kept confidential. This is where **virtual private networks**, or **VPNs**, enter the picture. VPNs are one means of securing communications between outside users and the network. VPNs will be discussed in depth in later chapters.

Summary

In this hour, you've learned what a network is, how a network works, the varieties of networks available, and how the Internet relates to your network. In the next hour, you'll learn about the benefits of networking—why networked computers are better than nonnetworked computers.

Q&A

Q *What is a network?*

A A network is any collection of items linked together to pass on information or physical goods.

Q *What are the different physical topologies used on computer networks?*

A The bus, star, and ring are physical topologies. Although the ring topology looks like a star configuration, it actually provides a logical ring that moves the data in a circular path from device to device.

Q *What are some of the varieties of computer networks?*

A Some of the most common types of computer networks are local area networks (LANs) and wide area networks (WANs).

Q *What is the relationship between an intranet and the Internet?*

A An intranet is a private network that makes use of the same software and protocols used for the Internet.

HOUR 2

The Benefits of Networking

In this hour, you have the opportunity to learn about the following topics:

- ▶ Computing before computer networks
- ▶ The first computer networks
- ▶ How resources were shared before networking
- ▶ Downsides of *not* networking your computers
- ▶ The benefits of networking

Have you ever thought about what life would be like if human beings did not have what Alexis de Tocqueville, the French observer of early America, called a natural propensity to organize things at the drop of a hat? Just think about it—everything would be local. There would be no national brands and very little standardization. There might not be a post office. There would not be a standard currency.

Why? Because all these things rely on highly organized networks—the postal service, sales distribution networks, and even the set of national currency issuing banks. Without networks, many of the things we take for granted in our daily lives, from the measures we use to the mediums of exchange, could not exist.

A network is first and foremost a system that enables communications among multiple locations and people. A network also creates synergy, where the sum of the whole is potentially greater than the sum of the parts. In this hour, you learn how computer networking can benefit users.

Computing Before Computer Networks

Assume that you have a time machine and can go back in time 40–50 years to examine the computers that existed then. Chances are that you wouldn't recognize much about them. The computers that businesses and the government were then using were huge water-cooled behemoths the size of rooms. In spite of their bulk, they weren't powerful by today's standards; they could process only very small programs, and they usually lacked sufficient memory—that is, the physical part of the computer where the computer stores the 1s and 0s of software and data—to hold a whole program at one time. That's why computers are always shown spinning huge reels of magnetic tape in old movies—the tapes held the data that the computer wasn't using right at that moment. This model of computing now seems antiquated, but 40–50 years ago, it was state of the art.

In those days, computers offered very little interaction between the user and the system. Initially, there were no interactive video display screens and keyboards. Instead of sitting at a terminal or PC typing characters and using a mouse, users submitted the work they needed the computer to do to the computer operator, who was the only person allowed to directly interact with the computer. Usually, the work was submitted on punched paper tape or punchcards.

A great deal of the time, computers were kept in climate-controlled rooms with glass walls—hence the slang name *glass house* for a data center. In any case, users submitted their jobs on punch cards that were then run in batches on the computer—one or two batches per shift—from which we derive the term batch processing. Batch processing was a situation common in early mainframe environments in which many tasks were scheduled to run at a specific time late in the evening. The user never directly interacted with the computer in batch processing. Debugging programs was much more difficult then!

Given the lack of interaction between users and computers, it's not at all difficult to believe that computers at that time couldn't interact well at all. A large IBM computer simply couldn't talk to a Honeywell or Burroughs computer. Even if they had been able to connect, they couldn't have shared data—the computers used entirely different data formats; the only standard at that time was ASCII. ASCII is the American Standard Code for Information Interchange, a way that computers format 1s and 0s (binary code, which it can understand) into the alphabet, numerals, and other characters that humans can understand. The computers would have had to convert the data before they could use it...which, in those prestandard days, could have taken as long as reentering the data.

Even if the computers had been capable of understanding each other's data formats, the data transfers would have been relatively slow because at that time there was no way to link computers together. Even between computers made by the same manufacturer, the only way to transfer data was to send a tape or a large hard disk to the recipient of the data. This meant physical delivery of disks to each new location that needed a copy of data, which was certainly not fast when compared to modern networks.

Fortunately, the U. S. government's Advanced Research Products Agency had funded a small program operated by Bolt, Beranek, and Newman (BBN), a computer and technology firm in Cambridge, MA. BBN's job was to figure out how to enable computers to interact with each other. BBN figured out how to tie computers together using phone lines and **modems** (devices that can convert the 1s and 0s of digital data into sound waves that can be transmitted over phone lines) to transmit data that had been packaged into small fixed-length pieces called **datagrams**, or **packets**. The technology of converting data into packets was called **packet-switching**, and it is the single most important development in the history of computer networking.

Networking's Breakthrough: Packet-Switched Data

This section provides a basic exposition of packet-switching, which will help you understand how networks work because packet-switching is how all computer networks—from your network to the mighty Internet—move data around.

Packet-switched data is important for a variety of reasons:

▶ It enables more than one stream of data to travel over a wire at a time.

▶ It makes implementation of error correction relatively easy, meaning that errors that occur when data is being sent from one place to another can be corrected.

▶ It enables data to be sent from one computer to another over multiple routes, depending on which routes are currently open.

Initially, packet-switching can be difficult to understand. Nonetheless, if you want to understand how networks function, packet-switching is a central concept that you've got to assimilate. Here's a brief thought experiment to help explain how packet-switching works.

Assume that you are an author writing a manuscript that must be delivered to a wonderful editor who lives a thousand miles away from you. Also assume (for the purposes of this thought experiment) that the postal service limits the weight of packages it carries, and that your entire manuscript is heavier than the limit. Clearly, you're going to have to break up the manuscript in a way that ensures that your editor can reassemble it in the correct order without difficulty. How are you going to accomplish this?

First, you're going to break up the manuscript into standard sizes. Let's say that a 50-page section of manuscript plus an envelope is the maximum weight that the postal service will carry. After ensuring that your manuscript pages are numbered, you break the manuscript into 50-page chunks. It doesn't matter whether the chunks break on chapter lines, or even in the middle of a sentence—the pages are numbered, so they can be reassembled easily. If any pages are lost because of a torn envelope, the page numbers help determine what's missing.

Breaking up the manuscript into equal-sized chunks with a method of verifying the correctness of the data (through the use of the page numbers) is the first part of packetizing data. **Packetizing** is the process by which a computer breaks a single large chunk of data into smaller pieces that meet the standards for maximum chunks of data allowed to be transmitted over a network. The page numbers, which are a property of the data, are used to determine whether all the data has arrived; in networking terms, this is called a checksum. When data is packetized, the computer checks the values of the 1s and 0s in the data and comes up with a number that it includes in the packet of data. We'll see how checksums are used a little later.

Second, you put the 50-page manuscript chunks into envelopes numbered sequentially—the first 50 pages go into envelope number 1, the second 50 pages go into envelope number 2, and so forth until you've reached the end of the manuscript. The sequence numbers are important because they help the destination computer reassemble the data in proper order.

The number of pages in each envelope is also written on the outside of the envelope; that is equivalent to a data packet's size—if the size is wrong when the packet gets to the destination, the destination computer will discard the packet. (This is one of several reasons why this can happen—to be discussed a little further on.)

Last, you write your editor's address as the destination and your address as the return address on the outside of the envelopes and send them using the postal service. Figure 2.1 diagrams our hypothetical envelope and the relationship each element has to a data packet in a computer network situation.

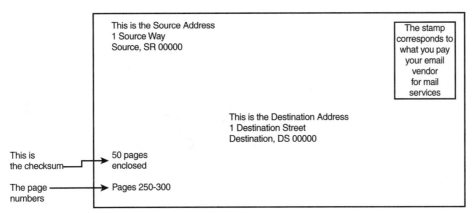

FIGURE 2.1
The various parts of the envelope and how they correspond to the parts of a data packet.

The route the envelopes take while in transit between your mailbox and your editor's desk is unimportant. Your editor gets mail from a different post office, but uses the same service, so the envelopes go through out-of-town mail. Some of the envelopes might be routed through Chicago; others might be routed through Dallas—it's not important as long as all the envelopes get to the editor (see Figure 2.2). If the number of pages your editor receives does not match the number of pages written on the outside of the envelope, the editor knows that something's wrong—the envelope came unsealed and pages fell out, or someone tampered with the contents. If you had sent your editor something over the Internet, the process would work the same way—the packets could have been routed through many different machines before arriving at your editor's computer.

In networking terms, each finished envelope is a packet of data. The order in which your editor—or a computer—receives them doesn't matter because the editor (or the computer) can reassemble the data from the sequence numbers on the outside of the envelopes and from the checksum (the number on the outside of the envelope detailing how many pages to expect in this envelope).

For each whole, complete, and correct envelope your editor receives, she will send you an acknowledgement so that you know she received it. If an envelope fails to arrive or is compromised in some way, your editor will not acknowledge receipt of that specific envelope. After a specified time, if you don't receive acknowledgement for that packet, you resend it so that the editor has the entire manuscript.

Packet-switched data doesn't correspond perfectly with this example, but it's close enough to give you a reasonable idea of the process.

FIGURE 2.2
Data packets can
follow several
paths across the
Internet.

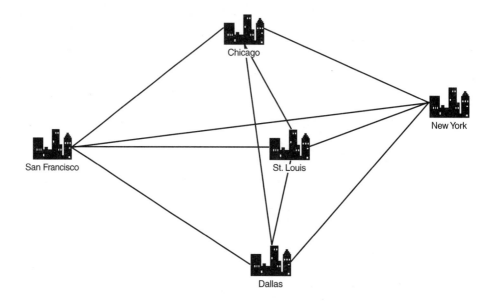

Mail can travel from New York to San Francisco across any combination of
these routes.

Any data you send over a computer network is packetized—from the smallest
email message to the largest files transferred across a wire. The beauty of packet-
switching networks is that more than one computer can transmit data over one
wire at a time. You can have a lot of packets of data from multiple machines
without confusion because each data packet (like each envelope in the preceding
example) has the following elements:

▶ A **source address**—This is the return address, or where the packet came
from.

▶ A **destination address**—This is where the packet is headed.

▶ A **sequence number**—This explains where this packet fits in with the
remainder of the packets.

▶ A **checksum**—This ensures that the data is free of errors.

Because each computer has a different address (called a MAC address, as
explained in the next hour), transmitting data is essentially a process of sending
mail from one piece of hardware to another electronically.

The importance of standards with respect to packet switching can't be overstated. The success of packet-switched networks depends *entirely* on the widespread adoption of standards. Networking is an endeavor where cooperation is rewarded; no matter how brilliant a new program is, if it doesn't meet a standard or if the standards aren't adequately public to allow other vendors to build devices that use it, it will fail.

Life Without Computer Networks

Transferring data between computers before networks was clearly difficult, but in those days, there was no alternative. Now networks are ubiquitous. But what would your computing life be like without a network?

Inefficient Resource Sharing

If you didn't have a network, you wouldn't be able to share the resources on your computer with others—or use their resources either. What are the ramifications of this?

Sneakernet

Back when ethernet networking was invented, computer users who were networked came up with a clever name for sharing files from files stored on computers that were not connected to the network. They called it **sneakernet**. What it meant was that if a user wanted to move files between nonconnected computers, she had to copy the file to a floppy disk, walk to the other machine (hence the *sneaker* in sneakernet), and copy the file to the other computer.

Needless to say, sneakernet is not an efficient way to move or manage files. It is time-consuming and unreliable to begin with, and it works easily only for files small enough to fit on a floppy disk. The worst thing about it is that data is decentralized, meaning that every user can conceivably have a different version of a particular file stored on her nonnetwork-connected computer. The chaos that ensues when users need the same version of a file and don't have it (usually because the file changes as users copy it to their machines and work with it before copying it to the next machine) can be truly horrific.

No Shared Software Applications

Disconnected computers also suffer from another malady: They can't share software applications. When computers are not networked, every application must be installed on every computer if data passed by sneakernet is to be effective. If a user doesn't have the application that created a file stored on her computer, the user can't read the file, period.

Of course, if you can't share applications, that means no one can share their calendars or contact lists with other users, let alone send them email. Not being networked can hinder communications.

No Shared Printer Resources

If computers aren't networked, the only way they can share devices like a printer is by using manual switch boxes that select which computer's printer port connects to the printer at any time. This is not simply an inconvenience; it can be harmful to your pocketbook. Some printer manufacturers do not warranty a printer that has been connected to a switch box; switch boxes can damage printer electronics.

No Internet!

Nonnetworked computers can't share a common connection to the Internet. In fact, without networks, there wouldn't even *be* an Internet! The increasing popularity of the Internet combined with a desire to reduce Internet-account costs has provided a reason for many people to build small networks—just so that they can connect all their users to the Internet through one connection.

Slo-o-ow Communications

Suppose that the only way you could get some commodity you use frequently—say, gasoline—was by mail order. Also suppose that you could get it only in bucket-sized increments. It would take forever to get your gasoline—and even longer to fill the tank on your car.

That's what networking by floppy disks is like. Floppies hold very little data, and trying to do useful work while exchanging disks is an exercise in frustration. The recent advent of high-capacity removable-media drives, such as Iomega's Zip and Jaz drives and newer media such as rewritable CD-ROMs and DVD-ROMs, partially ameliorates this situation, but it does not solve the underlying problem: the lack of real-time connectivity a network provides.

No Centralized Data Management

When computers are not networked, there is no way to manage them collectively and ensure that they share common configurations and access to data.

This means that administration is costly and time-consuming. Configurations cannot be standardized unless the person in charge of the computers repeats installations and configurations on each system, which at best is redundant and wasteful of effort and resources.

Expense

Nonnetworked computing is expensive because of the labor costs, the cost of lost worker productivity, and the capital costs of multiplying the cost of resources by the number of computers. In other words, if your computers aren't networked and all your users have to print, you might have to purchase a separate printer for each user. Contrast this with networked situations in which a single printer can serve 15 or 20 users. The cost savings are huge.

Benefits of Networking

The preceding paragraphs pointed out the downsides of computing in a nonnetworked environment, but they did not enumerate the benefits...

Simplified Resource Sharing

Resource sharing is easier over a network; whether the network uses a peer or client/server configuration is immaterial.

Shared Disk Space

Networked computers can share their hard disk space with each other. At first glance, this doesn't seem momentous; after all, many computers have large hard drives. But it's not the file-storage capabilities that are important here—it's sharing applications and files. It is satisfying to be able to find a copy of a file you require, copy it to your desktop computer, and work on it without leaving your chair.

Shared Applications

Although sharing files is an important reason for networking, sharing applications is another, equally important reason. Shared applications can be as prosaic as using a copy of Microsoft Word stored on another user's drive or as elaborate as a groupware application that routes data from user to user according to complex preset rules.

A **groupware application** (also called **groupware** or **collaborative software**) is an application that enables multiple users to work together using the network to connect them. Such applications can work serially, where (for instance) a document is automatically routed from person A to person B once person A is done with it, or it can be software to enable real-time collaboration. IBM's Lotus Notes software is an example of the former, and Microsoft's Office 2000 has some real-time collaborative features.

Examples of shared applications include **group calendaring**, which allows your staff to plan meetings and tasks using a centralized schedule instead of 20 different ones, and email, or electronic mail, which is widely called the killer app of networking. Email and other network applications are discussed in more depth in Hour 12, "Network Applications."

By the Way

In on the Kill

The term **killer app** is not pejorative. In spite of what might be a sensible conjecture about its meaning, it does not refer to viruses or other malicious software. Instead, a killer app is an application that is so useful that it increases the demand for computer resources. Email is the killer app of networking because when it was introduced, it allowed users to hold serial conversations in a common workspace that didn't require paper files and running around with memos. Email is a great way to send off quick messages that aren't really sufficiently meaningful to merit a memo. For example, email is great for project tracking: Workers can send a two-line message to their boss telling her what the status is on a project, and the boss can assign work and send out group messages quickly and efficiently without wasting paper.

Shared Printers

A third aspect of resource sharing is shared printers. As noted earlier in the discussion of the disadvantages of nonnetworked computers, standalone printers—that is, printers attached to computers that aren't networked—represent a significant capital expense. Printers typically also cost a lot to run—they consume ink or toner when they print, and inkjet and toner cartridges are typically expensive.

A visual example of resource sharing can be seen in Figure 2.3.

Networking Is Faster

Given everything else that has been said in this hour, it seems obvious that networking is faster than not networking. And, in fact, it is faster. Just think about it:

▶ No more printing memos—Use email!

▶ No more running from desk to desk to check everyone's availability for a meeting—Use the group calendar!

▶ No more wondering whose Rolodex has the name of the person you need to call—You can get it from the contact database.

▶ No more racing around from computer to computer to get the file you need—Just copy or open it from the network drive.

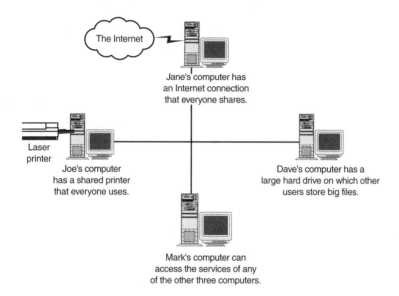

FIGURE 2.3
Resource sharing with a computer network.

Centralized Management

If you were a preschool teacher with a bevy of three-year-olds, you wouldn't try to manage them all individually. Instead, you'd try to do activities in groups. Imagine trying to fill the needs of 25 three-year-olds, each engaged in a different activity—the mind boggles at the management strategies you'd need.

Yet a great many of these same people, faced with a computer network, continue to treat network users' needs totally outside the context of the network. All too often, system administrators wind up running from desktop to desktop, installing, fixing, and managing entirely unique system configurations. This is extremely inefficient—and it wears down the patience of the network users and the technical person whose job it is to support them.

A better solution to managing networks is to centralize management functions and standardize application software across entire organizations. Once computers are networked, there are a host of software utilities (Microsoft's Systems Management Server, HP's OpenView, IBM's Tivoli, and Symantec's Norton Administrator for Networks, among others) that enable the administrator to diagnose and fix problems and install and configure software. These utility suites allow a network administrator to collect and standardize computer configurations from across a network—and very often, to install software on users' computers without leaving her desk (bad for personal fitness, good for the network).

To find out more about managing networks, look at the network administration chapters in Part V of this book, "Introduction to Network Administration."

The initial installation and learning curves are a lot of work for the administrator, but once the initial installation is finished, the administrator's life gets easier. Centralized management saves time and money (two things accountants appreciate) as well as the goodwill of the users and the credibility of the administrator (two things the users and administrators appreciate). Networking is worth the investment and time.

Summary

Clearly, when computer resources are shared through a network, you reap a variety of benefits ranging from reduced costs to ease of use to simpler administration. The cost savings and per-worker productivity gains represented by networks will be appreciated by companies trying to economize; from the worker's viewpoint, she has received a bonus because she doesn't have to chase down information anymore. If applications such as email, calendaring, and contact management are added to the mix, the network begins to establish synergistic relationships (that is, relationships that produce more value than the sum of their parts would suggest) between users and data. A well-designed and functional network allows groups of people to interact in ways that extend their natural capabilities and enables them to accomplish a great deal more than they could without the network.

Q&A

Q *What is the name of the technology that enables computer networks to exist?*

A Packet-switching makes computer networks possible.

Q *What sorts of computer resources can be shared on a network?*

A Networks enable the sharing of all sorts of things—drives, printers, and even connections to the Internet.

Q *What are some of the reasons that centralized management is useful for networks?*

A Centralized management of a network enables more efficient administration, the automated installation of software on network users' desktop computers, and easier desktop computer configuration management.

PART II

The Basics

HOUR 3

Getting Data from Here to There: How Computers Share Data

In this hour, we will first discuss four common logical topologies, starting with the most common and ending with the most esoteric:

▶ Ethernet
▶ Token Ring
▶ FDDI
▶ ATM

In the preceding hour, you read a brief definition of packet-switching and an explanation of why packet switching is so important to data networking. In this hour, you learn more about how networks pass data between computers. This process will be discussed from two separate vantage points: logical topologies, such as ethernet, token ring, and ATM; and network protocols, which we have not yet discussed.

Why is packet switching so important? Recall that it enables multiple computers to send multiple messages down a single piece of wire, a technical choice that is both efficient and an elegant solution. Packet switching is intrinsic to computer networking—without packet switching, no network.

In the first hour, you learned about the physical layouts of networks, such as star, bus, and ring technologies, which create the highways over which data travels. In the next hour, you learn about these topologies in more depth. But before we get to them, you have to know the rules of the road that determine how data travels over a network. In this hour, then, we'll review logical topologies.

Logical Topologies

Before discussing topologies again, let's revisit the definition of a topology. In networking terms, a **topology** is nothing more than the arrangement of a network. The topology can refer to the physical layout (which we discussed in Hour 1, "An Overview of Networking," and really deals with the wiring, more or less) or the logical layout of the network.

Logical topologies lay out the rules of the road for data transmission. As you already know, in data networking, only one computer can transmit on one wire segment at any given time. Life would be wonderful if computers could take turns transmitting data, but unfortunately, life isn't that simple. Computers transmitting data have all the patience of a four-year-old waiting in line at an ice-cream parlor on a hot summer day. As a result, there must be rules if the network is to avoid becoming completely anarchic.

In contrast to physical topologies, logical topologies are largely abstract. Physical topologies can be expressed through concrete pieces of equipment, such as network cards and wiring types; logical networks are essentially rules of the road that those devices use to do their job. In other words, this is software.

Ethernet

When packet switching was young, it didn't work very efficiently. Computers didn't know how to avoid sending data over the wire at the same time other systems were sending data, making early networking a rather ineffective technology. Just think about it—it was similar to two people talking on the phone at the same time.

Ethernet, invented in 1973 by Bob Metcalfe (who went on to found 3Com, one of the most successful networking companies), was a way to circumvent the limitations of earlier networks. It was based on an IEEE (Institute of Electronic and Electrical Engineers) standard called 802.3 CSMA/CD, and it provided for ways to manage the crazy situation that occurred when many computers tried to transmit on one wire simultaneously.

CSMA/CD Explained

The foundation of ethernet is a method of transmitting data called **CSMA/CD**, or **Carrier Sense Multiple Access/Collision Detection**. It sounds complicated, but it's quite simple; it's a protocol based on common sense. Here's how it works, in a blow-by-blow account.

In an ethernet network

▶ All computers share a single network segment, called a collision domain. A **collision domain** is the group of computers that communicate on a single network wire, also called a segment. The segment is a collision domain because if there's more than one computer in it, it's a cinch that at some point those computers are going to try to transmit data simultaneously, which is a big no-no.

▶ Each computer in a collision domain listens to all transmissions on the wire.

▶ Each computer can transmit data only when no other computer is currently transmitting.

▶ Each computer listens for a quiet time on the wire (this is the carrier sense multiple access) in CSMA/CD). When the network wire is quiet (which is measured in nanoseconds—network quiet has no relationship to human quiet), a computer that has packets of data to transmit sends them out over the network wire. If no other computers are sending, the packet will be routed on its merry way.

▶ When two computers transmit packets at the same time, a condition called a collision occurs (this is the *collision detection* part of CSMA/CD). In terms of networking, a collision is the thing that happens when two computers attempt to transmit data on the same network wire at the same time. This creates a conflict; both computers sense the collision, stop transmitting, and wait a random amount of time (in nanoseconds) before retransmitting. The phrase "random amount of time" is important because it's key to reducing collisions and it's unlikely that more than one computer on a network will randomly select the same number of nanoseconds to wait until resending.

The larger the collision domain, the more likely it is that collisions will occur, which is why ethernet designers try to keep the number of computers in a segment (and hence a collision domain) as low as possible.

Take a look at Figure 3.1 to see a diagram of an ethernet topology.

If a second computer tries to transmit data over the wire at the same time as the first computer, a **collision** occurs. Both then cease transmitting data, wait a random amount of time for a quiet period, and transmit again; usually this solves the collision problem. It is really that simple.

CSMA/CD, as personified in ethernet, does have some problems. Sometimes a network card goes into a mode in which it fails to obey CSMA/CD and transmits all the time—this is called **jabber**, and it's caused either by faulty software or a defective network card. Other problems can be caused by a segment with too many computers, which causes too many systems to try to transmit at each quiet time; this can cause **broadcast storms**. Fortunately, newer forms of ethernet (specifically **switching**, which we'll discuss further on) can circumvent these limitations by segmenting the network very tightly.

FIGURE 3.1
An ethernet topology: Only one computer can transmit data at a time.

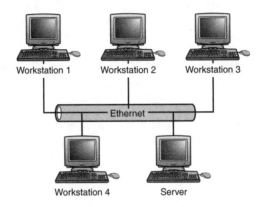

Ethernet's Nuclear Family

Ethernet is broadly used to describe both the logical topology that uses CSMA/CD and the physical topologies on which CSMA/CD networks run. All the basic ethernet topologies are described in IEEE standard 802.3. The members of the nuclear family are listed here:

- 10BASE-2, or coaxial networking. The maximum segment length of 10BASE-2 is 185 meters. This is a dead technology and is not used for new installations.

- 10BASE5, or thicknet. Thicknet is also called **AUI**, short for **Attachment User Interface**. AUI networks are an intermediate step between 10BASE-2 and 10BASE-T. 10BASE5 is a bus interface with slightly more redundancy than 10BASE-2. The maximum length of a 10BASE5 segment is 500 meters. Like 10BASE-2, this is a dead technology and is not used for new installations.

- 10BASE-T, which runs over two of the four pairs of unshielded twisted-pair wire. In 10BASE-T, the maximum cable length from the hub to a workstation is 100 meters. 10BASE-T is pretty much dead technology at this point.

Fortunately, the ethernet standard has grown to include faster networks and fiber-optic media. The newer members of the ethernet family are described in IEEE Standard 802.3u, and include these:

- ▶ 100BASE-T, also called fast ethernet, in which data travels at 100 megabits per second over two pairs of unshielded twisted-pair copper wire. The maximum cable length between the concentrator and the workstation for fast ethernet is 20 meters, and it requires Category 5 cabling standards. (Cable standards will be discussed later.)

- ▶ 100BASE-FX and 100-Base-FL, which is fast ethernet running on optical fibers. Because optical fibers can carry data much further than copper wire, 100BASE-FX and –FL have much greater maximum cable lengths than 100BASE-T.

- ▶ 1000BASE-T, also called gigabit ethernet, allows data to travel at one gigabit (1000 megabits, or ten times faster than 100BASE-T) per second. Currently, 1000BASE-T is used mostly for servers and for organizational backbone networks, but over time that will surely change. By the next edition of this book, it will probably be common to have gigabit ethernet to the desktop. This topology runs on CAT 5E or CAT 6 copper wire and over fiber.

Token Ring and FDDI

Ethernet CSMA/CD networks provide a relatively simple way of passing data. However, many industry observers correctly note that CSMA/CD breaks down under the pressure exerted by many computers on a network segment. These observers are correct; the squabbling and contention for bandwidth that is part and parcel of ethernet does not always scale efficiently.

In an attempt to circumvent this problem , IBM and the IEEE created another networking standard called 802.5. (Does anyone see a pattern here? Every new invention is built to rectify the older standard's shortcomings.) IEEE 802.5 is more commonly identified with token ring; FDDI also uses the 802.5 method of moving data around networks.

Token ring works very differently from ethernet. In ethernet, any computer on a given network segment can transmit until it senses a collision with another computer. In token ring and FDDI networks, by contrast, a single special packet called a *token* is generated when the network started up and is passed around the network. When a computer has data to transmit, it waits until the token is available. The computer then takes control of the token and transmits a data packet. When it's done, it releases the token to the network. Then the next computer grabs the token if it has data to transmit (see Figure 3.2).

FIGURE 3.2
A token ring topology (FDDI works in the same fashion): The only computer that can transmit is the computer holding the token.

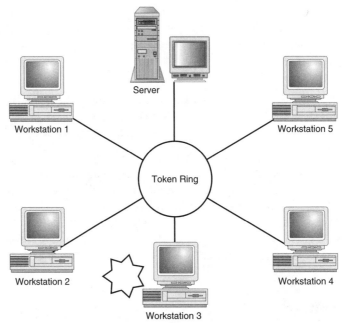

Has data to transmit.
It has taken the Token (an electronic message that's passed around the network)
and only it can transmit. When it's done transmitting data, it returns the Token to the ring,
where the next computer that needs to transmit will pick it up.
FDDI works basically the same as Token Ring.

In comparison to the contentious nature of ethernet, token ring and FDDI appear quite civilized. These two logical topologies do not have collisions in which multiple stations try to send data; instead, every computer waits its turn.

By the Way

Token-Ring Teaching

Token ring's underlying methodology worked to my advantage while a teaching assistant in grad school. To reduce my tuition, I taught a couple of sections of freshman composition, and one of the sections was particularly fractious—students would interrupt each other willy-nilly, which got in the way of teaching and learning. So I brought in a koosh ball (one of those little rubber hairy plastic things that were all the rage in the early 1990s) and announced that only the student with the koosh could talk. It took a couple of classes for the rules to sink in, but once they did, the class was much more civil—and a better place for learning. Who says high technology has no place in the real world?

Token ring suffers slightly fewer bandwidth-contention issues than ethernet; it holds up under load fairly well, although it too can be slowed down if too many computers need to transmit data at the same time.

Despite its load-friendly architecture, IBM held token ring as a proprietary topology for too many years. By the time it allowed other manufacturers to begin making devices for token ring, the battle for market share was already lost to lower-cost ethernet devices. It also never really evolved to transmit data as fast as ethernet, which might have sealed its fate. Currently, token ring appears to be dying out one network at a time, and I haven't installed a new token ring device in about four years.

Asynchronous Transfer Mode (ATM)

ATM networking is the youngest of the topologies described here. It was designed to circumvent the shortcomings of existing topologies, and hence it was created from whole cloth. Unlike ethernet, token ring, or FDDI, it can natively carry both voice and data over network wire or fiber. ATM transmits all packets as 53-byte cells that have a variety of identifiers on them to determine such things as Quality of Service.

Quality of Service in packet data is very similar to quality of service in regular mail. In regular mail, you have a choice of services: first class, second class, third class, bulk mail, overnight, and so forth. When you send an overnight message, it receives priority over first-class mail, so it gets to its destination first.

A few bits of data in a packet of data indicate the quality of service required for that data. When the Quality of Service feature is implemented—as it is in ATM and Internet Protocol version 6 (IPv6)—you can send packets based on their need for bandwidth. For example, email is relatively low priority and might be given third-class service; video or audio content, which has to run constantly, gets a higher priority.

ATM is fast. At its slowest, it runs at 25 megabits per second; at its fastest, it can run up to 1.5 gigabits per second (which is why phone companies use it for some of the huge trunk lines that carry data for long distances). In addition to its speed, ATM is exponentially more complex than either ethernet or token ring. Most commonly, the 155 megabit per second speed of ATM is used for applications in which quality of service and extraordinary speed are required.

Currently, ATM equipment is both esoteric and expensive. Fore Systems and IBM have both invested heavily in ATM-to-the-desktop technology (that is, they use

ATM to link servers and workstations) and are banking on the need for multimedia networks over the next several years. ATM standards and interoperability are still touch-and-go, however.

Unfortunately, ATM, like token ring, has largely been eclipsed in the consumer market by Fast ethernet and Gigabit ethernet, which provide comparable performance at lower cost.

That just about wraps up the discussion of logical topologies. Now it's time to discuss protocols.

Network Protocols

At the base of a network system is the physical topology. On top of that is the logical topology. And on top of the logical topology are **protocols**. If the idea of "on top of" or "beneath" doesn't make sense, don't worry; it's based on a system for describing how networks work called the OSI model, which is described in the following section.

Network protocols consist of sets of rules for sending and receiving data across a physical network and the software that puts these rules into practice. Logical topologies instruct the hardware how to packetize (or "frame") and transmit data across the physical topology; protocols handle the translation of data from applications (that is, software) to the logical topology.

If that all sounds confusing, don't worry. The next couple of pages discuss how protocols work, what some of the most popular protocols are, and how they're organized. Here is a list of the protocols you are most likely to run across:

- ▶ TCP/IP
- ▶ IPX
- ▶ NetBIOS/NetBEUI

To understand what network protocols are, you have to understand what they do and their function in relation to the rest of the network. To begin, let's examine the most popular theoretical model of networking: the OSI model.

The OSI Model (And Why You Should Be Familiar with It)

During the 1980s, a group called **Open Systems Interconnect**, or **OSI** for short, attempted to create a logical arrangement for the various parts that make up a network. In the long term, their efforts were futile (practically no one runs OSI protocols), but they did create a great model to explain how a network should work. The model is called the OSI seven-layer model, and it's a tremendously useful theoretical picture of how network functions should be distributed among the various bits of a network. The OSI model is useful to know, and it's worth memorizing because its theoretical model is useful for debugging network problems ranging from design issues to snafus with connections (see Figure 3.3).

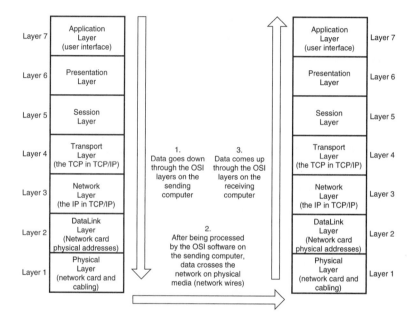

FIGURE 3.3
The OSI model shows how data is moved in a network.

The OSI model is not particularly complicated. The trick is to remember that as the OSI layer numbers increase from 1 to 7, so does the **level of abstraction**. The lower the layer, the less abstract and more concrete it is. Each layer communicates only with the layer directly above or below it while moving data from electrical impulses on a wire into data on your screen. If we return to the postal metaphor from Hour 2, "Why Build a Network?" as an analogy, OSI becomes even easier to understand:

> **Layer 7 (Application)** is the software applications that you use on your screen. Layer 7 is concerned with file access and file transfer. If you have ever used applications such as FTP or Telnet, you have interacted with an example of Layer 7. In the postal model, the Application layer corresponds to writing a letter. This is where applications such as Microsoft Word and Excel run.

Layer 6 (Presentation) deals with the way different systems represent data. For example, Layer 6 defines what happens when it tries to display UNIX-style data on an MS-DOS screen.

Layer 6 doesn't really have an analogue in the postal model, but if it did, it would be like rewriting the letter so that anyone could read it (which, as you can see, doesn't make much sense in a physical context). Probably the best analogy is to a translator; using the postal model again, assume that your letter is being sent to Mexico. A translator (equivalent to Presentation-layer software) can translate the data in your envelope into the local *lingua mexicana*. Like the letter in the example, data is mutable and protean and can be rearranged to fit the kind of computer on which it needs to run.

Layer 5 (Session) handles the actual connections between systems. Layer 5 handles the order of data packets and bidirectional (two-way) communications. In a postal metaphor, the Session layer is similar to breaking a single large document into several smaller documents, packaging them, and labeling the order in which the packages should be opened. This is where streams of data get turned into packets.

Layer 4 (Transport) is like the registered-mail system. Layer 4 is concerned with ensuring that mail gets to its destination. If a packet fails to get to its destination, Layer 4 handles the process of notifying the sender and requesting that another packet be sent. In effect, Layer 4 ensures that the three layers below it (that is, Layers 1, 2, and 3) are doing their jobs properly. If they are not, Layer 4 software can step in and handle error correction, such as resending packets if they are corrupted or missing. (**Dropped** is the usual term for a lost packet.) For what it's worth, this is the layer where the *TCP* in TCP/IP works.

Layer 3 (Network) provides an addressing scheme. If you send someone a letter, you use a street address that contains a ZIP code because that's what the post office understands. When a computer sends a data packet, it sends the packet to a logical address, which is like a street address. This layer is where **Internet Protocol**, the *IP* in TCP/IP, and Novell's **internetwork packet exchange**, or **IPX**, work.

Layer 3 works with Layer 2 to translate data packets' logical network addresses (these are similar to IP addresses, about which you'll learn in a few pages) into hardware-based MAC addresses (which are similar to ZIP codes), data frame numbers, and so forth and move the packets toward their destination. Layer 3 is similar to the mail-sorting clerks at the post office who aren't concerned with ensuring that mail gets to its destination, per se. Instead, the clerks' concern is to sort mail so that it keeps getting closer to its destination. Layer 3 is also the lowest layer that typically is part of an operating system.

Layer 2 (DataLink) is a set of rules burned into chips on network interface cards, hubs, switches, routers, and whatever else works on the network. In our postal model, this layer represents a set of rules governing the actual delivery of physical mail—pick up here, drop off here, and so forth. This is where the rules for ethernet, token ring, FDDI, ATM, and so on are stored. It's concerned with finding a way for Layer-1 stuff (the cards, hubs, wire, and so forth) to talk to Layer 3. Layer 2 is where network card addresses become important. Layer 2 also re-packetizes data inside **frames**, which are for all intents and purposes the packet type used by hardware devices to send and receive below the Layer 3 threshold.

Layer 1 (Physical) is similar to the trucks, trains, planes, rails, and whatnot that move the mail. From a network perspective, this layer is concerned only with the physical aspects of the network—the cards, wire, and concentrators that move data packets. Layer 1 specifies what the physical aspects are, what they must be capable of doing, and (basically) how they accomplish those things. This condenses to cable specs, physical jack specifications, and so on.

If you refer back to the description of packet data in Hour 2, you'll realize that if data packets are to pass over the network, the network (like the postal service) has to accomplish several tasks successfully:

- ▶ It has to be capable of transmitting data across a physical medium (copper wire, optical fiber, or—in the case of wireless networks—air).

- ▶ It must route data to the correct location by MAC address (**Media Access Control address**, a unique 48-bit address assigned to each network device).

- ▶ It must be capable of decoding the type of data received when it arrives at the destination.

- ▶ It must be capable of checking the correctness of the transmitted data.

- ▶ It must be capable of sending messages to acknowledge that a particular packet has been received.

- ▶ It must be capable of interacting with users through an interface that displays the data.

As you can see, the various layers of the OSI model accomplish these goals admirably. OSI, however, has seldom been implemented as a network protocol; instead, the existing protocols—mostly TCP/IP—were refined using the powerful OSI reference model as a guide.

TCP/IP

If you've read anything about the Internet that's deeper than a newsweekly's puff piece, you've probably heard of **TCP/IP**, or **Transmission Control Protocol/Internet Protocol**. TCP/IP is the protocol that carries data traffic over the Internet. Of all the network protocols in the marketplace, TCP/IP is far and away the most popular.

The reasons for TCP/IP's success, however, do not stem from the popularity of the Internet. Even before the current Internet boom, TCP/IP was gaining popularity among business networkers, college computer-science majors, and scientific organizations. TCP/IP has gained popularity because it is an **open standard**—no single company controls it. Instead, TCP/IP is part of a set of standards created by a body called the **Internet Engineering Task Force (IETF)**. IETF standards are created by committees and are submitted to the networking community through a set of documents called **Requests for Comments (RFCs)**.

RFCs are draft documents freely available on the Internet that explain a standard to the networking community. All RFCs are considered "draft" documents because any document can be superseded by a newer RFC. The reason for this focus on RFCs is that they form a large part of the basis for the various standards that make up Internet networking today, including TCP/IP.

If you're interested in examining an RFC to see how standards are defined, just do a Google search for "RFC1918" (a common RFC referring to private networks); it will generally lead you to a list of other RFCs. They aren't always easy reading, but if you understand the fundamentals, they offer a tremendous amount of information. And who knows? You might see a way they can be improved— there's no reason why you can't suggest changes if you see the need.

TCP/IP Defined

But what exactly is TCP/IP? It is many things. For one thing, the name TCP/IP is a bit misleading—TCP/IP is just shorthand notation for a full **protocol suite**, or set of protocols that have standard ways of interacting with each other. TCP and IP share the name of the whole protocol suite because they form the bedrock of the whole protocol suite; they are respectively the transport (OSI Layer 4, which regulates traffic) and the network (OSI Layer 3, which handles addressing) layers of the TCP/IP protocol suite. The suite includes, but is by no means limited to, the ways of transmitting data across networks listed in Table 3.1.

TABLE 3.1   Some TCP/IP Suite Members and Their Functions

Name	Function
TCP	Transmission Control Protocol. Ensures that connections are made and maintained between computers.
IP	Internet Protocol. Handles software computer addresses.
ARP	Address Resolution Protocol. Relates IP addresses with hardware (MAC) addresses. **RARP**, or **Reverse ARP**, does the opposite.
RIP	Routing Information Protocol. Finds the quickest route between two computers. Offers a maximum of 16 "hops" between routers before deciding that a packet is undeliverable. Good for smallish networks, not so good on the Internet.
OSPF	Open Shortest Path First. A descendant of RIP that increases its speed and reliability. Much used on the Internet as it accepts 256 "hops" between routers before it decides that a packet is undeliverable.
ICMP	Internet Control Message Protocol. Handles errors and sends error messages for TCP/IP. The most common use of this is the ping command, which is used to determine whether one network device can communicate with another network device.
BGP/EGP	Border Gateway Protocol/Exterior Gateway Protocol. Handles how data is passed between networks. Used at the edge of networks.
SNMP	Simple Network Management Protocol. Allows network administrators to connect to and manage network devices.
PPP	Point-to-Point Protocol. Provides for dial-up networked connections to networks. PPP is commonly used by Internet service providers as the dial-up protocol customers use to connect to their networks.
SMTP	Simple Mail Transport Protocol. How email is passed between servers on a TCP/IP network.
POP3/IMAP4	Post Office Protocol version 3/Internet Message Advertising Protocol version 4. Both set up ways for clients to connect to servers and collect email.

As you can see, there are quite a few pieces in the TCP/IP protocol suite, and this is just the beginning—there are a whole bunch more that we're not going to discuss here. If you want to see the whole of TCP/IP in all its glory, read the RFCs.

All these protocols are necessary at some point or another to ensure that data gets where it's supposed to be going. The pieces listed in Table 3.1 are standards at this point, but the process of defining standards is far from over.

In contrast to the OSI reference model's seven layers, TCP/IP uses only four layers—some of which amalgamate several OSI layer functions into one TCP/IP layer. Table 3.2 compares OSI and TCP/IP layers.

TABLE 3.2   Contrast Between TCP/IP and the OSI Model

OSI Layer	TCP/IP Layer	TCP/IP Applications and Protocols Running at This Level
7 (Application)	TCP Layer 4 (Application)	FTP (File Transfer Program)
6 (Presentation) 5 (Session)		Telnet (terminal program) SMTP (mail transfer) POP3 and IMAP4 (mail clients)
4 (Transport)	TCP Layer 3 (also called Host-to-Host; a host is any system running TCP/IP)	TCP (Transmission Control Protocol) UDP (User Datagram Protocol)
3 (Network)	TCP Layer 2 (Internet)	IP (Internet Protocol)
2 (DataLink) 1 (Physical)	TCP Layer 1 (Network Interface)	Hardware (network cards, cables, concentrators, and so on)

From this table, you can see that TCP/IP accomplishes the functions required in the OSI reference model.

IP Addresses

TCP/IP got its start as part of the UNIX operating system in the mid-1970s. Networkers who had previously relied on **UUCP (UNIX-to-UNIX copy)** to copy files and mail between computers decided that there had to be a better, more interactive way to network, and TCP/IP was born. Given the academic heritage of placing material in front of the academic community for critical review and discussion, it was a natural progression to include TCP/IP in the RFC process, where its standards have been set ever since.

The original specification for TCP/IP was open ended—or so the designers thought. They created an address space, or standard way of writing addresses, which set up 2 to the 32nd power addresses (4,294,967,296 separate addresses). In the days when TCP/IP was still young, the thought that four billion computers could exist was a bit of a stretch, especially because computers—even cheap ones—cost $5,000–10,000 each. However, with the increased popularity of the Internet, these IP addresses have been disappearing at a tremendous clip.

More Space!

Why are IP addresses so important? Well, in the postal-mail metaphor we've been using for our network, every person has a unique name and address. The Internet likewise requires unique names and addresses; and once the current IP address space of four billion-plus addresses are used up, there won't be any more addresses. That's why the next generation of Internet Protocol, called IPv6, is so important—it increases the number of addresses to such a great number that it will be a while before we're in danger of running out of addresses again.

By the Way

IP addresses have disappeared so fast because of the way the addressing scheme is designed. All IP addresses are written in dotted decimal notation, with one byte (eight bits) between each dot. A dotted decimal IP address looks like this:

`192.168.100.25`

Because each number is described by one byte, and because each byte is 8 bits (or binary 1s and 0s), each number can have a value of anything from 0 to 255. Because there are 4 numbers with 8 bits each, the total address space is said to be 32 bits long (4*8 = 32). So the preceding address, in binary, looks like this:

`11000000.10101000.01100100.00011001`

There are 32 characters in the binary address, divided into four eight-bit groups, or **octets**. This is where the *32-bit* title comes from—it's literally 32 binary ones and zeroes. T.S. Eliot wrote the famous *Four Quartets*; networkers have the not-so-famous, but undeniably more useful four octets in every IP address that exists.

With a 32-bit address space that can handle four billion addresses, you might think that the Internet would never run out of IP addresses (or that it would take a while at any rate). Unfortunately, that's not the case. IP addresses are allocated to organizations that request them in what are called **address blocks**. Address blocks come in three sizes, based on the **class** of address. And once you've read about IP address allocation in the following sections, you'll agree that the present method of allocating IP addresses is inefficient given the way the Internet has grown.

Class A Addresses

Class A addresses, of which there are very few (if any) left unused, have up to 16,777,216 addresses. It uses 24 of the 32 bits in the address space read left to right. A Class A address looks like this:

```
X.0.0.0
```

The number represented by the X is one fixed number from 0 to 126. The first octet (that X again) in a Class A address always begins with binary 0. This number is used as the first number before the leftmost dot by all the IP addresses in a Class A address space.

The other three octets, or all the numbers represented by the 0s in the preceding example, can range from 0 to 255. Because three of the four available numbers are used to create unique IP addresses, and three-quarters of 32 is 24, a Class A network has a 24-bit address space. Collectively, Class A addresses use up 50 percent of the available addresses of the IPv4 address space, or 2,147,483,648 of the 4,294,967,296 total available addresses.

Class B Addresses

Class A addresses provide 16 million IP addresses per network. The next increment, Class B, has a total of 65,536 IP addresses per network. A Class B address looks like this:

```
X.X.0.0
```

All Class B addresses begin with a binary 10 in the first octet. Class B addresses compose 25 percent of the available IP address space. This means that Class B addresses account for 1,073,741,824 of the 4,294,967,296 available IP addresses.

The numbers represented by the Xs are fixed numbers ranging from 0 to 255. The numbers represented by the 0s (the other two octets) can range from 0 to 255. Because the two rightmost dotted numbers are used to create unique IP addresses, and because one-half of 32 is 16, a Class B network has a 16-bit address space.

Class C Addresses

The smallest increment of IP addresses available to an organization is Class C. In a Class C network, only the rightmost dotted decimal number can be used for a total of 256 IP addresses.

The first octet of all Class C addresses begins with a binary 110. Class B addresses compose 12.5 percent of the available IP address space. This means that Class B addresses account for 536,870,912 of the 4,294,967,296 available IP addresses.

Here's an example of a Class C address:

x.x.x.0

As with the Class A and B examples just presented, the numbers represented by the Xs are fixed numbers that range from 0 to 255; the rest of the octets, represented by the 0, can range from 0 to 255.

Other Network Classes

In addition to Classes A, B, and C, there are two other network classes:

▶ Class D. The leftmost address always begins with binary 1110. Class D addresses are used for multicasting, or sending messages to many systems at once. This isn't commonly used, but there are applications in which many computers need to receive the same data in order to provide redundant systems. There are 911 systems that use multicast because it helps ensure that all systems receive all messages and thereby leads to greater uptime and redundant behavior (albeit at greater cost).

▶ Class E. The leftmost address always begins with binary 1111. Class E addresses are reserved for experimental purposes.

Why IP Address Allocation Is Wasteful

Under the current 32-bit Internet address scheme, organizations must select a network class that will provide enough IP addresses for their needs.

The few remaining Class A addresses could potentially be assigned to organizations that need more than 65,536 (Class B-size) IP addresses, even if the organization doesn't require anywhere close to 16 million addresses.

Class B addresses are likewise assigned to organizations that require more than 256 IP addresses, whether or not they require anywhere near 65,536 addresses.

Class C addresses are, fortunately, available for small networks. However, keep in mind that if you take a full Class C, you have 256 addresses, even if you require only 20 addresses.

Fortunately, several solutions are on the horizon. The first is **CIDR**, or **Classless Inter-Domain Routing**, which enables several Class C addresses to be combined. As an example, using CIDR, if you need a thousand network addresses, you can get four 256-address Class Cs and combine them for a total of 1,024 addresses (256*4=1024), rather than tying up a whole Class B address of 65,536 addresses. CIDR, or **supernetting**, as it's been called, has become a means of efficiently allocating network addresses without wasting large chunks of class B address space.

Also on the horizon (and getting closer, but not being implemented as fast as we'd like) is IPv6, or the next generation IP protocol. IPv6, in contrast to current IP (IPv4), has a 128-bit address space (versus a 32-bit address space for IPv4) and is laid out in a slightly different way than IPv4. The following listing compares an IPv4 address with an IPv6 address:

IPv4 Address:	X.X.X.X	Each X represents 8 bits in dotted decimal notation (1 through 255)
IPv6 Address:	x:x:x:x:x:x:x:x	Each X represents 16 bits, written in hex notation (0 through F)

By the Way

Binary Versus Hex

IPv6 addresses are written in hexadecimal, or base-16, numbers. Hex is used because if each 16-bit number between the colons were written out in decimal, the address would be huge. (Remember that 16 bits can represent any number from 0 to 65,536.)

If you're not familiar with hex notation, don't worry. There's an old conundrum that will mnemonically help you remember how it works:

How does a programmer count to 16? Zero, One, Two, Three, Four, Five, Six, Seven, Eight, Nine, A, B, C, D, E, F.

By using hex notation, it's possible to represent an IPv6 number in something approaching comprehensibility: `FEDC:BA98:7654:3210: FEDC:BA98:7654:3210`. Fortunately, IPv6 also does a lot of self-configuration, so you won't have to worry about this.

IPv6 will essentially eradicate the address-space problem with IPv4. Recall that 32 bits represent an address space of over 4 billion different addresses. Now, let's extrapolate. If 32 bits is equal to 4,294,967,296 different addresses, we add one more bit (to make a total of 33 bits) and we have 8,589,934,592 addresses. Make it 34 bits, and you have 17,179,869,184 addresses.... Now keep doubling that number with each additional bit until you get to 128 bits, and you'll see that the number continues to get larger very quickly. To kill the suspense, I'll tell you that if you continue doubling the quantity represented by a string of bits until you hit 128 bits, you'll wind up with 340 billion billion billion billion (340 times 10 to the 38th power). This means that there would be 67 billion billion addresses for every square centimeter on the earth's surface. In other words, we're not going to run out of addresses anytime soon if we use IPv6.

Currently, the most popular method of getting around the IP address squeeze is **Network Address Translation**, or **NAT**. With NAT, an organization doesn't need a lot of Internet addresses, but rather needs addresses for systems that must be accessed from the Internet. The NAT device translates internal addresses (which might be on private network spaces, discussed later) to Internet addresses, and acts as the Internet face of the internal network. If you have a cable or DSL router that uses the 192.168.1.0 network for the computers on the "inside" (non-Internet) side of the network, your router is doing NAT. Over time, NAT—in conjunction with firewalls for security—has proven to be the easiest way to stretch the limited address space of the Internet.

IPv4 is currently the world's most popular protocol. It's the backbone of the Internet, and most large networks rely on its standardization, interoperability, and reliability. If you elect to run your network on it, there will initially be an added dimension of complexity. However, once your network is set up to use IP, it will be capable of talking to any other computer of any type—from a personal computer to a mainframe—that can speak TCP/IP. It's the universal solvent of networking.

IPX

Internetwork Packet Exchange (IPX) is Novell's answer to the complexity of IP. Novell designed IPX in the early 1980s before the current furor over IP and the Internet, and it shows. IPX is a relatively efficient protocol that does several things for which network administrators are duly grateful:

- ▶ Unlike IP, IPX can configure its own address. This is very useful, particularly when there are a lot of systems to install.

- ▶ IPX is a "chatty" protocol. That is, it advertises its presence on the network. This characteristic is okay on networks with finite boundaries because the bandwidth it uses is not too bad. On a huge network (a WAN, for example), the chatty nature of IPX can become quite troublesome because it can overwhelm low-bandwidth WAN connections.

On the whole, IPX is easy to install and simple to use. Unfortunately, it's not an open standard; it's controlled by Novell. In spite of its ease of use, even Novell has acknowledged that IPX will eventually bow out in favor of IP.

IPX has lost in the face of the IP onslaught. The only network operating system that continues to use IPX is Novell's NetWare, and even NetWare now supports IP natively.

NetBIOS and NetBEUI

Network Basic Input/Output System (NetBIOS) and **Network BIOS Extended User Interface (NetBEUI)** are single-site network protocols. NetBEUI is based on a way of passing data called **server message block (SMB)**, which relies on computer names to resolve destination addresses.

Although NetBios is still an integral part of Windows operating systems, NetBEUI has really fallen by the wayside and Microsoft no longer supports this network protocol in the newer releases of its desktop OS and NOS (Windows XP and Windows Server 2003 respectively). You can, however, still implement NetBEUI (although it isn't supported) by downloading the protocol from Microsoft. NetBEUI is not the most secure of the network protocols. For small LANs, even Windows peer-to-peer LANs that don't require Internet access, you can implement NWlink (IPX/SPX) or use a set of private IP addresses. (For information about configuring TCP/IP see Hour 14, "TCP/IP.")

Summary

Whew! You covered a lot of ground in this hour to ensure that you have a grasp of network topologies and protocols. You should have a good foundation for the next several chapters in which you'll learn the specifics of computer and network hardware and software. With the theory presented in this hour and the knowledge of network hardware that's coming up, you'll have the basic knowledge to design your network.

Q&A

Q *What are the actual breakdowns of Class A, B, and C addresses?*

A There are actually limitations on which numbers can be assigned to each address class. These limitations are specified in RFC 796 and later related RFC documents. The breakdowns are as follows:

- ▶ Class A addresses range from roughly 1.X.X.X to 126.X.X.X, where the Xs represent any number from 0 to 255.

- ▶ Class B addresses range from 128.0.X.X to 191.255.X.X.

- ▶ Class C addresses range from 192.0.0.X to 223.255.255.X.

IP address numbers are assigned through the Internet Assigned Numbers Authority (IANA) through Network Solutions, Inc., in Virginia.

Q *What happens if I need a Class C address, but have to use the addresses in a WAN in which routers pass data between networks at different locations?*

A Believe it or not, this is not a problem. In an attempt to allocate IP addresses as efficiently as possible, the designers of IP made provisions for subnetting, which means breaking a given address space (such as a full Class C address of 256 IP addresses) into smaller units. Data is routed between the subnets according to the way the network is divided.

For example, consider a Class C network with the network number 192.168.10.0. This network has 256 IP addresses ranging from 192.168.10.0 to 192.168.10.255. Suppose that you have 25 users in separate locations. The first subnet covers addresses 192.168.10.1 through 192.168.10.26. (Remember that the 0 address is usually reserved for the network address itself.) The next network's rightmost number ranges from 26 to 51, and so forth. This arrangement enables a network to appear to be one network—192.168.10.0—to anyone outside the network (in other words, on the Internet) but actually to be many smaller networks.

HOUR 4

Computer Concepts

This hour is a primer on basic computer concepts. In this hour, you'll learn the following:

- ▶ How computers work
- ▶ The varieties of computer hardware
- ▶ What software is and what it does
- ▶ Basics of operating systems

Networks are made of computers in the same way a band is made of musicians. Each computer—and each band member—is unique, and in the right circumstances, they all work together. If they don't, all you get is chaos.

Similarly, networks require that certain conventions be observed when computers are networked. Although each computer is unique, it nonetheless works in the same fashion as the other computers on the network. If you understand how a computer works, you'll be better prepared to understand how networks work.

We're not asking that you become a guru, but given the fact that networks hook computers together, it seems pretty apparent that a basic understanding of the hows, whys, and wherefores of computers helps ensure a better, more global understanding of networking.

Computer Hardware

When you get right down to it, computers have two components: hardware and software. **Hardware**, as you have probably guessed, is the physical components that make up a computer. It includes, but is not limited to, the following items:

▶ The CPU (Central Processing Unit)

▶ Memory

▶ Disks

▶ Add-in adapters, including important ones such as Network Interface Cards (discussed more later)

▶ Printer and communications ports

In the next few pages, you'll get a very high-level virtual tour of a PC. Although the descriptions will most correctly describe an IBM-compatible PC (the most common kind of personal computer), the concepts presented here also hold for Macintoshes, UNIX boxes, and any other computer designed with a modular, expandable architecture. Don't get hung up on the type of computer; the basic concepts are what is important.

The CPU

When you remove the cover from a personal computer, the first thing you should see (after you have cleared away the tangle of cables) is one (or more) large square section of metal and ceramic with a fan, all mounted on a circuit board, attached to the electronics, that dwarfs everything else completely. That's the **Central Processing Unit (CPU)**—or "the chip" as people familiar with computers call it. A CPU is, in principle, nothing more than a chip of silicon that has had several layers of microscopic transistors etched and doped into it using extremely delicate and complex processes.

The CPU is usually mounted on a circuit board which mounts into a **socket** on the motherboard. A **socket** is a slot in the motherboard designed to provide many connections for devices such as CPU, memory, and adapter cards. They'll be discussed later in this chapter.

The CPU is the *sine qua non* of personal computing—without it, there would be no computer. The CPU is the device that takes all the 1s and 0s that make up the input from the keyboard, the mouse, the disks, the network, and whatever else you have in your system and processes it so that you can accomplish whatever it is you want to accomplish—see a display on a video screen, type a letter, create a spreadsheet...whatever.

But don't get the idea that CPUs operate entirely on their own; CPUs are usually mounted in a **motherboard**, which is a large printed circuit board that has several systems on it to enable data to be sent to and received from the chip.

Motherboards come in a dizzying array of varieties and are available from many different manufacturers. Here's a tip: Buy name brand motherboards, and fewer problems will ensue.

CPUs are **microprocessors**—that is, they have multiple microscopic transistors in logical arrays. The earliest microprocessors had only a few hundred transistors per chip; modern microprocessors, such as Intel's current chips, Sun Microsystem's SPARC chip, and Motorola's PowerPC chip, , may have more than five million transistors on a square the size of your thumbnail. And the next generation of chips are projected to have up to fifteen or twenty million transistors—an astronomical increase in power.

Memory

A CPU is a microprocessor, but all chips are not microprocessors. Some chips are built as arrays that can hold the 1s and 0s that the CPU is processing; these are memory chips. When these chips are arranged into groups, the resulting memory devices are called **Single Inline Memory Modules (SIMMs)** or **Dual Inline Memory Modules (DIMMs)**. SIMMs and DIMMs used to be the most common way to add memory to computers; when you buy memory from a retailer, you're buying memory modules instead of individual memory chips. You'll also hear about **DRAM (dynamic RAM)** and **SDRAM**, let alone **RamBus** and other memory architectures. In spite of the difference in nomenclature, all memory works in essentially the same fashion: Put a charge across it, and it will hold 1s and 0s that the CPU can access. The key point with respect to memory is to make certain that memory you purchase is the same sort that your computer requires.

The purpose of memory chips is not solely to provide a workspace for the CPU. Memory is also used to provide CPU-speed access to data. If the computer had to read data from tapes or disks each time it needed the next batch of data or instructions, computers would be terribly slow—far too slow to be useful. But the use of memory, specifically **random access memory (RAM)**, has led to computers being fast and useful for most users.

Here's an example that might help. Suppose that you are following a complicated recipe. It's got 50 ingredients (it's a very complicated recipe) and 39 steps. Imagine what would happen if you had no counter space and no table space to store your instructions and ingredients. Here's what might happen: Each time you were ready to perform the next step, you would have to leave the kitchen, go to the bookcase, find the book, open it to the correct page, figure out where you were, read the next step, replace the book, and then remember the next step. That, by itself, would slow you down pretty significantly.

To complicate matters further, suppose that you have a bunch of ingredients stored in cupboards, refrigerators, and freezers. Each time the instructions would say that you need a new ingredient, you would have to go to the appropriate storage location, find the ingredient, measure out the correct amount, close the package, replace the ingredient, and then bring the ingredient back to the kitchen. This organizational nightmare would pretty well guarantee that even if you could cook, the process wouldn't be pretty—the slowness might cause the food being cooked to be unappetizing.

It's the same way for computers. The CPU is the kitchen, where the work gets done. The bookcase is one piece of local storage (such as a hard drive), where the **program**, or cookbook, is stored. The cupboards, fridge, and freezer are where data is stored, and the counter is your memory.

Just think about it; if you had enough counter space, you could load up all the pieces you need to follow your recipe—the directions and the ingredients—and the cooking process would go much faster. You could conceivably still cook without the counter space, but without it, you have to go to storage for each item, and that makes the whole process less efficient.

By the
Way

Be Smart—Add Memory!

That's why analysts from think-tanks, such as the Gartner Group and the Meta Group, say that memory is often more important than CPU power: Memory is fast storage. Typically, a computer can access memory chips very fast; memory access speeds are measured in nanoseconds (millionths of a second). Contrast this with the fastest hard drives, which have millisecond access times, which are an order of magnitude or three slower—a thousand times slower. Kind of makes you want to fill your computer with as much memory as you can afford, doesn't it? Even if a computer has a very powerful processor, it will run slowly if it is short of memory. By contrast, a less powerful CPU armed with a lot of memory can outrun a more powerful but memory starved CPU.

Memory is great for ensuring that computers run fast. However, there's one thing memory can't do, and the next section explains what.

Disks

Memory makes a computer run faster. This is good. However, RAM is **volatile**, which means that it only works when the computer is turned on. Because RAM is made of chips that depend on an electrical power source to store data, when the power is cut, it can no longer store anything. And because you don't want to retype everything every time you turn on the computer—that was, after all, one of the reasons you bought a computer in the first place: to replace the typewriter that made you do that—there ought to be a way to store data so that it can be retrieved the next time you turn on the computer.

That's why disks were invented. Hard disks fulfill two of the most common needs of the computer: Disks store data in a **nonvolatile** state (that is, the data stored on disks doesn't disappear when the power is cut), and they act as additional (very slow) memory when the computer needs more memory than is physically installed.

The technology behind disks is not new. A Sony Walkman uses basically the same technology to read (or write) to a cassette tape. Almost all tapes and disks are members of the **magnetic media** family, which simply means that these devices store data—whether that data is a Pink Floyd MP3 on your hard drive or your presentation to the boss on a floppy disk—by manipulating the position of the north-south poles of tiny magnetic particles.

Disks and Magnetism

How, exactly, do disks work? Magnets have two poles—north and south. Remember that computers only use 1s and 0s? Well, 1s and 0s are binary—that is, they are either 1 or 0; there's nothing in between. Fortunately for those of us who need to store data, north and south on magnetic particles are also binary, and the computer can use the orientation of microscopic magnetic particles to correspond to the 1s and 0s it needs to function. A magnetic particle with the north pole facing up might be a 0, and a particle with the south pole facing up might be a 1—just what we need to store data.

By the Way

For a long time, disks did not have very large capacities—a drive that could store a **megabyte** (a million characters) was a huge drive 30 years ago and cost half a million dollars. Today, we can store twice that much data on a floppy disk that sells for 30 cents, and it's possible to get hard disks that store one hundred **gigabytes** (a billion characters) of data or more for a couple of hundred dollars. The trend has been that storage capacities get larger and the cost per unit of disk storage gets cheaper over time.

Modern disks for personal computers generally come in one of two varieties: IDE and SCSI. These are simply different methods by which hard drives connect to computers. Because devices of one type are not compatible with devices of the other type, it's important to know a bit about them.

Integrated Drive Electronics (IDE) (also known as **ATA**) is a standard for hard drives that places the electronics that control the drive directly on the drive itself. IDE/ATA supports up to two drives connected to a single cable and disk sizes up to 528 megabytes. A more recent version of the IDE standard, called **Extended IDE (EIDE)**, can support larger disks; it's now common to see EIDE disks with capacities of up to one hundred twenty gigabytes. EIDE is now often called "Ultra DMA." You'll usually find these drives sold as ATA these days, but they're just IDE with a different name, as the interface is the same as IDE.

Small computer system interface (SCSI) is a standard for connecting all sorts of devices to a computer. SCSI (pronounced "scuzzy") enables up to seven devices to be connected to the computer in a chain (see Figure 4.1).

FIGURE 4.1
A typical SCSI device chain with a hard drive, a scanner, and a tape drive connected.

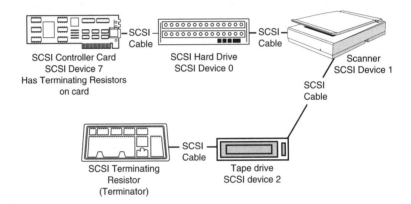

Newer SCSI devices enable up to fifteen devices to connect to a computer on one chain of devices. Each device on a **SCSI chain** (that's what a series of connected devices is called) has a number called (not surprisingly) a SCSI ID that enables the computer to locate that device when needed. Each end of the SCSI chain must be terminated, which means that a special device called a **terminating resistor** must be plugged in to the end of the cable. The terminating resistor essentially ensures that the impedance of the cable remains consistent along its length. SCSI comes in a variety of speeds ranging from SCSI-1 at 5Mbps (not so fast) to Ultra3 SCSI, which operates in excess of 160Mbps. The beauty of SCSI is that all SCSI is backward compatible, which is a fancy way of saying that old devices can connect to newer SCSI controllers and still work (although the entire SCSI bus slows down to the speed of the slowest device to which it's connected).

Of the two standards, IDE/ATA is usually simpler to set up because it supports only hard drives and supports only two hard drives per cable. IDE/ATA equipment is also less expensive than SCSI equipment, which is good to know if you're on a budget.

On the other hand, SCSI is faster and more versatile; if you're setting up a server computer, SCSI drives are almost always a better choice than IDE/ATA drives. And for some computers (notably Macintoshes and most commercial UNIX systems), you don't have a choice.

Of course, drives don't operate on their own; they have to connect to something. What drives connect to is described in the next section.

Add-In Adapter Cards

At the beginning of this hour, you learned that the CPU fits into a socket on the motherboard. In addition to the socket for the CPU, the motherboard has sockets for aftermarket devices that handle several of the computer's functions. These devices, which fit into sockets called expansion slots on the motherboard, are called **adapter cards**. These are an electronic assembly that connects to a computer through a standard interface (see the following section, "Slot Interfaces") called a *card slot*. Adapter cards can provide a variety of services to the computer, including video, network, modem, and other functions as required.

It is safe to make the claim that without IBM's decision to adopt a modular design for its initial personal computer, and the computer industry's following suit, modern personal computers wouldn't have become the powerful and adaptable machines that they are today. The modularity and adaptability of the IBM PC drove the personal computer's explosion of popularity in the early 1980s. In fact, the computer industry's rapid growth can be attributed to the adapter-card standards promulgated by IBM for the early PC.

Adapter cards handle a wide array of functions, including the following:

- ▶ Network adapters connect computers to the network.
- ▶ Video adapters provide a way for the computer to display images on a video monitor.
- ▶ Drive controllers connect floppy and hard drives to the system.
- ▶ SCSI controllers connect any devices that use the SCSI interface to the computer.
- ▶ Sound and video cards enable a variety of media types—from CD to MP3—to be played on your system.

This list is not comprehensive; it does not include all the different types of adapter cards. Nonetheless, it does cover all the devices you are likely to encounter in a common computer.

Slot Interfaces

Although most motherboards have expansion slots, the expansion slots on all motherboards are not the same. Various computer manufacturers have devised different interfaces for cards used in their systems; in general, the interfaces are not compatible with each other.

For Intel-compatible computers, the most common slot designs are, in order of age from oldest to youngest, ISA, EISA, and PCI. ISA stands for **Industry Standard Architecture**, which was what IBM called this interface when it initially created it in the early 1980s. ISA has a 16-bit data path (which means that it can move only 16 bits of data simultaneously), and it runs at 8 megahertz, even if the rest of your computer is blazing along at 2.4Ghz or more. EISA, or **Extended ISA**, was an attempt to extend the ISA interface by increasing the data path to 32 bits and increasing the speed to 32 megahertz. One good side benefit of EISA is its backward compatibility—or its capability to be used with older equipment. ISA cards can be used in EISA slots (but not the other way around)—they just don't get the speed and performance benefits of EISA.

As of this writing, ISA, EISA, VESA-Local Bus, and several other slot interfaces are dead technology. I haven't seen a new computer with any of the preceding interfaces for some years.

Peripheral Component Interconnect (PCI) is the current standard that has supplanted the old bus interfaces. PCI was the result of an initiative by Intel, the microprocessor manufacturer, to allow add-in adapters to run almost as fast as the system in which they are installed. PCI is blazingly fast, offering data transfer rates of up to 128 megabits per second.

Current systems use PCI slots to ensure good performance. Older systems based on 386, 486, and some Pentium microprocessors usually have ISA with a few faster slots, either EISA or PCI.

For Macintosh computers, there are two slot types: Nubus and PCI. The Nubus interface is found on older computers such as Mac II series machines that use various levels of the Motorola 68000 microprocessor. The PCI interface is found on the newer Power Macintosh computers that use the Motorola PowerPC chip, such as the G4 and G5. Interestingly, the PCI slots used on Power Macs are the same as the slots used on IBM compatibles, and it is possible (in some cases) to use PCI adapter cards interchangeably.

UNIX-based systems—such as Sun's SPARC systems, IBM's RS/6000s, Hewlett-Packard's HP9000 series, and Digital's Alpha-based systems (the Alpha also runs Microsoft Windows NT)—are now largely converted to PCI buses. Even so, the selection of adapter cards that work is largely tied to OEM system vendors, which can be costly. The cost of hardware on proprietary UNIX systems is one of the reasons why the UNIX-like Linux operating system is so popular; Linux runs on standard-issue PCs, which cost much less than proprietary hardware.

Intel-compatible computers have the largest market segment and the widest selection of add-in cards. As a result, the following sections primarily focus on cards designed to fit into Intel-compatible PCs.

Network Adapter Cards

If you want to connect a computer to a printer, you use a printer port. If you want to connect a computer to a network, you use a **Network Adapter Card** or **Network Interface Card** (the terms are synonymous), usually called either **network cards** or **NICs**, respectively. Network cards are available from a wide variety of manufacturers and in a variety of interfaces including Ethernet, Token Ring, ATM, and FDDI, which you'll remember from Hours 1, "An Overview of Networking," and 3, "Getting Data from Here to There: How Networking Works."

Network cards are seldom difficult to install. Typically, you turn off the power to the computer, open the case, find a slot that matches the card's interface (it'll usually be ISA, EISA, or PCI), center the card above the slot, and press the card firmly into the slot to seat it. Once you have done that, turn the computer back on. When the computer is fully running, you can install the **device drivers**, or software that enables the computer to talk to the network card. Once the device driver software is installed, you usually have to reboot your computer one more time to load the driver and be able to connect to the network.

One important thing to remember about network adapters is that every card is assigned a unique 48-bit number (that is, a 6-byte number; remember that 8 bits equals 1 byte, so 48 bits equals 6 bytes) called a **MAC address**. MAC is an acronym for **Media Access Control**. The network wire, network cards, and concentrators are also collectively called **network media**, which is where the *media* in Media Access Control comes from.

Video Adapter Cards

If you ask people to point to "the computer," some will point to the monitor on their desks rather than the box containing the CPU. Although they'd be incorrect in defining a monitor as the computer (the box that holds the CPU, motherboard, power supply, and adapter cards is, strictly speaking, the computer), they'd be making a powerful point that you'd do well to heed. Human beings are, by and large, visually oriented creatures. In general, things that are visually catchy get higher priority and garner more attention than things that aren't visually catchy. The computer box beside your desk just doesn't create visual interest. This would explain why Compaq and Apple (among others) now offer the CPU in bright colors because it will add visual interest and emphasis to the computer itself.

By contrast, the monitor *is* visually interesting because it's colorful and full of motion. Computer monitors get attention out of proportion to the amount of actual work they do. The keyboard and mouse are where the user's part of the work is done, and the system box actually does the computing, but the monitor is what we see, and therefore is what we respond to.

Because what we see on a video monitor screen is such an important part of how we interact with computers, the **Video Adapter Card**, or **video card**, is obviously an important part of the system. Video cards take the digital information the computer uses internally and converts it to an analog, or waveform, format that can be displayed on a computer monitor.

The minimum standard for video displays on modern Intel-compatible computers is called **VGA**, or **Video Graphics Array**. In order to meet the VGA standard, a video card must be capable of displaying an image that is 640 pixels wide by 480 pixels tall, in at least 16 colors. (A **pixel** is a picture element; just picture one square in a grid, and you've got the basic idea of a pixel.) VGA is a useful standard because so many manufacturers adhere to it as a baseline for their video adapters; almost all Intel-compatible video adapters have a VGA mode.

However, VGA is limited—640 by 480 with 16 colors does not provide particularly good screen resolution; it can't display images and colors very accurately. In an attempt to get around the limitations of VGA, video adapter manufacturers created several standards that extend VGA and make it more useful for computer users who actually have to spend time working at a screen: **Super VGA** (800 pixels wide by 600 pixels tall by 16 colors) and **Extended VGA** (usually 1024 pixels wide by 768 pixels tall). Additional display settings for some adapters offer increased **color depth**—or the number of colors on the screen—that ranges from 256 colors up to 16.7 million colors, which is photograph quality.

Color Depth

Color depth can get a bit confusing, especially if you do not need high-end video or graphics editing capability. But there's a very simple way to understand all the terms that surround video adapter color depths; it's common sense once you know how to interpret it.

256-color screens are sometimes called 8-bit color. This is because 8 bits (or eight 1s and 0s) are required to tell the computer what color to display in each pixel. Because 8 bits can be combined into 256 different combinations, that gives us 256 colors.

The next step up from 8-bit color is 16-bit color. 16-bit color simply uses 16 bits to describe each pixel—but what a change! With 16 bits, you can have up to 65,536 simultaneous colors onscreen. You might hear 16-bit color referred to as **high color**.

Beyond 16-bit color is 32-bit color, also called **true color**. Using 32 bits to describe the color of a pixel, you have up to 16.7 million color possibilities. In many cases, using 32-bit color in conjunction with a very high-quality monitor and video card, you cannot see the difference between a monitor screen and a photograph.

By the Way

Drive Controllers

Floppy drives, hard drives, and tape drives have to connect to the system to be useful. Drive controllers provide that connection. As noted earlier in this hour, most common drive controllers operate in the IDE, EIDE, or SCSI standard. The rule of thumb is to use SCSI drive controllers for servers and IDE drive controllers for desktops because SCSI is fast and expandable and IDE is simple. Drive controllers are available in ISA, EISA, and PCI interfaces; if your motherboard has PCI slots, use a PCI controller no matter what kind of drive you use because the PCI interface will increase performance.

SCSI Cards

Although SCSI cards were mentioned in the preceding "Drive Controllers" section, it's only fair to give them their own section because they enable a broad array of devices to connect to computers. In addition to hard drives, SCSI adapters can connect to scanners, removable-media drives from companies such as Iomega and Pinnacle Micro, sensor test equipment, and other devices. If you're faced with a limited budget and the probability that you'll need to expand a computer system, put a SCSI card in your system. It enables you to connect a range of peripherals using only one adapter card, thus reducing cost and complexity.

Operating System Software

Computer hardware is great, but it doesn't get you anywhere by itself. Hardware requires software, usually operating system software, to do anything useful. An **operating system**, or **OS**, is the software that enables users and applications to interact with the computer hardware. An OS is essentially a set of baseline functions for the computer. There's no reason why each program couldn't essentially contain an OS and boot the system, but an OS essentially frees application designers from having to redesign the world each time they write software. The OS also offers consistent user and programming interfaces and standard ways of doing simple tasks such as copying data between applications.

There are a variety of operating system types:

- ▶ **Single-tasking systems**, such as MS-DOS—These can do only one task at a time.

- ▶ **Multitasking systems**—These can run several tasks simultaneously.

- ▶ **Single-user systems**—These are intended for use by one user at a time on one machine at a time.

- ▶ **Multiuser systems**—These are intended to support many simultaneous user sessions on one computer.

These distinctions are important when you select the various components of your network, so remember these terms.

Multitasking Versus Single-Tasking Systems

Just as with everything else, there's more than one type of multitasking. This probably sounds a bit disingenuous—if an operating system can do more than one thing at a time, it can do more than one thing at a time, right?. But it bears a bit more explanation.

An MS-DOS system (which you're not likely to encounter any more) can, for all practical purposes, run one program at a time. DOS does not offer multiple sessions, so what you see on your screen is basically all that the computer can do at one time.

DOS also doesn't have a windowing system. This means that each program in DOS fills up the whole screen. If you use DOS' task switcher, you can switch between different full-screen instances of programs, but when a program isn't in the foreground filling the screen, it's inactive.

Some operating systems are multiuser—which means that they can support multiple users, each user having a unique session. UNIX is probably the best example of a multiuser system, although Digital's VMS and Linux also fit into this category. In multiuser systems, one computer runs one or more sessions simultaneously, and each user has a device called a terminal. **Terminals** are devices that look like a monitor but offer some additional connectivity services over either serial connections or networks.

ASCII terminals are generally connected via a serial port (a COM port, for PC users). ASCII terminals work at the command line—they don't have a graphical interface. X Terminals, by contrast, are usually network-connected devices that use Ethernet or Token Ring, and they offer a **graphical user interface (GUI)** called X Window that appears in many forms (GNOME, KDE, CDE, OpenLook) and works in ways similar to Microsoft's Windows or the Mac's interface.

Multitasking systems are systems that can do more than one task at a time. All multiuser systems are multitasking, but not all multitasking systems are multiuser. UNIX supports terminals to its command-line interface, and it can multitask. By contrast, Windows systems are multitasking but not multiuser (at least, not unless you install the added-cost Windows Terminal Services, which makes a Windows Server operating system multiuser as well as multitasking).

There are two types of multitasking: cooperative and preemptive. Rather than go through all the technical jargon about how the OS kernel handles task switching and so forth, we'll use an analogy to illustrate the difference between these two methods: Multitasking can be likened to managing preschool children.

Cooperative multitasking, performed by Microsoft's Windows 3.x products and the backward-compatible parts of Windows Me, is like having one toy (the operating system resources) that must be shared by several preschoolers (the software applications). Further, in the cooperative multitasking model, the teacher (or task switcher, or scheduler), who ideally should be ensuring that the toy is passed equitably, sits in the corner not doing much. In this model, the preschoolers are responsible for cooperatively relinquishing the toy when they're done with it and gracefully passing it on to the next child in line.

Clearly, this is not a recipe for successful multitasking. To return to the analogy, preschoolers are not known for their ability to cooperate when sharing resources. Invariably, one child will refuse to relinquish the toy and the whole system comes to an abrupt, screeching (and crying) halt. In the computer model, when one application hogs all the resources and the system "locks up," it's called a **system crash**. This is when preemptive multitasking becomes a more desirable model.

Preemptive multitasking is what happens when we have several preschoolers and only one toy, but with one major difference: The teacher is actively involved in governing the sharing of the toy. When one child has had the toy for a fixed period of time, the teacher takes it away, whether or not the child protests, and passes it on to the next child, and so forth. In other words, the teacher preempts the child's request to hang on to the toy, and so the toy, or resource, is successfully shared, even if one child protests. Preemptive multitasking is the model used in Linux, UNIX, Microsoft's Windows enterprise operating systems (Windows 2000, XP, 2003, and so on), and NetWare.

If you're using a server, you almost certainly want to ensure that the server operating system preemptively multitasks. Preemptive multitasking is also desirable for many client applications because it offers the user the ability to close from a crashed applications without being forced to restart the operating system.

Mac OS

In the early days of Windows, many Macintosh users complained that Microsoft had "stolen" the look and feel of the Macintosh. Apple invented the Macintosh OS, also called *the System*, in 1984. It is a clean and spare interface, well-suited to nontechnical users; this, combined with the Macintosh's reputation for never making the user worry about the computer hardware (Macintosh operating systems software ran only on Macintosh computers), led users to develop a near-fanatical devotion to Apple.

Mac OS initially came with a proprietary network called LocalTalk, which eventually turned into AppleTalk. With the rise of the Internet, MacTCP arrived and enabled Mac users to connect to the Internet and use TCP/IP standards.

Since about 2000, Apple has extensively rewritten its operating system software to create *OS X*, an operating system constructed around the UNIX-based **Mach microkernel**. It's a fully preemptive operating system, and it acts a lot like a high-end UNIX technical workstation with a really user-friendly interface. It's been quite reliable and has made further inroads into the artistic/technical community. For instance, the flagship version of DigiDesign's industry-standard ProTools recording software runs on the Mac.

Windows Systems

As mentioned in the preceding section, Microsoft planned to co-develop OS/2 with IBM, and in fact did share development efforts until version 1.3. However, in the early 1990s, Microsoft's plans changed, and Microsoft moved away from the OS/2 model to create an enterprise-class workstation and server operating system that could run on more than just Intel-compatible computers. Microsoft's name for this system was **Windows NT**, and it has led to Windows 2000, Windows XP, and Windows 2003. These are enterprise-class operating systems that offer multitasking, reasonably good user interfaces, reasonably good reliability, and the widest selection of applications currently available.

Windows NT—Why Is It Called That?

The derivation of the name Windows NT is unknown. However, there's a lot of speculation. Windows NT was initially assumed to mean Windows New Technology. Later, it became known that the Windows NT development team had several key people who had been involved in the development of Digital Equipment Corporation's VMS operating system—and WNT is VMS with one letter moved forward. Conspiracy buffs, take note!

By the Way

Windows NT was created from the ground up to serve two functions. One was to be an **enterprise-class server operating system**, which means that businesses could run their systems on it and be confident that it would work well for them.

The other function was to be a workstation-class operating system. In this context, the word **workstation** takes on a slightly different meaning from the way we've been using it. Up until now, workstation has meant a client system on a network. In the UNIX parlance that Microsoft appropriated, a workstation is a machine that has a great deal of processing power and a powerful, flexible, fast operating system that can run huge applications, such as engineering apps, digital video or audio editing, or financial data calculations.

In any case, Microsoft succeeded with NT. As a server operating system, it was reasonably fast and easy to administer, although it had a variety of interesting behaviors—the **Blue Screen of Death**, or a crashdump screen with a blue background, is legend among system administrators. The workstation client OS, Windows NT Workstation, was a fully preemptive 32-bit operating system that can run on Intel-compatible processors.

After the first several releases of Windows NT, Microsoft changed the name to Windows 2000, then Windows XP, then Windows 2003. The look and feel have changed a bit, but enterprise-class Windows operating systems remain relatively easy to network. In my opinion, the more recent releases are a great deal more stable than older versions.

As a network client, Windows enterprise operating systems are unparalleled in terms of their options. They can natively connect to almost any network without third-party software, and their connectivity is reliable. The Windows interface is ubiquitous and is easy for users of earlier Microsoft operating systems (Windows 95/98/ME), which means that users have a simpler learning curve. Windows enterprise operating systems also have relatively secure logins and entirely separate security for each user. We'll take a closer look at Windows enterprise operating systems in Hour 15, "Microsoft Networking."

UNIX

The last operating system we'll deal with for network client personal computers is UNIX. UNIX began as an experiment in a Bell Labs computer lab about 30 years ago and is now the preeminent server and workstation operating system. UNIX runs on almost every type of computer ranging from Intel-compatibles to high-end multiprocessor transaction servers used by banks, public safety agencies, and other institutions.

UNIX, like its younger sibling Windows NT, is a fully preemptive operating system. Unlike every other operating system we've discussed, it's often shipped with the source code (the set of instructions written in a computer language such as C) that runs the system. Most commercial operating system vendors do not provide source code because they believe it is proprietary. With UNIX, you often get the source code, which means that if you can program a computer, you can customize the operating system. In fact, it's pretty much necessary to customize the OS to do what you want—it's standard operating procedure!

Since the mid-1990s, a new variant of UNIX called Linux has sprung up and received a lot of media attention. Essentially, Linux is a UNIX-like operating system written in such a fashion as to evade the copyright restrictions on UNIX while retaining the look and feel. Linux is almost entirely unencumbered by the copyright restrictions on commercial UNIX systems, and the source code is always there for the taking. Linux is probably the best operating system on the planet at the moment from a cost/benefit perspective because for the cost of a CD from a Linux distributor (some of the most popular are Red Hat, Debian, SuSE, Mandrake, Slackware, and Yggdrasil), and a bit of time spent on the learning curve, it's possible to have the capabilities of a high-end UNIX workstation on an Intel-compatible PC. We'll discuss Linux more in Hour 16, "UNIX and Linux Networking."

UNIX has an undeserved reputation for complexity. This is because of the command-line interface that lies at the heart of UNIX. However, there is a standard graphical interface for UNIX, and it's called X Window; there are several slightly different versions of X graphical interfaces (in UNIX, they're called window managers) including Motif/CDE, fvwm, and Open Look—with Motif/CDE being the most common. On Linux, the typical window managers are called GNOME and KDE, and there are virtual religious wars over which is the better environment; in my opinion, both are excellent and well-constructed. The varieties of X Window managers provide slightly different visual schemes, but all work in ways similar to Microsoft's Windows or the Macintosh's graphical interfaces, with point-and-click functionality fully enabled.

As a network client, UNIX works extraordinarily well. Its default network protocol is TCP/IP, which is the protocol of the Internet, and UNIX (or, more properly in this case, Linux) servers are the foundation of most of the Web servers on the planet.

We'll take a closer look at UNIX in Hour 16.

That pretty well wraps up our overview of operating systems. The next thing you have to understand is network applications, which are (as noted earlier) the raison d'être of many a network.

Summary

At the beginning of this hour, we noted that it's necessary to know the parts in order to really know the whole. This hour was written to assist you in doing just that. By understanding something about computer hardware and operating system software, you have hopefully gained a global understanding of how a computer works and what client operating systems are.

These are important, material concepts. If you don't know how a computer works, what the parts of a computer are, or what an operating system is, you really can't understand a network at the build-it-yourself level. So make certain that you've assimilated these concepts—not doing so can make networking more difficult than it needs to be.

Q&A

Q *Why are there different types of adapter-card slots?*

A The primary reason is that newer slot designs are faster.

When IBM first released the IBM PC in 1981, it had seven adapter card slots that ran at 8 megahertz and passed data 8 bits (1 byte) at a time. Over time, this became too slow, so the slots were expanded to handle 16 bits (2 bytes) at a time.

Even this proved too slow, so EISA, VLB, and the newest standard, PCI, were invented to speed up the movement of data between adapter cards and the CPU.

Q *What are some of the criteria that are useful for selecting an operating system?*

A First and foremost, compatibility with the applications you'll be using on the network is desirable. An operating system can be great—but if it doesn't support your application, you're up the creek.

Next, look for the features that do the most for you. If you need an operating system that supports multiple user IDs logged in to different servers, OS/2 works. If you need to ensure that each application runs in its own memory space and can't crash other applications, try one of the Windows enterprise-class operating systems. For computers that are connected to a network sporadically, such as laptops, Windows XP or 2003 Professional will work, although technical users might want to try Red Hat Linux.

HOUR 5

Network Concepts

In this hour, you have the opportunity to learn about the following topics:

- ▶ What networks are made of
- ▶ Network-specific hardware
- ▶ Network-specific software

By this point, you have had the opportunity to learn some basic computer concepts and how they relate to networking. This hour introduces and explains basic network concepts in some depth. Some of the concepts covered in this hour have been mentioned earlier but are discussed here in greater depth.

What Networks Are Made Of

In Hour 4, "Computer Concepts," you learned about the hardware and software that comprise computers. In this hour, you're going to revisit both hardware and software from a network-specific perspective. The preceding discussion of computers looked at them as standalone devices, not connected to anything else. Now, we're going to see how to take that hardware and software (and some other devices mentioned only in passing, such as hubs and MAUs) and discuss how they fit together to create a coherent system.

Network-Specific Hardware

Network-specific hardware comes in two varieties. The first variety is computers that have been specifically built for networking but that could function without a network. The second variety is hardware such as network hubs, switches, cables, and routers that have no function outside a network context.

Servers

In the first two hours, you heard the term server used to describe a computer that shares its resources with other computers over a network. In the following sections, you learn more about servers—what they are, how they are different from regular computers, and what they're used for.

What Is a Server?

A **server** is a powerful computer that shares its resources with other computers on a network. In brief terms, that's what a server is and what it does. But a server is a great deal more—and, surprisingly, often a great deal less—than your desktop computer. Server hardware is usually built around two primary needs: moving data quickly and ensuring the safety and integrity of data.

For starters, a server is usually a great deal more powerful than your desktop computer. Even if your desktop computer has a ten-zillion-Hertz Perfectium VII processor, chances are that it lacks the I/O, or **throughput** (generally, a loose measure of the speed at which a particular piece of hardware can move data), to adequately service other computers' needs. No matter how fast your desktop computer is, if it can't move data off disks and onto a network wire quickly enough, it is not much use as a server. It's like a car's doughnut spare tire—a desktop computer can function as a server computer in a pinch, but you don't want to make a regular practice of using it as your mission-critical system.

In basic terms, a server has as powerful a processor—sometimes even more than one—and as much memory as you can afford to put into it. Typically, a server is more powerful than your desktop systems. Although important, processor speed and memory are not the best measures of a server's usefulness, as you are about to discover.

A server usually provides some form of insurance against disaster; most desktop computers don't. To return to the motor-vehicle metaphor, servers have systems to deal with disasters for the same reason that 18-wheeler highway trucks have dual tires. If one of the dual tires blows, the other one can keep supporting the load, and the truck doesn't crash. In server terms, the "backup tire" is called **redundancy** or **fault tolerance** and is a cornerstone of server architecture. Ultimately, fault tolerance simply means that your system is less likely to completely crash as a result of hardware failure. In the subsequent pages, you'll learn about I/O and fault tolerance as they apply to servers. We'll cover redundancy in more detail later in this hour.

The Need for Speed

Server speed can be measured any number of ways. Most server speed measurements are processor based and thereby largely meaningless to most users. The only speed tests that are worthwhile for servers measure the real-world performance of the server—that is, how fast it can move data.

Real-World Study Guides

As a rule, the large-format computer weeklies such as *InfoWorld*, *Network World*, and *CommunicationsWeek*, offer real-world testing that applies to the average network. It is well worth your while to search their archives on the Web; their reviews generally offer a worthwhile perspective on hardware.

Did you Know?

Pure speed testing does not offer much value. Although processor speed certainly should be a consideration, it's not the only measure of a server's adequacy. The types of add-in cards that fit into servers has largely ceased to matter because almost all servers made today contain a **PCI bus**. Maximum available disk space or maximum available drive bays are the next consideration—how much disk can the system handle? And, for systems that are critical, it's worth looking for ways to provide disk redundancy so that disk hardware failure doesn't automatically mean that the server is down.

No matter how fast a server operates, other computers on a network see only how fast it transmits data. A server that can't pass data to multiple clients efficiently is perceived as slow, even if it actually runs tremendously fast. As a result, server I/O (**I/O** is a term to denote input/output) is extremely important. Typically, servers have two potential I/O bottlenecks: limitations on the speed of a network card and limitations on the time it takes to read and write to the server's hard drive.

Network Card Speed

The speed of the network card is determined by two things: the **bus** of the card and the **speed** of the card. The bus of the card has ceased to matter because the PCI bus overwhelmingly dominates the field. PCI is the dominant add-in card attachment method because it enables data to flow between the computer and adapter cards much faster than any alternative.

The speed at which the card transmits data is determined by the network type. If your network topology is 10BASE-T ethernet, you can't transmit data faster than 10 megabits per second; if your topology is 1000BASE-T or ATM, you might be capable of transmitting data at 1000 megabits per second (*Mbps*, a term you'll see a lot going through this book).

If you're having trouble rationalizing these network speeds, consider the following: At 10 megabits per second (standard ethernet speed), it's possible to copy a 1-megabyte file in significantly less than 15 seconds. At 100 megabits per second, you can copy a 10-megabyte file in about the same time as the 1-meg file on the 10BASE-T network. At really high speeds (ATM or Gigabit ethernet, which move data at 1,000 megabits per second), the same transaction occurs so fast it barely even registers. Because the slowest networks you're likely to encounter for servers are about 100BASE-T ethernet, speed shouldn't be a concern unless the network is poorly designed and has a lot of users competing for network resources.

Hard Drive Speed

The speed of a server's hard drives is determined by two things. As with network cards, the first is the bus type of the hard drive controller card. All things being equal, the faster the bus of the hard drive controller card is, the faster the computer can read and write to and from the disk. The second limitation on the speed of hard drives is the interface. Even though IDE drives have become much faster in recent years, they are still not as fast as SCSI drives, so SCSI has become a server standard. When purchasing hard drives, look at the drive's speed in **revolutions per minute (RPM)** and its access time in milliseconds. Look for 10,000 RPMs or faster and the lowest possible access time; this will ensure that you get the fastest drive.

Redundancy—RAID, High Availability, and Fault Tolerance

If your data is on one disk, that's good. If your data can be copied across two disks so that either disk can break and you don't lose data, that's better. If you can chain three or more drives together so that if you lose one drive, the remaining drives can reconstruct the data on the broken drive, that's better still. Remember that redundancy increases reliability. That's why it's used so often in servers, where no one can afford to lose data.

SCSI cards, as you may recall from Hour 4, can have up to seven devices per SCSI chain. This means that you can use some special SCSI controllers to set up multiple hard drives on one chain that is very resistant to data loss. This type of setup is called **RAID**, for **redundant arrays of inexpensive disks**; the special SCSI controllers that handle RAID are called **RAID controllers**. RAID operates using a variety of methods commonly referred to as "levels" ranging from 0 to 5. Most people only need to know about levels 0, 1, and 5 because they seem to get used the most.

RAID 0

RAID 0 is best described as several hard drives connected to a computer with no redundancy. The purpose of RAID 0 is simply to increase throughput—if data is spread over several drives, it can be read from and written to the drive more rapidly. But servers need redundancy, so RAID 0 is used only for workstations. RAID levels 1 through 5 are commonly used for servers where fault-tolerance is important.

RAID 1

RAID 1 is disk mirroring or duplexing. In **disk mirroring**, two SCSI drives of the same size connect to the RAID controller card, but the computer sees them as one drive. For example, in a RAID 1 configuration, if you connect two 4-gigabyte drives to the computer, the computer sees only 4 gigabytes of disk space rather than 8 gigabytes. This happens because the RAID controller arranges the disks so that all data is written identically to both disks. In a RAID 1 configuration, one drive can fail and the other drive can continue working—the users never know that a drive has failed. In some systems, it's possible to connect each drive to a separate SCSI controller so that there is no single point of failure—either disk or either controller in a mirrored set can break, and no data or function will be lost.

RAID 1 is useful for a variety of reasons. It provides reasonable disk security and prevents downtime. Nonetheless, it's got several failings: It does nothing to accelerate reading data from disks, it cannot reconstruct missing data, and it is expensive.

RAID 1 is expensive because all hardware is redundant and set up in a fault-tolerant configuration. This means that the server would need two drives for each logical unit of disk space. Here's how it works: To provide 4 gigabytes of storage, it would be necessary to purchase two 4-gigabyte disks and mirror them so that each disk had exactly the same information.

Despite its expense, mirroring is often the easiest means of providing redundant disk space. When a disk drive goes bad, replacing the blown disk and mirroring the good disk to the new disk will often suffice to put a computer system back on track.

The performance of RAID 1 is quite good because each time the computer reads from disk, it reads from two disks at once and can get data from both disks simultaneously. The speed of writing data to disk is slightly slower because data is written to two drives, which the computer must keep in synch.

RAID 5

RAID 5 addresses the shortcomings of RAID 1 admirably. RAID 5 typically requires a minimum of three disks of equal capacity (compared to RAID 1, which requires two disks), but the net improvement is worth the cost. In a RAID 5 configuration, all data is spread across multiple disks in a process called **striping**, which is the process by which a RAID drive controller card writes data across multiple disks. Additionally, information about the file called **parity data** is also saved on all three disks. What this means is that any single drive in a RAID 5 set can fail and the parity data on the other two drives can be used to reconstruct the data on the failed drive.

RAID 5 offers another advantage: raw speed. Because any given file is divided into smaller pieces and stored on multiple disks, any time a user requests a file from the server, three disks read it simultaneously. This means that the file is read in to memory and out to the network more rapidly, which keeps your users happy.

RAID controller capabilities vary widely. Some require a tremendous amount of human configuration, and some (such as HP's AutoRAID units) can largely manage themselves after being given some basic parameters.

RAID 7 and Hot Swapping

Beyond RAID 5, there's a proto-standard called *RAID 7* or **JBOD (Just a Bunch Of Disks)**—we're not making that up—in which data is striped with parity data to more than three physical disks. (Raid 5 uses three disks; JBOD uses more than three disks.) It's not entirely standard, but it can provide even greater data security in the event of a disk crash.

RAID is good, but it still doesn't complete the topic of redundancy. If a drive fails when it's in service, it must be fixed. However, network administrators are sometimes caught in a bind when a drive fails; in many cases, networks simply cannot go down except for extremely rare scheduled maintenance. So how does a network administrator replace a failed drive in a production server where the application doesn't allow for downtime?

The answer is with **Hot Swappable capability**. When the hard drives in a computer system can be removed and reinserted while the system is running, the drives are called **hot-swappable**. The "hot" in hot-swap simply means that the system keeps running while the disk is replaced, and the "swap" is obvious—the bad disk is removed and a working disk is inserted in its place.

Fortunately, many RAID controllers also function in a "real-time" mode that enables drives to be pulled out of the system and replaced while the computer is on, or, as noted previously, hot swapping. Hot swapping is commonly used on RAID systems; when a drive is removed and replaced, many RAID controllers can automatically copy data to the new drive. For users, there's no effect other than a slight slowdown (see Figure 5.1).

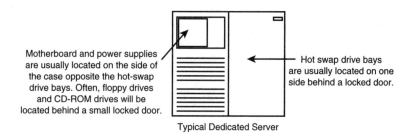

Motherboard and power supplies are usually located on the side of the case opposite the hot-swap drive bays. Often, floppy drives and CD-ROM drives will be located behind a small locked door.

Hot swap drive bays are usually located on one side behind a locked door.

Typical Dedicated Server

FIGURE 5.1
A server with hot-swappable drives and drive bays on the right side of the case.

Hot swapping is not something you can do with your average desktop system. First, most desktop systems don't have RAID controllers. Second, most desktop systems don't have **hot-swappable drive bays**, special drive bays in the case from which a drive can be installed and removed in real time. Typically, server manufacturers such as IBM, Dell, and Hewlett-Packard offer hot-swap bays in their workgroup (mid-line) and enterprise (high-end) servers. Most manufacturers require that you mount a hard drive in a special cradle that protects the drive and connects it to the hot-swap drive bays.

High Availability and Fault Tolerance

Some computer systems run applications so critical that downtime (that is, time when the system is offline and the application isn't running) is not an option. Examples of such systems include 911 systems, banking systems, and the like. These systems must be operational around the clock; when they aren't, bad things happen.

But everyone knows that computers break. Everyone's got a horror story of the time his computer crashed and he couldn't finish a paper for the teacher, send that important email, or whatever.

So how do network and systems administrators get around the inevitability of computer failure?

The answer is either Fault Tolerance or High Availability. These two terms refer to two entirely different methods used to ensure that systems can stay online and active in the face of hardware and sometimes software failures.

Fault Tolerance, at base, means that every component in a particular computer is **duplexed**, which is just a fancy way of saying that there are two of each device. Fault-Tolerant systems such as Stratus Computers' ftServers are built like this. If one component fails, another piece of hardware picks up the load and ensures that the users don't see downtime—runtime never stops until the whole computer system is shut down, so there's no interruption in service.

The methods Fault-Tolerant systems use to detect component and software failure are too complex to be adequately described here, but in the main they work very well. Fault-Tolerant systems also command a premium price, which many critical-system customers are willing to pay for the peace of mind.

Hard drives can be fault tolerant. In fact, almost every component can be. Typically, servers offer options for redundant hard drives, power supplies, and sometimes even motherboards. The rule to remember is that as you increase the redundancy and fault tolerance of your system, you increase the price of the system.

High Availability, on the other hand, also called **clustering**, is an arrangement that uses several computers to ensure that an application never shuts down because a computer fails. In a High Availability cluster, typically two or more computers are connected to a shared disk. At any point, one of the computers is running an application stored on the shared disk. If the computer running the application fails, control of the shared disk passes to another computer, which starts the application so that users can work.

Unlike fault-tolerant systems, highly available systems don't run continuously through component failure. A highly available system will show a brief interruption in service and then continued runtime. Examples of highly available systems include Microsoft's Windows Clusters, IBM's HACMP, Hewlett-Packard's MC/ServiceGuard, and Sun's SunClusters.

The advantage of High Availability is cost. The hardware for a highly available cluster may cost less than a Fault-Tolerant single system.

Neither fault tolerance nor High Availability are definitively better than the other. Both are useful, and their proper use depends entirely on the criteria brought to the network design. We'll discuss network design later in the book, including how to define the criteria for building a network.

Table 5.1 shows a comparison of fault-tolerant versus high-availability runtime.

TABLE 5.1   Comparison of Fault-Tolerant Versus High-Availability Runtime

Fault Tolerant (Runtime Does Not Stop for Component Failure):
Runtime ————————————
Outage

High Availability (Brief Interruption Followed by Restoration of Service):
Runtime ——— brief outage ———————
Outage   ———

Runtime is defined as time during which a system is operating—that is, the users can get to it and it is doing whatever it is supposed to be doing (serving Web pages, serving files, collecting and forwarding mail, whatever).

An **outage** is time when a server is *not* doing what it's supposed to be doing. This can be scheduled (maintenance outages) or the result of a malfunction of some sort.

In a Highly Available configuration, outages are part of the deal—if the primary server fails, there's a brief time lag until the backup server kicks in and takes over the primary server's function. By contrast, in Fault Tolerant configurations, components can fail (and be replaced) without generating outages.

Did you Know?

Name Brand Servers

Typically, when you purchase a server for a business application, it's a good idea to go with an established brand such as IBM, Hewlett-Packard, Dell, or any of the other first-tier manufacturers. This reasoning is not based on blind brand loyalty. Instead, it stems from the major manufacturers' capability and commitment to design, build, and troubleshoot their own systems. Servers are too important to slap together from parts; if a home-built server fails, it's up to the person who built it to get it fixed—and he might not have the knowledge or resources to do so. By contrast, first-tier manufacturers' technical support and service personnel often have exceptional knowledge of their products as well as access to the system designers. In the main, first-tier manufacturers discover bugs sooner and issue patches faster than do smaller or no-name manufacturers, which means that your server is more reliable.

Concentrators: Hubs, Switches, and Other Network Hardware

In Hour 1, "An Overview of Networking," you first became acquainted with hubs, switches, and other networking devices. In the following pages, you will learn how they work, starting with the simplest networks and going to the most complex.

Ethernet 10BASE2

As you might recall, one network topology didn't use hubs, switches, or MAUs: **Ethernet 10BASE-2**, also called **thinnet**, uses coaxial cable that runs from computer to computer. In spite of the fact that ethernet 10BASE-2 doesn't use hubs, an explanation of how ethernet 10BASE-2 works is helpful in understanding the role of hubs in topologies such as 10BASE-T, token ring, and FDDI.

Ethernet 10BASE-2 runs on coaxial cable from computer to computer (see Figure 5.2). All data travels along this single wire whether its destination is the next computer on the wire or 20 computers down the wire. This wire is called a **segment**. For all practical purposes, each segment functions as though it were a single piece of wire. Here's a list of the conditions that must be met for 10BASE-2 to work:

▶ All the data must travel on this wire between all destinations.

▶ All computers must be attached to this wire so that they can "listen" to the network wire to see whether any other computers are transmitting data.

▶ Only one computer on a segment can transmit data at any given time. Computers can transmit data only when no other station is transmitting data.

FIGURE 5.2
An ethernet
10BASE-2 network.

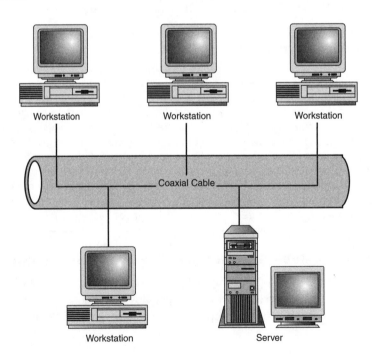

In Figure 5.2, the wire that connects all the computers is called a segment. A segment is not one piece of wire; it's actually composed of a series of shorter wires that each begin and end at a computer. At each end of the segment is a device called a **terminator** that essentially marks the end of the network. (There's a bunch of electronic theory behind termination that involves using resistors to stop electrical bounce, and so on, but that's outside the scope of this book.)

If any one of the pieces of wire that runs from computer to computer in an ethernet 10BASE-2 segment breaks or (in some cases) if a computer crashes, the network crashes. Why?

Well, because the termination on the segment will be missing. Because the termination will be gone, computers will lose the capability to determine whether any other computers are transmitting data on the wire. Because the computers can't communicate, they will drop any connections they have with other systems on the network.

Clearly, ethernet 10BASE-2 is a fragile technology if it can crash when one wire breaks. Even though ethernet 10BASE-2 is fragile, the three conditions listed earlier in this section must be met for effective networking. So the challenge is to figure out how to create a **logical segment**—that is, a network segment that mimics the effect of a single wire without being so fragile and temperamental that a single disconnection brings down the whole Net.

10BASE-2 has been superseded by versions of ethernet that use unshielded twisted pair (UTP) wiring such as 10BASE-T and 100BASE-T. It's unusual to find 10BASE-2 networks anywhere any longer. At this point, you might be asking why we're discussing it at all, since it's an outdated technology. Here's why: The basic functions of ethernet (a bus topology in which all computers listen on one wire properly terminated to kill off electrical bounce, CSMA/CD) is more easily pictured using a 10BASE-2 network than a 10BASE-T network. Fundamentally, both networks operate the same way, but 10BASE-2's physical layout makes it easier to associate with the characteristics of ethernet than later networks. This is why in network diagrams, ethernet is shown as a bus, whether or not it uses 10BASE-2, to remind us of the fundamentals of ethernet.

In Search of a Logical Segment: Hubs (Concentrators) and Switches

Enter the concentrator(also know as the hub, switch, MAU, and "that box that everything else connects to"), which is nothing more than a central junction that eliminates the need to have the coax bus of 10BASE-2 running all over the place. These devices share a single function—to create logical network segments. In networks that use concentrators, the individual pieces of wire that connect computers no longer run from machine to machine. Instead, they run from the concentrator to the workstation in a star configuration. This point-to-point wiring is also called "home running" wire because each wire goes from a central point (home base) to the field (offices, desks, cubes, and so on) (see Figure 5.3).

FIGURE 5.3
A star configuration with a hub (also known as a concentrator) at the center.

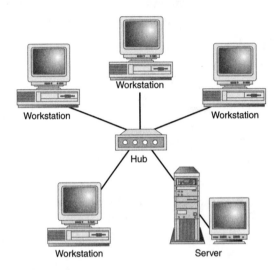

The presence of a concentrator of some sort (ethernet hubs or switches, token ring MAUs, ATM switches, what-have-you) ensures that no single network wire can break and bring down the network. A concentrator essentially is a complete segment in a box. If a wire from Data Terminal Equipment, or DTE (anything that can connect to the network—computers, printers, routers, and so on) is connected to a port on the concentrator, the concentrator can communicate with that port. If nothing is connected to a port, the concentrator bypasses that port and does not (unlike ethernet 10BASE2) see the lack of a connected port as a break in the network wire.

Given how complicated this arrangement is, another analogy is in order. Imagine a trucker whose truck is loaded in such a way that all the packages he carries must be unloaded in a particular order. He has to stop at John's house first, then Mary's, then Angela's, then Beth's, and then Mark's. If he gets to Mary's house and she's not there, he can't unload her packages—and he's stuck. He can't go to the next station (Angela's) because he can't deliver Mary's package first. He can't bypass this "break" in the system. The break in the system is equivalent to a break in the bus on a 10BASE-2 network

Another (more sensible) trucker has packed his truck so that he can get to any package at any time without difficulty. If he gets to Mary's house and she's not there, he just doesn't deliver the package and proceeds to the next delivery. He can bypass "breaks" in the system, which is what a concentrator helps a network do.

Concentrators increase the reliability of a network by ensuring that the segment is not interrupted or broken. In general, concentrators are "intelligent" enough to know when a device is connected and when one is not. In this way, concentrators have increased the reliability of networking adequately to make networking a mass-market technology.

The reliability of concentrators, however, is only the beginning of the story. The third condition we set forth—that only one computer on a segment can transmit data at any given time and computers can transmit data only when no other station is transmitting data—opens up several new issues.

Device Contention

If only one computer on any given segment can transmit data packets at any given time, the possibility that any single computer can grab hold of the network segment long enough to transmit data packets decreases as the number of computers on that network segment increases. When more than one computer or other network device has to transmit data packets at the same time, there are conflicts, and the network slows down. This process is called **device contention**, and it means that a single shared resource—in this case, the network segment—cannot service all the requests it receives in an efficient manner.

Most small-to-medium sized networks operate with a single logical segment, or only one wire, so that only one computer can transmit data at any time. At the same time, computers have become much faster and have developed ever more rapacious appetites for **network bandwidth**, or the time during which they can transmit data packets. As a result, many networks have excessive amounts of device contention and operate slower than users would like.

The solution to device contention demands that two additional conditions be met:

▶ Any equipment that can decrease device contention must be directly **backward compatible** with existing equipment.

▶ Any standard that can be applied to reduce device contention must work with current standards.

Network equipment manufacturers, faced with a steadily increasing demand for network bandwidth and the need to retain compatibility with the existing installed base of network adapters and concentrators, were in a conundrum. They had to reduce the number of stations contending for bandwidth on a given segment and at the same time increase connection speed.

To accomplish these goals, network manufacturers invented **switching technologies**. A network switch (which is available for all topologies, from ethernet to token ring to FDDI to ATM) essentially creates a separate segment for each port on a switch (see Figure 5.4). Because only one computer per segment can transmit data at any given time, this clearly frees up computers to establish connections to other computers connected to the switch and transmit data with much less contention for bandwidth.

Another use for switches is to segment networks by connecting switch ports to older shared-media (single-segment) concentrators to create several smaller network segments, thereby increasing the per-computer bandwidth and increasing the response time of the network.

FIGURE 5.4
A network segmented through the use of a switch.

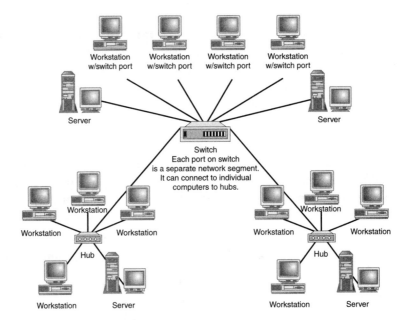

Premise Wiring: Cabling

No matter how well a network is designed, no matter the quality of its individual components, if the wire that joins the computers isn't installed properly, the network will not work well. Network cabling is the invisible yeoman of the network. When it works well, it goes unnoticed; when it doesn't work, it can be very difficult to diagnose without very sophisticated tools.

In general, there are three types of network wiring: coaxial, twisted pair, and fiber. Each type of cabling has different requirements if it is to meet network standards and work properly. The next sections list those requirements and explain what they mean.

Coaxial

In spite of being dead technology, coaxial cable, used for ethernet 10BASE-2 networking, has simplicity on its side. Because no concentrator is needed, it is less expensive than ethernet 10BASE-T, token ring, FDDI, or ATM. However, it's a dead topology; don't use it unless you have no other choice.

With ethernet 10BASE-2, up to 255 devices can be attached to a single segment, although once again, that maximum is not advisable. The maximum total length of a segment is 185 meters.

The wire used for coaxial networking is usually industry-standard RG-58 cable, which closely resembles the wire used to bring cable television in to your home. RG-58 cable has a solid copper center conductor and a braided outer conductor (see Figure 5.5). RG-58 is 50 ohm cable and requires termination at both ends of each segment using a 50 ohm terminating resistor (usually just called a **terminator**). Each computer attaches to the segment with a T-connector, which fits in to the back of the network card in the computer (see Figure 5.6).

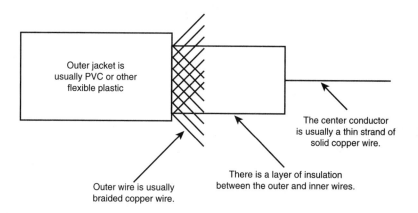

FIGURE 5.5
A simplified representation of a section of coaxial cable.

Outer jacket is usually PVC or other flexible plastic

The center conductor is usually a thin strand of solid copper wire.

Outer wire is usually braided copper wire.

There is a layer of insulation between the outer and inner wires.

Diagram of Coaxial Cable

FIGURE 5.6
A simplified repre-
sentation of a T-
connector and a
terminator.

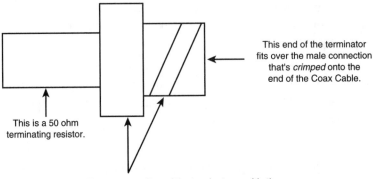

This end of the terminator
fits over the male connection
that's *crimped* onto the
end of the Coax Cable.

This is a 50 ohm
terminating resistor.

These two sections of the terminator provide the
connection to the end of the 10Base-2 Coax Cable.
It twists on with a very coarse thread;
the connector is called a *BNC connector*.

Unshielded Twisted Pair

The next step up from coaxial cable is **unshielded twisted pair**, or **UTP**. UTP is far and away the most common wire used for networking.

The UTP wires used for networking are eight-copper-conductor, four-pair wires very similar to the wire the phone company uses when it wires a home. The main difference between phone wire and UTP is that phone wiring generally has only two pairs of wire (four wires) and UTP has four pairs (eight wires). The wire must be terminated at each end of a point-to-point wire run according to very strict standards set forth in EIA 568B. EIA 568B specifies the order of the wires in the female jack (or the male patch cord) when viewed from above. Here is the order in which wires must be terminated (when viewed from the top) according to the 568B scheme:

Pin	Wire Color
1	White and Orange
2	Orange
3	White and Green
4	Blue
5	White and Blue
6	Green
7	White and Brown
8	Brown

If the cables are not terminated in this order at each end of the cable, they won't transmit data properly. Odd pin numbers are always white combined with another color.

Additionally, twisted-pair wiring comes in several levels, ranging from Level 1 (or Category 1), often used for telephone applications, to Level 5 (or Category 6), which is certified for data transmission up to 350 megabits per second. Twisted pair cables come in six categories; the following list provides you with an understanding of the various cable applications:

▶ Category 1 is not rated for performance.

▶ Category 2 is used for telephone wiring and is rated to a maximum data rate of 1 megabit per second.

▶ Category 3 is the lowest level that can be used for networking. It is used for ethernet 10BASE-T and has a maximum data rate of 16 megabits per second. Although Category 3 is rated for 10BASE-T, Category 5 is now much more common because it supports both 10BASE-T and faster speeds such as 100BASE-T.

▶ Category 4 is used for token ring and ethernet 10BASE-T. Its maximum data rate is 20 megabits per second.

▶ Category 5 is used for ethernet 100BASE-T and has a maximum data rate of 155 megabits per second. This is currently the most common cable; in fact, many companies are wiring everything in their offices (both phone and data) with Category 5 cable because it can be used for everything from basic two-wire phone services to ATM.

▶ Category 6 is used for ethernet 1000BASE-T (gigabit ethernet). It's rated for 350Mbps over 4-pair unshielded twisted-pair wire.

To maintain the maximum data rate, the wires must be handled and terminated, or connected, according to EIA 568B standards. If the wires are not correctly handled and terminated, much of their potential data rate can be jeopardized.

Always Install the Best Cable

If you're building a copper-wire–based network, it does not make sense to install cable less than Category 5 because installing Category 5 wire can extend the life of your network. Category 5 standards specify that the wires in twisted-pair cabling maintain their twist, or the braiding that leads to the name twisted pair, within $\frac{1}{2}$ inch of the final termination point. Category 5 also has strict standards for the radius of bends in Category 5 wire and so forth.

Did you Know?

Another reason to install the best cable you can is that the cost of the cable itself is negligible—it's 10 cents a foot or thereabouts. The installation is what's expensive, so don't skimp on the cable; drive a good bargain on the installation. And always always always always install two cables instead of one. The cost of doing so is not much higher than installing one cable, and it provides tremendous expandability.

The maximum distance for ethernet 10BASE-T using twisted-pair wires is 100 meters between the concentrator and the computer. For ethernet 100BASE-T, the maximum distance is 20 meters between stations—quite a reduction in length!

Unshielded twisted pair is currently the cable standard for most networks. It is relatively inexpensive, easy to install, very reliable, and easy to maintain and expand. If you elect to use twisted-pair cable for your network, find a professional cable installer if you must run wire through the walls and ceilings of your location. Fire regulations typically require that your installer follow building codes when installing cable. Cable run through open ceilings must be plenum rated, or capable to withstand certain environmental and fire conditions without giving off toxic gases in a fire. Cable run through walls is often different than cable run through ceilings, and only your installer will know the local fire codes well enough to install the correct cable types in the correct locations.

Optical Fiber

The last type of network cabling is **optical fiber**. Optical fiber has taken on a mystique within the networking community over the last several years. Initially, the expense of fiber was such that it was used only for creating high-speed links between concentrators and other esoteric applications. However, the advent of ethernet 100BASE-FX and 1000BASE-T, both of which can run over fiber, as well as FDDI and ATM topologies, has brought fiber closer to the mainstream.

Rather than using electrical impulses transmitted over copper wire, optical fiber transmits network data using pulses of light. In spite of its increased acceptance, optical fiber remains extremely expensive to install and maintain. The average network administrator lacks the skills to run fiber and terminate it properly at each end.

Termination of optical fiber is both difficult and chancy. Unlike copper wire, the finished end of a piece of optical fiber must be polished and capped with a special tip that fits into special receptacles on network cards and concentrators. If the polishing and grinding of the end of the cable is off in any way, the cable will not work.

Despite the care that must be lavished on optical fiber infrastructures, fiber has certain advantages because of its unique way of passing data. First, fiber is secure. Copper wire gives off electrical impulses that can be recorded through inductive sensors; optical fiber does not. Optical fiber can carry data at very high bit rates—over a gigabit per second!

Ultimately, the cabling type you select depends on your needs. If you're just starting to network and you want to become familiar with basic software and hardware, try coaxial networking with two or three machines. If you're installing a network that must be reliable yet cost-effective, try twisted pair. And if you've got to provide your users with huge amounts of high-speed real-time data, install fiber.

Software: Server Operating Systems

Just as network clients must have operating systems loaded for the client machines to function, a network server must have an operating system (refer to Hour 4 for explanations of the most popular client OSes). The chief differences between desktop operating systems and Server Operating Systems are, not surprisingly, scale and resources.

Typically, Server Operating Systems are optimized differently than desktop operating systems. A desktop operating system is designed to provide the user at his desktop workstation with the best possible performance for the application currently being used. By contrast, a Server Operating System's charge is to balance the needs of all users accessing the server rather than giving priority to any one of them.

In the following sections, you will learn about three server operating systems and one peer configuration. Because this book is devoted to beginning networkers, the Server Operating Systems listed here are all primarily used on Intel-compatible systems.

Novell NetWare

Novell NetWare, currently at version 6.5, is the oldest PC-based product in the Server Operating System category. In the early 1980s, it was Novell, founded and led by Raymond Noorda, who led the charge into personal-computer networking.

NetWare is an intense and complex product. By contrast with other, newer Server Operating Systems such as Microsoft Windows XP, it's less intuitive.

In the file, print, and directory services arena, NetWare is a formidable contender, offering a full suite of file, print, and web services. Novell is also making forays into the Linux arena.

In Figure 5.7, the image is not the NetWare command prompt; instead, it shows Monitor, the application most commonly in the foreground on NetWare server screens. Monitor allows the administrator to access a variety of information about the current state of the server, ranging from available memory to disk space.

FIGURE 5.7
A Novell NetWare console Monitor screen.

Unlike many newer PC-based Server Operating Systems, NetWare was not designed with the Internet in mind. A great many of the design choices Novell made appear to have been an attempt to simplify networking enough to make it palatable for PC users.

In the first place, Novell did not build native support for TCP/IP, the language that computers use to communicate across the Internet. Novell had good reason for this: When NetWare was developed, TCP/IP was a relatively new and immature protocol standard; it required a great deal of manual configuration, and maintaining it was difficult.

Given the complexity of TCP/IP and the technical skills of its target market group, Novell decided to develop a simpler protocol. Novell's proprietary network protocol was called **Internetworking Packet Exchange/Sequenced Packet Exchange (IPX/SPX)**; in many ways, it was ideal for PC networking. IPX was and is largely self-configuring, easy to install, and simple to maintain.

Did you Know?

For More on Protocols

Recall the discussion of protocols at the end of Hour 3, "Getting Data from Here to There: How Networking Works." Protocols are the languages that computers use to speak to one another.

Unfortunately, as the Internet revolution picked up steam (and TCP/IP with it), Novell's position deteriorated because NetWare is fundamentally founded on IPX networking. Current versions of NetWare natively use IP, and this has helped NetWare's popularity.

Microsoft Windows Server 2003

Beginning in the late 1980s, Microsoft decided that it needed a high-end Server Operating System to compete with NetWare and Unix. After a ferocious three-to-four year struggle (aptly described in Pascal Zachary's book *Showstopper*), Microsoft had what it had set out to create: Windows NT. Initially, Windows NT version 3.1 (the first version, but renumbered to match the existing version of 16-bit Windows) was all one product—there was initially little if any differentiation between versions used for servers, and versions used for workstations. By the time Microsoft released Windows NT 3.5 in 1995, Microsoft had created two different versions of the operating system: Windows NT Workstation (profiled in Hour 4) and Windows NT Server. To date, these have evolved into Windows XP Professional for the workstation market and Windows Server 2003 for the server market. For all intents and purposes, both operating systems are built on the same basic platform, but Microsoft's Server products have a rich set of utilities and tools the Workstation product lacks. The ability to connect to all sorts of networks was built into Windows XP from the start. Additionally, Windows Server 2003 can handle the server portion of network application work, which makes it an ideal application server platform. It uses the familiar Windows interface that simplifies administration—Windows XP is admirably well-suited to small organizations because of its point-and-click administration. For the vast majority of beginning networkers, Windows Server 2003 is probably the easiest enterprise-class network OS to install and maintain. Do not construe that statement to mean that the Windows NOS is simple; it is not. But in comparison to other Server Operating Systems, Windows Server 2003 has a certain amount of familiarity because it uses the ubiquitous Windows interface.

For the vast majority of beginning networkers, Windows 2000 Server is probably the easiest enterprise-class network OS to install and maintain. Do not construe that statement to mean that Windows 2000 is simple; it is not. But in comparison to other Server Operating Systems, Windows 2000 has a certain amount of familiarity because it uses the ubiquitous Windows interface.

UNIX

As mentioned in the UNIX client workstation section in Hour 4, UNIX is the result of Bell Labs' innovations some 30 years ago. It is a fully preemptive Server Operating System with a rich interface unmatched by any other operating system. Unfortunately, with UNIX's richness comes a tremendous degree of complexity. UNIX can accomplish almost any task a computer can do, but the complexity of the interface has unfortunately led to UNIX being maligned as user hostile. In spite of a much-undeserved reputation for difficulty, UNIX makes a fast file and print server and offers perhaps the best application services of any network OS presented here.

As with Windows server products, UNIX can operate as either a client or a server on a network. For the most part, there's little or no difference between a client UNIX system and a server UNIX system except for the power of the hardware—the server should be more powerful than the workstation—and the tightness of the security. UNIX comes with such a rich feature set that it seldom needs third-party software to administer its users. It's possible to create shell scripts, perl scripts, and compiled C programs to take care of mundane tasks on most UNIX systems.

Because of its age, UNIX is a very stable platform. However, UNIX is not produced by any single vendor; instead, a host of vendors purvey UNIX, and each version is slightly different. As a result, there is a lack of shrink-wrapped applications, or applications ready to install right out of the shrink-wrapped box. In recent years, UNIX vendors have tried repeatedly to create a standard for UNIX to ensure binary compatibility, which simply means that an application, once compiled, can run on a variety of different operating systems. Unfortunately, this has met with only limited success; hopefully, the threat of Microsoft's Windows server products will make the UNIX vendors rally around a standard.

UNIX is best suited to networks in which an experienced system administrator is in charge. Its complexity makes it unsuitable for the casual user or part-time system administrator, but in the hands of a truly knowledgeable system administrator, UNIX can accomplish almost any task reliably and fast.

Linux

Linux is to UNIX as a child is to its parent.

In the late 1980s and early 1990s, UNIX gained popularity at a staggering rate. The only problem for most noncorporate users was that the cost of UNIX was far beyond most individuals' means, and the few UNIX-like operating systems of reasonable cost (such as Minix, an operating system designed by a Dutch professor for teaching purposes) were judged inadequate by the user (hacker) community.

This gap is why UNIX-like systems couldn't last long given the open-standards basis of UNIX and its derivative operating systems. In 1991, Linus Torvalds, building in part on the success of Richard Stallman's GNU project (`www.gnu.mit.edu`), created a new, UNIX-like operating system that he fancifully called **Linux**. The fledgling operating system was rapidly adopted by the Internet hacker community, who began to extend Linus' creation tremendously. Now, 12 years later, Linux is the fastest growing server operating system in terms of percentage growth from year to year. It's inexpensive, it's open source (which is a way of saying that when you buy the programs, you also get the source code and the rights to modify and rebuild, or **recompile**, the programs to make them do what you want), and it's supported by a cast of—hold your breath—*millions*. Some 40 million Linux systems (that number might already be out-of-date by the time you read this) are online at this time, running all sorts of applications ranging from Web servers to mailservers to engineering workstations to who knows what else.

Like UNIX, its progenitor, Linux is based on the POSIX standard, which in turn is heavily reliant on the open standards promulgated by the Internet Engineering Task Force, or IETF. This means that it is a pretty fundamental embodiment of the rules that make the Internet work, just like UNIX. It also has all the toys that UNIX does—shell scripts (DOS users, think "batch file on steroids"), C, C++, Java, Expect, Perl, Eiffel, and other compilers, and a pair of wonderful windowing desktops called GNOME and KDE. Linux users reading this take note: Both GNOME and KDE are fine accomplishments, and I won't make pronouncements as to which is better.

From a pure networking perspective, Linux has tools to hook up to almost anything. It can network using TCP/IP; that's basic. It can use SMB (server message block) and act like a Windows server. It can run IPX and act like an old NetWare server. Linux is arguably the most popular Web- and mail-server platform on the Internet, in large part because it is inexpensive and nowhere near as complex as naysayers claim.

Linux is not a proprietary product available from one vendor. It's typically packaged in **distributions** from vendors who package the software and source code with some of their own improvements. The current leading vendor in the United States is probably Red Hat (`http://www.redhat.com`), although there are other, perfectly acceptable distributions from Debian (`http://www.debian.com`) and SuSE (`http://www.suse.com`). I've used all these distributions at one time or another, and all are good distributions. There are even more: TurboLinux, Lindows, Mandrake, Yggdrasil...the list goes on and on.

Often, software compiled on one distribution of Linux will run on another without **porting**, or working on the source code to ensure compatibility. Even if it doesn't, Linux's software development tools are second to none, meaning that debugging problems with programming is not horribly difficult.

For a more complete story of the development and rise of Linux, read *Just for Fun: The Story of an Accidental Revolutionary* by Linus Torvalds (yes, *that* Linus) and David Diamond. It's largely Linus' first-person perspective and is a quick and entertaining read.

Client/Server Versus Peer Network Configurations: A Quick Guide

So far in this book, we have mentioned the terms client/server and peer networking several times. In the following brief sections, you learn what client/server and peer really are, and what ramifications they have on you.

Client/server and **peer** are terms that describe the logical relationship between computers on a network. Remember that a logical relationship is not the same thing as a physical relationship—computers can operate in either client/server or peer on any network topology, from 10BASE-2 to FDDI.

Client/Server Networks

In a client/server network, the computers are divided into servers and clients. The **server** is usually a dedicated, powerful machine bearing all the hallmarks of servers as described earlier in this hour; the **clients** are usually less powerful than the server and connect only to the server through the network. Figure 5.8 shows an example of a client/server network.

FIGURE 5.8
A client/server network.

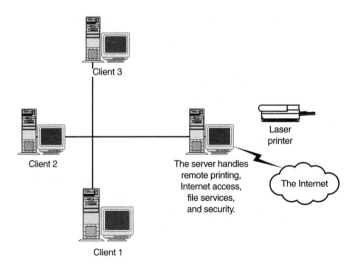

The benefits of a client/server configuration (or **architecture**, as it is sometimes called) are mostly of interest to people who rely heavily on the network's reliability. They include the following benefits:

▶ Centralized management of network resources

▶ The capability to set stringent and rigorous controls on security, file access, and other potentially sensitive material

▶ A significant reduction in management at the client

▶ The capability to secure and back up data from the server

▶ The capability to "scale"—that is, to increase in size gracefully

In the client/server relationship, clients can see only the server; they cannot see each other. This arrangement results in greater security and increased "replace-ability"—if a client workstation fails, it is possible in a client/server architecture to simply replace the client workstation with a comparable machine. If the applications are run from the server's hard drive, once the new computer is connected to the network, the user will have access to most of what he had before the work-station failed.

The downsides of client/server are less apparent:

▶ Client/server networks cost more to implement than peer configurations because of the cost of the server—a dedicated machine that no one uses as a workstation.

▶ The server becomes a single point of failure. If it breaks, the network is down. Many servers have fault-tolerant features (as do RAID servers, described earlier in this hour)—fault tolerance is truly necessary for client/server networks.

Client/server is almost always the architecture on which large enterprise networks are built. Reliability and scalability are almost always the stated reasons behind this choice, but make no mistake about it—data security and centralized manage-ment, which are big dollar savers, are also a large factor in the choice of the client/server network.

Peer Networks

At the other end of the spectrum is the peer network. In a peer configuration, all user workstations also handle some server functions. For example, one machine with a large hard drive might be used to store some of the users' files. Another system, connected to a printer, might share that printer with other workstations.

The chief fact about peer networking, though, is this: In a peer network, there is no server, and all computers can be used as user workstations (see Figure 5.9).

FIGURE 5.9
A peer network.

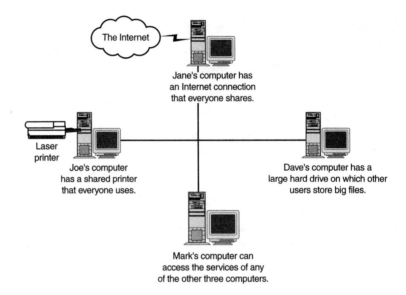

The Internet

Jane's computer has an Internet connection that everyone shares.

Laser printer

Joe's computer has a shared printer that everyone uses.

Dave's computer has a large hard drive on which other users store big files.

Mark's computer can access the services of any of the other three computers.

A peer network has some distinct advantages:

▶ Ease of installation and configuration

▶ Inexpensive compared to client/server networks

However, peer networking has several downsides that (in the author's opinion) outweigh its benefits:

▶ It has a total lack of centralized control, which means that a peer network is basically unmanageable.

▶ It is tremendously insecure—security on a peer network is almost nonexistent.

▶ It is unreliable. Peer networking relies on the vicissitudes of user workstations, which means that the network can be seriously disturbed if (for example) the workstation to which the printer is connected is rebooted or locks up.

Peer networking is suitable only for the very smallest networks—those people who build to teach themselves networking or those in an office with no more than three or four computers.

This winds up the discussion on what makes up a network. In the next hour, we'll revisit the ways in which networks pass data between computers and look at how networks pass data to other networks.

Summary

In this hour, you had the opportunity to learn about the hardware used to connect computers, as well as some basic concepts about network layout. In the preceding hours, you learned about basic computer concepts and how networks pass data; in subsequent hours, you'll learn how to extend your network beyond the confines of the local office.

Q&A

Q *What are some compelling reasons why you might want to use fault-tolerant hardware?*

A Fault-tolerant hardware is worth the cost whenever you need a computer to be up and running 24/7/365 because the hardware can partially fail without ceasing to work altogether. For this reason, banks, insurance companies, hospitals, and other round-the-clock businesses use highly fault-tolerant systems.

Q *What are some of the reasons that could drive the decision to use a switch rather than a shared-media hub?*

A There are many reasons, but these are some of the most common situations in which switches are better choices than hubs:

▶ Networks that have a lot of traffic and tend to slow down because of bandwidth contention

▶ A local network that has grown to too many users to comfortably share one collision domain or token ring

▶ Networks that must be segmented for security or performance reasons

Q *What are the circumstances in which a peer network might be more useful or appropriate than a client/server network?*

A Here are several situations in which a peer network might be more appropriate than a client/server network:

▶ When the network consists of only two or three computers

▶ When resources are extremely scarce and a separate computer can't be allocated as the server

▶ For small home networks

HOUR 6

Extending Your LAN: Wide Area Networks

In this hour, you'll have the opportunity to learn about the following aspects of networking:

▶ Definition of a Wide Area Network (WAN)

▶ How WANs are put together

▶ What the digital phone service is and why WANs need to use it

▶ How you can use the Internet to help you assemble your WAN

How often do you send overnight-delivery packages? If the answer is "often," you understand the need to be able to move information over long distances rapidly. It isn't a new problem.

Sending information over long distances has traditionally been a struggle for humankind. Before the advent of electricity, people moved information quickly by using smoke signals or fast and lean modes of transportation such as the Pony Express or the railroad. With the coming of electricity, telegraphs could suddenly send messages much faster—a message sent from New York could conceivably be in San Francisco almost instantly.

Despite its speed, the telegraph still had drawbacks. The information it transmitted was encoded, and therefore required a specially trained person to decipher the data; in addition, it could carry only limited amounts of data.

Early networks suffered from some of the same problems as earlier technologies: They were slow, too. Over time, however, networking companies have invented ways to hook together networks that allow users spread out across the world to have access to the same data in real time. That is discussed in this hour.

What Is a WAN?

As you learned in Hour 1, "An Overview of Networking," sometimes networks are distributed over too great a geographical area to make networking them feasible using regular network cards, concentrators, and wiring. When multiple local area networks (explained in Hour 3, "Getting Data from Here to There: How Computers Share Data") in different locations need to be connected, the result is a WAN.

As you remember from Hour 1, a wide area network (WAN) is so named because it is a network that links together geographically dispersed computer networks. A WAN is basically two or more LANs tied together using high-speed phone lines (such as **T1s** or **56K frame relay**). Beyond that, it is difficult to make generalizations about WANs other than saying that they link many sites into common resources. What matters is that there are LANs at either end of it (or, if it's a large WAN, that it ties together two or more LANs).

Because WANs serve many purposes, it is sometimes difficult to precisely define the term. Should the systems connected to a WAN all be interactive desktop computers? If a network is linked only for internal email and other communications tasks, is it a WAN or just an expensive private Internet (also called an **intranet**)? Is an **extranet** (a system linking your system with your suppliers' and customers' systems) a WAN?

Here are several examples that explain the astonishing versatility (and bewildering elusiveness) of WANs:

- ▶ If you've recently purchased anything at a retail outlet with a credit card, chances are good that your card's credit was examined over a very slow WAN connection to the cashier's computer. The cashier's computer is certainly not a computer in the sense that we usually think of a computer—it has only a limited set of functions and an extremely limited purpose—but it does data lookups in corporate databases across leased phone lines. Is this a WAN? It certainly is, according to the working definition given previously.

- ▶ Your international company has installed groupware at all its remote locations around the world. To ensure that email and groupware messages and data replication work reliably, the company builds a private network using leased lines instead of using the Internet as a backbone. The users at one site do not directly access the resources of users at another site. Is this a WAN? The answer, again, is yes.

▶ Your international company has installed groupware at all its remote locations around the world. To ensure that email and groupware messages and data replication work reliably, the company builds a **Virtual Private Network (VPN)**—a method for connecting networks that uses the Internet to carry data, which is discussed at length later on—using the Internet as a data conduit. The users at one site can access the resources of users at another site. Is this a WAN? Yep!

▶ A small company with a regional presence (such as the Northeast or Northern California) has to provide its traveling sales representatives with access to the central network resources. The company does so by using a private dial-up link into its network; the company also uses the Internet (for the more far-afield reps) as a way to carry traffic in and out of its LAN from distant locations. Is this a WAN? Yes.

These kinds of networks have all been considered WANs; the concept has expanded to include all of them. In the final analysis, a WAN is just a way to extend your network resources beyond the local area. In the age of the Internet, there are a host of ways to do so, ranging from expensive digital phone lines to VPNs, from dial-up network access to other ways that haven't been invented yet.

However, the basic WAN configuration (in which computer users on multiple LANs share resources) is the focus of this hour (see Figure 6.1). WANs built for special purposes are not strictly applicable to this discussion; simply being aware that they exist as viable alternatives is quite enough.

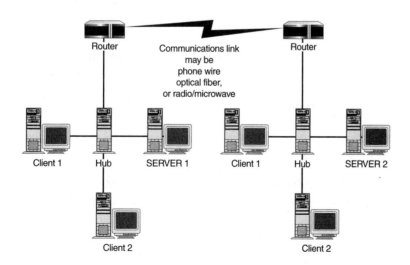

FIGURE 6.1
A basic WAN configuration.

WANs, more than LANs, require a great deal of planning on the front end if they are to function effectively. They require that a company's Information Systems staff develop a variety of competencies ranging from the relative simplicity of data networking to the arcane voodoo of the public telephone network. But more than anything else, WANs need a purpose. WANs built without a specific, articulated, clear, and broadly accepted purpose are nothing more than money pits. Before you build a WAN, ask yourself the following questions to ensure that you need one:

▶ Do users in multiple locations need to have real-time access to a common database, such as a transactional system?

▶ Do your remote locations already have LANs, or are they mostly home offices or one-person offices?

▶ What are the services you want to share across a WAN? Database? File services? Email? Web? Something else?

▶ Are your remote sites capable of administering their end of a WAN, or will you need to hire traveling system administrators?

▶ Are you willing to pay the costs of high-speed digital phone lines?

If you have users who need real-time access to a common database, a WAN can offer real value. But if you're dealing with small or home offices, you will likely require significant system administration to ensure that your end users (who are probably not computer gurus) can actually get their work done. System administration costs are often relatively hidden, but they often make up the greater part of the **total cost of ownership (TCO)** of a WAN (or even of a large and complex LAN). Administration costs can and will increase the overall operating costs of the WAN if you don't plan for them. Make certain that the return is greater than the cost. It is very easy to spend several tens of thousands of dollars a month on a WAN, and if you don't recoup it through increased services or productivity, it will become a drain instead of a help.

WAN Hardware

Several pieces of hardware can be used to link LANs. Of these, the most common devices are routers. Bridges are older devices that aren't used much any longer, but we'll discuss them because you might encounter them at older sites. And **gateway** has become an amorphous term more often used to denote a router, although there are a few gateway devices that *aren't* routers.

Bridges

A **bridge** is a network device that essentially does what its name describes: bridges two LANs together into one very big LAN with a *very* slow connection in the middle. The difference between a bridge and a router is based on the way they link networks. In a telecommunications network, a bridge is a hardware device or software that copies Layer 2 packets (see the following By the Way) from one network to another network. For example, two LANs can be connected with a bridge, a digital phone line, and another bridge at the other end. A bridge connects networks at the hardware level. If you connect two networks by bridging them, they'll essentially be one segment with a very slow link. Bridging is not the best way to handle WAN connections unless it's absolutely necessary because bridging passes broadcast traffic—messages sent to every machine on an particular network—which can waste quite a bit of WAN-link bandwidth.

Networking Theory Help

If you want to brush up on your networking theory and the seven layers of the OSI model, Hour 3 has a description of the OSI model and a discussion of protocols. A good understanding of the OSI model is very useful when learning the functions of a network.

By the Way

In general, a bridge is a **router** that's been configured to bridge networks at OSI layer 2 rather than OSI layer 3, which is where routers work. When a bridge links networks, for all practical purposes, users see a larger version of their current network—they can access remote resources using the same methods they use in their local LAN. Bridges, however, are slow and resource intensive, which is why most interLAN networking today is routed, not bridged. The "Routers" section a bit later in the hour will help you understand the differences between routers and bridges.

Bridges are often used for networks that use protocols that cannot be routed (for example, NetBIOS or NetBEUI). However, these protocols can be carried over a bridge because the bridge works at the Data-Link layer (which is still concerned with hardware) rather than the Network layer (where data packet routing depends on software).

Gateways: Protocol Translators

The term **gateway** can refer to a variety of different devices. At its most basic, a gateway is a device that acts as a two-way path between networks. For example, in an Internet-connected network, a proxy server can be a gateway between the internal network and the external Internet (see Figure 6.2).

FIGURE 6.2
These proxy
servers are acting
as gateways.

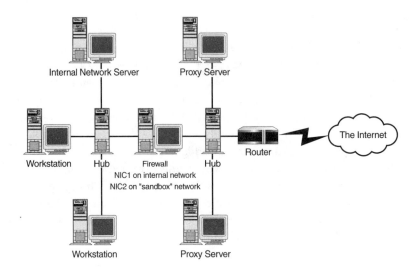

Another common use of the term gateway is any device that passes IP packets from one network to another network around the Internet. Routers and bridges loosely belong to the global group called gateways, but the gateways discussed in this section have specific purposes other than routing packets between networks or bridging networks.

Gateways link networks together. As noted earlier, gateways are different from bridges in that they can create junctions between dissimilar networks; this can come in very useful for networks that do not run TCP/IP. Gateways that can translate one protocol to another are called **protocol translators**, devices that can translate between two network protocols. Typically, protocol translators translate NetWare IPX to TCP/IP so that users on an IPX network can access the Internet or IP resources.

Protocol translators are not commonly used to link LANs into WANs; these days, protocol translators are often used to translate between NetWare's IPX protocol and the TCP/IP protocol so that an IPX-based network can connect to the Internet. If you have chosen to build (or have inherited) a NetWare LAN, protocol translation might be the best way to provide Internet access to your users. However, NetWare's main protocol, IPX, is routable, so a router is probably a better choice if you want to join two LANs into a WAN.

Routers

A **router** is a device that handles the traffic flow for data packets that are not addressed inside the local network. In other words, a router is the long-distance post office sorting machine that passes data between multiple networks. It works at the OSI Network layer (Layer 3), which means that it must be capable of understanding the data packets so that it can route them to their destinations. Routers are essentially computers optimized for handling packets that have to be transferred between separate networks. Not surprisingly, routers attempt to send packets from their source to their destination in the fastest way possible, which (as you'll see) is not always the absolute shortest path.

On a network, packets with destinations on the local network go directly from the sending machine to the destination machine without any intermediaries. However, if the destination address of a packet is outside the local network, the sending machine sends it to the router (which the sending machine knows as the default gateway) and has no further interaction with that packet. When the router receives a packet destined for a point outside the local network, it looks to see if it has a route to get the packet to that destination network; if it does (or if it has a default gateway of its own), it will send the packet to the next stop.

Routing between LANs, as you recall from Hour 2, "Why Build a Network?," is like a postal system or a courier network. A package traveling from New York to San Francisco might travel through a hub in Memphis or Chicago and be re-sorted in Reno before heading to its final destination. If the package has to be hand delivered quickly, you could do that, but the cost would increase significantly. And hopefully, the package won't get routed the long way around because that tends to be inefficient and difficult to trace.

In the same fashion, routers send packets according to the available routes between networks and try to determine the shortest possible route at any given time. How does a router do this? Well, inside a router (which is actually a very powerful computer—you'll see why in a moment), there's a set of data called **routing tables**. Routing tables are dynamic—they are updated by routing protocols called **Routing Information Protocol (RIP)** or **Open Shortest Path First (OSPF)** that constantly pass messages between routers to ensure that all routers have the most current data regarding available routes.

Routing tables contain all the possible routes that the router is aware of; the router consults them to determine whether it has a route to a particular destination address. A router is sort of a combination travel agent and personal assistant—it is always looking for the best possible route at the least possible cost. The process of sending a packet closer to its destination is called **routing**.

Explanation of Routing

When a router takes a packet and sends it closer to its final destination, we say that it has **forwarded** a packet. In the simplest terms, that's what a router does: It forwards packets toward their destinations. And it tries to do so at the least possible cost—which is a tricky concept that has to be explained next.

Cost, for a router, is not measured in dollars and cents. Instead, it is measured in hops. Every time a packet is routed between one router and another, a number in the data packet called the hop count increases by 1 (this is usually called "incrementing the counter"). If the hop count reaches certain preset limits (for example, the RIP enables a maximum of 16 hops between the source and the destination), the packet might be discarded as undeliverable because the routers have not been able to deliver the packet to the destination address in 16 hops.

For routers, however, cost is not the absolute variable it is in the physical world because it isn't much more expensive to go "the long way" from an origin to a destination when dealing with the Internet. Note these two facts:

▶ Data (which is basically just pulses of electricity) moves at the speed of light (or very close to it over copper wires), so it would take a pretty serious out-of-the-way, roundabout route before the additional distance made a truly significant difference in speed.

▶ The Internet was designed to be redundant (remember, it was created for military use during the Cold War). The planners of the Internet had to deal with military demands for a network that could still find a way to get data from point A to point C when point B (which was on the route from A to C) had failed (ostensibly because an ICBM had wiped out a city or something like that). The planners had to figure out a way to route data redundantly: If the first route fails, try the second, and so forth.

Fortunately, we've rarely seen the redundancy of the Internet significantly tested, although the September 11th terrorist attacks did put some strain on a variety of networks passing through lower Manhattan. Fortunately, the design is solid because the network reroutes data packets all the time as a result of events such as extreme terrorism, natural disasters, and power failures such as the 2003 power failure on the east coast.

How Routers Route Data: Gateway Protocols

Routers variously use one or more of four pieces of the TCP/IP protocol suite to determine which route a packet should take to a given destination at any time. These four pieces are collectively referred to as **gateway protocols**, a needlessly confusing term. Gateway protocols are members of the TCP/IP protocol suite that routers use to determine the best route for data packets. Rather than gateway protocols, a more descriptive and accurate term would be **router protocols** because routers use them to determine the proper way to forward data packets.

These four pieces are called **Routing Information Protocol (RIP)**, **Open Shortest Path First (OSPF)**, **Border Gateway Protocol (BGP)**, and **Exterior Gateway Protocol (EGP)**. Don't be scared off by the names; they're really very easy to understand.

Two of these four protocols (RIP and OSPF) are called interior gateway protocols; they deal with routing data only within a self-contained network such as a LAN or WAN. The other two protocols (BGP and EGP) are called exterior gateway protocols and are used to route data outside a LAN or WAN.

Interior Gateway Protocols: RIP and OSPF

In Hour 3, you learned the names of two of the protocols that TCP/IP uses to figure out the best way to send packets: RIP and OSPF. Of the two, RIP is the older routing standard and has limitations on how well it can route data when the network is changing constantly. RIP is **static**; that is, it has rigid settings that allow for a maximum of 16 hops, which means that it doesn't work very well in large network settings (such as, not surprisingly, the Internet). OSPF, on the other hand, is **dynamic**. It can change its routing strategy according to the current conditions on the network—so if your main router has gone down for some reason, OSPF can adapt and send data packets through your other router (if you have one).

These protocols are used in private networks, or what technical types call **Autonomous Systems (AS)**. An AS is a collection of routers that are all related and that all route data using the same gateway protocol (RIP or OSPF).

For a great many WANs, RIP suffices to handle interoffice data routing. The rise of the Internet has made router manufacturers simplify the basic configuration of their routers so that users don't often have to worry about RIP and OSPF directly. Instead, when the router is set up, the administrative user adds some static routes to the routing table in one or more routers.

Network providers ranging from your local phone company to Internet service providers have realized that they have to be responsible for configuring routers that connect to their networks, so they've developed significant competencies in installing, configuring, and troubleshooting routers. Even so, try to have a reasonably technically literate person on staff (even if that person is you). Even if that person isn't directly managing the system, she will be able to translate the technology issues into business issues that executives can understand.

Cisco Systems is arguably the largest manufacturer of routers and routing technology products today. It sponsors a broad range of educational programs designed to help budding system administrators and network administrators get up the curve on the **IOS (Internetwork Operating System)** software that runs on its routers. Further, Cisco Systems' classes provide an excellent base in practical TCP/IP. Such programs are well worth investigating.

Exterior Gateway Protocols: EGP and BGP

Sometimes, however, you have to send packets out to the wide world. That means your packets have to be sent over the Internet. To do this with something approaching effectiveness, you have to use BGP or EGP, your exterior gateway protocols.

Remember the acronym AS (for Autonomous System or private network) that was just introduced? Well, BGP and EGP are what routers use to send data packets between ASes. In other words, if you route within your own private network, you only need RIP and OSPF. However, when you start sending data to other people's networks (for example, an extranet), you need BGP or EGP.

Border Gateway Protocol (BGP) is a newer version of EGP, which is largely out of date these days. Whereas RIP and OSPF look at packets and try to route them to a destination inside the network, BGP and EGP look at packets and route them to the outside world. BGP is newer and is preferred to EGP because of its increased flexibility and configurability.

BGP relies on TCP to ensure that packets get delivered—another example of the tremendous degree of integration and efficiency in the TCP/IP protocol suite. BGP has an optimized routing table procedure, which means that it doesn't waste network bandwidth. It also detects when a particular route has failed, which, given the size of Internet routing tables, is no small feat.

One thing to keep in mind: More than one router running BGP can be used inside a single private network (or AS), but this requires that the private network have a router running RIP or OSPF as well. If RIP or OSPF isn't running inside the network while several routers inside the network are running BGP, the BGP routers start routing packets to each other—each expecting the other to forward the packets to an external network. This creates an infinite loop and crashes the system. Once again, careful planning can help you avoid this kind of mistake.

In summary, Table 6.1 offers a breakdown of the basic TCP/IP routing protocols. With this chart, you can see the various functions that interior and exterior gateway protocols accomplish.

TABLE 6.1   Routing Protocols

Type of Protocol	Protocols Included in This Heading	Explanation	Notes
Routing protocols Used to route local network.	RIP (Routing Information Protocol)	RIP enables packets to be routed a maximum of 16 times.	RIP is common, packets inside a but is being superseded by OSPF.
	OSPF (Open Shortest Path First)	OSPF uses a link-state algorithm to determine the current best route. No maximum number of hops during routing.	
Gateway protocols Used to route packets to networks outside the local networks.	EGP (Exterior Gateway Protocol)	Sends packets to destinations outside the local network.	Is being superseded by BGP.
	BGP (Border Gateway Protocol)	Sends packets to destinations outside the local network.	

Using Routers to Make the Internet Efficient: Classless Inter-Domain Routing (CIDR)

Although the current IP supports several billion hosts, that's simply not enough anymore. More and more, enterprises are getting a whole Class B (65,536 IP addresses) or a whole Class C (256 IP addresses) when they actually require significantly fewer IP addresses than are allocated under the current domain rules. This process is rapidly leading to a shortage of available Class B and Class C addresses—even though many of those host IP addresses are unused. Also, the size of the **routing tables** in routers are exploding, which means that the Internet runs slower. This is bad all around.

What's the Network Called?

Hour 3 discusses the network and broadcast addresses of TCP/IP networks. Remember that the network address is the section of the address that identifies which network the computer is on, rather than the specific computer. For example, `192.168.1.X` is a network address for computers where X can range from 0 to 255. The broadcast address is the address that can be used to send messages to all machines on the network. Traditionally, the broadcast address is the highest number in the local network; in the preceding example, `192.168.1.255` is the broadcast address.

Classless Inter-Domain Routing (CIDR), pronounced "cider", provides a method for circumventing the limitations of standard IP address allocation. Essentially, it enables multiple Class C addresses to be combined, circumventing the "16 million or 65,536 or 256 host addresses and nothing in between" Class A, B, or C allocation method (that's why it's called **classless**). This technique is generally called **supernetting** because instead of taking a large network and breaking it down into smaller component networks, it's combining smaller component networks into one larger network.

The authors of RFC 1519, which describes CIDR, explained the reason why they invented this protocol: With CIDR, a business that would have taken a whole Class B address and left most of it unused—remember that a Class B network has 65,536 addresses—would now be capable of combining as many 256 IP address Class C networks as they required. In other words, CIDR makes more efficient use of IP addresses than standard Class A, B, or C address allocations, which respectively provide 16 million, 65,000, and 256 addresses per class.

Why is this important for your network? There are three reasons:

▶ CIDR makes more efficient use of a shrinking pool of IP addresses than standard Class A, B, or C IP address allocation. Because modern networks commonly connect to the Internet, they require IP addresses. The more efficiently we use IP addresses, the longer we'll be able to add new networks to the Internet.

▶ CIDR potentially represents an additional layer of complexity to the routing tables. As CIDR becomes more common, your network is going to require either more or faster routers because the size of routing tables is primed to explode.

▶ If one of your suppliers or customers uses CIDR, your equipment has to be capable of supporting it. It's better to be prepared for it by ensuring that your routers can support CIDR (ask the manufacturer), as well as the various gateway protocols. By ensuring that your routers have support for CIDR at the outset, you will avoid a whole series of headaches. Until IPv6 (with its 128-bit address space and nearly unlimited number of IP addresses) is widely implemented, CIDR is going to be an essential if not central part of IP routing.

Other Router and Packet-Routing Functions: Authentication and Encryption

Now you know how routers function in general terms. What else can they do? Fortunately, the answer is that routers can add security to your WAN. If your WAN is accessed by many users, or if it passes over high-speed digital phone lines or the Internet, your WAN is a potential target for a **cracker** (a person who maliciously breaks into data networks to steal, damage, or otherwise compromise data). How can you avoid this?

Well, you can begin by using the features built in to your routers. A lot of modern routers can strengthen network security while they route packets. Although routers are not **firewalls** (computers dedicated to security), they have a limited capability to verify that data has come from where it claims to have come from (the process of authentication). Routers can also encrypt data so that it can't be read without the appropriate key; this is called encryption.

Routers with Security or Light Firewalls?

Strictly speaking, authentication and security aren't router features; they're firewall features. But increasingly, router manufacturers are including security functions, so we've written about them. Cisco provides IPsec firewall/routers, as do Nortel and other networking vendors.

By the Way

Authentication

Authentication is simply the process of ensuring that data comes from the place it claims to come from. Let's go back to our postal metaphor: Generally, you trust that the return address on a letter is accurate. However, if the return address on your Visa bill is suddenly different and you are told to send your payment to a different company name and address, you would be suspicious that someone was trying to defraud you.

In the same fashion, firewalls that run in tandem with routers can check whether a data packet came from the computer it claims to have come from. This technology is not perfect, but it is becoming increasingly popular as **spammers**, or junk emailers, have taken to routinely appropriating other people's Internet addresses to send their junk mail. If the packet contents don't match where the packet says it is from (as is the case with some spam, or junk email), routers can be instructed to discard the packets and send an alarm to an administrator.

Encryption

Encryption is simply taking one string of data and using a system to render it into a form that can't be read directly. For example, solve the following encryption. Hint: It's a famous quote.

```
up cf ps opu up cf
```

In this example, a simple phrase is rendered unreadable by simply taking the plaintext, or unencrypted phrase ("to be or not to be") and changing it to **ciphertext** by changing each letter to the letter immediately following it in the alphabet ("t" becomes "u," "o" becomes "p," and so on). When firewalls and other such devices perform encryption, it is similar, although the encryption schemes are much more complex than the one used in this example.

To explain the previously used terms a bit better, plaintext indicates text of a message in human-readable format. In other words, "*to be or not to be*" is an example of a plaintext message.

By contrast, ciphertext is the text of a message that has been encoded so that it isn't readable without being decrypted into plaintext. In other words, "up cf ps opu up cf" is an example of a ciphertext message.

By the Way

Diffie-Hellman Encryption

If you're going to encrypt data that you send over the Internet, try to use Diffie-Hellman data exchange. In this system, encryption keys are exchanged; the software uses those keys to generate a third key, called a session key. The session key is used to encrypt data before it is transmitted. With Diffie-Hellman, the encryption keys themselves are never passed over the network, which makes stealing them more difficult.

Public-Key Encryption

Public-key encryption is one of those neat things that you wish you knew when you were a kid. It's the ultimate way to encrypt stuff. If you would have had this when you were a kid, you could have hidden the secrets of your club in the treehouse and no one would ever have decrypted them.

Public-key encryption is based on esoteric mathematics that deal with factoring really big prime numbers. The only thing you have to know is that public-key encryption offers the potential for great security.

Encryption key is a series of letters and numbers used to make plaintext messages into ciphertexts. An encryption key's security depends on how long it is. For example, a 40-bit key can be broken with today's powerful computers; this level of encryption (often called "weak encryption") might lawfully be exported from the United States. However, 128-bit encryption is much more difficult to break and cannot be lawfully exported from the United States.

In theory, key length can be infinite. Each successive bit added to the end of a key makes it exponentially more difficult to decrypt a message. Thus, some people build 4096-bit keys, which (in theory) could take longer than the life of the universe to decrypt—At least until a math whiz comes up with a method for rapidly factoring large keys.

In public-key encryption, each person who sends and receives messages has two keys: a public key and a private key. Public keys are widely distributed and anyone can know them; private keys are kept private. Messages encrypted with a user's public key can only be decrypted with that user's private key and vice versa.

If Fred wants to send Ginger a message, he encrypts it using Ginger's public key (which she's given to him or made freely available). When Ginger gets the message, she decrypts it using her private key, which she alone knows. When Ginger replies to Fred, she encrypts the message using Fred's public key and Fred reads it with his private key.

At this time, encryption and authentication are not part of any standards. IPv6, the next generation Internet Protocol has encryption and authentication built into the protocol, which will make it much easier to have secure data routing over the Internet.

High-Speed Data Access

WANs typically link to each other using high-speed digital phone lines. Although most digital phone services do not run as fast as the local LAN, they do provide sufficient bandwidth to allow users to access resources with reasonable performance. Digital phone services are available in a dizzying array of speeds, services, and prices; the following sections give you an opportunity to learn about some of them.

Digital phone lines convert the sound of your voice into digital data. Digital phone lines work better for computers because computers transmit information digitally. Digital phone lines are often used for WANs where data is transmitted at high speeds over long distances.

Analog phone lines transmit the sound of your voice as a waveform (like a radio wave). Analog phone lines are common (chances are that analog phone lines are what your home phone is plugged in to). To transmit data over an analog phone line, you must convert it from digital data to sound—that's why modems (devices that convert data to sound) make funny sounding squawks and hisses. That's digital data being converted to sound.

Satellite Broadband

There are also alternatives to local phone lines. Some companies link their networks into WANs using satellite links, which are tremendously expensive. Nonetheless, this type of networking is rapidly becoming more popular, particularly in parts of the world in which the telecommunications infrastructure is limited.

Trunk Lines: T1 and T3

Trunk lines are the backbone of long-distance packet-switched networks. With speeds as low as 128 kilobits per second and as high as 45 megabits per second, they cover a broad range of networking needs. At the low end, they can provide Internet services to LANs or can link LANs at speeds just fast enough to be useful for long-distance networking. At the high end, they have enough bandwidth so that a user might never suspect that the computer she is accessing is hundreds or thousands of miles away.

Types of Trunks

The trunk lines system, dating to the 1960s, was the first digital phone line system. The original transmission rate (1.544 megabits per second) is the T1 line, often used to interconnect WANs. Another level, the T3 line with a bandwidth of 44.736 megabits per second, is also available. T3 lines are commonly used by large corporate WANs and Internet service providers—they're tremendously expensive and outside the realm of most networking budgets.

Trunk lines are entirely digital. T1s use four wires and provide full-duplex (two-way simultaneous transmission) capability. The T1 digital stream consists of twenty-four 64 kilobits-per-second channels bonded together to create the 1.544 megabits-per-second rate. The four wires on which T1 circuits were originally carried were usually copper twisted-pair wiring. Modern T1s can operate over coaxial cable, optical fiber, digital microwave, and other media. You can use the T1 service in a variety of ways; almost anything is possible. The plethora of options available for T1 service can make deciding what you want a daunting task. The next few paragraphs help explain the possible selections.

Possible Uses for Trunks

Although all trunk lines are digital phone services, all trunks do not carry data. A T1 line, for example, can carry up to 24 separate voice phone lines. Alternatively, it can carry up to 1.544 megabits per second of data. A third possibility is that it can use 12 voice channels (half the available channels) and use the remaining bandwidth (about 768 kilobits per second) to carry data. A fourth possibility is that it can use only a small percentage of the bandwidth for a **fractional T1**. A final possibility is that you can use a T1 line to carry ISDN Primary Rate Interface, which is yet another variety of digital phone service.

All these possibilities are available through your local phone service. The difference between the kinds of trunks listed here is based on their use, not from any inherent difference. All the aforementioned services can be carried over exactly the same type of trunk line. This is why knowing a bit about trunks is useful before you begin to order a digital phone service for your WAN.

Provisioning Trunks

When you order a trunk line from your local phone company, the phone company is going to ask how you want to *provision* it. This means that you have to explain how you are going to use the **circuit**, which is the phone company's term for any line it drags into your space. Depending on your application, you might want the trunk for voice traffic, for data traffic, or some combination of the two. For small-to-medium-sized WANs, you normally will be using either a fractional or full T1. Large WANs sometimes use fractional or full T3 lines, which can carry up to 45 megabits per second. Chances are that you won't encounter a T3 unless you have a connection to a major corporate data center, or work for either an Internet service provider or a local phone company.

Leased Lines

Trunk lines are often called leased lines. When you purchase fractional or full T1 data services from a telephone company, you get what is called a **point-to-point line**, which means that it is a circuit that carries data only between two specific points. Those two points can be two of your offices (in which case, you would have a WAN), or one end could be your office and the other could be an Internet service provider's location that would connect you to the Internet. Because these lines go between two points and are used by only one entity (one company or organization), they are called **leased lines**.

Frame Relay

Frame relay is one of the methods used to carry data over digital phone lines such as T1s and 56Ks. Frame relay is commonly used to connect to the Internet, as well as being used to link multiple sites.

Frame relay is easy to use but makes less efficient use of the available bandwidth than does a clear channel line. Why? There are two reasons:

▶ **Committed Information Rate (CIR)** from your vendor. A CIR is a measurement of the worst possible performance you'll get over your frame line; typically, it is half the bandwidth of the line. In other words, if you order a 128 kilobits-per-second frame line, you usually get a 64 kilobits-per-second CIR. This means that during periods of heavy traffic, your connection could drop to a maximum speed of 64 kilobits per second, rather than the 128K maximum speed the line is rated for.

▶ Your computers have to packetize their data to send it through your local LAN. For packetized data to travel across frame relay, the router has to repacketize the data into specially formatted data packets called frames that can be routed over frame relay lines.

Frames, like data packets inside a LAN, have source and destination addresses, checksums, and the rest of the features of packets. This means that frame relay effectively puts packets into packets and sends them off. This process is like putting a completely addressed envelope into a larger envelope when it is sent to an out-of-town location. Clearly, this is wasteful: The weight of the extra envelope (packet) makes the postage heavier, so it costs more to send. Likewise, the extra data in each frame (used for labeling and controlling data) reduces the amount of data that can be sent. And the reverse must happen at the receiving end—the data must be extracted from the frame and the packet, adding further latency.

Clear Channel

The alternative to frame's inherent inefficiencies is clear channel. Clear Channel Signaling (CCS)—which also stands for Common Channel Signaling, a term that means exactly the same as Clear Channel Signaling—is a way of sending all the instructions on how to move data (also called **signaling**) over a channel separate from the data. This means that there is less overhead for data—there isn't a need for the phone company to frame your data packets in its data frames—so you get a higher throughput. CCS is expensive, however. Be prepared to pay as much as one and a half times the price of frame relay for clear channel.

Trunk Line Speeds

The vast majority of trunk lines sold are T1s and various fractional permutations thereof. Table 6.2 lists the most common T1 speeds available, from 1.544 megabits per second (Mbps) to 128 kilobits per second (Kbps).

TABLE 6.2   T1 Speeds

Full T1	Fractional T1
1.544Mbps	128Kbps
	256Kbps
	384Kbps
	512Kbps
	768Kbps
	896Kbps
	1.024Mbps
	1.152Mbps
	1.280Mbps
	1.408Mbps

This is not a complete list; instead, it lists the most common speeds. Remember that a T1 line has 24 channels—when you purchase and provision your T1, you will be able to join, or bond, the channels in 64K increments all the way up to a full T1.

T1 lines offer tremendous flexibility. They are not inexpensive—some telephone companies routinely charge $3,000 or more a month for a full T1—but if you need to connect a WAN, a T1 is one of the premier methods.

Bandwidth Pricing

Phone companies have a bewildering array of methods to calculate digital phone line charges, and these charges differ from phone company to phone company. Before you purchase, shop around. More important than name recognition is the CIR and the reliability of the carrier.

By the Way

Digital Subscriber Lines (DSL)

The telephone companies' latest entry into the digital phone line market is **Digital Subscriber Line (DSL)** service. DSL is at least as fast as a T1, but unlike a

T1, DSL runs over standard two-wire telephone wire. DSL service used to be very expensive, and phone company expertise in provisioning and installing it was inexact. However, the phone companies responded to the challenge posed by cable modems and have made DSL both affordable and easy to provision. These days, it's possible to get DSL service for $50 a month or so, and they can be sold by ISPs, not just the phone company. They provide an excellent means of connecting to the Internet.

Benefits of DSL

DSL services offer tremendous bandwidth benefits to users lucky enough to live where the service is available. They can carry a lot of data at very high speeds, and prices are being reduced at a breakneck rate to provide incentives for consumers to invest in this technology. Another distinct plus is that DSL services can run over the same copper wire that your regular phone lines use—**unconditioned two-wire copper**. This means that the installation costs for DSL services will be much less than for T1 service.

The Downside of DSL

In spite of its upsides, DSL has a potentially deadly downside. In most cases, the maximum distance for DSL circuits is less than six miles. In other words, if the distance between your office and the telephone company's central office is more than six miles, you can't use the service. This is not an issue for metropolitan WAN builders, who are very likely to be within easy walking distance of their phone company's central office, but it represents a potential problem for adding DSL capability to suburban WANs.

DSL Configurations

DSL is available in a variety of configurations:

- For Internet access, Asymmetric Digital Subscriber Line (ASDL) is usually requested because the data flow coming into the network operates much faster than the data routing out of the network. This is not as useful for WANs as it is for Internet access, where data coming into the network is more important than data going out. A lot of home-based DSL uses this particular flavor because most users will download a great deal more than they'll upload.

- More useful for WANs are High-speed Digital Subscriber Lines (HDSL). HDSL transmits data at symmetrical speeds at T1 data rates (1.544 megabits per second) over distances of 12,000 feet or less. Telephone companies have used HDSL lines to provision T1 lines for ages because HDSL can be installed much faster than regular T1 or T3 wiring.

▶ Rate Adaptive DSL (RADSL) is a useful tool for WANs that are more spread out. RADSL can change its speed in response to line conditions. It can work farther from central offices than the rest of its siblings, but it still has trouble beyond six miles. This isn't used very much any longer.

▶ The fastest member of the family is VDSL, (Very high bit-rate Digital Subscriber Line). These lines go as little as 1,000 feet, but they can operate at LAN speeds (10 megabits per second) or faster. If you have to build a campus WAN, VDSL is a great solution. VDSL is very expensive, but it still costs less than a fractional T3. This is also not used very much any longer because increases in fiber optics and WAN technology have rendered it unnecessary.

Service Level Agreements and Quality of Service Agreements

When you order digital phone lines, make certain that you write out and contract a Service Level Agreement (SLA) or a Quality of Service (QoS) guarantee. These are powerful tools to hold WAN downtime to a minimum.

As a network builder, you will necessarily be responsible for the network under your control. Unfortunately, once you have a WAN, you are also responsible for one item that is not totally under your control—the digital services that tie your WAN together.

Given the phone companies' propensity to accidentally disconnect lines and the like, it is well worth your while to hammer out an agreement that defines the percentage of uptime your digital lines will have. This agreement is usually called an SLA. Typically, SLAs provide for fiscal relief or refunds if you suffer network downtime in excess of what is specified in the agreement and is an incentive for the carrier or service provider to keep the lines up and running as much as possible.

QoS agreements, on the other hand, are concerned with ensuring that you get the service you pay for. If you have a 128 kilobits-per-second fractional T1 line with a CIR of 64K, get a guarantee that your slowest data rate (the CIR) will be 64K and that you will receive proportionate dollar relief from the carrier or service provider in the event that the data rate drops below 64K.

Given that a WAN is an organizational tool, SLAs and QoS agreements provide you, the network builder/designer/administrator, with a powerful tool to ensure uptime. That is more important than anything else on a WAN—because if the WAN goes down, there is no WAN, just a lot of unhappy users.

Can the Internet Help You Build Your WAN?

Given the high costs of digital phone service, building a network with a lot of remote sites linked with digital lines can get very expensive very quickly. Part of the expense is inescapable; to connect networks together on a reliable ongoing basis, digital phone service is necessary. However, there are additional, incremental costs of developing a private WAN, such as the cost of one or more system administrator's salaries and the overhead that comes with the management of a private network.

One way to reduce the administration costs of your WAN is to **outsource** it, or hire someone else to handle the interLAN networking for you. Initially, the businesses that accepted WAN outsourcing jobs came from the pool of computer systems integration and administration firms; often, they were large consultant groups trying to use WAN management as a new source of revenue. These firms operated on a consultative basis, and the costs of their service reflected it: The cost of hiring a computer consultant to manage a WAN was capital inefficient because consultants typically charge on an hourly basis, so the clock was always ticking.

As the Internet has grown, however, large Internet service providers have gotten involved in the business of providing WAN services. Their business model differed from the consultants' in one major fashion: They viewed their connection services instead of their expertise as the service being sold. The ISPs elected to absorb a large chunk of the cost of integrating digital phone lines and WAN technology, choosing instead to make their money on the network service being provided. Of the two models, the consultative is more lucrative, but the ISP model is more likely to survive because it is following in the phone system's footprints by providing a for-cost service and inexpensive integration.

In any case, the ISP model has another net positive: ISPs essentially are nothing more than computer-based routing networks. Because the ISP has a computer-based network, it is a cinch to set up reliable, relatively secure WANs for their clients. How do they do it? Well, they already have networking expertise; more importantly, they have networking infrastructures already in place. The ISPs' networking infrastructures is designed solely for the purpose of specifying how data routes from point A to point B and back again. If they set up their routers to route packets coming from certain networks only to certain other networks and use the Internet as a transport between ISP service locations, they have set up a type of

WAN called a Virtual Private Network (VPN). For all practical purposes, a VPN accomplishes the same tasks as a totally dedicated point-to-point digital phone line-based WAN, but in general it costs less and requires less end-user maintenance. As long as the ISP is doing its job, the costs of maintaining internetwork links should be included in your monthly ISP fee.

There are a few important caveats about VPNs. First, a VPN uses the Internet to route some or all of its data. Clearly, the Internet as it currently exists is not a terribly secure place. There are ways to capture a lot of network traffic if someone knows how. (Trust me, someone does know how to capture data traffic.) If that person captures traffic containing your unencrypted credit card information or sensitive memos, you could be in serious trouble. If you decide that a VPN sounds like a good idea, spend some time learning about computer security (discussed in Hour 19, "Security") and take the time to implement it properly. VPNs are a great solution to the age-old battle between cost and features, but only if they're put together correctly. If you do it right, you can leverage the power of the Internet for your needs—which is not an inconsiderable accomplishment.

So Who Needs a WAN, Anyway?

WANs are usually set up by large companies or organizations that want to establish significant network presence in multiple offices around the nation or the world. They are not inexpensive, but the benefits can—if correctly designed and configured—outweigh their costs many times over. If data on a server can be replicated to a group of users who need it to serve clients adequately (and thereby retain the clients), the WAN has done its job. If the WAN can be turned to proactive uses such as tracking packages for clients or (my all-time favorite example) managing flight data at airports, it has become a **Value-Added Network (VAN)**, where its services become the product that clients purchase.

Summary

In this hour, you learned some basic concepts about what constitutes a WAN and some of the hardware that WANs use. You also learned something about digital phone service, which lies at the core of WAN architecture.

In the next hour, you'll learn about the other outside-the-local-LAN network— remote access.

Q&A

Q *What is a WAN?*

A Any situation in which computers are networked can be a WAN if it also fits the following conditions:

- ▶ It connects to private networks.

- ▶ It transmits data over telephone lines (in general; microwave transmission is the one obvious exception).

- ▶ Users can be authenticated at both ends.

Q *What kind of phone lines can WANs use?*

A There are two basic types of lines that can be implemented for a WAN:

- ▶ Standard dial-up lines.

- ▶ Digital phone lines such as frame relay, or T1 service.

Q *What are the upsides and downsides of VPNs?*

A A Virtual Private Network (VPN) has the following pros and cons:

- ▶ Upsides: VPNs are relatively inexpensive and use Internet-standard protocols.

- ▶ Downsides: VPNs aren't as secure as "private" WANs.

Remote Networking

In this hour, you have the opportunity to learn about the following aspects of remote networking:

- ▶ What remote networking is
- ▶ The history of remote access
- ▶ Why remote networking is becoming more important
- ▶ Remote access requirements
- ▶ How remote access works using PPP and SLIP
- ▶ Using VPNs and the Internet for remote access
- ▶ Remote networking security
- ▶ Using the Internet for remote access
- ▶ Remote networking hardware

Although business paradigms continue to shift and evolve, it's clear that a great deal of business is accomplished on the run as employees travel from location to location. And although the number of workers who are considered telecommuters is hard to quantify, a large number of people find it advantageous to be able to access their employer's network from home or any location.

Remote access employs a number of different connectivity strategies that allow users to connect from a remote connection to a corporate, institutional, or even a home network. Dial-up modems have always provided one way of "dialing into" a corporate network, but higher speed connections and the Internet has expanded the possibilities including the use of Virtual Private Networks over the Internet. In this hour, we will explore these different strategies for remote connection.

A Brief History of Remote Access: Remote Control and Remote Node

Before the explosion of the Internet, users who needed remote access to their network resources did not have many options.

Remote Control

The first remote access was really UNIX's telnet program. UNIX users need to be able to connect to their UNIX host system when they are not directly connected to the system's main character-mode terminal. The result of this need was and remains telnet. Telnet is a program used by UNIX (and eventually by many other operating systems) that offers a user the capability to open a command-line session across a network. In a telnet session, the user sees only a few characters that make up a screen image, while all the processing is being done on the remote system. For the user, there's no difference between a telnet session 1,000 miles away and a telnet session from a computer right next to the UNIX machine.

The first PC remote access solutions were built using telnet's remote-control behavior. It's not surprising that remote control was the first method of remote access used for personal computers since initially, personal computers weren't considered sufficiently powerful to do any processing locally.

Consequently, in the early days of PC remote access, when users requested a way to get to their applications and files from on the road, an Information System (IS) person would arrive at his desk with floppy disks in tow and install remote control software—such as Symantec's pcAnywhere, Stac's ReachOut, or Traveling Software's LapLink—on both the user's desktop and the laptop computers. The IS person would then instruct the user to put the desktop system into a mode in which the computer waited for a call while the user was out of the office. The user would take his trusty eight-pound laptop on the road, and if he needed to read email, check a schedule, gain access for any other reason, he would dial in to the desktop computer. The screen of the desktop computer would appear on the laptop, and the user could slo-o-o-owly read email or work with other applications. When the session was over, the user disconnected the laptop's modem and that would be the end of data access for that session.

The use of remote control stemmed from the use of applications that depended on a server to operate—these applications had to be spawned across a network, and even if the remote computers had been connected by some sort of dial-up networking, a phone line's bandwidth would have been insufficient to run them. So in early remote access, users only got to see a remote desktop screen on their laptop screens. They couldn't save data from a remote control session to their laptops' hard disks; thus they couldn't do any real work unless they were connected to their network. This model was inefficient, but it was all that was available at the time.

Remote control applications are still used for certain applications in which sending an image of the desktop screen is more efficient than sending actual data over the phone wire. For example, a firm that has a huge database would not want users to try to run reports and queries across a phone line masquerading as a network wire; it would be too slow. So they run the queries on the server, and the client laptop sees only screen data. It isn't a perfect solution, but in certain potentially bandwidth-wasteful applications, remote control is more efficient than its competition, remote node, discussed in the next section.

In recent years, Microsoft, Citrix, and Sun have breathed new life into the remote control paradigm with their introduction of terminal-based networks. In Microsoft's Terminal Server and Citrix's WinFrame, Windows applications run on a central server, and only a picture of the screen (a bitmap) gets transmitted over the network. In Sun's model, the same thing happens except that UNIX applications are distributed—that is, they're set up so that one piece of the application runs on the server and another piece runs on the client computer.

This model offers compelling advantages for some networks. If a network has a high proportion of workers who move from space to space, terminal servers using distributed applications in a remote-control configuration makes sense because the users' session settings can move from position to position.

There *is* one area where remote control has increased and, in fact, has become one of the preferred methods for remote access to computers: system administration. Some organizations have elected to avoid phone support for their workers, preferring instead to simply install a system management remote control agent on each end-user PC. With the agent in place, a user can report a problem with his computer and an administrator can use the agent to temporarily take over the user's desktop across a network. Note most of the time, dial-up remote control is too slow for this sort of administration, so it's used over a network such as Ethernet or Token Ring, both with 10 megabits per second or more. The administrator sees what the user sees at his desktop and can interact with the user to either teach him or diagnose (and fix) symptoms. This significantly reduces administrations costs for PCs because the system administrator only needs to actually go to a user's desk if the user's computer is so broken that it can't support the remote control agent software. Microsoft, IBM, HP, and a host of others have built excellent client systems.

However, for systems on which users need to have significant local storage and processing, this model fails. This leads into the next discussion: remote node networking.

Remote Node

Over the last several years, a variety of items have come together to enable many more computers to join networks from remote locations as opposed to remote-controlling a remote computer on a network. These factors include the following:

▶ An increase in the processing power of laptop computers

▶ The exponential increase of Internet use

▶ An increase in the installed base of reasonably good quality analog phone lines and in consumer software to use them for network (as opposed to remote control) access

▶ The increase in high-speed data access provided by cable modems and DSL

▶ Increased numbers of TCP/IP implementations designed to work over phone lines

▶ The introduction of IP Security (IPSec) and implementations that enable VPNs to work using the Internet as a medium

These changes in the computer and networking arena enabled remote node networking to become preeminent. **Remote node** means that the computer in the field connects to the central network over one of a variety of media (dial-up phone lines, the Internet via high speed cable or DSL, radio networks) using a network protocol, such as TCP/IP. Once connected, the remote computer becomes a network client just like any other client on the network.

By the Way

What Is IPSec?

IPSec, which is short for IP Security is actually a suite of cryptography-based protection services and security protocols that can be used to secure internal networks and also secure data on remote access and Virtual Private Network connections.

By the Way

Not All Remote Clients Are Equal

Actually, what you just read is not quite true for analog phone lines, radio networks, and other low-bandwidth connections. They will use the same protocols as faster networks, but they tend to run much more slowly, which places limits on what services are realistically available to them. For instance, a network client located on a LAN has a 10 megabits per second connection (or faster), but low-bandwidth remote-node connections usually max out at between 9600 and 33.6 kilobits-per-second. A low-bandwidth remote node connection is therefore an order of magnitude or two slower than the LAN connection.

Remote node is important because it enables a variety of changes to the remote access model. Essentially, the model changes: In remote control, you have a highly graphical dumb terminal session (in which you see a picture of the server computer's screen but can't copy data to your local hard drive); but in remote node, your computer is part of the network. This means that even though the overall connection speed doesn't change, the user gets benefits—such as being able to compose mail and schedule meetings offline—and then sends them when he connects using a phone line.

Being a part of the network has other benefits as well. Because a computer connected as a remote node is part of the network, it can use standard network services, such as telnet, FTP, ping, and (far more important) email and Web services such as POP3 for mail and HTTP for the Web.

Dial-Up and Remote Node Are Synonymous

If you have ever used a dial-up connection to the Internet, you have used a remote node session. The protocols used for Internet dial-up access are coincident with the protocols used for remote node access.

By the Way

The importance of remote node is in what it can do for disconnected users. Because the connection over a phone line mimics being connected to the LAN while using the modem as a network card, the user simply has slower access to all the same resources that he has when connected to the network in the office. So far, this is not an improvement over remote control.

However, in a remote node network connection, the software the user requires to get a job done is stored on the local laptop drive. The application isn't passed down the wire in remote node; only data, such as email or Web pages, are transferred across the network.

Because data is passed over the phone wire just as if it were an in-office network connection, the user can save the data locally. Why is this important? Because if a user needs a file, he only has to dial into the network, change to the network drive, and FTP or copy the file to his hard disk. Although the transfer will be slower than a full-bandwidth LAN connection, when the user is finished copying the files, he can disconnect from the network and still be able to work on the copy of the file made on the laptop's hard drive. That by itself is enough to justify remote node access, but it can do more. The user can also work offline and compose new emails or calendar appointments.

The next time the user connects, he can send the prepared email and schedule data, and receive his email on the laptop's hard drive; then the user can go offline and read it while not connected.

Clearly, remote node is more desirable for most applications than remote control. And that's a good thing because remote node is remote networking. Remote node connections are based on Internet standards that ensure that you can dial your client laptop in to any host server that runs the same group of Internet-standard protocols.

Remote Access Requirements

Unlike LANs, which tend to require a whole pile of special cable, wire, and other equipment, remote networking using phone lines is refreshingly simple. For the most part, all you need are two computers, two modems or other telephony devices, a standard phone line, and some industry-standard software.

You know about the computer; we discussed that in Hour 3, "Getting Data from Here to There: How Computers Share Data." As long as the computers at both ends of a modem connection can share files and so forth, the type of computer does not matter. The main thing to remember is that there must be a computer at each end of the connection.

The modems or other telephony devices, on the other hand, have not been discussed yet. The following sections acquaint you with modems and ISDN terminal adapters, which form the basis of many remote networking solutions.

Modems

The term **modem** stands for *modulate-demo*dulate. This means that a modem takes digital data sent from your computer's serial ports and modulates it into an analog, or sound, form that can travel over the regular phone lines. At the other end of a modem connection, another modem translates the analog signal back into digital so that the computer on the other end can read it (see Figure 7.1).

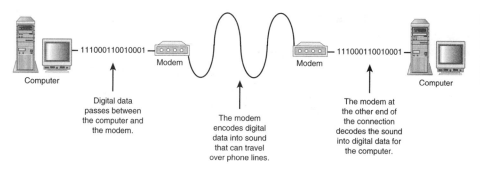

FIGURE 7.1
A modem connects to a computer and changes the data from digital to analog.

Digital data passes between the computer and the modem.

The modem encodes digital data into sound that can travel over phone lines.

The modem at the other end of the connection decodes the sound into digital data for the computer.

"Why are modems necessary at all?" you ask. "Why not just transmit the data digitally? We've just learned about digital phone lines."

Modems are, unfortunately, still necessary for the vast majority of users who need to access networks. Most current telephone installations are standard two-pair (that is, four wire) copper cables that are designed to carry only analog signals. In fact, the regular phone wires running into your house have more in common with the wires connecting speakers to a stereo than to a T1 or a LAN wire. So we're stuck with modems—at least until the phone company starts making home phone service digital. And that's not going to happen very soon.

Modems Use Bandwidth for Error Checking and Data Correction

By the Way

Modems were invented to circumvent the need for expensive digital phone lines. Initially, modems ran at 300 bits per second or slower—it could take a couple of minutes for a whole page to show up on your screen at that speed—and gradually got faster until they reached the current ceiling of approximately 53 kilobits per second (which is asymmetric, or nonsymmetric—that is, in one direction; there's a 53 kilobits-per-second download speed, but the maximum speed in the other direction is 33.6 kilobits per second). Modems are not terribly efficient devices because a very high proportion of the data they transmit is dedicated to catching and correcting data transmission errors. Nonetheless, modems are the most common way for a remote user to tie into a network.

With a modem, the user has a significant degree of involvement in the connection process. The user has to dial the modem when he wants to connect to the corporate network; there is no **dial-on-demand**, or automatic connection, when he selects a resource not stored on the laptop. Also, modems are usually sensitive to the quality of the phone line. If our user is calling from Outer Mongolia and trying to get a fast connection, he had better forget it—there will be too much distortion in the phone lines to get a good connection (if he can get connected at all). Poor phone line quality is not limited to out-of-the-way locations, however; because of increasing pressure on the phone companies to service increasing numbers of users, line quality can be iffy even in major metropolitan areas.

Establishing a Better Modem Connection

In cases in which you have a "bad" modem connection (based on the bits per second), disconnect and redial. You can often get a better connection by simply reconnecting.

Modems can be purchased as standalone units or (if you have a lot of users who need to connect) in special boxes called **modem racks**, which you'll learn more about in a few pages. All things considered, modems represent a cost-effective, technically acceptable solution for remote users.

Protocols

Once the hardware is in place, it is time to begin considering the network protocols that will connect remote users' computers to the main network. Ninety-nine percent of the time, the protocols used to connect remote users will be members of a special subset of the TCP/IP protocol suite that handle transferring data over phone lines. These special protocols are PPP and SLIP.

By the Way

Protocols Dictate the Rules for Data Communication

For additional information on network protocols, refer to the protocol section in Hour 3.

PPP

Of all the protocols used to control and manage the transfer of data over telephone lines, **Point-to-Point Protocol (PPP)** is far and away the most popular. PPP was developed to provide a way to network computers that did not have network cards and required a modem or ISDN terminal adapter to make an effective network connection. PPP is an Internet standard.

PPP has several requirements that remain the same from system to system. First, PPP needs to know several parameters:

▶ The phone number of the system to which it will connect.

▶ A Domain Name Server (DNS) address. DNS services are very important to networks because DNS servers provide a lookup table that enables a computer to reconcile a numeric IP address (such as 192.168.207.124) to a name such as foo.bar.com.

▶ Whether the remote computer has a fixed IP address or it will be assigned an address when it connects with the server. Server-assigned IP addresses are assigned by a server running the Dynamic Host Configuration Protocol (DHCP), yet another subset of TCP/IP. DHCP is used when you have a finite pool of IP addresses—for example, from address 192.168.1.1 to 192.168.1.254 (that's 255 addresses)—and a larger pool of users—for example, a thousand users vying for those 255 addresses). DHCP enables IP addresses to be assigned as required; when they aren't used, the addresses return to the common pool from which they are drawn as required.

▶ If the computer will be connecting to the Internet, it needs a default gateway setting (the IP address of the router or gateway that connects to the Internet). In many PPP implementations, you can tell the dialing computer to acquire this information from the server into which it dials.

Once these parameters are set up, it's time to dial. (Each operating system has slightly different procedures for setting up parameters. It's part of Microsoft Windows 2000 Professional's and Windows XP's Dial-Up Networking).

Depending on which software you use, your computer might ask you for a user ID and password. Once you have keyed them in, the system authenticates your login and switches to PPP data handling. After the system has switched to PPP data handling, it is possible to access the host network via TCP/IP.

By the Way

> **The Point to Point Protocol Provides Flexibility and Security**
>
> For a dial-up protocol, PPP offers a rich feature set. It can carry multiple protocols (TCP/IP, IPX, and NetBEUI) at the same time, and it can use a variety of methods for authentication including the vaunted Kerberos system in which passwords never pass across the wire. More about authentication and security can be found in the network administration chapters in Part V, "Introduction to Network Administration."

PPP is remarkably reliable for a dial-up protocol. If the line is clean, PPP usually does not spontaneously disconnect unless no one has used the connection for a while. It's a great, elegant solution to a vexing problem (see Figure 7.2).

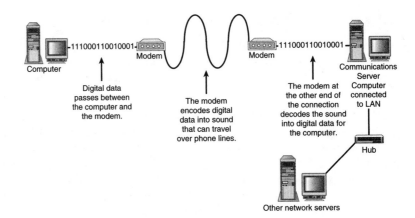

FIGURE 7.2
A typical remote-node dial-up connection configuration using PPP.

SLIP

Serial Line Internet Protocol (SLIP) is an older cousin of PPP. It requires that you specify even more parameters than PPP, and there is little guarantee that it will connect; SLIP must negotiate the size of the largest data packets that both ends can handle before it begins transmitting user data.

Essentially, SLIP is out-of-date. However, you might run across it on older systems particularly systems running UNIX. If you have the opportunity to upgrade it to PPP, do so—PPP is faster and better. SLIP unfortunately requires a great deal more from the user than does PPP, and it's less efficient—every remote user must have a unique IP address.

Authentication and Security

A modem waiting for a call is a gateway to the world just waiting to be cracked. If a modem is left waiting for a call and no security is in place, the server computer cannot verify that users who dial in are actually who they say they are. Even simple network passwords are better than nothing.

Passwords alone, however, do not ensure that all users who connect are authorized to access the internal network. This is because passwords are sometimes passed in plain text (that is, unencrypted text) over a PPP network connection, so any user who can "listen in" on a successful login session can capture that user ID and password for use at a later date. Although this particular situation is not common by any means, it illustrates some possible weaknesses in security.

To ensure dial-in security, there are several measures you can take:

▶ Ensure that the system logs all incoming calls and login attempts. This can help locate users who are trying to guess passwords.

▶ Limit login attempts to three or fewer, and lock out any user who has not produced a correct password for a given user ID after three unsuccessful attempts to log in.

▶ Use **access tokens** (small calculator-like cards that produce numbers that constantly change) in addition to user IDs and passwords. Access tokens are particularly difficult to crack because anyone logging in must have access to a known and trusted user token in addition to a valid user ID and password.

▶ Change the PPP settings so that the remote user has a secure login. Security protocols such as **Challenge Handshake Authentication Protocol (CHAP)** and **Password Authentication Protocol (PAP)** can help secure the login process.

▶ Force users to change their passwords frequently.

No matter how secure you make your network, don't ever stop trying to make it more secure. Security is a process, not a destination. Hour 19, "Security," discusses security in more depth and can help you establish behaviors to make your network more secure.

Using the Internet for Remote Access

Dial-up strategies were really the only method of establishing a remote connection with a private LAN or WAN. The Internet now provides us with another possibility for remote access: the Virtual Private Network, or VPN. A VPN is a secure connection that is established over the Internet between the remote user and the corporate network. The VPN is basically a conduit that moves the private data across the public Internet.

To take advantage of VPN for remote access, an organization will need to provide for the appropriate infrastructure as follows:

▶ Invest in a contract with a national or international dial-up Internet service provider (ISP) to provide local dial-up phone numbers.

▶ Provide cable modem or DSL service to users who require high-speed remote access.

▶ Set up a server/VPN hardware between the organization's network and the Internet to authenticate users using VPN software.

While using the Internet ad, a conduit for remote access is a little more complicated than using dial-in connections (as discussed earlier in the hour). There are a bunch of advantages of sourcing remote access to a third-party provider and then using VPN clients to enable all remote clients (low and high-bandwidth) to connect to the network.

► There's only one pathway into the network (via the Internet), and ideally the VPN server is sufficiently well-secured to discourage or limit break-ins.

► There's no need to manage many high-speed data circuits, such as T1s.

► A dedicated provider, whose sole business is competently providing network access, provides the service. Contrast this with your business—do you want to provide network access or concentrate on core business issues?

If your organization is set up to doing everything locally, dial-in servers that manage PPP connections and authentication are a great way to ensure good security on your network. But if you have users who are far away—from Boston to San Francisco, for example—you might want to try using the Internet as the media to connect your remote offices.

VPN is ultimately much more flexible than users trying to actually dial-in to the company network. Although dial-in remote access and VPN both require a remote access server to authenticate remote users to the corporate network, dial-in requires corporate modem pools to service dial-in customers. In the case of a VPN, the only additional hardware that needs to be deployed is the VPN remote access server. Then, any user any where in the world, who can connect to the Internet, can access the corporate network provided that he has a username and password that will allow a connection through the VPN remote access server. Cisco Systems, Microsoft, and a host of others provide VPN software that uses IPSec for authentication and security. In the long term, this might prove to be the most efficient method for providing remote users access to secured networks.

In the case of Microsoft's various server products, VPN server capabilities are built into the network operating system's **Remote Access Service (RAS)**. Figure 7.3 shows the RAS snap-in in Microsoft Windows Server 2003, which is used to manage and configure VPN access to the LAN.

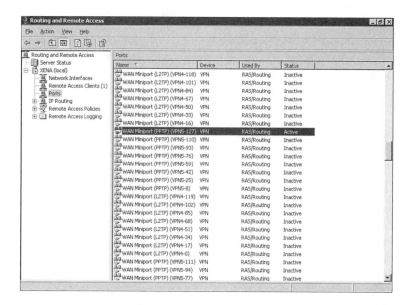

FIGURE 7.3
Network Operating Systems such as Microsoft Windows Server 2003 provide utilities for configuring and managing VPN.

Remote Access Hardware: Build or Buy?

Even though Internet-based remote access is becoming increasingly common, some organizations are going to build their own remote access solutions. The following discussion deals with the ramifications of doing so, and provides some insight into what's involved in building a robust remote-access architecture.

Remote access hardware comes in a variety of permutations from a huge number of manufacturers; it would be pointless to attempt to list them all here. Instead, this section focuses on the build or buy question that faces people who have to purchase and deploy remote access solutions.

Whether to build or buy a remote access solution is a difficult question. The answer depends on a variety of variables, including your company's size, how fast your company is growing, how many people will be using the remote access system at any given point in time, and how easily it should be upgradeable.

The process of selecting hardware for a heavily user-interactive application growing by leaps and bounds has been compared to buying clothes for a child. By the time you get the clothes home and get the child dressed, more often than not, the kid has outgrown them. Alternately, if the clothes do fit, the child doesn't like them and won't wear them. It's a damned-if-you-do, damned-if-you-don't situation. But over time, a rule of thumb has emerged for remote access equipment: Figure out how many simultaneous users you will have and then at least double that capacity. That way, your first-year expansion is manageable.

Building a Remote Access Solution

If you have only a few users, it is possible to create a remote access solution based on connecting two or more modems to a server computer. Most server operating systems offer solutions for remote node access, including Microsoft's Remote Access Service (RAS) and Novell's NetWare remote connection services. UNIX and Linux distributions also provide remote access services.Typically, a remote access server built entirely on Intel-compatible computer architecture has only one piece of hardware that is not on other computers: a **multiport serial board**. Because most Intel-compatible computers have only two serial ports to connect to modems, multiport serial boards that enable the addition of up to 16 additional modems per card offer much needed expandability.

Systems built on a computer architecture have a variety of positives, including the capability to use an operating system's built-in security and login handling. Typically, homebuilt remote access systems provide very good performance at a reasonable cost. The downside of building your own remote access server solution is that it can be difficult to support if you have a problem. All too often, the operating system vendor blames a problem on the multiport card vendor, and vice versa, which gets you nowhere.

Buying Turnkey Remote Access Solutions

The alternative to building a remote access system from standard hardware and parts is to purchase a **dedicated system**. Dedicated systems usually do not follow standard Intel-compatible architecture and might or might not interface directly with your network operating system. In spite of their proprietary architecture, or nonstandard vendor-dependent designs, many of the dedicated remote access solutions available in the market offer great value for what they do. Shiva's LANrover and CUBIX's communications server solutions are two of the most popular dedicated remote access systems. Shiva offers a special authentication package with its products. Other manufacturers, such as MultiTech, offer network–login-based remote access solutions that handle the network connection as part of the login software.

In the case of VPN, a number of companies also provide VPN hardware, including Cisco and Nortel. In the case of Cisco, an entire line of VPN routers are available that provide data encryption and a Web-based device manager. Many of the VPN routers available are in many cases deployable right out of the box and provide a good alternative to attempting to deploy VPN as a service of a particular network operating system.

Summary

In this hour, you learned what remote access is and why it has become so important over the last several years. You have also learned about some of the alternative ways of deploying a remote access system.

This is the end of Part II of this book, "The Basics"—hopefully you are now fluent in basic network concepts. Part III, "Building Networks," talks about building a network, starting at the planning stages, and winding up with the products that enable you to accomplish what you require.

Q&A

Q *What are some of the factors driving the growth of remote access?*

A Government regulations, employee morale, and the ADA are some of the reasons for the growth of remote access.

Q *What is remote control?*

A Remote control is a method of remote access in which a user at a remote computer sees a picture of the screen of the dial-up host computer. ReachOut, pcAnywhere, Remotely Possible, and LapLink are examples of remote control software.

Q *What is remote node?*

A For all practical purposes, remote node is a network connection made across a phone line rather than across a network wire.

Q *Which dial-up protocols are commonly used for remote node?*

A Point-to-Point Protocol (PPP) is most commonly used with a very few installations still using the older Serial Line Internet Protocol (SLIP) for dial-up connections.

Q *Which protocols can run simultaneously over a remote node connection?*

A TCP/IP, IPX, and NetBEUI can all run together over a remote node connection. Doing so, however, is relatively inefficient because multiple protocols can generate more traffic than the network topology can carry. In other words, running multiple protocols simultaneously can cause network traffic jams.

PART III

Building Networks

HOUR 8

Network Criteria

In this hour, you have the opportunity to learn about the following topics:

▶ Networks and best practices

▶ The steps to create and maintain your network: plan, design, implement, and tune

▶ Security and best practices: passwords and disaster recovery

Building a network, even a small one, requires a solid knowledge base of networking concepts and also careful planning. Much of the subject matter of this book relates to the basics of how networks work and are implemented.

Planning and implementing a new network is even a challenge for the seasoned professional, so an experienced network administrator will embrace the concept of **best practices**. Best practices provide a framework or checklist for completing a series of tasks, and using best practices to remain focused and organized is essential when networking computers and other connectivity devices.

Best practices are really a variety of practices that collectively cover most of the dilemmas and unforeseen crises that crop up. They don't necessarily provide pat answers; instead, they provide a global framework or map; even if you get lost, you can retrace your steps and figure out where you are at any point in the process.

Best Practices and Networking

Nearly every job or human endeavor can be quantified in terms of best practices. The term best practices was actually coined by consultants in the 1980s to describe the institutional behaviors that had become ingrained and codified into standard operating procedures. Healthy organizational use of best practices can provide an organization with a sensible, flexible set of rules that provide conceptual guidelines for decision-making.

Best practices exist for networking; they transcend operating systems, hardware platforms, network topologies, and every other fast changing component of networking. Instead of dealing with specifics, they're a set of concepts, which you can apply with great flexibility in a variety of situations.

Because computer and networking technology evolves so quickly, having best practices that can be applied no matter the network operating system or the hardware provides you with the ability to remain focused on the big picture rather than becoming fixated on the minutia. Some of the benefits of using best practices (in a very generic sense) are as follows:

▶ Best practices offer a perspective that enables network planners to step out of the upgrade cycle long enough to take a long hard look at their current practices. Rather than focusing on today's problems, best practices provide a perspective with which to examine the infrastructure and procedures of the underlying pieces and determine whether they are working together in productive fashions.

▶ Best practices offer a way to assess policies and procedures, codify those policies and procedures that work, and discard those that are nonproductive or counterproductive. As you assess your organization in preparation for a network or network upgrade, remember that there is no one single set of best practices for everyone. What is best for one organization is not necessarily best for another. Every organization is different from every other organization; as a result, best practices cannot be slavishly copied from a successful organization—your organization must define them for itself.

▶ Best practices must be tested to demonstrably produce good results; they must be assessed, discovered, written, refined, and applied systematically. After this process, they must be reassessed to ensure that they reflect real concerns and can reliably ensure superior performance when implemented. After this, they can be deployed.

▶ Codifying and instituting best practices often results in cost savings. Cost savings are not an automatic corollary of the institution of best practices; in fact, best practices might actually increase spending if that increase is necessary. However, in many cases, best practices save money by increasing efficiency.

With respect to networking, best practices are not an option if the goal is a robust, flexible, highly functional architecture. No one would ask an architect to build a small house only later to ask that it "evolve" into a skyscraper—but that's what routinely happens in networking. Nightmare tales of ad hoc networking are legend in the consulting world. An example that keeps rearing its ugly head is the company in which several well-meaning department heads each independently builds her own network, leaving the internal networking staff to Frankenstein stitch everything together at extraordinary cost and difficulty.

The complexity of data networks at even the small LAN level has made it imperative that network managers review the way they do their jobs to attempt to stem the flood of user-initiated requests, desktop configuration management problems, large-scale network management issues, and change requests. It is not uncommon for a network manager to find her time focused almost entirely on crises, leaving little time to deal with tactical and strategic organizational issues. Naturally, this crisis focus does little good, but instead accomplishes much that is bad. First, constant crises burn out network managers at an alarming rate; and second, crisis management creates an adversarial relationship between management and users.

Instituting best practices when a network is first being built is the best way to ensure that the network will function well, be manageable, and meet the goals set for it. Best practices related to networking revolve around capacity planning, interoperability, security, network monitoring, and the overall goals for the network implementation. In the following sections, we look at best practices that are related to building your network and how you apply best practices to various situations.

Best Practices and Specific Network Devices

You will also find that when you work with specific network devices such as network servers and routers, each manufacturer has bought into the concept of using best practices in terms of implementing and maintaining the device. The device documentation and help system (particularly in the case of network operating systems) helps you to work in a logical and methodical way as you deal with the idiosyncrasies of the device or platform.

By the Way

Planning Best Practices: Plan, Design, Implement, and Tune

There is an old saying that "change is the only constant." If you've ever doubted that, look at the change in networking from month to month, even week to week. The rate of change is so rapid that it's difficult to plan. Look at the evolution of the Internet, particularly the World Wide Web. We've seen the dot-com boom become the dot-com bust, and—in terms of networking—we have seen a seesaw battle from various network operating system companies as each software giant seeks industry dominance. Throw into the mix open source possibilities, such as Linux, and you can see that it is very difficult for the network professional to keep pace with the every changing industry.

Although keeping up with change can be discouraging, it is a necessity when dealing with network, particularly costs. Many of the latest and greatest technologies often can lower a company's total cost of ownership when building a network infrastructure. Let's look at some strategies for dealing with change.

Dealing with Change

If you were building a house, would you start nailing boards together willy-nilly, or would you work from plans? You'd probably work from plans. If you didn't, you might get a house...or you might not. You might create art, but you can't necessarily live in art (although Frank Lloyd Wright and Antoni Gaudie, if around today, wouldn't necessarily agree).

Even in cases in which you do have a plan for a house, you can face issues related to spur of the moment issues related to the latest and greatest building materials and changes you want to make in the plan as building is under way. The desire to make changes is always a temptation and sometimes a necessity.

That's what building a network can be like, even if you have a plan. Change really is the only constant. And in the network technology world, where the pace of change is breakneck, change is more than a constant; it's an annoying, cost—and morale—draining force that knocks on your door all the time. When you're building a network, because of the rapid steps in technology, it's especially important to ensure that you follow a reasonably logical process. Otherwise, you'll wind up with a heap o' technology that no one can make sense of. The process is, simply stated, plan, design, implement, and tune:

- ▶ Plan—Plan your network from a user perspective. Know what your network is for! It sounds simple, but if you don't know why you're building it, you're not likely to reap much benefit from it.

- ▶ Design—Design your network. What is design? A good definition is that it's taking a perfectly beautiful idea and proving why it won't work. Good engineers don't look for successes during the design process; they look for potential points of failure. That's a good way to look at designing a network. It must be capable of doing what you need it to do without breaking down at every turn.

Network design includes a variety of tasks, which we'll examine in more depth in the next hour. The chief task is **capacity planning**, or figuring how much your network will grow and trying to ensure that you have enough capacity to deal with network requirements. But the main trick to successful design (of any type) is to look for what *doesn't* work and to solve problems before you implement the design. Network design also includes **compatibility issues** in which you determine that all the pieces of the puzzle can work together.

▶ Implement—This is the point at which you take a perfectly good design and prove that the people who designed it didn't know what they were talking about. Implementation is the process of physically realizing the design. Inevitably, the design process has missed something, and the implementation stage is where it pays to be flexible, knowledgeable, and creative.

▶ Tune—Implementations always leave some loose ends, just like the first time you sewed on a button. Tuning is the part of the process in which you try to rectify the small flaws in your creation. Note that tuning is not intended to compensate for fundamental design flaws. Don't try to patch a network with a fundamentally flawed design.

Applying the Best Practices

To arrive at a passable standard that adheres to the best practices set forth, you need...a crystal ball. Because crystal balls are in short supply, you have to think hard about the future of your business, your organization, and technology—and extrapolate what you'll need a year from now to remain competitive, serve your users, and not break the bank in the process. If you're going to be responsible for capacity planning for a network (and if you're the person building the network, this is almost certainly the case), answer the following questions. They represent a starting point for your reflections. As you work through these questions, take notes and add questions of your own; remember, you know your business and your network better than anyone else.

1. How many workstations does your network have?

   If your network has 5 or 10 workstations, planning should be relatively simple. If, on the other hand, you have to support 500 workstations, you'll need to structure and plan in more depth. Large networks are a challenge because they require the delivery of high-quality services to a wide variety of users, most of whom can't be supported in a constant, one-on-one personal basis. This requires network management solutions, mass software distribution solutions, and finding a way to do open-ended capacity planning.

2. How many workstations will your network have a year from now?

   This question follows on the heels of the first question. The degree of growth can help determine what equipment you initially roll out. A 5-workstation network that will have 10 workstations the following year requires less overall power and flexibility than a 5-workstation network that will grow to 25 or 50 workstations. Clearly, if your network is growing at a rate that outstrips the ability of existing staff to service each user and each request manually, there'll be a strong need for the services mentioned under point 1.

3. Do you or will you provide file services for your users?

   If you do, you have to make provision for a file server. Discussed in earlier hours, file servers tend to be overbuilt; if you can afford more power than you need now, get it. If you centralize data storage, you need to plan to back up that data adequately—otherwise, your users will lose confidence in the shared network storage and won't use it.

4. Will you provide Internet email services for your users?

   If you do, you require a mail gateway. It's usually best to assign a single computer to accomplish this task. You'll need to contract with an ISP to handle your bulk mail, and you'll probably need to register a domain on the Internet.

5. Will you provide Internet access (the Web, FTP, Telnet services) to your users?

   If you're going to provide Internet access for your users, you need a router, proxy server, and firewall. You can also roll the email server into this system. Chances are, you'll also need to go to the ISP marketplace and select an Internet service provider who can provide you access across some sort of high-speed phone line (a T1, DSL, or other high-speed access).

6. Are there other services you're providing to your user base?

7. Do you now provide centrally administered remote access for your users? Will you ever have to provide centrally administered remote access for your users?

   Remote access is generally best provided by computers dedicated to the task of providing remote access. In most cases, this means implementing a server computer with Virtual Private Networking capabilities. For more about VPN, see Hour 7, "Remote Networking."

Questions Are Often Answered with Questions

As you use the best practices questions listed here to help you develop an approach to building a network, you will find that the answer to a question might actually generate additional questions. Make sure that you have all the facts and a solid plan before you begin the actual process of building even a small network.

One of the benefits of going through a question everything process is that if you do it right, the results are typically stellar, and people will hail you as an IT sage (although very few of us are recognized as geniuses in our own time, so you won't always get all the credit even when it is due).

What you want to create by answering these and other questions (questions that arise as you brainstorm the possibilities for your network) is a document that specifies what you want the network to be capable of doing. You should end up with a document that lays out the network requirements and overall functional design.

Even if you are feeling pretty good about the answers that you've formulated to the questions that have been discussed so far, you will find that two issues that can still give you major headaches (typically because the issues continue to evolve) are those of interoperability, a standardized network, and security. Let's take a look at these issues.

Interoperability and Standards-Based Networking

Although network and computer technology changes quickly, you don't necessarily have to concede that your network will be an outdated pile of junk as soon as new possibilities become available. You actually want to try and design your network so that it is as **future-proof**, or immune to abrupt technology shifts, as possible. Given that networking changes as rapidly as it does, you might be led to think that future-proofing is impossible, or improbable at the very least.

Fortunately, that isn't the case. As you might recall from Hour 3, " Getting Data from Here to There: How Computers Share Data " a group called the IETF sets standards for TCP/IP networking and publishes those standards in documents called Requests for Comments (RFCs). The standards set forth in the RFCs are available to any and all manufacturers who want to use them, and these mean that at least an attempt is made in the network engineering and software world to adhere to standards and provide products that will interoperate with both legacy and new products.

What does this mean in terms of best practices? First, it means that you should be aware of the various IETF and TCP/IP standards. You don't have to know them in detail, but you should at least know what is standard, what is pending standardization, and what is not. This allows you to select products that provide the greatest possibilities in terms of interoperability. The other benefit of deciding to use standards-compliant products is that it simplifies your purchasing decisions. If a vendor's products are **proprietary** (that is, they do not conform to open standards), they are automatically out of the running.

As a result, you should ask yourself whether you want to make your network standards compliant. In most cases, the answer is yes—it's a no-brainer—and you should make note of that decision, as you'll take that into account when you select hardware and software in the next hour.

Security

Best practices are required to ensure security as well. A network might work well and provide all its users with everything they need, but if one user illicitly sends one copy of data out of the building—either on a disk or over the Internet—and gives it to a competitor, you're up the creek without a paddle.

Although good network security certainly deals with issues related to your network users and the importance of company "secrets," security is also one of those information technology arenas that is evolving at a very rapid pace. This is largely Because of the number of hackers, crackers, and cyber-villains who have made it their life's work to punch holes in our computer network defenses, create viruses, and other **malware** (a collective term for viruses, Trojan horses, and other nasty software) and just generally annoy us by defacing our Web sites or messing with our email.

> ### Become a Security Expert and Enjoy Great Job Security
> The network security arena is the most rapidly growing area in the information technology field. Protecting a network has become almost more important than planning and implementing a network in terms of protecting important network data. Hour 19, "Security," discusses a number of the issues related to securing a network.

Because you certainly can't control the behavior of those who threaten the network from outside (although you can develop a strategy for blocking their attacks), you can institute best practices that will help secure the network internally. And this relates to user behaviors. Some of the best practices for security that you can institute include the following:

- Enunciate a set of rules for your end users.

- Define secure behaviors

- Figure out how to implement the preceding

- Test, verify, and restart the process

Mostly, though, remember that security is a process. You can never decide that the network is secure and all the work is done. Good security, as you'll find in Hour 19, requires monitoring and vigilance.

Enunciating Usage Policies and Procedures

When you set up your network, you must clearly define how users are and are not allowed to use data. Any violation of these rules, whether it be using floppy disks, Zip disks, CD-ROMs, DVDs, laptops, PDAs (Personal Digital Assistants) email, Web pages, unauthorized Internet access, or other parts of the network, *must* be punishable by sanctions up to and including dismissal and legal action.

These rules should be incorporated into an employee handbook (after all, data is just like any other company property) and should be acknowledged with a written and signed statement by the employee.

These rules should also be added to your growing list of information regarding what the network should do.

Defining Secure Behaviors

Because each company's business is different, we have not defined an exact set of rules. However, the following questions can help you figure out where your potential security holes are:

1. Do you have your servers physically secured?

2. Is each server's operating system "hardened" against common intrusions?

3. Are there controls in place to reduce Internet-based spyware, adware, and unwanted cookies?

4. Does each user have a unique password?

5. Are passwords regularly changed according to a schedule?

6. Is there a clearinghouse for passwords?

7. Are all logins and logouts and all file activity logged at the server?

8. Are all file-copy actions to removable media logged?

9. Do your users understand their roles in helping secure the network?

10. Do you have a way to monitor and audit security?

These questions represent only the beginning of the security questions you have to ask. Think about how your users work: Do they have read/write access to a corporate database? Do they have physical access to the variety of servers that make up the network? Just as with capacity planning, security is a subject that gets bigger the deeper into it you get. Go there anyhow—you'll be glad you did.

The purpose of these questions is to help you determine how you want your network to work. This material comes in useful in the hours ahead when you design and administer your network.

If you want to read more about security, go to Hour 19, which deals with these issues in more depth.

Monitoring

"You can't monitor what you can't measure." Whoever said that was *smart*. It's as true for networks as it is for anything else. If you're setting policies on your network, whether for access control, intrusion detection, performance, or what-have-you, you'll need to be able to monitor activity to ensure that your goals are being reached.

Why Monitor?

You don't need to be a large corporation's Network Operations Center (NOC, pronounced "knock") to need to monitor. If you've got a cable modem or DSL modem and your computer is directly connected to the Internet without a personal firewall, chances are good that your computer has been scanned for security vulnerabilities by someone who means you no good.

So why monitor? The average time online of a new, not particularly well secured system prior to being attacked and compromised is *three days*. Yeah, you read that right—three days. So it seems like a good idea to find some way of protecting your system and, more importantly, *auditing* the results.

How Do I Monitor?

We'll discuss this in more depth in the Hour 19. But at base, you need to be aware of the threats coming from the Internet and take action against them by configuring your existing software to remove vulnerabilities and by adding software that monitors remaining vulnerabilities. Attacks can come from anywhere, and you can only defend against attacks you know about.

Collating What You've Learned

At this point, you've answered (or thought about) a lot of questions regarding what your network should do and how you want it to work. This information can help guide you in the hours ahead, when you design, build, and administer your network. If you can, assemble the information you've gathered into a document so that you have the questions and answers available for later review. You'll find it useful for helping you get back on track as you go forward through the process.

Summary

In this hour, you learned about the issues related to using best practices to determine the infrastructure and the policies and procedures that define your network. Hours that follow expand on all these ideas. As you design your network, be aware of the issues we have raised here related to network planning, interoperability, and security.

In the next hour, you'll go through the process of designing your network, step by step. You'll bring all you've learned in the book so far to bear on the process—so reviewing what you've read up to this point would be wise.

Q&A

Q *How far into the future should you plan?*

A You can never plan too far ahead! If you know that your network is slated to grow, and you know how fast, your planning can accommodate the planned growth so that your design won't limit the possibility of expansion.

Q *Why is interoperability so important to network planning?*

A In basic terms, the need for interoperability affects everything else when you are planning a network. Software or hardware that does not work with other software or hardware (or that does so only under certain conditions) limits the capability of your network to grow.

Q *What are some "best practices" related network security?*

A Actually defining a set of rules and behaviors for your network users, detailing proper or best practices for their network use, will go a long way in helping to secure your important network data.

HOUR 9

Designing a Network

In this hour, you'll have the opportunity to learn about the following aspects of designing a network:

- ▶ Defining the "big picture" purpose of your network
- ▶ Determining the roles that will be filled by computer systems on the network
- ▶ Determining the type of network, client/server, or peer-to-peer that best suits your networking needs
- ▶ Diagramming the network—that is, getting down on paper the network infrastructure
- ▶ Reviewing and perfecting your plans
- ▶ Writing a specification that defines the network
- ▶ Building the network

In the last hour, we took a look at how you use best practices to logically develop the overall strategies and policies that define your network. In this hour, we take a look at more nuts and bolts issues related to creating a network, including how you define the network, establish the network blueprint, and then actually build the network.

Although advances in network hardware have made the overall process of actually connecting devices a much easier prospect, for example, you could actually build a network simply by purchasing the parts and following the instructions that explain how to insert tab A into slot B and so forth. Creating a network that can easily be maintained, secured, and grown (all networks must be scaleable or expandable) is much more than just assembling the various components.

Networks must also be designed to fulfill a particular purpose, and although it is difficult to quantify how much money a computer network actually saves or generates for a company, it is important to establish how the network provides a communication and data sharing environment for your company, institution, or even home office. Let's begin our discussion with a look at how you identify the uses for your network.

Step 1: Identify the Uses of Your Network

Every network is different. That point, as simple as it is, cannot be overstressed. Just as every human being is different, or every snowflake is different, every network is different. Networking is one of the few nonartistic human endeavors in which every system, once created, grows in its own way.

Why? Because every network has a collection of individual users who, being human, bring their own baggage to the use of the network. The users working in productive concert with the network designers collectively make a network usable and functional (or conversely, dysfunctional and counterproductive). So at the very beginning of the process, you have to define the purpose (and hence, the goals) for the network.

Defining the Organizational Purpose

What does your organization do? Are you a writer who works from home and has to network to ensure that the rest of the family has access to much constrained computer resources? Are you a member of a small consulting firm that uses computers to handle job requests, client tracking, and billing? Are you in a department of a large corporation that has been given the mandate to automate its job processes? Or is it one of the zillion other jobs out there?

No matter what your organization does, its network has to accomplish only one task to be considered successful. It has to ensure that whatever your organization does, it can do it better, faster, and more efficiently because of the network. If the network doesn't do that, it will be a failure, regardless of the quantity of premium technology and quality of service.

The first order of business is determining the reason why you or your organization requires a network. This process can be likened to a journey of a thousand miles starting with a single step; like all journeys, it has the potential for peril or chaos because you have to reconcile management's reasons for networking with users' needs. The first steps on your journey lead to the desk of the most senior manager to whom you can get access. Make an appointment to meet with him and talk about two things: what the organization's core business is now, and how he wants to change or improve the business processes that support the core business.

This meeting should *not* involve a broad discussion of what networks can do in general but a more specific discussion of what a network could do for your company. You need to pin down the core purpose of how the network will make the company a more productive place.

Any questions you pose should be open ended; try to see whether the manager has a vision related to the company's future, and try to understand what that vision is and what its ramifications are as related to computer and networking technologies.

Companies Are Much More than a Mission Statement

For what it's worth, interviewing key managers or corporate officers will supply you with much more information on a company's goals and purposes than the corporate mission statement. Mission statements are often designed for the company customers and are particularly tailored for company brochures. The better your understanding of the company and its reason for being (besides making money) can only help you better plan and implement your network.

By the Way

Once you've interviewed the senior executive and documented his responses, start talking to the rank and file or the folks on the production floor. Sit with them and find out what they do. Be up-front about the purpose of your visit; it will help break down suspicion that you're there to increase their workload. If you can, try to work with several employees over the course of a couple of days to see what they do and how they do it.

Once you understand some of the various tasks necessary to ensure that the organization fulfills its purpose, it's time to ask the employees what, specifically, would make their jobs easier. Don't fish for computer-related improvements; instead, get concrete, productivity enhancing, job life improving answers such as "if I could find a way to track all the phone conversations everyone has with Mr. X, I would be better prepared when he calls me." Clearly, whatever gives rise to this kind of response doesn't necessarily require a computer to rectify (a public notebook could also work quite well in this example), but it offers an insight into a deeper question: *How can we all have the same information so that our clients don't think we're clueless?* Such a question can be parlayed into a piece of a **specification**, which is discussed later in this hour.

The ultimate goal of these informational interviews is to derive a set of visions, current behaviors, desired results, and desired processes. Once you have these, you can attempt to distill the deeper organizational issues related to improving the overall performance and success of the organization. Some of the bullet points that might result from your research follow:

▶ Increased responsiveness to customers

▶ Increased ease of access to customer data

▶ More up-to-date information

▶ Capability to handle an increase in business

▶ Increased flexibility in order handling

These are typical goals of an organization, but they are generic. It's very likely that the responses you receive will be more specific than these, and will strictly address the issues your management and your users face every day.

Quantifying the Network

After you have completed your interviews and distilled the information in a document that lists the core issues that affect what purposes the network must fulfill, you are ready to actually quantify the network—meaning that you can actually look at issues related to implementing the resources that will effectively serve your user base. First, *determine how many users your network will have.* Do not mistake this number for the number of computers on the network; that's the next question, and the two are emphatically not the same thing. One computer can adequately serve multiple users if they don't have to interact with it on a constant, real-time daily basis. The one-computer-per-desktop model works for many offices—particularly in cases in which users work constantly on productivity software including word processing, database, and spreadsheet applications—but it doesn't hold true everywhere. For example, in a factory floor shop, one computer used for laser-based barcode inventory control might serve 20 or 30 users. A healthcare practice might have a few public computers so that doctors can key their patient reports, but they probably wouldn't be dedicated systems. Instead, each doctor would log on, briefly enter a report, and then go on to the next patient.

Whatever the situation, determine how many users the network will serve. Nearly every network will grow over time, so keep expandability in mind. However, also keep in mind that initially you need a count of current users and those who will need to access network services when the network is first rolled out.

After you have figured out how many users you have, look at who those users are. Are they management who will use the computer primarily for administrative purposes such as memo writing and messaging; will they be office workers; or will they be people on a production floor? This is a very important part of the process because it leads to the next question: *How many computers will the network have initially?* Actually, the question is really this: *How many computers will have only one user, and how many will be shared by many users?*

After you have determined how your users will interact with the network, it is possible to *determine how many computers your network will have.* It's a simple matter: Look at how your users will interact with the network and determine whether the ratio of computers to users is one-to-one or one-to-many. If you have a one-to-one ratio, your user count equals (or, in client/server networks, is just shy of) the number of computers. If you have a one-to-many ratio, it's quite likely that you will have to allocate computers according to job function. In other words, if you have a group of users who has a computer only for checking work in and out with a barcoding system (common in some manufacturing settings) or for checking in parts picked in a warehouse, you'll have only as many computers for that group as will concurrently use them: If you have a single user queuing up at a time, one computer will do. If you have 10 users queuing up and their tasks take time (say, more than half-a-minute each), you might want several computers. Once again, the number of computers you allocate to user groups will depend on your organizational needs. As with anything else, think it through and try to **rightsize** (that is, design enough capacity but not too much or too little) your design.

Step 2: List Which Tasks Happen at Which Computers

The second step in the network-design process seems terribly obvious: Know which applications and tasks have to be performed at each of the computers on your network. Unfortunately, it isn't quite as straightforward as that; this step is less about following the workflow trail than it is about continuing the rightsizing process.

In networking, rightsizing is a process that starts early on and continues well after the initial rollout of the system. It starts with knowing the physical limits of your network (how many users, how many computers), but it certainly doesn't end there. It isn't enough to know how many systems are out there; you also have to know how powerful each computer should be, and what each computer should be capable of.

For example, the barcoding computers mentioned at the end of the step 1 section generally don't have to be very powerful; they're doing one task that does not require much processing horsepower or memory. Neither do they need soundcards or particularly high-end video adapters.

On the other hand, some users will need all these things and more. Let's look at a couple of hypothetical cases that illustrate how to determine the quantity of horsepower and the range of features a given network system will require.

The Many-User Computer

Computers used by many users can be built minimally, as in the warehouse barcode example, or with all the bells and whistles. As with any other system, the amount of power and features depends on the application. Some of the possibilities related to computer configuration are as follows:

▶ Simple task—simple computer: A computer, such as the one that would be involved in the warehouse barcode example, wouldn't need an exceedingly fast processor or huge amount of memory or a giant hard drive. Because video quality and sound capability are not an issue, even a legacy computer already available at the company would suffice. In case of new hardware, a minimum configuration system would certainly provide more than enough power. Because it is difficult to even buy a computer with less than a Pentium IV processor and 128MB of RAM, you could definitely go with a bargain-basement model in terms of features. You would need to configure the computer hardware, however, to run the barcode software and the operating system required.

▶ Complex task—powerful computer: Although multiuser computers used in a warehouse or manufacturing environment might not require a high-end configuration, you will run into situations in which you have to configure computers that will be accessed by numerous users and, because of the task they serve, require a powerful and feature-rich configuration. For example, you might deploy a kiosk computer that requires sound and multimedia capabilities and also is configured with a touch screen. We have all seen these types of computers serving as informational kiosks in shopping malls.

▶ Multiple tasks—single user computer: Single-user computers generally occur in office environments. No matter the job title, many people have become **knowledge workers** because their currency is dealing with information—formatting, managing, and analyzing data. Depending on the nature of their jobs, they tend to require higher-end computers to begin with, but they also have widely varying connectivity requirements. For example, some workers might be able to leave their work behind at the end of the day and require no remote access; other users might require two or more computers to be able to do their jobs. Again, as in the other scenarios listed here, you must determine the tasks that will be accomplished on the computer and then configure the computer hardware so that it will run the operating system and application software that will allow the individual to be productive.

Even knowledge workers will require different classes of computers. Many users might be able to do their job with minimal configurations, whereas others—who you could label as "power users"—require computers that can run more complex software applications. This typically requires a more robust hardware configuration. Users who travel might require a laptop configuration that gives them power on the road but also supplies them with all the capabilities that they would need from a desktop computer when they are in the office.

Working with Users on the Go

Laptops do not generally fit neatly into overall network schemes. It's not because they are not standard desktop computers; instead, laptops are an oddity because of the way they connect and disconnect from the network using **PC card** network cards and modems.

This isn't to say that it isn't possible to integrate laptops into a network plan. Just be aware that doing so requires additional foresight and planning.

By the Way

As you can see from the discussion in this session, you really have to spend some time determining what people will be doing with their computers and how these computers must provide them with the technology to get their jobs done. You can't just configure a generic computer for every user; you must make sure that each computer is configured with the appropriate features (and power) as defined by the tasks that will be accomplished.

Step 3: Selecting the Type of Network: To Centralize or Not to Centralize

Another issue related to building your network is how centralized the network administration and security must be for the network to run effectively. Typically, the centralization issue is most related to scale and the nature of business. (That is the nature of the data and its overall importance to the business.) Small businesses that only have a few users who need to share data and other resources (such as printers) typically do not require an extremely centralized network, nor do they require a separate server or network operating system, which can be a great cost saver for a small office or company. Let's take a brief look at peer networks, and then we can discuss centralized server-based networks.

Peer-to-Peer Networks

Peer-to-peer networks, which are supported by most desktop operating systems such as Microsoft Windows XP and the various distributions of Linux, allow users to share directories and folders with each other with little interaction from a network administrator. Each resource is secured by its own password. (This can include printers and other devices.) In terms of network administration, each user really becomes the administrator of his own peer computer. In terms of security, peer networks are not all that secure because people often readily supply the passwords to co-workers. However, in an environment in which the data shared by these workers is not of a highly proprietary nature, users can readily communicate and collaborate on a network that is easy to get up and running.

For example, Microsoft Windows XP (both the Professional and Home versions) provides a Network Setup Wizard that actually walks you through the process of configuring a small peer network. Figure 9.1 shows the Network Wizard Setup screen where you define the name of your network. In the Windows environment, a small peer network is referred to as a **workgroup**.

FIGURE 9.1
Microsoft Windows XP provides a Network Setup Wizard for creating a peer network.

Not only does the Network Setup Wizard make it easy to connect to other users who are running Windows XP, but also a disk can be created during the Network setup process that allows you to bring other versions of Windows, such as Windows 2000 or Windows 98, quickly into the network configuration.

A Simple Network Does Not Mean a Secure Network

Peer-to-peer networking can be accomplished by connecting computers via wireless or wire media and then taking advantage of the peer networking capabilities of most desktop operating systems now available. Although these networks are extremely easy to get up and running, they can turn out to be a security nightmare. Users control the various security levels placed on shared files, and issues related to secure connections to the Internet also arise. Just having a few users should not be the only criteria you use when determining if a peer network will work for you. Even small companies often use server-based networks because of the security that they provide in terms and data access and protection from malicious activity from outside the network.

Server-Based Networks

The alternative to the peer network is the centralized network that uses a server or servers to centralize the administration of the network. This model also provides for centralized security. Users log on to an authentication server and, once on the network, can only access resources that they have been assigned rights to by the network administrator.

In terms of network scale, you will find that the server-based model is required when you go beyond 10 users (because most desktop operating systems only allow 10 connections at a time). However, it isn't necessarily the number of users who dictate the **client/server model** (meaning client computers gain access via a centralized server) but the level of security that you require to protect the valuable company data.

Client/server networks are definitely more secure. Their files are usually stored in a central location and are backed up on a regular basis. User access tends to be controllable.

Server-based networks often require that you deploy a number of different server types. Some of these servers are

> ▶ **File Server**—A file server's job is to provide a central location for the company's data. The network administrator can actually assign different levels of access to each file contained on the file server. Some users can have full access (meaning that they can even delete files on the file server), whereas other users may only be able to access a file or files in a read-only mode (meaning that they cannot even edit the file).

> ▶ **Print Server**—A print server hosts a printer or printer on the network. It not only allows the network administrator to control print jobs, but it also provides the memory and hard drive space to spool print jobs in the print queue as each print job waits to be printed.

▶ **Communication Server**—A server that provides a communication platform for the network. For example, Microsoft Exchange supplies an email, calendar, and contacts platform that allows users to communicate and share appointment, address book, and meeting information. Other examples of communication server software include Lotus Notes and Novell GroupWise.

▶ **Application Server**—A server that hosts applications, including specialized data. Application servers provide the backend processing power to run complex databases and other applications. User computers require a client application to access the services provided by the application server. Microsoft SQL server and Oracle are two examples of client/server database environments.

▶ **Web Server**—A Web server can host internal and external corporate Web sites. Even companies that do not deploy a Web server on the Internet can use a Web server internally (typically referred to as a **intranet**), allowing network users to view and share information.

A number of other specialized server types can also be deployed on a network—for example, DNS and DHCP servers. We will look at these specialized servers in Hour 14, "TCP/IP."

One server type that was not included on our list is the authentication server. This server allows users to log on to the network. Each network operating system supplies authentication servers. We will discuss some of the network operating system platforms in Part IV, "Network Operating Systems and Providing Network-Wide Services."

File Servers and Security

You can see that making users log on to the network and using file servers to store and serve up data greatly enhances the level of security for a network. As already mentioned, file servers allow you to assign access rights down to the file level (meaning below the folder or directory level, which is a limitation for peer networks). Typically, file server security for PC-based operating systems follow some fairly simple rules:

▶ **Inheritance**—Security inheritance works similarly to financial inheritance; what a parent has can be inherited by a child unless it is blocked by third parties. In security inheritance, a user gets access to a particular directory (for example, F:\DIRECTRY). Whatever access a user has to F:\DIRECTRY is inherited by any and all subdirectories of F:\DIRECTRY (for example, F:\DIRECTRY\ONE, F:\DIRECTRY\TWO, and so forth). Inheritance is a useful tool to ensure that a user has as much access as he requires to a given part of the server's disk.

▶ **Access rules**—In general, users are limited to three levels of access to a given file or directory on a file server:

  ▶ No Access, which often means that users cannot even see the file or directory.

  ▶ Read-Only Access, which means that users can view the contents of a file or directory but cannot modify it.

  ▶ Read-Write Access, which means that a user has the access rights to view and modify files and directories.

Various network operating systems enable additions to these three basic access rights, but by and large it should be possible to ensure reasonably good security using only these three rules.

Windows Networks Provide Two Access Permission Schemes

Access rights can actually be more complicated than you might realize from this basic discussion. In fact in the Windows networking environment, you might actually have to deal with share access permissions and also NTFS permissions. NTFS permissions can be assigned to files on NTFS formatted drives (NTFS stands for NT File System) that will interact with any share level permissions that have been set. We discuss NTFS permissions versus share permissions in Hour 15, "Microsoft Networking."

Did you Know?

Each network operating system uses a slightly different model for protecting files on a network server. We will discuss these in the context of each network operating system in Part IV, " Introduction to Network Administration."

Easier Backup

A great benefit to storing network files on a centralized server is the fact that the files can be backed up simply by duplicating the server's hard drive to tape or some other media. If that doesn't sound like a compelling advantage, here's an example that will explain why it is.

Assume that your network has 50 user workstations. If all the users store their files on their workstations, you'll have to back up all or part of their hard drives to ensure that no data is lost if a system crashes. Further suppose that each user has 50 megabytes of files on their workstations' hard drives (for many users, a very conservative estimate). Backing up this quantity of files across the network for this many users could take 10 or 12 hours and be a nightmare to manage.

By contrast, backing up a server's hard drive with an attached tape drive or some other backup device can take as little as an hour or so. Clearly, backing up files from a single server to a tape drive takes less time and is more controllable.

There are many varieties of tape drives:

▶ 4mm digital audio tape (DAT) drives that handle up to 8 gigabytes of storage

▶ Digital linear tape (DLT) that handles 20 to 40 gigabytes of storage

▶ Advanced intelligent tape (AIT) that backs up as much as 50 gigabytes per tape

Most tape drives handle only one tape at a time. However, devices called **tape changers** can handle whole libraries of hundreds or thousands of tapes. The kind of tape drive you select depends on what your needs are today and what you expect them to be in the foreseeable future. Remember that the amount of data that seems huge today will seem a pittance tomorrow.

Easier Configuration Management

Storing files on a server offers compelling advantages. However, there is more to centralized management of a network than simply storing files on a server. As a guideline, if you have more than 10 workstations, it's necessary to find a way to inventory the hardware, audit the software on the hard drive, install new software, and ensure that the workstation adheres to configuration standards.

Configuration management is the art (or science) of using a central console to ensure that user workstations have the correct hardware and software installed and that the software and hardware is set up according to consensus and preset standards. Configuration management software is complex, make no mistake about it. It's usually composed of a hugely complex database with a proprietary front end that allows a network administrator to view and modify the configurations of users' workstations. Most management software requires that each system have an **agent** (a piece of software that interacts with the administrative database) installed on the workstation; often, agents can be installed automatically as a user logs in to the network.

There is a payoff, however, for mastering the intricacies of configuration management software. Network administrators who install and rigorously use configuration management software report that they have better control over their users' workstations. They can inventory the network very quickly, and install and upgrade software for many users simultaneously. In addition, they can set up alarms that register unauthorized tampering, which helps keep the theft of hardware and unauthorized employee installed software under control.

A variety of manufacturers—including McAfee, Microsoft, Tivoli, IBM, Digital, Hewlett-Packard, and others—make high-quality network management tools. Many packages are modular, so you don't have to purchase the whole package to get the modules you need.

Even if you do not elect to have an in-house network administrator, you can still benefit from configuration management software. Many third-party consultants sell network troubleshooting services. If the consultant is authorized to access your network to perform upgrades and fixes, you can successfully outsource your network management.

Choosing a Topology

Whether your network is going to be client/server or peer, you have to select a topology. Because peer networks are by practice used to keep the overall cost of the network down, you will use a hub or switch and configure a simple Ethernet star network. In terms of server-based networks, you will also typically use some variety of star-configuration Ethernet (10BASE-T, 100BASE-T).

Your network topology, however, might also be dictated by the network architecture that you deploy. Most networks now use some flavor of Ethernet. For example, if there is a compelling reason for you to deploy an IBM Token Ring network, you will be working with a logical ring topology. In cases in which you have to expand a LAN beyond one location, you might also become involved in a FDDI implementation. Remember that FDDI actually uses a redundant ring topology.

Step 4: Making It Real—Drawing the Network

By the time you get to this step, you should know the following:

- ▶ The organizational purpose of the network
- ▶ The specifics of the network's use (which users do which tasks)
- ▶ The quantity of both users and computers
- ▶ Whether the network will be centralized or decentralized
- ▶ The network topology you plan to use

Of all the steps in this process, this is the most fun. Once you know the basics of your network, you're ready to go to the whiteboard (or easel). Get a set of markers in at least four or five colors, go to the whiteboard, and then start drawing your network.

Get a Big and Flexible Picture on a Whiteboard

For what it's worth, a whiteboard is much more valuable than paper for this process because it allows you to make revisions on-the-fly without starting from scratch each time.

Drawing the Logical Network Diagram

The first drawing you make is the **logical diagram**. It details the applications that have to run on workstations and which resources workstations have to be able to access.

1. Start by drawing a workstation for each type of user (for example, one warehouse floor computer, one analyst's computer, one accounting computer, one secretary's computer, and so on). Just make a circle for each computer; draw them in a line across the top of the whiteboard or page (see Figure 9.2).

FIGURE 9.2
The first stage of the logical network diagram.

Analyst   Partner   Secretary   Warehouse

◯   ◯   ◯   ◯

2. Underneath each computer, list the applications it has to run (see Figure 9.3). This could include word processing, spreadsheets, email, scheduling, and more for a user's desktop computer, or a single application for a dedicated machine, such as a factory or warehouse inventory computer or an in-office computer dedicated to routing email.

3. Make a list of the resources each workstation computer will share. In general, peer networking has a lot of these shared resources (such as printers, scanners, shared modems, and so on); client/server networks will have fewer shared resources. No matter whether you've elected to use client/server or peer, add these resources in to your diagram (see Figure 9.4).

4. If the system will participate in a network-wide security scheme, note which group of users has login access to the various pieces of the system (see Figure 9.5). For example, business desktop users can log in to the file server,

warehouse supervisors can log in to the transaction server, and administrators can log in to anything anywhere. This step helps ensure that you provide the correct levels of security.

	Analyst	Partner	Secretary	Warehouse
	○	○	○	○
Applications	E-Mail	E-Mail	E-Mail	Barcode
	Word Proc	Word Proc	Word Proc	Tracking
	Spread Sheet	Spread Sheet		Application
	Statistical	Trading Software		
	Software			

FIGURE 9.3
The second stage of the logical network diagram, showing the applications needed.

	Analyst	Partner	Secretary	Warehouse
	○	○	○	○
Applications	E-Mail	E-Mail	E-Mail	Barcode
	Word Proc	Word Proc	Word Proc	Tracking
	Spread Sheet	Spread Sheet		Application
	Statistical	Trading Software		
	Software			
Shared	Printer	Printer	Printer	Nothing

FIGURE 9.4
The third stage of the logical network diagram, showing the shared resources.

	Analyst	Partner	Secretary	Warehouse
	○	○	○	○
Applications	E-Mail	E-Mail	E-Mail	Barcode
	Word Proc	Word Proc	Word Proc	Tracking
	Spread Sheet	Spread Sheet		Application
	Statistical	Trading Software		
	Software			
Shared	Printer	Printer	Printer	Nothing
Security	File Server	File Server	File Server	Transaction
	Internet	Internet	Internet	Server

FIGURE 9.5
The fourth stage of the logical network diagram, showing security concerns mapped.

5. Add the workstation operating system to the bottom of the list (see Figure 9.6). The OS is usually something like Windows XP, a Linux flavor, or Macintosh. Although UNIX can be used as a client, outside of academic computing centers and high-end engineering workstations, it is (sadly) not common as a workstation OS. If you have more than one workstation OS, ensure that you have more than one computer drawn—each workstation OS should be shown on a separate machine.

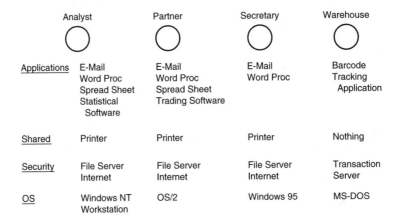

FIGURE 9.6
The fifth stage of the logical network diagram, showing the operating system for workstations.

	Analyst	Partner	Secretary	Warehouse
Applications	E-Mail Word Proc Spread Sheet Statistical Software	E-Mail Word Proc Spread Sheet Trading Software	E-Mail Word Proc	Barcode Tracking Application
Shared	Printer	Printer	Printer	Nothing
Security	File Server Internet	File Server Internet	File Server Internet	Transaction Server
OS	Windows NT Workstation	OS/2	Windows 95	MS-DOS

6. Add the quantity of each type of workstation to the bottom of the list (see Figure 9.7).

FIGURE 9.7
The sixth stage of the logical network diagram, showing the quantities of each type of workstation.

	Analyst	Partner	Secretary	Warehouse
Applications	E-Mail Word Proc Spread Sheet Statistical Software	E-Mail Word Proc Spread Sheet Trading Software	E-Mail Word Proc	Barcode Tracking Application
Shared	Printer	Printer	Printer	Nothing
Security	File Server Internet	File Server Internet	File Server Internet	Transaction Server
OS	Windows NT Workstation	OS/2	Windows 95	MS-DOS
Quantity	6	2	4	2

Now comes the fun part. Draw lines from each workstation type to each system to which that workstation type requires access. In other words, if an accounting PC requires file storage resources on a file server, select a colored marker, draw a line between the two systems, and write the name of the resource the workstation client will use. If a workstation has a shared printer, ensure that other systems that have to use it are connected to it using lines of a different color than the first.

If a router provides connectivity between the network and the workstations, but must first route data through a server, draw that full path as well in yet another color.

Make certain that each connection documents the network protocols that will carry the traffic. For example, a great deal of Microsoft networking is done using NetBEUI; NetWare uses IPX and TCP/IP; Internet-standards–compliant networks use TCP/IP. Many networks use a single protocol, but it is entirely possible for multiple protocols to run side by side on a network. (That situation is just not very efficient.) If you're not certain which protocol a particular service will use, put a question mark next to its connection line and make a note to find out as soon as possible which protocols will work there. Remember: Finding out what you don't know is almost as important as finding out what you *do* know.

When you're done, you've got...abstract string art! Actually, you have created a web of dependencies you can use to determine which computers need access to which resources (see Figure 9.8). Copy what you've done on the whiteboard into your notebook for future reference.

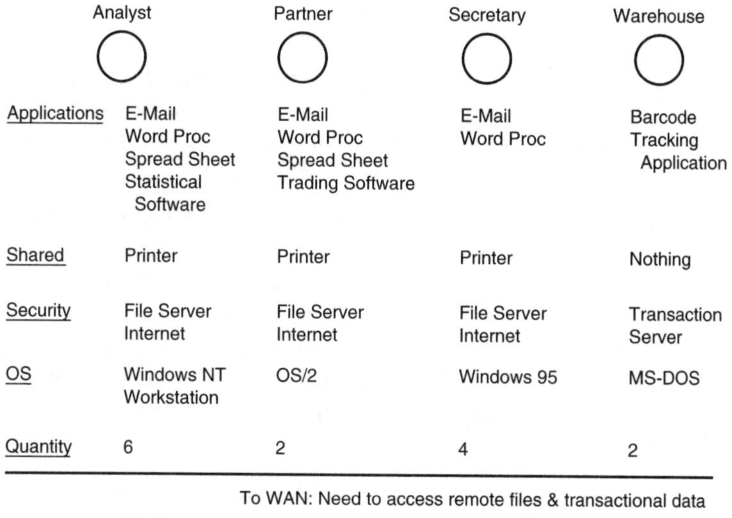

	Analyst	Partner	Secretary	Warehouse
	◯	◯	◯	◯
Applications	E-Mail Word Proc Spread Sheet Statistical Software	E-Mail Word Proc Spread Sheet Trading Software	E-Mail Word Proc	Barcode Tracking Application
Shared	Printer	Printer	Printer	Nothing
Security	File Server Internet	File Server Internet	File Server Internet	Transaction Server
OS	Windows NT Workstation	OS/2	Windows 95	MS-DOS
Quantity	6	2	4	2

To WAN: Need to access remote files & transactional data

FIGURE 9.8
An example of a finished logical network diagram.

Once you have determined the various resources that have to be shared (which was probably rendered much simpler by drawing it than by trying to create a comprehensive list), you're ready for the next great task: drawing the physical network.

Drawing the Physical Network Diagram

▼   Drawing the physical network really isn't as hard as it sounds. If you already
know which clients have to be connected to specific resources and which topology
you'll be using, you're halfway there. Let's assume that we are going to deploy an
Ethernet network (because this is the most commonly deployed network architecture).

1. Start by drawing the physical center of your network, such as a switch or a
   hub. If you are deploying a network of any size, a switch would be more
   practical. Switches are now priced such that it makes sense to take advantage of their greater capability to control bandwidth; in fact, you might
   actually find it difficult to purchase hubs that are even configured with a
   high density of ports.

> **Switches Allow You to Segment the Network**
>
> Because nearly everyone embraces Ethernet as the network architecture of choice,
> it makes sense to use hubs to segment the network. This allows you to chop a
> large collision domain into small subsets, which allows you to better use the avail-
> able network bandwidth.

2. Draw as many boxes as you need for additional switches or hubs that you
   will use. Connect lines between the switch and the segments; each of these
   lines represents the cable that connects the ancillary switches or hubs to the
   central switch.

3. Next, draw the servers and mark them as connected directly to the switch
   (see Figure 9.9). A server connected directly to a switch offers compelling
   advantages in terms of performance at the workstation because the server
   has a direct connection to the port to which the workstation is connected.
   This holds true even if a workstation is connected through a secondary
   switch or hub connected to a switch port; the collision domain of individual
   switches or hubs are usually fairly small, so there isn't much competition for
   bandwidth.

4. Refer to the drawing of the logical network and do some analysis. Look at
   which workstations require access to which servers and try to group them
   together.

5. Once you analyze the relative bandwidth requirements of your users, you're
   ready to start figuring out which class of user has to connect to which
   device.

▼

Take the time to think about this. If users don't have sufficient bandwidth initially, they will have network problems and consequently lose faith in the network. It's important to roll out systems that work for the users; otherwise, the network has no credibility. Figure 9.10 provides an example where a centralized switch is used and hubs provide connections for each segment.

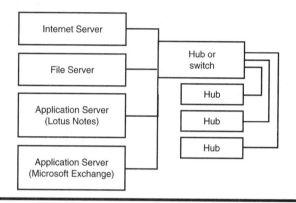

FIGURE 9.9
The completed connectivity diagram.

Now that you've drawn your network both logically and physically, you have a body of work you can use to see whether what you've done makes sense. One of the benefits of working graphically is that you can begin to see how your users are grouped based on common access. If you begin seeing patterns in how users work and you're using a switch, you might elect to extend the pattern and formalize it. For example, all accountants need to have access to the inventory data, so the user group called Accountants is granted that right globally.

Once you have made any changes to your network drawings based on any patterns you've discovered (such as to segment or not to segment your network), you're ready to start drawing the workstations and connecting them to the appropriate network device (a hub or switch port). When you do this, make note of how many of each type of computer are connecting to each port; that way, you can ensure that you connect only as many workstations to each hub as each hub has ports.

Once this process is done, you'll have a set of drawings that provide you with connection-oriented data you might otherwise have missed. These drawings will enable you to quantify the number of hub and switch ports you'll need for your network.

FIGURE 9.10
The physical net-
work drawing.

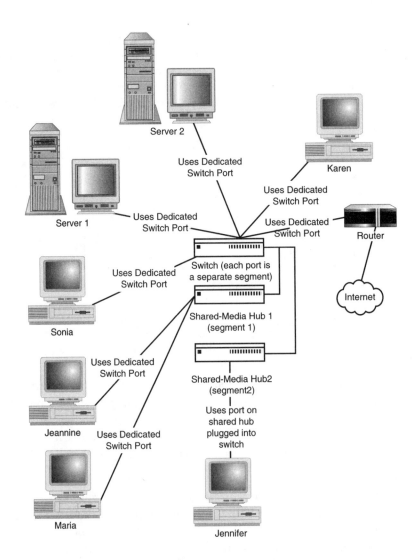

Step 5: Writing the Specification and Getting Others' Input

Once you've gotten this far, you have enough data to write a document that includes the following:

▶ The organizational purpose of the network

▶ The specifics of the network's use (which users do which tasks)

▶ The quantity of both users and computers

▶ Whether the network will be centralized or decentralized

▶ The network topology you plan to use

You also have a pair of diagrams that portray the logical and physical connections required by the network. Pat yourself on the back—you deserve it. You've created the basis for an initial specification document, which enumerates all the preceding points and includes the diagrams.

Once you created the specification document, you're ready to meet with other users to look over the plans and ensure that all the bases are covered.

Create Your Network Using Software

If you want your diagrams to look cleaner than hand drawn diagrams, several manufacturers provide software that simplifies the process of drawing networks. All the diagrams in this book were created using Microsoft Visio.

By the Way

Writing the Specification Document

Now is the time to actually write your specification for the network. The specification document should take into account all the points in the preceding section and list, quite specifically, the various uses of the network. Specifications do not have to be long, but they must be complete and clear; as English teachers are prone to say, "it should be as long as it needs to be—but no longer."

The purpose of a specification document is twofold: to limit the scope of the network design and to provide a reference document for network administrators.

A good specification document helps limit the insidious process called **scope creep** (a process in which the scope of a job creeps bigger and bigger while the job is in progress) in which a plan gathers additional tasks as it is executed. This is why it's so important to get buy-in from other users. If other users keep demanding new features ("let's just add this one new feature, it's not much, it won't slow things down"), the network may never be built. However, if the network builder can point to the specification document and ask whether the feature is included, he might be able to build the base network before beginning to add additional features.

The other purpose of a specification document is to ensure that the network builder and subsequent network administrators have a reference guide to the underlying design of the network. It's surprising how easy it is to forget the basic specs of a network if you're not confronted with them every day. The specification document provides a reference for the details that can easily be forgotten.

The specification document should include, at the very least, the following information:

- ▶ Why are you building the network?
- ▶ What will the network be used for?
- ▶ How many people and computers will the network have?
- ▶ Will the network be peer or client/server?
- ▶ What is the network architecture (such as Ethernet)?

Note that the answers to these questions are the same things you knew when you started this section. If you can, include in the specification document some of the following as well:

- ▶ What applications will each computer type run?
- ▶ What access rights will each user have?
- ▶ How will the network's center (the hubs and switches) be organized?
- ▶ What are the planned administrative user IDs and passwords?

Anything that concerns the network that has been planned or can be standardized is fair game for this document. Add it so that you'll have something to refer to when the going gets confusing. The more detailed the specification document is, the more useful it will be.

Writing a specification should be done over the course of a few days. Review it frequently to ensure that it contains the depth of information you require, and try to avoid using buzzwords. As much as acronyms can ease discourse for people who are conversant with them, they do very little except increase technophobia in users who don't know what they mean. And that's important because once you're done writing the specification, it's going to be reviewed by users, among others.

Meeting with Other Users

Once the spec is written, convene a working group of the people whose work will be affected by the network. This group will probably include a couple users, managers, and senior-level people, as well as a technology consultant or in-house IS (if either of these positions exist).

Use the information you have acquired at the meeting to revise your network specifications. Give revised copies of the specification to the attendees and get them to provide approval of the specification as articulated in that document. Getting concerned parties to sign off on a specification can save you untold hours of grief later in the process by inhibiting scope creep.

Step 6: Building the Network

After you have diagramed the network and written and then revised the specifications for the network, you are ready to build the network. An important step in building the network is purchasing the hardware that will actually make up the network.

Computer hardware is evolving at a rapid pace, so any recommendations that you might have collected related to hardware purchases really become meaningless even if only a short time passes. You need to spend a great deal of time researching the hardware you will deploy: the servers, client computers, and network connectivity devices.

Selecting Network Hardware and Software

Selecting the hardware and software for your network really requires a lot of research and patience. Keep in mind interoperability and expandability. Check out Hour 10, "Selecting Network Hardware and Software," for more information.

By the Way

Once you've settled on the hardware, you're ready to begin building the network. The next hour describes the various rationales behind selecting specific pieces for your network (which you can review when you write the specification document described in this hour). Hour 11, "Assembling a Network," gets into actually building the network.

Summary

In this hour, you examined the process by which your network is designed. In the next several hours, you'll work through some of the specific parts of designing your network, including selecting the network hardware type, the network operating system, and the network protocol.

Q&A

Q *Why is it important to identify the desired use of a network at the outset of the design process?*

A Doing so ensures that the network is built to serve the organization's needs.

Q *Why is it important to determine the computers on which network tasks will run?*

A By determining the location of a given process, you help build a list of criteria that can determine the configuration of your network.

Q *Why is a public examination and discussion of network plans useful?*

A A public examination allows you to measure the function of the network in relation to users' needs and to ensure that the planned network can accomplish the functions outlined earlier in the process. It also allows you to establish buy-in from network users and corporate officers. They all need to feel that they were intimately involved in the planning process because network implementation is often a high-ticket budget item.

HOUR 10

Selecting Network Hardware and Software

In this hour, we will select the type of network and architecture you deploy:

- ▶ Selecting the network topology and architecture
- ▶ Understanding interrupts and I/O addresses
- ▶ Deploying peer-to-peer networks versus server-based networks
- ▶ Selecting your client operating systems and network operating system
- ▶ Working with network protocols

This hour includes a look at network clients and network operating systems and the different LAN protocols that can be used so that your network devices can communicate.

Making the Right Choices

We have already discussed issues related to planning and documenting your new network. In this hour, we take a look at making decisions related to the actual physical infrastructure of the network and the client and server operating systems that you will deploy on the network.

So, in essence, this hour is about making the right decisions for your network. If you're building a two-computer home-office LAN, you don't need the same equipment as a fully staffed office or a national organization. However, because any network might need to grow, you also need to keep scalability (or expandability) in mind as you choose the software and hardware that will make up the network.

Selecting a Network Architecture

Actually choosing a particular network architecture such as Ethernet or Token Ring not only affects the topology of the network, but also will affect the cost of the network, the available bandwidth, and the potential expansion of the network.

Although most new networks use Ethernet (typically 100BASE-T), there are alternatives. For example, IBM Token Ring provides a token-passing environment that is actually considered more reliable than Ethernet during periods of very heavy traffic. Token Ring is often employed in banking and financial circles because of this fact. However, the cost of Token Ring hardware and its overall slower speed makes Ethernet the most logical choice for most networking situations.

Ethernet is also the easiest network architecture in terms of shopping around for wiring, network cards, switches, routers, and other equipment. Even the most bare-bones computer equipment store will provide connectivity devices and Ethernet NICs.

As mentioned in Hour 3, "Getting Data from Here to There: How Computers Share Data," Ethernet has been around since the early days of the PC revolution and provides a number of different flavors such as 10BASE-2, 10BASE-5, and 10BASE-T. You will find that the 10BASE-2 and 10BASE-5 implementations of Ethernet are basically dead technologies, and you will certainly have to search around to even find one of these Ethernet types that is still up and running. Although 10BASE-T has been the Ethernet standard for several years, nearly all new deployments of Ethernet will be 100BASE-T. It won't be long before Gigabit Ethernet becomes a viable option for even the smallest of Ethernet networks.

Although 99% of the time you will probably go with Ethernet (definitely if you decide to go wireless), keep in mind that there are other architectures such as IBM Token Ring. And in cases in which you are connecting different LANs to a high-speed backbone, you might also have to deal with FDDI or an ATM deployment. Make sure that you do your homework and look at your network not as it will be today but in the future—meaning that you need to know whether the network will need to grow a lot or just a little and how this will affect the cost of the network over time and the bandwidth available to your network users.

By the Way

Ethernet Is the Most Used Network Architecture

Given its ubiquity, Ethernet 100BASE-T is the clear choice for the vast majority of networks. It's inexpensive, it's everywhere, it's integrated into almost every new network device, and every network equipment manufacturer offers it. It's also standardized to a very high degree, which helps ensure interoperability between equipment made by different vendors. You probably already know that ISPs use Ethernet connections and NICs to connect home and small office users to DSL and cable modem networks for Internet access.

Working with Ethernet 100BASE-T

So, for the sake of discussion, let's say that you are definitely going to go the Ethernet route (meaning 100BASE-T). 100BASE-T is extremely versatile in terms of typical everyday networking. It is widely available, scales beautifully, is simple to install and maintain, and is extremely reliable. There is also a plethora of manufacturers who make network cards for everything from Intel-compatible desktop systems to Macintoshes to laptops—you can find a 100BASE-T Ethernet card for almost any system.

Additionally, 100BASE-T cabling offers an upgrade path. If you use the proper type of wire or cabling (called 568A or B and described in this section), the network can support 100BASE-T networks. This upgrade path is part of what makes 100BASE-T a solid choice for a network topology. And because you can chain 100BASE-T hubs together (remember that hubs are necessary), it's possible to increase the size of a network relatively simply.

By the Way

Using a Crossover Cable

Actually, it's not strictly true that a network of only two computers running 100BASE-T needs a hub. If there are only two computers on a 100BASE-T network, they can connect using a special RJ-45–ended cable called a **crossover cable**. Crossover cables are designed to enable hubs to connect to one another, but they can be used to join two 100BASE-T computers as well. However, omitting the hub in a two-computer 100BASE-T network is not advisable—how will you add a third computer without a hub? And never doubt that the third computer will make an appearance eventually. A crossover cable is wired as follows, with RJ-45 plugs:

CROSSOVER CABLE WIRING:

Pin 1 connects to pin 2

Pin 2 connects to pin 1

Pin 3 connects to pin 6

Pin 4 connects to pin 4

Pin 5 connects to pin 5

Pin 6 connects to pin 3

Pin 7 connects to pin 7

Pin 8 connects to pin 8

If you anticipate that your network will grow, 100BASE-T is a great topology to start with. For one thing, it offers options for the network connection type. 100BASE-T Ethernet is the simplest Ethernet that offers both joined by crossover cables) and switching a technology that uses a device resembling a hub but works faster by creating separate network segments for each connection between computers (which provides you greater control over your network bandwidth).

Also, 100BASE-T is a standard for network peripherals such as network printers and the new network copier/printers—almost all these devices have a 100BASE-T port. Also, routers and bridges typically require a 100BASE-T connection to connect to a network. So the 100BASE-T topology is widespread and versatile.

Here's a recipe for the ingredients necessary for a 100BASE-T network:

- ▶ Two or more computers. Almost all computers can use some form of Ethernet, from laptops to desktop PCs to UNIX systems and Macs.

- ▶ One 100BASE-T network card per computer.

- ▶ One hub/switch with enough ports to connect all your computers.

- ▶ Enough patch cords to connect each network card's RJ-45 socket to the hub's RJ-45 socket. A **patch cord** is an eight-conductor cord (meaning four pairs of wires) with an RJ-45 jack at both ends. (It looks like a really fat phone cord.) Patch cords are available premade at computer stores for a couple dollars a cable. Buy premade cables; they're cheaper and guaranteed to work. Shop around; prices vary widely. For Ethernet 100BASE-T, Category 5 or 5E cables are adequate; for Ethernet 1000BASE-T running over copper cables, you'll want to use Category 6 cable, which is rated for higher speed.

100BASE-T is a star topology, which means that everything has to connect to a concentrator—or, more correctly, a hub or switch.

By the Way

Using Small Network Hubs or Switches

Be aware that many small Ethernet hubs and switches (small in terms of the number of ports they provide) have a special port designed specifically to connect your hub to other hubs (or **stack** them, in the parlance). If you connect a computer to this port (usually port 1), that computer won't be capable of using the network because the hub doesn't use the stacking port like the rest of the ports. The problem is that stacking ports usually don't look different from regular ports. So read the documentation on your hub to find out whether it has a port dedicated to stacking and save yourself some frustration.

Fortunately, 1000BASE-T running over copper wire is physically identical (at least, in form factor) to 100BASE-T. The chief difference is that the cards and switches must support 1000BASE-T, and cable really needs to be Category 6 rather than Category 5 or 5E. So once you know how to put together a 100BASE-T network, you have most of the basic skills to put together a 1000BASE-T network that uses copper cable.

Selecting the Network Type: Client/Server or Peer to Peer

Earlier in the book, we spent a lot of time discussing the various upsides and downsides of client/server and peer networking strategies. In the next couple of pages, you will have the opportunity to see how you can quantify your decision to go with client/server or peer. Remember that two important issues related to choosing the type of network is going to be scale and cost. A small office with little or no expansion needs certainly doesn't need to deploy an expensive network server and run a network operating system so that users can share a few files and a printer.

Let's discuss client/server or server-based networking. We can then take a look a peer-to-peer networking.

Client/Server Networking

Pure client/server networking has two basic criteria: Services and authentication are provided by a centralized server. Workstations on the network do not require services from other workstations on the network. The whole service architecture of the network resides on one or more redundant, protected, regularly maintained and backed up servers dedicated to specific tasks—file services, Internet/WAN connectivity, remote access, authentication, back-end distributed applications, and so forth.

In other words, workstations connected to the network see only servers—they never see one another. A client/server network is a one-to-many scheme with the server being the one and the workstations being the many. Note that this is the model used by large commercial Web sites, such as Amazon, where the client is essentially a small graphical front end that is delivered fresh from the server each time it's opened, and a large server architecture at the back end that handles ordering, billing, and authentication. No user of Amazon knows that another user is currently online—there's no interaction between users, just between the servers and the client system.

The client-server model is useful for large businesses that have to manage their computer users' computer resources efficiently. In a pure client/server environment, a great deal of the software that clients use at their workstations is stored on a server hard drive rather than on users' own hard drives. In this configuration, if a user's workstation fails, it's relatively easy to get him back online quickly—simply replace the computer on the desktop. When the user logs back in to the network, he will have access to the applications needed to work.

The TCP/IP-based technology of the Internet has changed the accepted definition of client/server somewhat, with the focus being on distributed applications, where a thin client (such as a Web page application running in a browser) works in tandem with a much larger server. The advantages of this model stem from the application's capability to run in a browser. Because browsers are universal—that is, can run on Windows machines, Macs, UNIX boxes, and other systems—applications can be distributed quickly and effectively. To change a Web-enabled application, only the copy at the server need be changed because the changes will be distributed when users open the new page.

Client/server is appropriate if one or more of the following conditions apply to your situation:

▶ Your network is large. (Large is relative; I'm talking about more than 10 computers.) On a larger network, it's not wise to leave resources entirely decentralized as you would on a peer-to-peer network.

▶ Your network requires robust security (Internet access, secure files, and so forth). Using secure firewalls, gateways, and secured servers ensures that access to network resources is controlled.

▶ Your network requires that data be free from the threat of accidental loss. This means taking data stored on a server and backing it up from a central location.

▶ Your network needs users to focus on server-based applications rather than on workstation-based applications and resources—meaning that users access data via client/server based technologies such as large databases, groupware software, and other applications that run from a server.

Peer Networking

Peer networking is based on the idea that any computer that connects to a network should be capable of sharing its resources with any other computer. In direct contrast to client/server, peer networking is a many-to-many scheme.

The decentralized nature of peer networking means that it is inherently less organized. Peer networks that grow to more than a few computers tend to interact more by convenience or even chance rather than by design. In this respect, peer networking is similar to the Internet; there are hard-and-fast rules about basic hardware and software interaction and standards, but specific connections between computers occur in unforeseen ways. Peer networks are curious for that reason; the connections between systems tend to evolve over time until the network reaches an equilibrium. However, there is a significant amount of wasted resources while the network is finding its balance.

Note that the peer networks we're discussing here deal with the basic network services outlined in the prior section: file services, print services, and so on. Peer file sharing through KaZaa, Gnutella, and other services use the peer many-to-many model, but are using such a small subset of services that they scale to many thousands of users. Most network services require too many system resources to scale as well as the aforementioned peer networks—which are actually peer network applications.

Peer networking is appropriate for your network if the following conditions apply:

▶ Your network is relatively small (really fewer than 10 computers, although depending on the number of users accessing any one computer for resources, you could get by with 15 to 20).

▶ Your network does not require robust security regarding access to resources.

▶ Your network does not require that data be free from the threat of accidental loss.

▶ Your network needs users to focus on workstation-based applications rather than on server-based applications and resources—meaning that users run applications such as productivity software (Microsoft Office, for instance) that is installed on each individual computer. Each user is really working in a closed system until he has to access data on another peer computer or print to a shared printer.

Most of the time, home networks can use peer networking without a problem. The only piece of the network that really needs to be centralized is Internet access, and that is often provided via a combination device that serves as a hub/switch/router and a firewall.

By the
Way

Server-Based and Peer Networking on the Same Network

In some situations, you might find that you need a server-based network. However, you also want to make it easy for users to collaborate, so you allow workstations to share resources through peer networking. These two environments can certainly coexist. Just keep in mind that allowing peer networking degrades your ability to secure the network, and files that would typically reside on a file server might end up on individual workstations, making it more difficult to back up important data.

Now that we've looked at client/server networking and peer networking, let's take a look at client operating systems—specifically those that provide peer services—and then we can tackle network operating systems. The next section provides an overview of client operating systems that provide peer networking. We will then focus on peer networking with Microsoft Windows because it is the most prevalent operating system seen at the desktop.

Peer-to-Peer Operating Systems

In a peer-to-peer network, there is no Network Operating System (NOS) *per se*. Instead, each user's workstation has desktop operating system software that can share resources with other computers as desired. Typically, operating systems include the capability to configure a protocol and share resources. Most peer OSes provide a relatively limited range of sharable devices, although file sharing (or shared disk space) and networked printing are relatively standard features.

Some of the possibilities as far as client operating systems that provide peer services are as follows:

▶ Microsoft Windows—Microsoft Windows has provided peer networking capabilities since Microsoft Windows for Workgroups 3.11. Each of the subsequent versions of Windows has provided greater peer capabilities. Microsoft Windows XP (both the Home and Professional versions) even provides a Network Setup Wizard that makes it easy to configure a Windows **workgroup** (a workgroup being a peer network). We will look more closely at Windows peer networking in the next section.

▶ Linux—Linux is fast becoming a viable operating system for both the home and workplace. A number of Linux distributions are available that vary in their degree of "user friendliness." Linux provides a number of ways to share files and other resources such as printers. Linux provides the Network File System (NFS), where a Linux computer can act as both a server and a client. To include Linux computers in a Windows workgroup, you can configure SAMBA. SAMBA derives its name from Server Message Block, which is an important part of the NetBIOS protocol. SAMBA is available with most distributions of Linux.

▶ Macintosh OS X—Although our discussion has centered around Intel-based computers, we should mention the peer networking capabilities of the Apple Macintosh and its various offspring such as the Mac PowerBook. Peer networking has been part of the Mac OS since the beginning.

By the Way

Peer Networking Operating Systems and the Wonders of TCP/IP

In Hour 4, "Computer Concepts," you learned about client operating systems. If you review the list of operating systems presented there, you'll find that many of them are capable of working in a peer-to-peer environment. Since the early 1990s, almost every client/single-user operating system has been shipped with at least a limited collection of network protocols and tools. This means that almost every client OS can be used to build a peer-to-peer network.

One confusing fact is that in a TCP/IP network, all computers are *de facto* peers. This means that any computer that has a full suite of TCP/IP utilities can interoperate with any other computer on the network. As a consequence, the characteristics and functions of a particular machine (processor speed, disk space, application services, and so on) tend to determine which machines are servers and which are workstations. This is a relative flattening of the PC-network hierarchy.

Windows is certainly the most dominant desktop operating system in terms of installations. Let's take a closer look at peer networking with the latest version of Windows, Microsoft Windows XP.

Peer Networking with Microsoft Windows XP

As already mentioned, Windows for Workgroups was the original "do-it-yourself" network for Intel-compatible personal computers. It was designed around Microsoft's MS-DOS operating system and Windows shell. A number of different versions of Windows have come (and gone); we've seen Windows 95, Windows 98, Windows Millennium Edition (Windows Me) for the home user, and Windows NT and Windows 2000 for business network users. The current version of Windows, Windows XP, comes in two versions: Home and Professional.

By the Way

Two Versions of Windows XP

Microsoft provides two versions of Windows XP: Home and Professional. The Home version is designed for the home or small office user who will work in a Microsoft workgroup (meaning a peer network). Windows XP Professional provides additional features and is designed to serve as a client on a server-based network. Don't buy the Home edition if you are going to implement a client/server network.

As already mentioned, Microsoft's peer networking products are based on the idea of a workgroup, or a set of computers that belong to a common group and that share resources among themselves. Microsoft peer networking is actually quite versatile, and can include computers running any version of Microsoft Windows.

Additionally, on a given physical network, multiple workgroups can coexist. For example, if you have three salespeople, they can all be members of the SALES workgroup; the members of your accounting department can be members of the ACCOUNTS workgroup. Of course, there is a common administrative user with accounts on all machines in all workgroups, so central administration is possible to a limited extent, but it isn't an efficient administrative solution.

Windows peer networking is very straightforward. Computers running Windows XP (or earlier versions of Windows) are configured so that they are in the same workgroup. This can be done in the Windows XP Computer Name Changes dialog box (shown in Figure 10.1), which is reached via the System's Properties dialog box (right-click on My Computer and select Properties).

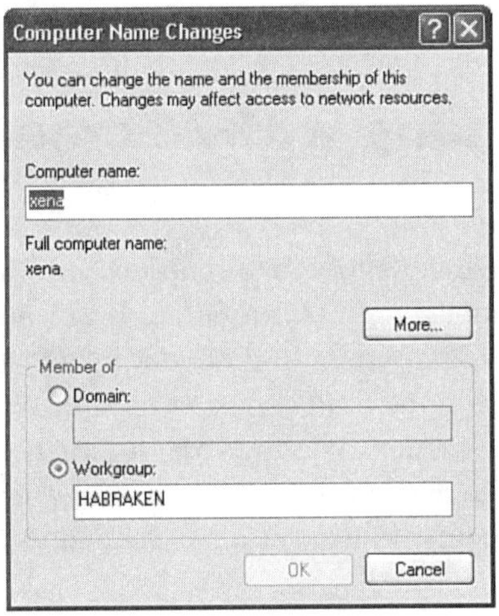

FIGURE 10.1
Configure a Windows XP computer to be part of a workgroup.

The alternative to configuring the workgroup manually is to use the Network Setup Wizard.

The wizard walks you through the steps of configuring the workgroup and can even generate a diskette that can be used to add other Windows computers to the workgroup, even computers running earlier versions of Windows. You start the wizard via the Windows Control Panel; select the Network and Internet Connection icon in the Control Panel, and then select Set Up or Change Your Home or Small Office Network. Figure 10.2 shows the wizard screen that allows you to select a connection method.

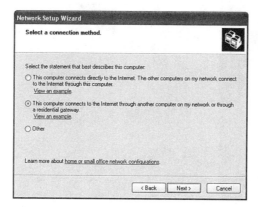

FIGURE 10.2
The Network Setup Wizard walks you through the steps of creating the workgroup.

Once the workgroup is up and running, any user in the workgroup can browse the workgroup for shared folders and printers. Folders that are accessed regularly can be mapped to a member computer as a network drive. Workgroup computers and their shared resources can be viewed using the My Network Places window. Figure 10.3 shows the two members of a workgroup named Habraken.

Remember that Peer Networks Are Decentralized

For resources to be available for the workgroup, such as folders and printers, each individual user will have to share the folders and the printers that need to be accessed by the workgroup.

By the Way

Although workgroups are extremely easy to set up and manage (because each user really manages the resources that they offer up to the workgroup), they do pose problems in terms of protecting important data (either from accidental deletion) and don't make it easy to set up any sort of backup schedule to provide some redundancy to the workgroup. Workgroups are fine in situations in which users can collaborate in a friendly atmosphere and have enough computer savvy to make sure that important data is used appropriately (and backed up). Because each resource (such as folders) can require a separate password, any more than a few users can create an overall environment of chaos. When you have more than 10 users, you certainly want to look at the option of deploying a server running a network operating system, which is our next topic.

FIGURE 10.3
Workgroup members can browse the workgroup member computers.

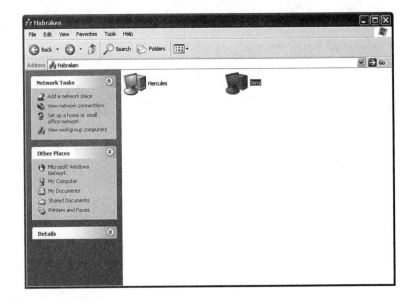

Network Operating Systems

If you're building a network with a sizable chunk of centralized services, one of the following client/server Network Operating Systems is for you. Whereas peer-to-peer networks are similar to a cooperative group of people with diverse functions but no single leader, a client/server network is similar to a hierarchy—the server is the leader, the one with all the knowledge and the resources.

The following brief sections describe a selection of network OSes, which are used in client/server networks. We'll look at the following network OSes:

▶ Novell NetWare

▶ Microsoft Windows Server

▶ Linux/UNIX

Let's begin our discussion with NetWare, really the first major player in the network operating system market. We can then take a look at Microsoft Windows server products and then discuss the Linux/UNIX platforms.

Novell NetWare

In the early days of PC internetworking, Ray Noorda's Novell invented NetWare. It came as a balm to early PC-networking system administrators who were used to dealing with the innumerable networking schemes that appeared in the early to mid-1980s. NetWare provided reliable, secure, and relatively simple networking; in the early years, the business world snapped up as many copies as Novell could turn out.

Over the years, NetWare matured. Its focus broadened beyond the local LAN into WAN configurations. With the advent of NetWare 5 and NetWare Directory Services (NDS), Novell had a product that enabled a global network to provide its users with the same resources, no matter where on the network those users logged in. It was on a roll.

But in 1994 and 1995, two things happened that made Novell stumble badly. The first was the introduction of Microsoft's Windows NT, which Novell failed to view as serious competition. Microsoft's aggressive marketing and the ease of use of Windows NT quickly made inroads into Novell's market share.

Novell's second slip was in failing to realize that the rise in public consciousness of the Internet fundamentally changed the playing field for NOS manufacturers. Novell had used its IPX protocol for close to 15 years, and under then Chairman Robert Frankenberg, it saw no reason to change.

Novell has certainly made up for a number of earlier missteps in relation to NetWare. The NOS now embraces TCP/IP as its default network protocol. The latest version of Novell's NOS, NetWare 6.5, also integrates a number of open source services from the Linux platform including Apache Web Server, which is one of the most popular Web server platforms currently in use.

Administrative tools for managing NetWare have also been rather meager in earlier versions of NetWare. However, NetWare 6.5 provides a number of new tools, including the NetWare Remote Manager, which can be used to manage network volumes and monitor server settings. Remote Manager is accessed using a Web browser, which makes it easily accessible by an administrator from any workstation on the network. Figure 10.4 shows the NetWare Remote Manager in a Web browser window.

FIGURE 10.4
The NetWare
Remote Manager is
just one of the new
features available
in NetWare 6.5.

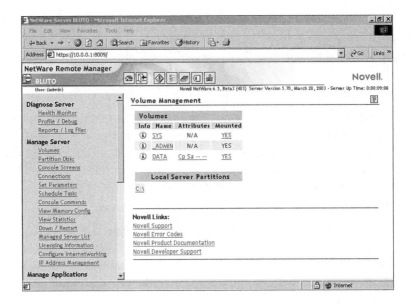

NetWare is appropriate for networks in a variety of situations. If you're building a small network, NetWare is fast (NetWare 6.5 is certainly easier to set up than earlier versions) and fairly easy to install and configure. The Novell Directory Service hierarchy for network objects (such as users and groups) has been upgraded to the Novell eDirectory, providing an easy-to-use hierarchical system for tracking servers and other objects on the network. NetWare can also accommodate situations in which your network spans multiple LANs (using WAN technology). It provides the scalability expected from a NOS platform.

Although new installations of NetWare have slipped, there is still a very large installation base of NetWare around the world. With recent changes to NetWare and changes in NetWare licensing structure, it is certainly worth your while to take a serious look at NetWare when you are working through the process of determining the best NOS for your network.

<table>
<tr><td>By the Way</td><td>Select the NOS that Makes the Most Sense for Your Network

These sections on specific network operating systems are not intended as recommendations, but rather should be considered starting points as you research the different NOS platforms available. Cost, scalability, and ease of administration—these are just a few of the factors that should be part of your selection process. For more about Novell NetWare, see http://www.novell.com.</td></tr>
</table>

Microsoft Windows Server

Windows NT Server, the first edition of Microsoft's popular server software, emerged out of the breakup of IBM and Microsoft's shared OS/2 initiative. Although Windows Server operating systems offer a fairly simple graphical user interface, it is a true multitasking, multithreaded network operating system.

Since Windows NT was introduced in 1993-94, Microsoft has weathered a storm of criticism regarding its reliability, scalability, and robustness. To be fair, some of this criticism has been deserved because some releases of the Windows network operating system have had a number of flaws. However, Microsoft has persevered and continued to refine its NOS as it passes through a number of product cycles (NT Server 3.5 to NT Server 4 to Windows 2000 Server) up to and including the current iteration, Windows Server 2003.

The biggest evolutionary jump, without a doubt, in the Microsoft server products was the upgrade of the Microsoft NOS from NT Server 4 to Windows 2000 Server. Microsoft's flat domain model was replaced by a hierarchical directory service called Active Directory. Active Directory holds all the objects that exist on the network including domains, servers, users, and groups. We discuss how the Microsoft domain model works in comparison to Active Directory in Hour 15, "Microsoft Networking." Active Directory allowed Microsoft to complete on a level playing field with NetWare's NDS (now eDirectory) and Sun's Network Information Service.

In terms of licensing, Windows server (whether we are talking Windows 2000 Server or Windows Server 2003) requires that you purchase server licenses and client licenses. We also discuss the different types of server licenses and some of Microsoft's new twists on licensing in Hour 15.

UNIX and Linux

Unlike NetWare or Windows NT, UNIX is not a monolithic operating system owned by a single corporation. Instead, it is represented by a plethora of manufacturers with only a few clear standouts. The most common UNIX systems are Sun Microsystems' Solaris, IBM's AIX, and Hewlett-Packard's HP-UX.

In the PC-hardware world, Linux, a UNIX clone, has trumped a wide variety of UNIX systems, including commercial variants such as Santa Cruz Operation's SCO UNIX, Novell's UNIXWare, and Sun's Solaris for Intel. Linux has also grabbed greater market share than other community-based operating system developments such as BSD (Berkeley Standard Distribution), OpenBSD, and FreeBSD.

UNIX and UNIX-like operating systems come in many flavors, and some features and commands vary widely between versions—but in the end, it remains the most widely used high-end server operating system in the world.

However, the UNIX world is fragmented by a host of issues that derive from UNIX's basic design: UNIX is open-ended and is available for almost any hardware platform. UNIX has existed for almost 30 years, and its design has been optimized and revised and improved to the point at which it is hugely reliable.

Unfortunately, the availability of UNIX across many different platforms has led to one significant problem that blocks its widespread adoption: Software written for one version of UNIX usually does not run on other versions. This lack of compatibility has led to UNIX receiving a dwindling share of the server market except at the very high end where absolute reliability is a must. Linux and the Open Source/GNU movement have ameliorated a good deal of the binary incompatibility issues by ensuring that the source code for most Linux-based software is available. This means that with a copy of Linux with a C-language compiler, it's possible to compile—that is, translate from source code to machine instructions—a very wide variety of software.

UNIX has a reputation for being difficult to master, a reputation which is almost wholly undeserved. It *is* complex; there's no doubt about that. But once the basics are assimilated (which *can* prove daunting), its raw power and versatility make it an extremely attractive server platform.

Interestingly, Linux, which is essentially a UNIX clone, has begun to make a great deal of headway in the server and workstation market. It has actually begun to put a dent in Microsoft's market share both in the server and desktop operating system categories.

In spite of its complexity, however, any version of UNIX makes a fine file, print, and application server. Because of 30 years of refinement, the reliability of a UNIX system is typically a step above that of other platforms. UNIX uses the TCP/IP networking protocol natively; TCP/IP was created on and for UNIX systems, and the "port-and-socket" interface that lies under TCP/IP has its fullest expression on UNIX systems.

Although purists certainly do not consider UNIX and Linux the same platforms, we will look more closely at these two server platforms in Hour 16, "UNIX and Linux Networking." Most of our discussion will actually relate to Linux because its open source development makes it a very inexpensive and also intriguing network operating system to explore. Linux has become a very cost-effective and viable alternative to some of the standard network operating systems, such as NetWare and Microsoft Windows Server.

A Word Regarding Network Protocols

Although selecting the appropriate network operating system platform is essential, selecting the network protocol that you will use to move data on your network is also important. Because most corporations, businesses, and home users want to be connected to the Internet, it has become essential that network servers and clients be configured for TCP/IP. As you've probably seen in the discussion of network operating systems provided in this hour, all the current versions of the most widely used server platforms have TCP/IP as their default protocol. In fact, you actually have to add additional network protocols if you want to use them.

We discuss TCP/IP in greater detail in Hour 14, "TCP/IP." And we have already mentioned other network protocols such as IPX and NetBEUI in Hour 3. NetBEUI is no longer supported by Microsoft's most recent versions of its desktop operating system and NOS: Windows XP and Windows Server 2003, respectively. In cases in which you do not want to run TCP/IP or want to run a secondary network protocol because of issues with IP subnet (discussed in Hour 14), you can run IPX/SPX or—as it is called in the Microsoft Windows world—NWLink. Even computers in a peer network can use NWLink.

IPX is actually self-configuring, making it a good choice for simple peer networking. It builds computer systems' network addresses (which, for IPX, are hexadecimal numeric) from a combination of administrator-specified server network-wire addresses and network card MAC addresses. This simplifies the process of setting up a network because once the network is physically connected, IPX can autoconfigure and begin routing data packets very quickly. Administrators do not have to install a separate network address at each computer (a feature that can save quite a bit of time). And IPX is fast.

However, IPX does have downsides. It's a broadcast-based protocol, which means that computers periodically announce themselves on the network. Such announcements use network bandwidth better used for actual data. And it isn't part of the TCP/IP protocol suite, so it doesn't carry Internet traffic.

Summary

In this hour, we discussed Ethernet and 100BASE-T, which is currently the most deployed network architecture. We also took a look at peer network versus server-based networking and discussed Microsoft peer-to-peer networking. Our discussion also included an introduction to some of the popular network server platforms available. You also learned that TCP/IP is really not only the network protocol of choice but also of necessity.

Q&A

Q *What is the most popular network architecture?*

A Ethernet has become the most popular network architecture. Most new implementations are now 100BASE-T installations, with advances in gigabit Ethernet making it a good possibility in the very near future.

Q *What are typical peer operating systems?*

A Peer operating systems currently available include Microsoft Windows XP (and earlier versions of Windows) and various distributions of Linux.

Q *What are the most common PC Network Operating Systems?*

A Network Operating Systems include NetWare, Windows Server 2003 (and Windows 2000 Server), and various UNIX platforms, as well as a number of Linux implementations.

Q *What is the de facto standard for network protocols?*

A TCP/IP has really become the *de facto* standard for networking and is embraced as the default protocol by most network clients, as well as network operating systems.

HOUR 11

Assembling a Network

In this hour, we'll cover the following topics:

- ▶ Good practices for working on computer hardware
- ▶ Understanding I/O and IRQs
- ▶ Installing adapter cards
- ▶ Working in the wiring closet: cables, connections, and connectivity devices

At this point, you've read about the theory of networks and how they work, and you have also been introduced to some of the popular network operating systems. In subsequent hours, you'll read more about specific network operating systems so that you can make an informed choice. This hour is a bit of a way station, or a turning point: It's a hands-on how-to-install chapter.

You've already learned how to identify network hardware, and in this hour, you'll pull it all together and deal with how to plug pieces of the network together.

This hour is meant to be used as a reference. It will familiarize you with installation processes for the various bits of hardware you've read about in preceding hours. It is not a comprehensive guide, however; it's intended to familiarize you with the process rather than provide a be-all and end-all guide to installation. With the information you'll learn in the next hour, you'll be able to do more detailed research and engage a network-cabling company with a certain measure of confidence.

Before Installation

Although computer hardware might look robust and impervious to damage, it's not. Computer and network electronics powered by electricity can, paradoxically, also be damaged by electricity. Although your computer hardware is powered by 120-volt wall current, don't assume that the motherboard or hub actually uses that much electricity. Most computers and networking equipment use 5 volts or so at the motherboard. Static electricity, which can build up to 20,000 volts or so, can wreck computer equipment by burning up the delicate wiring inside a silicon chip.

So that you don't inadvertently burn up some expensive piece of computer equipment while working on it, this section presents a few precautions you can and should take, both for your own safety and the integrity of the computer and networking equipment you're working on.

First, take precautions to prevent electrical-shock damage to yourself and the computer:

- ▶ Wear a wrist strap when you're working on a computer. A wrist strap is a small device that connects you (usually one of yours wrists) to the computer. This ensures that you and the computer have the same electrical potential; in layman's terms, it means that you won't be transmitting static to the computer and burning up parts while you're installing them. Wrist straps are available at computer stores for a few dollars. They're a great preventative measure—use them.

- ▶ Always shut the computer's power off before working on it. Sounds like common sense, but it's not. Installing an adapter card in a computer that's running is pretty well guaranteed to burn up the card, the card slot, and (very often) the motherboard, which is the big circuit board with all the slots in it.

- ▶ Always unplug the computer before you open it up to install equipment. Again, this might seem like common sense, but surprisingly few people think of it. It's a corollary to the preceding direction, and it ensures that the power is off, which is absolutely, positively, utterly necessary. In addition to the near certainty that you'll damage computer equipment by working with it while it's on, you're also taking a chance on damaging yourself—electrical shocks are neither pleasant nor particularly good for your health.

By the Way

To Unplug or Not to Unplug

There is a school of thought that not unplugging a computer actually grounds the computer better. This in theory is true, but making sure that no electricity is flowing to a motherboard that you are working on is more of an issue than grounding. If you use an antistatic wrist strap or, even better, an antistatic mat, you shouldn't have any worries related to static electricity. Always touch the metal frame around the motherboard before starting; this will discharge any static that might have inadvertently built up.

Next, take precautions when you're physically opening the computer's case and installing adapter cards:

▶ If you're opening the case and the top doesn't come off easily, don't force it. Forcing computer cases can damage the box and often the delicate electronics that make the computer useful. Force is a last resort.

Don't Just Rip into the Computer Case

Watch Out!

In the early days of PC networking, taking the top off a case was a risky proposition. The number of cables in an IBM XT was staggering. The arrangement of ribbon cables within the case generally ensured that if the case cover was yanked off unceremoniously, you were almost guaranteed to snag a cable and probably damage it.

Since those days, PC manufacturers have improved the cable routing inside computers quite a bit. In fact, most computers no longer require tools to open the case, and the components are increasingly modular, so it isn't too common for the case cover to catch on cables any longer. Nonetheless, it pays to be cautious. I recently disassembled a computer for which the case cover was part of the cable routing—it had clips into which cables slid to route around the inside of the box. If I'd just yanked the top off, I would have torn off at least two cables. Taking the time to figure out how the top should come off saved a lot of time and aggravation—and it was a great puzzle as well!

▶ Mark all cables and connections if you have to disconnect anything. This makes reassembling a disassembled computer much simpler. You can use a marker to label the cables, and you can also draw some diagrams depicting which cables connect to which devices. The best way to mark connections is the one that helps you reconnect what you disconnected. Masking tape and a Sharpie marker are your friends!

▶ When you're installing adapter cards, ensure that the adapter card and the adapter card slot have the same interface. In other words, don't put a PCI card in an ISA slot or vice versa. Doing so can damage the computer, the adapter card, and (more often than not) your bankbook—new parts are expensive!

Older Computer Expansion Cards Can Be Confusing

By the Way

Just for the record, here's a quick lesson in what adapter cards fit into which slot types:

▶ ISA fits into ISA, EISA, and some VESA slots. ISA cards have either 62 or 98 gold connector strips on the edge that plug into the motherboard slot; the connector strips are divided into one set of 62 connectors and one set of 36 connectors. ISA is for all intents and purposes dead technology.

▶ EISA cards fit only into EISA slots. EISA cards look like ISA cards with one cru-
cial difference: They have 100 connectors divided into one set of 62 connectors
and one set of 38 connectors. EISA, like ISA, is dead technology.

▶ VESA cards fit only into VESA slots. VESA cards vary from computer to computer. Fortunately, like ISA and EISA, they're mostly dead technology.

▶ PCI cards fit only into PCI slots. PCI cards are easy to distinguish from the other
cards because PCI connectors are much narrower and the entire connector is
smaller. PCI is pretty much the only game in the PC world at this point. So,
hopefully, you will not have to deal with a lot of legacy computers and the other
card types discussed here.

Remembering these points ensures that you won't accidentally try to force an ISA
card into a PCI slot.

Learning which adapter card interface is which is simply a matter of reading the
label on the adapter card's box and then looking at the edge connector (the gold-
striped thing) on the bottom of the card. After you have identified a few, you're a pro;
you'll identify adapter card interfaces in a snap.

▶ Don't use force to fit adapter cards into slots. This is a sure-fire way to damage the card and void the warranty. If a card doesn't fit, pull it out and look
at it. Is it the correct slot interface? Is the metal strip on the back of the card
(the "slot cover") in the way somehow? Close examination can often enable
you to figure out why a card won't fit. Sometimes it's necessary to bend the
bottom of the metal strip to fit—other times, the card just has to be rocked
in slowly and gently. This process can be tedious, but it prevents cracked
motherboards. You'll learn more about the process of installing adapter
cards in the next section, but this precaution deserves to be repeated
because it has caused more equipment failures than all the static in the
world.

▶ Use proper tools. It's tempting to use any old tool to work on computers
because they don't seem as mechanical as (for example) a car. Nonetheless,
make certain that your tools fit. Have a good Philips screwdriver and a nut-
driver set, if possible. Tweezers are useful for picking up small parts. A small
pair of needlenose pliers can come in handy as well. If any of your tools are
magnetized, either demagnetize them (heat works) or replace them—mag-
netism and computers just don't go together. And of course, to reiterate
what was said previously, use a wrist strap.

Working on networking equipment need not be difficult if you're careful. It's
mostly a matter of developing what writer Robert Pirsig calls *mechanic's feel*: a
sense of respect for the physical properties of an object and a gut-level understanding of how much force is enough. It's common sense; don't force anything
unless you have no other choice.

Installing Adapter Cards

Adapter cards are inescapable, particularly in the Intel-compatible computer world. Because very few computers come with built-in networking (although this is changing), at some point, you're going to have to take a deep breath, open a computer case, and plunge inside to install a network adapter card (whether you are talking a network card for a wired network or wireless network; wireless LANs are discussed in more detail in Hour 23, "Wireless Networking").

You should be aware of two things related to network cards and other device cards that you might install in a computer—Input/Output (I/O) addresses and IRQs (Interrupt Request). Because almost all expansion cards are now **Plug and Play** (meaning the operating system configures them automatically), you don't have to worry about manually setting I/O or IRQ settings. However, if you have to troubleshoot a malfunctioning card or are dealing with older hardware, it doesn't hurt to understand the basics of these settings.

Input/Output (I/O) addresses for network cards generally range from about 200h (decimal 512) to about 380h (decimal 896). 200h is actually a hexadecimal (base 16) number. Again, Plug and Play cards will take care of this for you. Table 11.1 provides a list of common I/O addresses.

TABLE 11.1 Commonly Used I/O Addresses

Device	Memory Address
COM1 (first serial port)	03E8
COM2 (second serial port)	02E8
LPT1 (printer port)	0378
IDE Hard Drive Controllers	170 or 1F0
Sound cards	220 and 330

Most network cards use addresses outside the commonly used list of addresses. But watch out! Some network cards might use memory address 0360. Although this address doesn't seem to conflict with anything, unfortunately, sometimes the software device driver takes up too much space. When this happens, the software device driver can take from 0360 all the way to 0380 in memory, which conflicts with the printer port at 0378.

When a device, such as a network card or a video card, has to get the full attention of the computer system, it uses something called an IRQ. An **IRQ**, or Interrupt Request, is just that—a request that the system stop whatever else it's doing at the moment and give its attention to the device requesting attention. Table 11.2 provides a listing of common Intel-based IRQ settings.

TABLE 11.2   Common Intel-Compatible IRQ Settings

IRQ #	Function
0	Reserved for use by the operating system (system timer).
1	Reserved for use by the operating system (keyboard controller).
2	Used to access IRQ 9 and above. Use only as a last resort.
3	Used for COM2 communications serial port (often built into the motherboard).
4	Used for COM1 communications serial port (often built into the motherboard).
5	Usually unused and available.
6	Reserved for use by the operating system (floppy drive controller).
7	Used for the printer port (also called LPT1).
8	Reserved for use by the operating system (system clock).
9	Usually available, but use as a last resort. Refer to IRQ 2.
10	Usually available.
11	Usually available.
12	Often used for bus mice (as opposed to serial mice, which connect to COM ports).
13	Often unused and available.
14	Usually used for Primary IDE disk drive controllers.
15	Reserved for use by secondary IDE controllers.

The important thing to remember when you install a network card is to try not to use the memory address or IRQ that other cards or the motherboard are using. If you do, the card will not work.

Now that you have a basic understanding of how I/O and IRQs work, let's actually take a hands-on look at installing a NIC into a computer.

Try it Yourself   **Install an Adapter Card**

This section provides a hands-on view of the process of installing an adapter card in a computer. Remember that these instructions aren't universal; computers vary widely. The basic idea is to understand the steps and adapt to what you find when you open the computer.

1. Shut off the computer's power and disconnect the power cord.

2. Identify the card. Put on a ground strap, take the adapter card out of its packaging, and examine it (see Figure 11.1). What is its interface (ISA, EISA, PCI)?

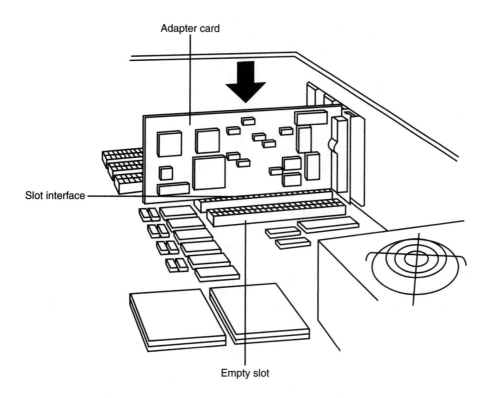

Adapter card

Slot interface

Empty slot

FIGURE 11.1
Determine the slot interface by looking at the edge connector—the shiny gold connectors at the base of the card.

3. Just about every new NIC that you buy will be PCI and will also be a Plug and Play card. Most operating systems (including Windows, Linux, and UNIX) have no problem recognizing "mainstream" NICs such as 3Com or Intel and setting the appropriate I/O and IRQ for the card. Some NICs that are considered **soft-set** cards might require that you install the card and then run software (that came with the card) before the OS can configure them. In the very rare situation in which you are dealing with some very old NICs, you might have to set switchblocks or jumper blocks, which are normally used to determine one or more of the adapter card's settings (I/O address, IRQ). Look at the surface of the card. If you see switchblocks or jumper blocks, refer to the manufacturer's documentation to determine what settings they manage.

▼

FIGURE 11.2
A jumper block and
a switchblock. The
jumper is a small
piece of metal and
plastic that makes
an electrical con-
nection like a primi-
tive switch.

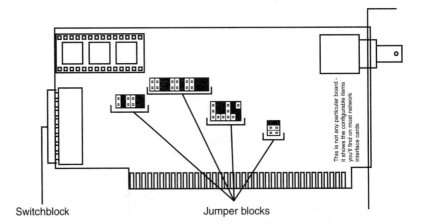

This is not any particular board - it shows the configurable items you'll find on most network interface cards

Switchblock   Jumper blocks

4. Once you figure out what card type you are working with (again, in most cases, we are talking Plug and Play), open the computer. While opening the computer case, rest the NIC on its antistatic packaging (usually a bag made of silver mylar plastic). Computer cases vary greatly: Some require that you unscrew the case (usually on the back), whereas others snap together. If the case cover doesn't lift off readily, don't use force; look for flanges and hidden hinges that could be preventing the case cover from coming off.

5. Select the slot in which you want to install the card and remove the slot cover—a small piece of sheet metal that covers the slot in the back of the computer when no card is installed (refer to Figure 11.1). The slot cover is usually held in with a 1/4-inch or 5/16-inch screw that often has a Philips slot as well. Save the screw after you've removed the slot cover—you'll need it to fasten the card when you're done.

6. Install the card. Take the card and line it up with the slot. Ensure that the sheet-metal piece that resembles the slot cover faces the outside of the computer. Once the card is lined up in the slot, gently but firmly press it into the slot. You might have to gently rock the card back and forth. When the card is fully seated in the slot, most of the connections on the bottom edge will be hidden inside the connector, and the part of the card that screws in will be level against the back of the computer's chassis. Screw the card in using the slot cover screw you removed earlier.

7. Finish up. Replace the case cover on the computer. Plug in the power cord and restart the computer. You'll have to install device driver software (used to enable adapter cards and other hardware to interact with the operating

▼

system; device drivers are discussed in Hour 4, "Computer Concepts") to make it work; read the manufacturer's directions to do so. Again, in the case of Plug and Play NICs, the operating system should recognize the new device upon startup and walk you through the process of selecting the best driver for the hardware.

See? Cards aren't so difficult to install after all. If you take a bit of time to do it correctly the first time, you can prevent the vast majority of headaches from damaged hardware. It's worth your while to look at your computer's manual and determine which slots have the same interface as the adapter card you want to install. If the computer has more than one slot with an interface that matches your adapter card's interface, use whichever slot is open—no slot is preferable to any other.

Installing Other Adapter Cards Is Really Straightforward

By the way, this procedure isn't limited to network cards. You install all adapter cards in more-or-less the same way. So once you know how to do it, you can become an installation fiend, putting cards in left and right, and wowing all your relatives (who will hail you as a computer expert and have you working on their PCs in short order).

By the Way

Working on Wiring: Closets, Cables, and Connections

After the network cards are installed, the next step is dealing with the wiring (unless you are working with a wireless network setup). The next sections focus on some of the issues related to wiring your network. It's basically a hands-on version of the wiring stuff you learned in Hour 5, "Network Concepts."

The Wiring Closet: The Network's Home Sweet Home

Most of the back end of a network (such as servers, hubs, switches, and routers) should be behind locked doors. It isn't because contact with the equipment is hazardous (it's not); it's that you don't want just anyone to have access to your servers and connectivity equipment. Just innocent curiosity could bring your whole network down, and there is always the chance of malicious intent and sabotage.

As a result, it's a good idea to set up a wiring closet if you're building a network to serve an enterprise—whether that enterprise is a business, a town hall, a library, or whatever. And a wiring closet doesn't have to take up a lot of space; it's perfectly acceptable for a wiring closet to simply be a centrally located closet that you can access to install electrical power and route cables. A lot of the time, the phone closet can double as a wiring closet without too much difficulty. In some cases, the wiring closet might also double as the server closet, so you might want to secure a space that will also allow you to deploy racks that contain your servers and other connectivity devices.

The basic wiring closet usually contains several items:

▶ **A set of 110 blocks**—A 110 block is a device, usually mounted on a wall, that has a row of RJ-45 jacks on it. Each jack is connected to a wire that runs out to a network wall jack elsewhere in the office. 110 blocks are also called patch panels (see Figure 11.3). It's possible to install and terminate your own patch panels. (It's pretty easy, in fact.) Because the wires that connect to the contacts on the back of the panel are color coded, it's difficult to make a mistake. Nonetheless, there are specialized tools involved, and it's wise to learn from someone who already knows how to do it. Be advised that the punch-down block (as the 110 block is also called) is fast being replaced by cable runs that directly connect to switches, or hubs, or other devices.

FIGURE 11.3
A patch panel or a
110 block.

▶ **One or more switches or hubs**—Switches or hubs (which you might also hear referred to as concentrators) tend to be stored in the wiring closet for two reasons. First, they're generally pretty small—they can fit in a briefcase if an ethically impaired person has the mind to steal one. Second, they make great listening devices; if a network card set up in a special way called promiscuous mode is plugged in to the concentrator, it's possible to read every data packet passing over the network. Because this represents a huge security risk, it's best to lock the concentrators away (see Figure 11.4).

▶ **Wiring bundles**—Because the wiring closet is where all your office network wiring converges, you'll usually have a bundle of cables connected to the 110 block. Wiring bundles represent one end of what can be an arduous task: running cables up hill, down dale, across ceilings, and down walls. If you have a lot of wiring to do, it's often better to let a professional pull and terminate your network wiring. Doing so reduces the aggravation factor quite a bit, and if anything is wrong with the cable, the installer will warrant it. In home networking situations (or a small office), you might be involved in pulling your own wiring though walls or ceilings.

FIGURE 11.4
A typical switch or hub.

Keep Your Cable Runs Away from Power Cables

Do not run network cables any closer than one foot (25 cm) from wall-current electrical cables because the power cable's 50 or 60Hz cycle can interfere with data transmission. Also keep your cables away from light fixtures in the ceiling if you are pulling cable along a drop ceiling.

Watch Out!

▶ **Patch cords**—Patch cords are the cables that connect the 110 block to the switch or hub (see Figure 11.5). You need one patch cord to connect one port on the 110 block to one port on the switch or hub. You will only need patch cords if you decide to include a 110 block in the closet. Patch cords are sometimes referred to as rat tails.

Wiring closets aren't absolutely necessary, but they do make life easier and more secure. And (for neat freaks) the best part of a wiring closet is that it keeps the messy part of the network behind closed doors.

Connecting a star topology network is really easy once the wiring between the 110 block/patch panel and the jacks in offices have been installed. You simply have to plug a patch cord in between the computer's 10/100BASE-T network jack (it's on the network card you installed earlier) and the 10/100BASE-T outlet in the wall, and then ensure that the corresponding port on the patch panel is connected to the concentrator (see Figure 11.6). It's really simple, which is why it's a great design.

FIGURE 11.5
An RJ-45 connec-
tor—a typical patch
cord (or network
cable end) used for
10BASE-T or
100BASE-T.

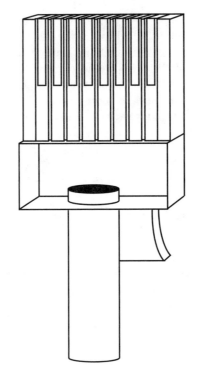

FIGURE 11.6
How computers are
connected in a
wiring closet/office
jack situation.

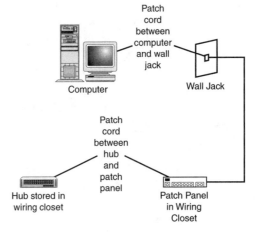

A Word About Wireless Networking

Obviously, the alternative to wired networks is a wireless network. Wireless networks can provide users a free run of the office because of the radio frequency technology used by wireless network cards and access points to communicate. Wireless networks also provide an excellent option for the home office, especially in situations when trying to pull wire in the home would be a real nightmare.

In purchasing wireless technology, there are issues with interoperability between devices, and there are also issues related to the range provided by wireless implementations, which can actually relate to building concentration. There is also the nagging issue related to security. We discuss wireless networking in more detail in Hour 23, "Wireless Networking."

Summary

Thunder is good, thunder is fine; but it is lightning that does all the work.

—Mark Twain

As this statement illustrates, theory is fine and good, but practice is what allows us to hone our skills. The best way to get your networking skills into shape is to work with a bias toward action.

If you learned anything in this hour, it's that the physical hookup of a network is one of the least significant hurdles to successful networking. At the same time, in many people's eyes, this is the most daunting part of the process. In my estimation, the best way to become proficient with hardware installation is simply to do it a lot. Use old computers (they're often pretty inexpensive) and work with them. Make mistakes; you'll learn from them. And in the end, you'll be more successful.

Q&A

Q *When installing adapter cards in a computer, what do you want to avoid?*

A Primarily, you don't want to damage the card either by handling it too roughly or by applying static shock. Both can damage a card badly enough to make it wholly inoperable.

Q *Why should a wiring closet be close to the center of an office space (if it's possible)?*

A In Hour 5, you learned that the maximum run of twisted-pair wire (CAT 5 or 6) is 100 meters. Keep the wiring closet central to your installation to avoid having to deploy additional switches or other devices to extend the network.

HOUR 12

Network Applications

In this hour, you will learn about the following topics:

- ▶ Defining network applications
- ▶ Introducing groupware
- ▶ Exploring the client and server aspects of groupware
- ▶ What groupware applications can do for you

Applications that a user runs from the network can take the form of productivity software (such as Microsoft Office or Sun's StarOffice Suite), which can also be installed and run on the user's computer. Whether run from a server or from individual desktops, the user experiences little difference. In terms of network administration, running the applications from the server does allow for easier updates and overall ease of administration.

Microsoft SharePoint Expands the Concept of Networked Applications

Did you Know?

Microsoft has recently released SharePoint Server, which enables a company to deploy a sharing environment for Microsoft Office users that makes it easy for them to share files on a network or over the Internet. SharePoint is designed to work with the latest version of Microsoft Office—Microsoft Office 2003.

Another commonly deployed network application is the network database. These database applications embrace a client/server model for data access—meaning that a client application on the desktop is able to access the resources on the database server. Most of the processing power in this model is on the back end or sever end. Examples of client/server databases are Oracle and Microsoft SQL Server.

Another category of network applications is **groupware**, which is typically a suite of products that allow users to communicate and collaborate. On the desktop, the client side of these applications are often referred to as a **Personal Information Manager**, or PIM.

Groupware applications embrace the client/server model of communication. A client runs on each user computer and allows the client computer to communicate with the communication server, which accumulates and holds the application data. Groupware products run on top of a particular network operating system. For example, Exchange Server from Microsoft is a groupware environment that runs on a Microsoft 2000 or 2003 server.

Three commonly used groupware product suites are Microsoft Exchange Server, Lotus Notes, and Novell GroupWise. Each of these groupware products offers several different communication and collaboration features. Some of the common features of groupware products are

▶ *Electronic mail system*—The groupware communication server serves as the mail server for internal email systems or Internet email.

▶ *Group scheduling*—A centralized scheduling system is maintained on the communication server.

▶ *Discussion groups*—Users can read and post messages to a discussion database. Discussion groups can be created for the discussion and development of projects by users on the network.

▶ *Information databases*—Databases such as an employee handbook and a centralized employee address book (including email and phone extension information) can be hosted by the communication server.

▶ *Task automation*—Forms can be developed that allow users to order office supplies online and invite users to a meeting.

The fact that all these communication resources are centrally held on the communication server means that any user on the network can access a particular service, such as email or the calendar/scheduling service. Even remote users can log on to the network and access the services on the groupware server.

By the
Way

PIMs Can Also Be Used on Standalone Computers

PIMs, such as Microsoft Outlook, do not necessarily need to be used in a network situation in which Exchange Server serves as the server part of the client/server relationship. Data related to an application such as Outlook can also be stored on the local client computer. This allows the user to organize her calendar, contacts, and email, but it does not provide the collaborative powers that Outlook would supply in a networked environment.

One of the most common uses of the PIM is as an email client. Email has become as important to human communication as the telephone. Let's begin our discussion of groupware and network applications with email systems.

Email

One of the important features provided by groupware is email. The sending and receiving of email, although transparent to the end user, basically works the same as postal or "snail" mail. You create your correspondence or email, address it, and then send it on its way. Your network email system actually takes care of the return address and routes your email across your local network and the Internet without any more concern for the route it takes than a paper letter. If it gets there, great; if not, it will provide you a notification that the message was undeliverable. However, I think all of us who use email on a daily basis are actually quite satisfied with our success rate in both sending and receiving email.

Email started out as a simple function of the early UNIX operating systems. Essentially, email was basically an automated file copying operation in which a text file containing a message was copied from your local UNIX system's hard drive onto a remote UNIX system's hard drive.

To get around the nonstandard and often incompatible email systems that permeated the early UNIX environment, a programmer named Eric Allman wrote a program called **sendmail**. Sendmail offered (and still does offer) a huge range of options for sending and receiving mail.

More recently, software developers have improved both on the concept of email and the software and protocols that are necessary to send and receive email. This means that a wide variety of email clients and email communication servers are now available. Most email systems for businesses now center around Internet standards and embrace the TCP/IP protocols **POP3** (Post Office Protocol version 3) and **SMTP** (Simple Mail Transport protocol). POP is the protocol used on the server that holds your email until you download it to your computer using an email client. SMTP provides a client computer to transfer mail to a mail server that then starts it on its journey over a intranet or the Internet until it reaches its final destination.

By the
Way

> **IMAP Is an Alternative to POP**
>
> POP3 is used by a client computer to collect its email from the mail server. IMAP is another email transport protocol that actually allows you to check your messages but does not remove it from the email server. This provides a user who works on several different computers (such as a salesperson on the road) or other mail-ready devices and wants to be able to view received email from any device or any location.

Proprietary Mail Systems

With the advent of PC-based networking in the early-to-mid 1980s, a raft of vendors began building proprietary mail systems to operate in various PC environments. These systems, which included Lotus cc:Mail, Microsoft Mail, and various packages built around Novell's MHS (Message Handling System), often attempted to rectify what their designers saw as shortcomings in sendmail.

Proprietary email packages for PC networks are typically very easy to install and configure. However, many of these systems have come and gone. Three of the most popular email and groupware platforms are now Microsoft Exchange, Lotus Notes, and Novell GroupWise. These platforms not only provide for the use of POP3 and SMTP to send company email using Internet standards, but they also provide a centralized server for the administration of the mail and communication services.

A downside of proprietary mail systems is that they do not work with each other without the intercession of a mail gateway, a computer that converts mail from one proprietary format to another.

Additionally, proprietary mail systems cannot route mail directly to the Internet. To do so, they require yet another mail gateway to convert mail to SMTP (Simple Mail Transport Protocol) format, the section of the TCP/IP protocol suite that handles mail routing.

Open-Standards Email

An alternative to proprietary mail systems is the use of open standards. As with all things networked, the Internet Engineering Task Force (IETF) has worked out nonproprietary standards for the function of email. When you see something referring to **Internet mail standards**, the IETF standards set forth in the Requests for Comments (RFC) documents are what's being referred to. Internet mail standards are surprisingly simple. As long as your network uses TCP/IP, it's possible to use Internet mail; all you need, really, is a server to run the server-side mail application software and the software to run at the client to retrieve mail from the server.

There are many different manufacturers of server and client Internet mail software. The beauty of the standards set forth by the IETF is that any client can work with any server as long as both pieces conform to the standards: SMTP for server-side work and POP3 or IMAP for the client side.

Common standards-compliant email include the following:

▶ Open-source sendmail, usually running on UNIX or Linux

▶ Commercial sendmail from `sendmail.com`, usually running on UNIX or Linux

▶ Procmail, usually running on UNIX or Linux

▶ Fetchmail, usually running on UNIX or Linux

▶ Microsoft Exchange Server running the Internet Mail Connector

Sendmail, procmail, and fetchmail are (mostly) open source. This means that you can download the code from the appropriate Web location (`http://www.send-mail.org` for open-source sendmail), configure and compile it on your UNIX or Linux system, and run it. Commercial sendmail and Microsoft Exchange are commercial solutions that offer vendor support.

Configuring Email

Getting a particular email client up and running requires that you install and configure the client to send and receive email. To configure the client, you must first configure an email account on the server for the client. For example, on a server running Microsoft Exchange Server, a new Exchange Mailbox is created in the Windows Active Directory, as shown in Figure 12.1.

FIGURE 12.1
Users require an
email account on
the mail server.

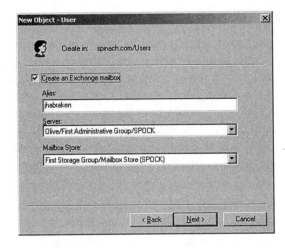

Once the account has been created (whether a proprietary platform account or
an Internet email account), the client application can be configured. For example, Microsoft Outlook actually walks the user through the steps of creating a new
account (see Figure 12.2), allows a number of different account types to be created—such as Microsoft Exchange, POP3, IMAP, HTTP (such as a Hotmail
account)—and can also serve as the client for a number of proprietary mail
systems.

FIGURE 12.2
The email client
must then be con-
figured to communi-
cate with the mail
server.

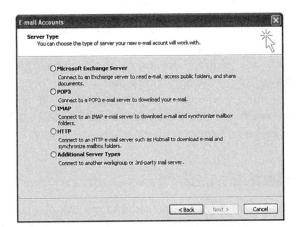

When configuring the email client, you will need to specify the user account, user
password, and the name of the mail server. When dealing with Internet email,
you must typically specify both a POP3 and SMTP server.

Understanding Multipurpose Internet Mail Extensions

Although being able to send text messages over a network or the Internet is an incredibly useful tool, the fact that we can attach files to email messages makes it a fantastic way to send all sorts of personal and professional items. There are application binary files (programs you can run on your computer), picture files, video files, sound files, and so forth. And until the advent of **MIME**, or **Multipurpose Internet Mail Extensions**, these kinds of files could not be carried over regular email channels.

As a result, the IETF decided to create a set of extensions for the SMTP mail standard that enabled files of many different types to be attached to email. Rather than defining all the file types and creating a new SMTP version each time a new file type came into existence, the IETF decided that it would create a system to which new file types could be added without changing the whole mail system. The IETF's standard turned out to be the MIME standard, which is used to copy files of many different types across the Internet.

As the Internet matures, many new file types will probably become available. However, MIME is sufficiently open-ended that it will support many new types of files. MIME is a useful tool; without it, the rest of the Internet-compliant email system would lose a significant portion of its utility.

Diagnosing Email Problems

Problems sending and receiving email usually boil down to problems with the client or problems with the mail server. This holds true no matter what mail system your network uses. Oh, and there is always that pesky problem that can shut down any client/server based system (such as email); I'm talking about connectivity issues. If there is a network problem, even a perfectly working email client and an email server that is up and running can't talk if the network infrastructure does not provide the appropriate connectivity. Remember that connectivity issues don't always relate to a bad switch or problem with cabling; other problems that control the capability of computers to communicate on the network can also be at fault.

Some simple questions that you can ask are as follows:

▶ Is the mailserver running? yes/no

▶ Is the remote (recipient) mailserver running? yes/no

Although these questions are fairly elementary, they do provide you with a start. Accurately diagnosing network communication problems requires a good understanding of the TCP/IP protocol stack and network troubleshooting. We will discuss TCP/IP in Hour 14, "TCP/IP," and network troubleshooting in Hour 21, "Network Administration Tips and Tricks."

Dealing with Spam

An absolute curse that everyone with an Internet email account deals with on a daily basis is spam. **Spam** is unwanted email, and it can fill your In box. It not only is a nuisance, but it also costs companies and institutions work hours and ultimately money. It is beginning to actually clog the Internet to the point at which it has become a major problem. Some spam is innocuous, but a lot of it is pornographic or otherwise unsuitable for work environments.

Higher-end email clients, such as Lotus Notes and Microsoft Outlook, provide filters that can be used to move spam directly to the trash bin, and some email clients can actually block spam based on email addresses or the domain of the sender. Also a number of other tools are on the market that do a good job fighting spam. The list that follows provides some of these; consider it a list of possibilities, not necessarily recommendations:

- ▶ CloudMark's SpamNet is an excellent spamfighter; it's an inexpensive subscription, and it works very well.

- ▶ Bayesian filters, which are available from a variety of sources on the Web, block spam based on local algorithms and what you select as spam.

- ▶ For people using Linux or UNIX and sendmail, SpamAssassin is a remarkably accurate server-based tool to help block spam. I recommend using it with Red Hat Linux 9 or higher; it works very well.

- ▶ Subscriptions are available to businesses to filter spam based on black hole lists such as the one maintained by the heroes at `http://www.mail-abuse.org`. They keep a database of known spammers and deny messages coming from those email addresses and domains.

- ▶ A good spam fighter that integrates well with Microsoft Outlook (and Outlook Express) is Mail Frontier Matador. It provides a home or corporate user with the ability to filter and block spam messages. More information on Matador can be found at `http://www.mailfrontier.com/`.

In corporate environments, it really falls on the network administrator to find strategies and set rules that will minimize spam on the corporate network.

You might want to devise a set of rules that must be followed by users on the network. For example, you might have a rule that dictates that network users do not sign up for any Internet services or special Web sites using their corporate email accounts. This is one way that the spammers build their long list of email addresses that will be deluged with unwanted email.

Scheduling and Calendars

Anyone who has worked in an environment that requires the staff to meet periodically knows how hard it is to schedule a meeting that works for all the potential attendees. I think everyone will agree that just tracking your own personal and business appointments can be problematic. We use every possible kind of system to stay organized: calendars, daily planners, and a lot of little scraps of paper.

Groupware products such as Microsoft Exchange and Lotus Notes also provide scheduling and calendar features that make it easy to schedule appointments, meetings, and other events. Let's look at an example of how this works in the Microsoft Exchange environment.

By the Way

Groupware Scheduling Features Do Not Embrace a Common Standard

There have been several proposed calendaring standards: iCal, ICAP, SSTP, and others. None of these have been embraced as an industry standard, and calendar software packages are still proprietary.

There seems to be little consensus among the proponents of various calendaring systems regarding form and function. Currently, Microsoft Exchange owns a surprisingly large share of this market, largely because of the lack of a real standard.

Rather than working on standards, several vendors are working on open source standards-compliant mail/calendaring clients. Hopefully, implementation will overtake design in this case and provide useful products from which a standard can be derived.

Each user's calendar (meaning her current schedule containing appointments and scheduled meetings) is held in folders on the Exchange server. This means that when any user attempts to schedule a meeting from Microsoft Outlook's Calendar feature, Outlook can actually check to see if the invitees for the meeting are available or busy. Figure 12.3 shows the Plan a Meeting window in Outlook 2003. Notice that an AutoPick button provides a user with the ability to find open time slots for the meeting that will accommodate all the attendees.

FIGURE 12.3
A user scheduling a new meeting has the calendar resources on the Exchange Server to accommodate the attendees' schedules.

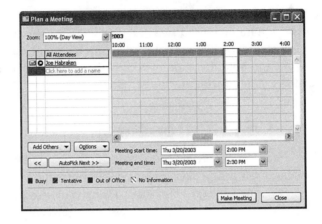

After the meeting is scheduled by the user, the meeting is posted to the Exchange Server. This process also sends out email meeting requests to all the attendees. Figure 12.4 shows a sample of a meeting request email.

FIGURE 12.4
Meeting requests are sent out to the invitees.

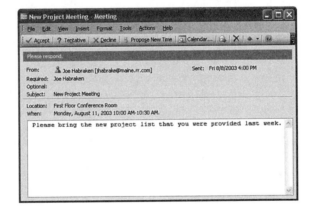

Because the Microsoft Exchange Server environment enables the Outlook client to reconcile all attendees' schedules with the meeting date and time, you have a system that should be foolproof in terms of scheduling meetings and other events. However, if users have not kept their calendars up-to-date, this system won't work any better than a paper calendar or the scraps of paper mentioned earlier.

Groupware products are not limited to just scheduling meetings. Tasks and appointments can also be assigned to users. For example, when a task is assigned to a user, the user then can accept or decline the task. Because messages are sent back to the originator of the task whether the user accepts or declines, groupware, such as Microsoft Exchange, makes it easy to track job assignments and their status.

Shared Calendars Keep Employees' Schedules Up-to-Date

Groupware products also make it easy for users to share calendars. For example, an executive assistant can be given access to the calendar of the corporate officer she serves, allowing the assistant to make and track the executive's appointments and meetings.

By the Way

Networked Contact Management

Another tool provided by groupware products is contact management. At its most basic, contact management allows a user to store names, addresses, email addresses, and phone numbers in a database. Not only can a user create her own contacts list in a groupware client, but she can also access group contact and distribution lists that make it easy to send email, phone, or otherwise communicate.

In networked environments, groupware contact software provides a way for a sales force to not only track its clients, but also track the most recent meeting it has had with clients; it can also, in some cases, automatically schedule a time for a next call after a preset amount of time has elapsed.

Like group calendaring, contact management software does not yet have an IETF standard, so for the most part, contact management software interoperates only with itself. You will find, however, that most contact management software—particularly those provided by groupware products such as Lotus Notes, Microsoft Exchange, and Novell GroupWise—do provide the ability to import and export data to and from other contact management software.

Creating a new contact in the different groupware products will vary; however, all the products provide a window that allows you to enter the information related to a particular contact such as name, address, phone number, and so on. Figure 12.5 shows the Outlook Contact window, which is used to enter information related to a new contact.

After the contact is entered, the information is then available to all the users on the network. This not only creates an environment in which client or customer data is readily available to all employees, but it also sets up a system in which contact data will more likely be updated because the contact records do not reside on individual computers; they are held on the server.

FIGURE 12.5
Contact information
is entered in a
simple-to-use
window.

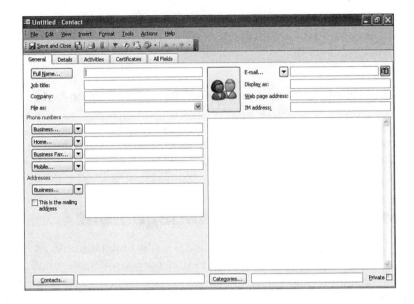

A Sampler of Network-Based Software

As already mentioned, a number of different groupware products are available. Each provides the standard groupware features such as email, scheduling, and contacts.

In the sections that follow, I will briefly discuss Novell GroupWise, Lotus Notes, and Microsoft Exchange/Outlook. You will find that each are remarkably similar at the user level. So, in terms of deciding to use a particular platform, you will really need to look at the server side of each groupware product and see how they will fit into your current network implementation.

Novell GroupWise

GroupWise is Novell's entry in the groupware category. It consists of a GroupWise client and server. The GroupWise server product can be deployed on a Novell NetWare server, and it can also be run on a Microsoft Windows server such as Microsoft Windows 2000 or Microsoft Server 2003. The GroupWise client can run on several different client platforms such as Windows, Linux, and the Mac operating system. Figure 12.6 shows the GroupWise client window on a Windows XP computer.

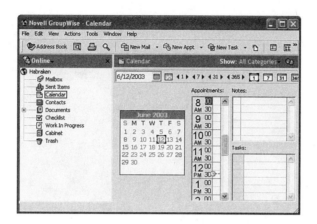

FIGURE 12.6
The GroupWise client window.

The GroupWise server product (version 6.5 as of the writing of this book) is fully integrated with NetWare's eDirectory hierarchical object database, so client accounts are actually created within the eDirectory.

The eDirectory Is the Latest Version of NetWare's Object Database

The eDirectory is the successor to the Novell Directory Services, or NDS. The eDirectory provides a branching, hierarchical database that is used to hold network objects such as network trees, servers, users, and other objects.

By the Way

Users are provided access to the GroupWise post office when their NetWare eDirectory user accounts are created. Figure 12.7 shows the eDirectory New User dialog box. To include a user in the GroupWise post office, the Add User to GroupWise Post Office check box must be selected.

How Can GroupWise Run on a Windows Server When eDirectory Is Required?

The eDirectory can actually be run as a separate service and does not require that your server operating system be NetWare. Check out http://www.novell.com for more about eDirectory.

By the Way

GroupWise actually provides all the tools that user's expect from a GroupWare product: email, calendar, contacts, and tasks. GroupWise also provides a slick Web interface tool that can actually be deployed and allow users that are on the road to access their GroupWise account via the Internet.

Lotus Notes

Lotus Notes also provides a client/server groupware platform that can be run on a number of different network operating systems such as Microsoft Windows, Sun Solaris, and Novell NetWare servers. The server side of the Lotus Notes platform is actually called Lotus Domino Server, and it can provide users with email, contacts, tasks, and different discussion and communication databases.

The Lotus Notes client runs on different client operating systems such as Microsoft Windows and Linux/UNIX implementations. Figure 12.8 shows the Lotus Notes client window.

The Lotus Domino server can actually be managed from a command-line interface or using the Domino Administrator. Either venue allows you to add Lotus Notes users, groups, and platform policies. Figure 12.9 shows the Domino Administrator window.

One of the real strengths of Lotus Notes (at least in my opinion) is the capability to create discussion databases. These databases are very much like Internet newsgroups in that users can post a particular message and then other users can post comments related to that message (or post a new message). This allows users to have an online dialog without having to clutter their email boxes. For example, several workers involved in the same project could design a discussion database and then post status information, tips, or even frustrations on the database.

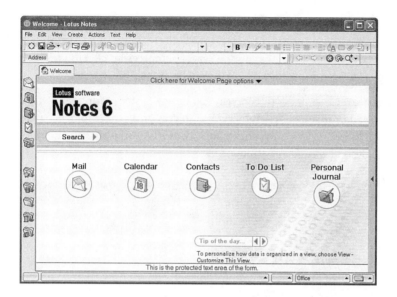

FIGURE 12.8
The Lotus Notes client.

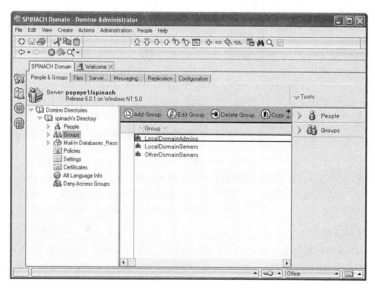

FIGURE 12.9
The Domino Administrator window.

Microsoft Exchange/Outlook

Although you have already seen some of the Outlook interface in figures in this chapter, let's discuss the server side of Microsoft's groupware product. Microsoft Exchange Server runs on a server class computer that already has the Windows network operating system installed on it. (The latest version of Exchange is designed to run a server configured with Windows 2000 Server or Windows Server 2003.)

Exchange Server is tightly wrapped with Microsoft's Active Directory (the hierar-chical database used to store objects on a Windows network). Users in the Active Directory gain access to the Exchange Server resources by clicking the Create an Exchange mailbox check box on their User Properties dialog box.

Exchange Server is managed using the Exchange System Manager, which allows the network administrator to manage mailboxes and public folders (such as those holding distribution lists and other public contacts). Figure 12.10 shows the Exchange System Manager window.

FIGURE 12.10
The Exchange System Manager.

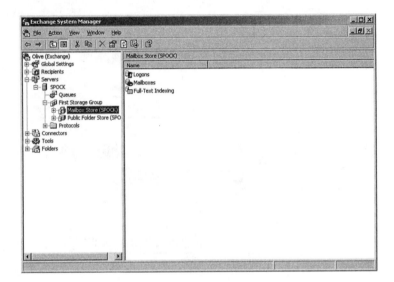

Outlook is closely linked with Microsoft's Office desktop productivity suite (prod-ucts such as Microsoft Word, Excel, and so on). In a special folder called the Journal, Outlook can log all documents generated in Office for future reference. This allows a user to track her activity in relation to her use of other Office appli-cations. Not only does the Journal track Office application use, but it also can be set up to track activities within Outlook itself, providing a user with an even high-er degree of organization.

The most current versions of Outlook (Outlook 2000, 2002, and 2003) support all mail protocols (POP3, IMAP4, HTTP) as well as Microsoft's proprietary Exchange-based mail systems and offer a variety of groupware applications that can be downloaded from the Microsoft Web site. Since its introduction, Outlook has become a fairly powerful mail client, and its groupware features have steadily gotten stronger. If there is a problem with Outlook, it is Microsoft's desire to use

active content including Web pages and programs embedded in emails that has caused many users to fall prey to **macro viruses**, which (for instance) send copies of infected messages to everyone in an Outlook user's contact list.

A Few Others

Although we have looked at what I consider to be the groupware big three in terms of user base, there are also a number of other products available on the market. Other products that fit into the PIM/groupware category include Symantec's popular ACT! product, Commence Corporation's Commence, and GoldMine. All have varying degrees of email integration, and all can share contact information. Each has its own proprietary scheduler, which for the most part does not interact with that of other systems. Again, most of these software tools do allow you to import/export data.

Summary

In this hour, we have explored groupware and some of the communication features provided by groupware products. We discussed email, scheduling, and contact management. We also took a look at some of the most popular groupware platforms.

Q&A

Q *What network model do groupware products embrace?*

A Most groupware products embrace a client/server model, where a desktop client is used to access information stored on a network server.

Q *Why are Internet/TCP/IP-standard applications more desirable than applications that use proprietary communications protocols?*

A TCP/IP is a vendor-independent standard; applications that adhere to it can work with other TCP/IP applications. By contrast, proprietary systems require expensive gateways to communicate with other systems; without a gateway, proprietary systems might not be able to communicate with other systems at all.

Q *What are some of the services that groupware products provide to users?*

A Groupware products provide email, scheduling, contacts, and a number of other collaboration features.

HOUR 13

Connecting to the Internet

In this hour, you will learn about the following topics:

▶ The origins of the Internet
▶ Connecting to the Internet
▶ Firewalls, proxy servers, and Network Address Translation
▶ Internet email
▶ The World Wide Web and other Internet services

Most of our discussion in this book, thus far, has related to local area networks, or LANs. The Internet, a huge network of networks, has become increasingly important for both personal and corporate computing. It really has become an imperative that users be provided with a connection to the Internet at the office and at home. In this hour, we take a look at the rise of the Internet and different ways that both corporate and home users connect to it. We will also look at some of the services that users take advantage of on the Internet, such as Internet email and the World Wide Web.

The Origins of the Internet

While there is a great deal of mythology and misinformation surrounding the origins of the Internet, most people were not even aware of this giant, worldwide network until the advent of the World Wide Web and the ability to quickly browse Web sites using a Web browser. In the United States, The Advanced Research Projects Agency (ARPA), an agency in the Department of Defense, began working on the idea of large-scale packet switching network in the 1960s. The idea was to connect research sites across the country (such as those at Universities), allowing researchers and ARPA officials to easily share information.

The development of this packet-switching network would require both network protocols that supplied the rules and transmission scheme for the data and the devices that would actually switch the data along a path that moved the data from the sender to the receiver. Named ARPAnet, the network actually spanned the United States by 1971.

> ### Where Was the First Node on the ARPANET?
> In 1969, the first node on the ARPANET was installed at UCLA.

While it certainly was not the very first protocol set that was developed for the ARPANET, TCP/IP (available in 1981) was mandated by the Department of Defense as the protocol to be used on all its computers for long distance communications in 1983 (meaning outside any short range WAN implementations).

ARPANET itself, however, didn't evolve into the actual backbone of what we know today as the Internet; it only provided the protocols and switching equipment that would be used to make the Internet a reality. In 1986, the National Science Foundation (NSF) built a network backbone using the technology and protocols developed for ARPANET. This NSFNET began as a network for educational institutions and NSF sites that actually evolved into the Internet. The NSF actually got out of the public Internet business in 1994, and this allowed Internet service providers to interconnect on the Internet through various network access points (some created by the NSF, and others created by companies such as Sprint).

So, although all of us who use the Internet for email, the Web, and other communication platforms can't really remember not having Internet access, it is actually not even twenty years old.

Let's take a look at some of the ways that we connect to the Internet. Then we can take a look at Internet communication tools such as Internet email.

Getting Connected to the Internet

To take advantage of the Internet, your company (or your home) must be connected to the Internet. This means that you have to establish a connection with the Internet backbone.

In most cases, this means establishing a relationship with an **Internet service provider (ISP)**. ISPs can offer a number of different services such as email, Web browsing, and so on. This is particularly useful for small companies (or home offices) that do not want to establish their own mail servers. Because even the smallest of businesses might want their own domain names, ISPs can also provide domain hosting (where they provide the DNS services for your domain) and they can host your Web site on one of their Web servers. You really have to decide if the size and mission of your company warrants you deploying your own DNS servers, mail servers, and Web servers when you initially shop around for your ISP.

In cases in which you work at a very large company, you can actually forgo using an ISP and deal with a company called an **Internet Access Provider (IAP)**. These companies—Sprint is an example—offer connections to the Internet backbone via trunk lines that are connected to the Internet backbone. Each trunk line is referred to as a **network access point**, or NAP. Most local ISPs (even big ones) connect to the Internet via an IAP.

Connecting via an IAP requires that you provide the entire network infrastructure for running Internet applications. You would have to deploy your own DNS servers, mail servers, and so on. In most cases, your company will probably deal with an ISP rather than an IAP.

Who Manages the NAPS?

The MFS Communications Company manages the various NAPs on the Internet backbone. Each NAP is actually referred to as a MAE or Metropolitan Area Ethernet. In Washington, D.C., the MAE is referred to as MAE East (and was the first MAE in the country). The MAE that serves Silicon Valley in California is referred to as MAE West.

By the Way

Choosing an ISP that meets all your needs can be tricky. You rally need to do some research and shop around. Here are some things that you should keep in mind as you choose an ISP:

- ▶ Is the ISP redundantly connected to its upstream link? It's important for you to know how many redundant links the ISP maintains with its "big brother" IAP. Redundant connections assure you of a more consistent connection through your ISP to the Internet backbone.

- ▶ Who will supply the equipment for the ISP/LAN connection? You need to find out whether the ISP provides and configures necessary equipment, such as routers, as part of the connection cost or whether you will have to purchase and maintain your own WAN connectivity devices.

- ▶ Can the ISP provide you with a pool of IP addresses for your network and obtain your domain name for you? Having your own pool of IP addresses to work with provides you with flexibility in bringing new clients onto the network and configuring Web servers or DNS servers that require fixed IP addresses. Having a pool of "legal" IP addresses is certainly not a requirement to connect to the Internet because there are alternatives such as proxy servers and Network Address Translation (discussed later in this hour).

► Will the ISP help you secure your IP network? You need to know what the ISP is willing to do to help protect your LAN from invasion over the Internet connection. Find out whether the ISP offers firewalls and proxy servers (discussed later in this hour).

► What kind of technical support is offered by the ISP? Find out whether the ISP offers 24/7 technical support.

Although cost can typically be a major concern when choosing an ISP, keep in mind some of these other points. An inexpensive connection that is often down or doesn't provide all the services and support that you need really isn't a savings.

Types of Internet Connections

The connection that you choose to connect to an ISP (or an IAP) can take a number of forms; we discussed a number of high-speed connection types in Hour 6, "Extending Your LAN: Wide Area Networks," such as T1 lines and Frame Relay. During your initial dialogue with a prospective ISP, you need to find out how much experience it has with the different WAN possibilities for connecting your company to it. An ISP with a proven track record of providing connections for businesses can also provide you with information on the type of connections it is providing to other clients.

In cases in which the cost of a dedicated high-speed connection such as a T1 line is out of the question because of cost (and need), home users and small offices are not necessarily relegated to the world of dial-up. Alternatives also exist that can supply a great deal of bandwidth. Let's take a look at the possibilities including dial-up.

Dial-Up Connections

Dial-up connections to the Internet use a modem to make the connection between a client computer and an ISP. The digital data from your computer—that is, the ones (1) and zeros (0)—must be converted so that it can be carried by the analog phone line. This conversion from digital to analog information is called modulation. When analog information is received on the modem connected to the ISP dial-in server, the data must be converted from analog back to digital. This process is called demodulation. The name modem is taken from *modulation* and *demodulation*.

An asynchronous modem is designed to move data over a regular analog voice-grade telephone line, and it is asynchronous modems that we use to connect a single computer directly to an ISP over regular phone lines. An asynchronous modem uses start and stop bits to let the receiving modem know when a particular packet of data starts and stops. Beyond the start and stop bits, many modems incorporate some type of error checking to ensure that the data is sent correctly across the telephone line.

Modem speed is measured in terms of the number of bits per second (bps) that can travel across the phone line. The fastest modems now available can operate at 56Kb (kilobits). Unfortunately, because of the nature of telephone lines, the fastest data speeds that can be attained are around 53Kb.

Modems are still fine in cases in which you want to send email and do some Web browsing; however, a modem connection is slow compared to other alternatives. It is, however, still the least expensive way of connecting to an ISP and taking advantage of Internet services.

DSL

Digital Subscriber Line, or DSL (which we discuss in relation to remote networking in Hour 7, "Remote Networking") provides voice and data communication over regular phone lines with speeds of up to 7Mbps. Because DSL runs over regular phone lines, you can be constantly connected to the Internet yet still make phone calls over the same phone line.

A number of the "Baby Bells"—such as Verizon and Qwest—provides DSL services. The amount of bandwidth you get depends on how much you want to pay. Different packages are available offering different connection speeds.

The DSL connection is provided to the home or office via a customer premise device (which you might have to pay for) that is typically referred to as a DSL router. These routers can be connected to a switch or a hub, which allows you to connect multiple computers to the DSL line. Figure 13.1 shows a Cisco DSL router, which is typical of the DSL devices supplied by the various DSL providers.

Although DSL is primarily marketed as a way for home users and small businesses to connect to the Internet, it is also a very good way for a remote user to connect to the Internet and then take care of remote networking strategies such as Virtual Private Networking. Check out Hour 7 for more about remote access strategies and Virtual Private Networking.

FIGURE 13.1
A DSL router serves as the customer premise device for a DSL connection.

Broadband

Another high-speed Internet connection strategy is broadband. Broadband connections are offered by a number of cable television providers across the United States. Broadband connections make use of a cable modem as the customer premise device. The cable modem isn't really a modem in the strictest sense of the term, and it takes advantage of the cable TV infrastructure. Data is moved on different frequencies (or channels, if you prefer). Upstream and downstream data typically require separate frequencies. Although cable modem technology and the methods for allocating bandwidth are still being developed, bandwidths in excess of 2Mbps (with the possibility of speeds up to 30Mbps) can be experienced using the technology (the more bandwidth you want, the more you pay the provider).

Most cable television providers now offer cable modem connections for home networks, small businesses, and even larger businesses. Even the basic home cable modem package will provide dynamically assigned IP addresses and enough bandwidth for five networked computers. It is a very good way to share an Internet connection in a home or small office situation.

Using Firewalls, Proxy Servers, and Network Address Translation

No matter what technology you use to connect to the Internet, you need to deal with issues related to protecting the network from outside attacks and supplying an IP address to each server and client on the network. Two ways of protecting your network are with the use of firewalls and proxy servers.

In the case of proxy servers, you also need to know how Network Address Translation (NAT) works, which is a method of assigning private IP addresses to the internal network. This actually can be used with a proxy server to protect the internal network from intrusion and also cut down on the number of real or "legal" IP addresses you lease from your ISP. Let's take a look at firewalls, and then we will discuss proxy servers and NAT.

Firewalls

To protect your network, you really need a firewall. A **firewall** is a computer or other device that sits between the router (or other Internet connectivity device) and your internal network. There are software firewalls and hardware firewalls (actual devices).

A firewall examines data leaving and entering the internal network and can actually filter the data traveling in both directions. If data packets do not meet a particular rule that has been configured on the firewall, data is not allowed to enter or leave the internal network. This means that firewalls not only protect a network from outside attack, but they can also control the type of connections made by users on the internal network to the outside.

Firewalls are categorized by how they deal with network traffic. The different types of firewalls are

> ▶ Packet filter firewall—This type of firewall uses a set of rules to determine whether outgoing or incoming data packets are allowed to pass through the firewall. The rules or filters designed to control the data traffic allowed by the firewall can be based on such things as the IP address, ports, and services of the sending device. Packet filter firewalls move data quickly and are the simplest type of firewall.

> ▶ Circuit level firewall—This type of firewall is similar to the packet filter firewall (in that it filters packets based on a set of rules), but it also can make packets sent from the internal network to a destination outside the firewall

appear as if the packets originated at the firewall. This helps to keep information relating to hosts on the internal network secret. Circuit level firewalls also can determine whether a connection between a network host and a computer on the other side of the firewall has been established appropriately. If the connection has not been established appropriately, the firewall can terminate the connection.

▶ Application-Gateway firewall—Application gateways use strong user authentication to verify the identity of a host attempting to connect to the internal network using a TCP/IP protocol such as FTP or Telnet. This type of firewall can also actually control the devices that an external host can connect to once the firewall has authenticated that particular user.

Firewalls are manufactured by a number of companies including Cisco, 3Com, and Ascend Communications. Firewalls come in a variety of models that have been designed to protect different sizes of networks. For example, 3Com manufactures the OfficeConnect Firewall line as a security tool for small companies. For larger enterprise networks, 3Com offers the SuperStack 3 Firewall.

If you want to protect a single computer from outside intrusion, you can use a software firewall. This is actually a recommendation from Microsoft for home users (because a number of communication flaws in Windows XP have been exploited of late by hackers). For example, Windows XP has a built-in software firewall, which is part of the XP operating system. Another popular software firewall is ZoneAlarm. You can get more information about ZoneAlarm at http://www.zonealarm.com.

Firewalls have certainly become a necessity, particularly for those of us who use Microsoft operating systems. We will take a look at the different types of attacks that hackers use to crack into internal networks in Hour 19, "Security."

Proxy Servers

Firewalls are all well and good, but a firewall by itself can still leave you open for trouble. Why? If your internal network runs TCP/IP, each computer has a unique address. And without getting into the subject too deeply, those internal IP addresses can offer the discerning and skilled cracker an opportunity to get into unauthorized areas of the network.

How do you avoid allowing users' TCP/IP messages and requests from advertising their IP addresses? With proxy servers, of course; a proxy server is a rather ingenious method of preventing internal IP numbers from being visible to the outside world without denying your users access to any of their beloved Internet resources. Proxy server software is available from a number of different vendors, including Microsoft Proxy Server, Netscape Proxy Server, and Sun's iPlanet Proxy Server.

How does a proxy server work? Well, you configure each user's TCP/IP software (on his desktop or laptop computer) to look for a proxy server at a specific IP address. When the user clicks a link in a Web browser, such as Netscape Navigator or Internet Explorer, the data packets sent to that Web site don't route directly through the firewall and out to the Internet. Instead, the proxy server captures the internal computer's request to show a Web page. Then the proxy server takes note of the IP address of the computer on the internal network and sends a request for the same resources the internal user made—but the request is coming from the proxy server's IP address, not the internal user's IP address. When answering data packets (in this example, the Web page) come in over the Internet, the proxy server collects and forwards them to the IP address of the network user who originated the request.

As a result, to any observer outside the network, all requests for resources (Web pages, FTP files, whatever) seem to come from only one computer. This is terribly frustrating for malicious users, but it should be some source of comfort for people trying to protect their networks.

This process of using private addressing on the internal network, which then is connected to the Internet via a proxy server with a valid IP address is called **Network Address Translation**, or NAT for short. Let's take a look at NAT.

Firewall and Proxy Server in One Device

Firewalls often also have proxy server capabilities, so you get a firewall and proxy server in one device. These firewalls/proxy servers provide the ability to configure NAT for your network.

By the Way

Understanding Network Address Translation

Network Address Translation (NAT) allows you to hide a group of computers (such as a network) behind one public IP address. In the UNIX world, this is known as IP masquerading. Basically, your network sits behind the NAT server, which also is typically a proxy server and/or firewall. This means that you only need one "legal" IP address for the server running the NAT software. The IP addressing scheme that you use on the computer network behind the NAT server is really up to you (although there are ranges of IP addresses reserved for this purpose, which I discuss in a moment).

Firewalls and proxy servers that offer NAT are configured with two network interfaces. So, a server running a firewall or proxy server software package would have two Network Interface Cards (NICs). One of the NICs is configured with an IP address provided by your ISP (or receives its IP address from the ISP's DHCP server) and is connected to the ISP (or IAP if you are a big company). The other NIC is connected to your network and configured with an IP address consistent with the pool of addresses you use for your internal network. When the classes of IP addresses (A, B, and C) were defined for IP version 4 by the Internet Engineering Task Force (IETF), a range of addresses in each class was blocked out for NAT, as shown here:

- ▶ Class A—10.0.0.0 to 10.255.255.255, with a subnet mask of 255.0.0.0
- ▶ Class B—172.16.0.0 to 172.31.255.255, with a subnet mask of 255.255.0.0
- ▶ Class C—192.168.0.0 to 192.168.255.255, with a subnet mask of 255.255.255.0

The great thing about using a proxy server for firewall with NAT capabilities (or a NAT server) is that you can use as many IP addresses as required internally. For example, you can treat your internal network as if it is a Class A or Class B network, which provides a huge number of addresses. Remember, NAT only requires one "official" IP address for the proxy or NAT server that sits between your network and your ISP.

Proxy servers and NAT not only provide security and filtering capabilities for large networks, but also a proxy server with NAT capabilities can offer low-cost connection options for small companies and home businesses that want to attach more than one computer to a single Internet connection.

Now that we have had a look at connecting to the Internet and methods for protecting the internal network, let's take a look at common Internet services. We will start with Internet email.

Internet Email

The most commonly used Internet service is, surprisingly, not the World Wide Web but email. You can use Internet email to answer clients' informational queries, to chat with friends, to provide a personal touch to your business transactions, and to pass along news—the possibilities are endless. This is referred to by some accountancy types as "making a good business case," which is to say that it can be used to do work. They're right; in a world in which the fastest customer service is barely fast enough, email can be used as a tool to decrease response time and increase client satisfaction.

Before you can decide on the best method to route mail to the Internet, you must know and understand the various tasks that have to be accomplished between the time your user sends email and the time it gets to the Internet proper:

▶ Email must be addressed properly. If you are sending email from a POP3 or IMAP4 mail system, your mail has to be addressed in the standard *username@domainname*.com format (such as foo@bar.com).

▶ The email client on a computer must have a connection to the Internet from where messages can be sent and received. This connection can use any media from wireless networks to regular phone lines. One of the best things about TCP/IP standard software is that it can run over almost any media; the software really doesn't care.

▶ You must send and receive mail from a recognized domain. This means that your company must have its own domain, or you send and receive your email via your ISP's domain. Bottom line, someone involved in the Internet connection process must have a domain.

Unless all three of these criteria are met, you aren't going to be able to send or receive email. Obviously someone, either your company or your ISP, must also deploy a mail server or servers. Both an SMTP and a POP3 (or IMAP) server must be in place to send and then receive messages from a client on the network, respectively. I discuss different communication software platforms that supply email servers such as Microsoft Exchange and Novell GroupWise in Hour 12, "Network Applications.

Email Was Not Part of ARPAs Plan

Surprisingly, email was not part of ARPAs plan as the protocols and devices were developed for large-scale packet switching networks. However, when it was introduced to the ARPANET in 1972, it quickly became the most used application on the network.

By the Way

The World Wide Web and Other Internet Services

Connectivity to the Internet actually offers a number of different communication platforms for a user. There is the World Wide Web, FTP, and Newsgroups (not to mention all the proprietary chat platforms, such as Microsoft Messenger and Yahoo Chat).

Most of us use Internet email (as already discussed in this hour) and also take advantage of the Web. If you have ever downloaded a file, you might also have used the **File Transfer Protocol (FTP)**, which was one of the first protocols available for the TCP/IP protocol stack for sending and receiving files. Web browsers such as Internet Explorer support FTP, so we aren't required to run a separate FTP client (which is discussed in a moment). Let's take a look at the Web and then discuss FTP.

Using the Web

The protocol and markup language that made the World Wide Web a reality were not developed until 1991. Scientists at the CERN research laboratory developed the Hypertext Markup Language (HTML) and Hypertext Transfer Protocol (HTTP) so that they could exchange information about their projects over their TCP/IP network.

> **HTML** is the file format used to create documents that can then be read by a Web browser such as Microsoft Internet Explorer or Netscape Navigator. HTML consists of tags that are used to format a document so that it can be viewed in a Web browser. HTML offers a rich environment for creating documents that include graphics, sound, video, and links to other HTML documents such as other Web sites.
>
> **HTTP** is the TCP/IP stack member that provides the connection between an HTTP client (a computer outfitted with a Web browser) and server (which would be a Web server). A Web client sends a connection-oriented request using HTTP (which uses TCP for the connection) to a particular Web server (typically using the URL or Uniform Resource Locator for the Web server, which is the DNS name for the server; see more about DNS at the end of the chapter).

The Web server holding the HTML documents or Web site requested by the Web client will respond to the client with a connectionless HTTP communication. This enables the Web client to access the actual Web site.

Just about everyone should be familiar with the different Web browsers or clients available, such as those provided by Netscape and Microsoft. As far as Web servers go, in the UNIX/Linux world, the Apache Web server is quite popular. Netscape offers the Netscape Enterprise server, which can run on Windows, Linux, and UNIX operating systems. Microsoft bundles Internet Information Server with Windows Server 2003 and Windows 2000 Server.

File Transport Protocol

FTP provides a file-sharing environment that can control access to the file server by requiring a login name and password. This means that the FTP server must validate a user and his password before he can access files on the server.

On the Internet, many public FTP sites allow an anonymous logon. This means that anyone can log on to the FTP site using a username of "anonymous." The password for an anonymous logon is often your email address. A site allowing anonymous logons is often referred to as an anonymous FTP site. Figure 13.2 shows Apple's anonymous FTP site that has been accessed using the Internet Explorer Web browser. Note that the command FTP replaces the HTTP in the address window because you are accessing an FTP site rather than a Web site (HTTP).

FIGURE 13.2
Anonymous FTP sites are common on the Internet.

Notice that on a Windows-based computer, the directories on the FTP site appear in the Internet Explorer window the same as local directories would. You are potentially accessing files that reside on a computer clear across the world, but the computer's connection to the Internet makes the directories and files appear as if they are local.

Because we use our Web browsers to access anonymous FTP sites, most of us have never had to use an actual FTP client. A number of different FTP clients are available and can be used to access FTP sites without using a Web browser. If you are accessing FTP sites that require a username and password, you will need an FTP client. You can find a number of freeware FTP clients (and some demos for commercial software) at www.tucows.com.

Figure 13.3 shows the WS-FTP client connected to Novell's FTP site. Notice that the split screen shows the local computer directories and the directories on the FTP site. This makes it easy to upload files to the FTP site or download files from the FTP site with just a couple of clicks of the mouse.

FIGURE 13.3
FTP clients make it easy to access an Internet FTP site.

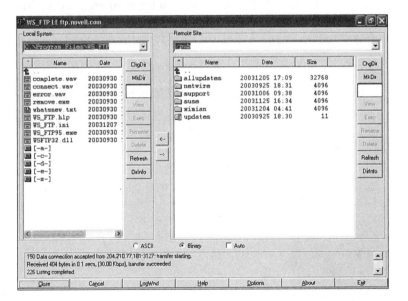

By the Way

FTP at the Command Line

If you don't want to download a separate FTP client and install it on your computer and you will download from servers that don't require a password, you will find that most operating systems such as the various UNIX/Linux flavors and Microsoft Windows allow you to access FTP sites by using the FTP command at the command line.

Summary

In this hour, you learned how the Internet got its start, as well as ways to connect a network or home computer to the Internet. We also discussed ways of protecting computers connected to the Internet through the use of firewalls and proxy servers. We also looked at Internet services such as email, the Web, and FTP.

Q&A

Q *What are some of the alternatives that you can use when you want to connect a network to the Internet?*

A You can use any of the WAN connection types, such as frame relay, that are discussed in Hour 6. You can also take advantage of newer communication strategies such as broadband and DSL. The type of connection you select will depend on the amount of bandwidth you need for your users, which directly relates to the size of your user base.

Q *If IP addresses are at a premium as your network grows, what network service can be used to negate the need for more public addresses?*

A Network Address Translation (NAT) not only provides a method of protecting a network via a proxy server, but it also allows you to use private IP addressing on the internal network and one public IP address to communicate with the outside world. This is not only a cost savings, but allows you to use Class A, B, or C ranges when you configure your internal IP addressing.

Q *What are two ways to protect an internal network from outside attack via the Internet?*

A Firewalls and proxy servers provide different strategies for protecting an internal network that is connected to the Internet. Firewalls allow you to control network communication from both outside and inside the network. Firewalls can filter traffic based on parameters that you set. Proxy servers enable networks to hide behind a public IP address; this means that data from the internal network is not addressed using the IP address of the network client.

PART IV

Network Operating Systems and Providing Network-Wide Services

HOUR 14

TCP/IP

In this hour, you will learn about the following topics:

▶ Understanding IP addressing

▶ Configuring network servers and clients for TCP/IP

▶ Working with DHCP

▶ DNS and FQDN to IP address resolution

▶ Getting a domain name

In Hour 3, "Getting Data from Here to There: How Networking Works," we took a look a brief look at the TCP/IP protocol stack and how it relates to the OSI model. We also discussed some of the protocols. An understanding of how TCP/IP is configured on network clients and servers and how the Domain Name Service, which translates IP addresses to DNS names (and vice versa) is essential for network administrators.

In this hour, we take a look at issues related to configuring the TCP/IP network protocol on network clients and servers. We also will explore the Dynamic Host Configuration Protocol and the Domain Name System. We will also discuss how you get a domain name for your company.

Understanding IP Addressing

As discussed in Hour 3, IPv4 addresses consist of 32 bits of information and are written in dotted decimal notation consisting of four octets in the format *x.x.x.x*. The usable pool of these addresses (usable for assignment to network devices and excluding the Class D and E addresses) has been divided into three classes of addresses:

▶ **Class A**—Used for very large networks and supplies over sixteen million node addresses for the network. Because of the way IP addresses are structured, a Class A network can serve a huge number of host computers (nodes); however, there can only be 127 Class A networks. ARPAnet (built in the early days of the Internet) is an example of a Class A network.

▶ **Class B**—Used for networks that still need a lot of node addresses, such as for large companies and institutions. There are 16,384 Class B network addresses available—with each Class B network supplying over 65,000 host addresses.

▶ **Class C**—Used for small networks. There are over two million Class C network addresses available. Class C networks only provide 254 node addresses.

Class A IP addresses are no longer available. (They are all assigned.) The only occasion when you will work with Class A addresses is in cases in which you are using Network Address Translation and a Proxy server on your network, meaning that you are using a Class A range of addresses as the private internal addresses. Class B addresses are assigned to large companies. (Microsoft is a Class B.) So, in most cases, unless you work for a fairly large company, you are probably going to be dealing with Class C addresses.

You can quickly identify the class that an IP address belongs to by looking at the decimal value of the first octet; each class (A, B, or C) has a specific first octet range:

▶ Class A (1–126)

▶ Class B (128–191)

▶ Class C (192–223)

Did you Know?

How Computers See IP Addresses

You have probably noticed that Class A ends with 126 and Class B begins with 128. So, what happened to 127? The 127 range is reserved and is used for loopback testing of the IP configuration of a computer (or other device).

> Computers see IP addresses as a bit stream, meaning in a stream of 1s and 0s. for example the IP address 130.1.16.1, would be represented in binary as
>
> `10000010 00000001 00010000 00000001`
>
> Notice that the bits have been divided into four groups of eight, or octets, just as the dotted decimal version of the address.
>
> This is how you convert dotted decimal numbers to binary (bits). Each octet has 8 bits. The decimal value of the bits in an octet from left to right are
>
> `128 64 32 16 8 4 2 1`
>
> So the decimal number 130 (the first octet in our address) is 128 + 2. This means that the first bit (the 128 bit) and the seventh bit (the 2 bit) are both turned on. (They are represented by 1s in the binary format.) To convert the decimal to the binary, you mark the bits that are on with 1s and the rest with 0s. The result is `10000010`, which is what we saw previously in the binary format of the IP address.

IP addresses really don't mean anything without an accompanying subnet mask. Devices on a network need to be capable of telling what part of the IP address is providing information related to which network the computer with a particular address is on and what part of the address actually refers to just the computer itself. This is determined by the subnet mask. Devices on the network use the subnet mask to "mask" out the portion of the IP address that refers to the network that the computer (or other device such as a router) sits on.

Each class has a default subnet mask:

- ▶ Class A—`255.0.0.0`
- ▶ Class B—`255.255.0.0`
- ▶ Class C—`255.255.255.0`

Without going into a lengthy and complex explanation of how computers and other devices use a subnet mask to determine certain information from an IP address, the default subnet masks provide some obvious visual clues. If you look at the Class A subnet mask, you will notice that 255 only appears in the first octet. In binary, 255 would be `11111111`, meaning that all eight bits are turned on. These "turned on" bits in the subnet mask actually mask out the first octet of any Class A IP address. This tells a computer that the first octet holds the network information.

Notice that all the other octets in the Class A subnet mask are `0`—this would be `00000000` in binary—and would not mask out the information in the second, third, and fourth octets. This enables these octets to be used for node addresses.

Each octet contains 8 bits. So in a Class A network, 8 bits are used to determine network information, and the other 24 bits are used for node addresses. This is why so many different possibilities are available for node addresses (over 16 million).

In the case of Class B networks, only the third and fourth octets are used for node addresses; this is because the first and second octets are masked out by the subnet mask and provide the network information. With only 16 bits available for node addresses, this means that Class B networks supply fewer node addresses (around 65,000).

Using this logic, you can see why Class C networks supply so few IP addresses (254). This is because only the fourth octet is reserved for node addressing, and the rest of the octets are used for network information. The subnet mask 255.255.255.0 masks out all the octets in a Class C address except for the last octet.

So, bottom line, every device on the network that requires an IP address must be configured with a unique IP address and the appropriate subnet mask. So, the next question is where do IP addresses come from and how do you get some?

Getting Your IP Addresses

If you are using Network Address Translation (NAT) to hide your network behind a firewall or proxy server with a public IP address, you don't need to worry about acquiring "legal" IP addresses for your network devices. ARIN (The American Registry for Internet Numbers), the organization responsible for leasing IP addresses, has set aside a range of addresses in each of the three address classes (A, B, C) for use with NAT. These ranges are

▶ Class A—10.0.0.0 to 10.255.255.255, with a subnet mask of 255.0.0.0

▶ Class B—172.16.0.0 to 172.31.255.255, with a subnet mask of 255.255.0.0

▶ Class C—192.168.0.0 to 192.168.255.255, with a subnet mask of 255.255.255.0

Now you will still need to acquire a public IP address for your firewall or proxy server that is supplying the NAT service. You can lease static IP addresses directly from your ISP. Charges vary from ISP to ISP, but based on my experiences with leasing additional static IP addresses for my own small business network, I have found the cost to be around $20 to $30 per month for each static IP address.

ISPs Prefer Dynamic Addressing

Most ISPs use a DHCP server to hand out IP addresses to subscribers. You will
have to call your ISP and discuss options related to static IP addressing.

By the
Way

If you work at a large company and need a large pool of IP addresses, you can go
to the actual source of IP addresses, ARIN to lease your addresses. ARIN is a not-
for-profit organization established to register (and administer) IP addresses for
North America, South America, the Caribbean, and sub-Sahara Africa.

The minimum number of addresses that can be leased from ARIN is 4,096, which
costs $2,500 per year. So, unless you work for a very large company, you will
have to acquire IP addresses from your ISP. For more information about ARIN,
check out its Web site at `http://www.arin.net/`.

IP Addressing Around the World

IP addressing for the rest of the world is managed by two other organizations. The
RIPE Network Coordination Centre handles Europe, the Middle East, and the parts of
Africa not serviced by ARIN. APNIC (Asia Pacific Network Information Centre) handles
the Asian Pacific region.

By the
Way

Configuring Network Devices for TCP/IP

One option for supplying devices (or nodes, as I mentioned earlier) on the network with IP addresses is to configure the computer or other device with a static
IP address and subnet mask. An alternative to static IP addressing is dynamically
assigning IP addresses (and other TCP/IP configuration information) using the
Dynamic Host Configuration Protocol (DHCP), which requires that a network
server provide the DHCP service. DHCP clients on the network receive their IP
addresses and subnet masks dynamically. I will discuss DHCP in more detail later
in this hour.

Static IP Settings on Servers

Network servers that provide services such as DNS (discussed later in this hour)
and DHCP (and other special servers such as Web servers, mail servers, and in
some cases print or file servers) require a static IP address.

Did you
Know?

Servers Providing Network Directory Services Require Static IP Addresses

Servers that provide directory services typically require a static IP address. For example, in the Windows Server 2003 environment, the Domain Controller providing the network with the Active Directory must be configured with a static IP address. The same is true for NetWare servers providing the eDirectory for the network.

Each network operating system (and client OS platform for that matter) will provide its own mechanism for configuring a computer with a static IP address and subnet mask. In most cases, the IP address and subnet mask can be configured during the process of installing the NOS on the server or can be configured after the installation has been completed.

Let's take a look at configuring a server running Windows Server 2003. The TCP/IP settings are configured in the Internet Protocol (TCP/IP) Properties dialog box (which is accessed via the Local Area Connection Properties dialog box for the server). Figure 14.1 shows the Internet Protocol (TCP/IP) Properties dialog box.

FIGURE 14.1
Entering an IP address and subnet mask on a Windows server.

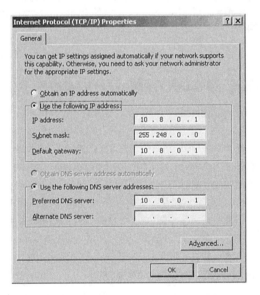

In Figure 14.1, you can see that the IP address and subnet mask are not the only information that you must provide when configuring a computer such as a server for the TCP/IP protocol stack. You must also supply the default gateway for the server, which is the router interface connected to the segment that the server resides on (more about router interfaces and IP addresses in a moment).

Another piece of information that must be included in the TCP/IP configuration is the IP address of the primary DNS server used for name resolution by the server. Large networks might deploy multiple DNS servers, so there is also the option of providing alternative DNS server IP addresses. In the case of Windows networks, you might also be deploying WINS servers, so the IP address of the WINS server would also need to be included in the TCP/IP configuration of the server (which is entered by clicking the Advanced button shown on the dialog box in Figure 14.1).

Did you **Know?**

What Is WINS?

On a Windows network that is running pre-Windows 2000 clients (such as the 9x family), you might need to deploy a WINS (Windows Internet Naming Service) server. Legacy Windows desktop operating systems still use NetBIOS names as the "friend-ly" naming system for the computers (as opposed to DNS on newer versions of the Windows OS). This means that clients on the network can eat up a lot of bandwidth sending out broadcasts that are used to resolve NetBIOS names to IP addresses. A WINS server takes care of the NetBIOS name to IP address resolution (and vice versa), which cuts down on client broadcasts and frees up valuable network band-width. For more about networking in the Windows environment, see *Sams Teach Yourself Microsoft Windows Server 2003 in 24 Hours*.

So, you can see that the TCP/IP configuration for a server requires more informa-tion than just the IP address and subnet mask. Configuring a server with an incomplete TCP/IP configuration is asking for communication problems between the server and the rest of your network.

Static IP Settings on Network Clients

Depending on the scale of the network, you can also configure your network clients with static IP addresses. You will find, however, that a network with even as few as 10 or 15 clients will require a great deal of your time in terms of config-uring them for TCP/IP. On larger networks, keeping track of the IP addresses that you have actually assigned and those that are still available can become a big headache.

This is why it makes sense to deploy a DHCP server. DHCP can configure a net-work client with an IP address and subnet mask and other TCP/IP configuration information, such as the default gateway and preferred DNS servers. Let's take a look at a better option for network client addressing—DHCP.

Understanding the Dynamic Host Configuration Protocol

The Dynamic Host Configuration Protocol (DHCP) evolved from a protocol called BOOTP. BOOTP was used to assign IP addresses to diskless workstations. BOOTP did not assign IP addresses, dynamically, however, but pulled IP addresses from a static BOOTP file that was created and maintained by the network administrator.

DHCP allows you to dynamically assign IP address to your network computers and other devices. IP addresses are taken from a pool of addresses and assigned to computers either permanently or for a fixed lease time. When you consider that you must configure every client computer on an IP network with such things as an IP address, a subnet mask, a default gateway address, and a DNS server address, you can see that there is an incredible margin for error.

DHCP actually simplifies much of the drudgery that would be involved in manual assignments of IP addresses. Most network operating systems—including Sun Solaris, the various Linux distributions, Novell NetWare, and Microsoft Windows Server 2003—provide the DHCP service.

So, how does DCHP work? Well, let's take a look at how a DCHP client (which is what you call a computer that is configured to receive its IP address dynamically) requests an IP address from a DHCP server.

When a DHCP client boots up for the first time, it goes looking for an IP address. The client initializes TCP/IP (a stripped down version) and broadcasts a DHCPDIS-COVER message, which is a request for an IP lease that is sent to all DHCP servers (addressed to 255.255.255.255, meaning all nodes on the network). This broadcast message contains the hostname of the client (which, in most cases, is also the client's NetBIOS name) and the MAC hardware address (the address burned into the computer's NIC) of the client.

In the next step, a DCHP server (or servers, if more than one is available) on the subnet will respond with a DHCPOFFER message that includes an offered IP address, an accompanying subnet mask, and the length of the lease. The message also contains the IP address of the DHCP server, identifying the server. The DHCPOFFER message is also in the form of a broadcast because the client does not have an IP address at this point.

When the client receives the first DHCPOFFER message (it might receive multiple offers, but it will go with the first appropriate offer that it receives), it will then broadcast a DHCPREQUEST message to all DHCP servers on the network, showing that it is accepting an offer. This broadcast message will contain the IP address of the DHCP server whose offer the client accepted. Knowing which DHCP server was selected enables the other DHCP servers on the network to retract their offers and save their IP addresses for the next requesting client. (Yes, it does sound a little bit like a used car lot.)

Finally, the DHCP server that supplied the accepted offer broadcasts an acknowledgement message to the client, a DHCPPACK message. This message contains a valid IP address lease and other TCP/IP configuration information. The client stores this information. For example, a client running a Windows operating system stores the TCP/IP configuration information in its Windows registry.

Deploying a DHCP Server

As already mentioned, most network operating systems can be configured to provide the DHCP service. We will take a look at providing the DHCP service on a network in Hour 17, "Common Network Services and How to Provide Them."

By the Way

Configuring a Network Client for DHCP

Configuring a network client or server as a DHCP server is very straightforward. Every client (or server for that matter) will provide a dialog box that allows you to configure settings related to the computer's network connection.

For example, if you look back at Figure 14.1, you can see that the server being configured in the figure could be made a DHCP client by clicking on the Obtain an IP Address Automatically option button. That's all there is to it. The computer is now a DHCP client.

Other client and NOS platforms also typically provide a GUI that allows you to configure the computer as a DHCP client. Figure 14.2 shows the Ethernet Device dialog box on a computer running Linux Red Hat. Note that this dialog box provides you with the option of configuring the computer as a DHCP client or with a static IP address.

A real time-saver related to deploying DHCP on your network is that most network clients are configured as DHCP clients by default. So, in most cases, you won't have to do any TCP/IP configuration on the clients. This allows you to spend your time setting up the pool of addresses and the other configuration settings required by the DHCP server.

FIGURE 14.2
Operating systems
provide a variety of
GUIs that make it
easy to configure
the TCP/IP proper-
ties for the
computer.

We will look at providing the DHCP service on a network in Hour 17. You will find that most network operating systems include this as a basic service of the NOS platform.

Understanding DNS

An solid understanding of how DNS works is essential for any network administrator or support staff. The **Domain Name System (DNS)** provides a hierarchical name resolution strategy for resolving a **Fully Qualified Domain Name (FQDN)** to an IP address. DNS servers provide this "friendly name" to logical address (the IP address) resolution on TCP/IP networks (such as the Internet) and are also capable of resolving IP addresses to FQDNs.

DNS was originally developed for the Internet, and you use DNS every time you connect to a Web address such as www.samspublishing.com. This friendly name is resolved by DNS servers on your network, with possibly help from DNS servers on the Internet, and the actual IP address of the Web site you want to navigate to is returned to your Web browser.

DNS and the Internet

By the
Way

In the 1980s, DARPA switched to TCP/IP as the protocol for the Internet. Needing a name resolution strategy, the Domain Name System was developed. During its development, it was determined that the naming system needed to be a distributed database, meaning that the information would be spread across the Internet on DNS servers that could query each other when name resolution was required for an unknown FQDN.

DNS servers talk to each other; this is how unknown FQDNs are resolved on the local network. So, all the DNS servers are really involved in a huge network. The DNS servers communicate by sharing information with their nearest DNS server neighbors. This allows requests and information to be passed around by DNS servers so that any FQDN can eventually be resolved. DNS servers learn from neighboring DNS servers, so this means that the local DNS database will grow as additional records are added to it because of local queries made for name resolution.

Before discussing how DNS works and how many DNS servers are really needed in different network situations, let's take a look at the DNS namespace. The DNS namespace provides the naming hierarchy for FQDNs.

The Domain Namespace

The domain namespace is the actual scheme used to name domains that are at different levels in the DNS domain hierarchical tree. The domain namespace also provides for how the down-level names of hosts (meaning individual computers and other devices on a network) are determined. Because of the way that the domain namespace hierarchy works, every host on an TCP/IP network (such as the Internet) ends up with a unique FQDN.

The domain namespace is divided into different levels or domains. Domain names can be up to 63 characters in length and must begin with a letter of the alphabet. Numerical entries and hyphens are also legal characters for domain names. Domain names are not case sensitive.

The domain namespace resembles an inverted tree. At the base of the DNS tree is the root domain. The Internet root domain is represented by a period. Below the root domain are the top-level domains. The top-level domains consist of suffixes such as .com, .edu, and so on. Some of the top-level domain names available are

- ▶ com—Used by commercial organizations. For example, samspublishing.com is the domain name for Sams Publishing.

- ▶ edu—Reserved for educational institutions. For example, une.edu is the domain name of the University of New England.

- ▶ org—Used by noncommercial organizations and institutions. For example, gsusa.org is the domain name of the Girl Scouts of America.

- ▶ gov—Reserved by the United States for governmental entities. For example, senate.gov is the domain for the U.S. Senate.

- ▶ net—To be used by companies involved in the Internet infrastructure such as ISPs.

- ▶ Country names—bs for the Bahamas, ga for Gabon, or uk for the United Kingdom.

- ▶ biz—A new top-level domain added recently to accommodate businesses.

- ▶ info—Another new top-level domain recently added, which can be used for informational Web sites (or just about anybody looking for a domain name).

Below the top-level domains are the second-level domains; these secondary domains consist of company, institutional, and private domains that we commonly use to access a Web site on the Web such as samspublishing.com (Sams Publishing's domain name). Under the second-level domains are found subdomains. These subdomains are typically used to divide a larger secondary domain into geographical or functional units. For example, if I have a company that uses the secondary domain name of *mydomain*.com and my business is divided into two distinct divisions (consulting and sales), I could create the two subdomains *consulting.mydomain*.com and *sales.mydomain*.com. The domain namespace and the second level domains that I have mentioned here are shown in Figure 14.3.

Second-level domains (and subdomains) will also contain hosts, which are the computers and other devices that reside within the second-level domain or subdomain name space. For example, if I have a computer named *admin1* and it is in the *sales.mydomain*.com subdomain, it will be referred to as *admin1.sales. mydomain*.com using the DNS naming conventions.

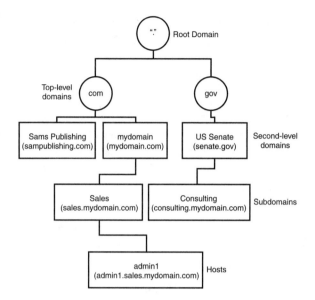

How DNS Works

Now that you have a feel for the DNS namespace, let's take a look at how DNS actually resolves IP addresses to FQDNs (and vice versa). First of all, there are two types of DNS servers: master and slave. The master server (which by definition would be the first DNS server you bring up on your network) is used to store the local name server database. This would be records for each host that provide the hosts FQDN and the accompanying IP address. So as far as creating records and fine-tuning the database are concerned, this is done on the master DNS server. Because a master is responsible for a certain part of the DNS database, it is referred to as being the master of its zone of authority.

> **DNS Zones and Records**
>
> Zones and different types of records play an important part in how DNS works. I discuss creating a zone and records in Hour 17.

By the Way

A slave DNS stores a copy of the master DNS database. This not only provides two options for computers attempting to resolve FQDNS, but it also adds some redundancy to the network. DNS service will continue even if the master DNS server goes down.

So, the DNS server (master or slave) will attempt to resolve FQDNs when requested by a network client (meaning a client in the DNS server's zone of authority). The client computers are capable of making requests of the DNS server because of an entity called the resolver. The resolver is built in to applications such as Web browsers that will require FQDN to IP address resolution.

When a client computer attempts to resolve a FQDN to an IP address, the resolver will check a local cache (if the resolver is set up to maintain a local cache; most network clients, no matter the OS, maintain a DNS cache) and see if the FQDN to IP address resolution information is available. If the information is in the cache, the process is over and the FQDN is resolved to an IP address by the client computer itself.

If the information is not available in the cache, the resolver software uses the IP address of the local DNS server, which is found in the client computer's TCP/IP settings, and sends a request to the local DNS server.

In cases in which the name to be resolved is for a host that is on the local network, the DNS server looks up the name in the DNS database and returns the appropriate IP address to the requesting computer. If the name is for a computer not on your domain, two things can happen: The name can be resolved using the cache maintained by the local DNS server; the server will cache or remember hostnames that it has previously resolved with the help of other DNS servers (such as those on the Internet). If the information is in this cache, the DNS server provides it to the requesting client.

In cases in which the information is not cached on the DNS server, your DNS server will contact the root server for the hostname's top-level domain by querying it with the host . The root server will use the hostname to determine the IP address of the authoritative DNS server for the domain that the particular host belongs to. Once your DNS server has the IP address of the other domain's DNS server, it can query that server, which will then supply the FQDN to IP address resolution information. The local DNS server can then pass this information on to the original requesting host.

Getting a Domain Name

Before you can configure a DNS server (or set up your network servers in some cases because the DNS hierarchy must be known for its configuration), you need a domain name. Also, if your company is going to have a presence on the Internet (particularly the World Wide Web), you need a domain name.

You can apply for domain names that end in `.com`, `.org`, or `.net` by contacting a domain name registration provider. (Sites ending in two-letter country codes are handled by other providers.) Whether you choose to be a `.com`, `.org`, or `.net` depends on the type of business you are conducting. Nonprofits would use `.org`, whereas `.com` is best for most businesses. In cases in which the domain name you want to use is not available in the `.com` realm, you can take advantage of the new suffix `.biz` for your business domain name.

A number of registration providers are available on the Web. For example, the InterNIC Domain Services, a registration provider at `http://internicdomainservices.com`, can be used to register your domain name. (This is just one of many providers and is only being used as an example, not as a recommendation.) InterNIC Domain Services also supplies a search engine you can use to determine whether the domain name you want to use is already taken.

When you apply for your domain name, you will also need to know how DNS services will be handled for your domain. Either you deploy your own DNS servers, or you use the DNS servers provided by the ISP that is connecting you to the Internet.

The cost of a domain name is fairly nominal when you consider that it can help to greatly increase the visibility of your company when used to establish your presence on the Web with a Web site. Believe it or not, the fees for registering and maintaining your domain name will vary among domain name registration providers. You should do a little research before you select a provider. Also be advised that ICANN (Internet Corporation for Assigned Names and Numbers) limits the leasing of a particular domain name to 10 years. To find a list of ICANN approved domain name providers, check out the ICANN site at `http://www.internic.net/`.

Summary

In this hour, we took a look at IP addressing and configuring network computers with IP addresses. We also discussed the use of DHCP to dynamically assign IP addresses to network clients and servers. We took a look at how DNS resolves FQDNs to IP addresses (and IP addresses to FQDNs) and looked at the domain namespace.

Q&A

Q *Why might a computer configured with a static IP address not be communicating on the network?*

A A simple typo, such as an incorrect subnet mask or default DNS server IP address, can keep a computer from communicating on a network. Always check your TCP/IP configuration for your device. In cases in which you have inadvertently used the same IP address on more than one device, both devices will be unable to communicate on the network.

Q *How does the deployment of DHCP cut down on TCP/IP configuration errors?*

A Because IP addresses, subnet masks, and other TCP/IP related information such as default gateways are dynamically assigned to nodes on the network by the DHCP server, the possibility of errors related to statically entering this data on each computer is dramatically cut down.

Q *How should I determine the domain name that I want to register for my company?*

A The domain name should be descriptive of your company and can be the company name or a descriptive term that describes what the company does. The domain name should be easy to remember (long or complex domain names aren't very good marketing strategies) and should be as unique as possible. Spend some time on the Web using a site that allows you to search for whether your domain name is available, and you might want to check out what types of companies have similar names to the name you want to use.

HOUR 15

Microsoft Networking

In this hour, you will learn about the following topics:

- ▶ The Microsoft logical network structure
- ▶ Installing and configuring a Microsoft server
- ▶ Configuring network clients and network protocols
- ▶ How resources are shared on a Microsoft network
- ▶ Managing a Microsoft server

Although certainly not one of the first big players in the network operating system market, Microsoft has been in the networking business since the early 1980s. Early networking efforts, such as the development of NetBEUI and OS/2, were collaborative efforts with IBM. LAN Manager was an early effort at Microsoft to develop a network operating system.

In 1992, Microsoft launched Microsoft Windows NT Server 3.1, which was the first version of its NT or New Technology network operating systems. The latest version in this line is Microsoft Windows Server 2003, and we will look at this NOS in this chapter. We will also take a look at how Microsoft's directory service provides the logical networking structure and how a server running Microsoft Windows Server 2003 shares resources and is managed.

Microsoft's Logical Network Structure

When Microsoft Windows NT Server 4.0 became available in the marketplace, Microsoft definitely had a hit on its hands. The Microsoft NOS made huge gains in the number of server installations worldwide.

Despite the fact that Windows NT Server 4.0 became a huge hit, it still only supplied a "flat" directory services model for managing users and resources. The basic administrative unit for the Microsoft network was the **domain** (and still is, but in a slightly different context, so read on). A domain can be defined as a collection of servers (although a domain only needs one server), client machines, users, and other network resources that are managed by a **domain controller**. The domain controller is a server running the Windows NOS, and it is responsible for user authentication and maintaining the database of user accounts and resources.

> ### Large Domains Required Backup Domain Controllers
> In situations in which a Windows NT domain grew a great deal or an administrator wanted to add some redundancy to the domain user database, backup domain controllers (or BDCs) could be deployed on the network. These servers also running the NT 4.0 NOS could authenticate users and replicate the user database with the main domain controller as well.

In the case of Windows NT, the domain model did not provide any type of branching, "tree" hierarchy such as was provided by Novell's NetWare Directory Service or NDS. (NetWare is discussed in Hour 10, "Selecting Network Hardware and Software.") So, the domain model really provided you with a kind of "bucket" or container in which you lumped all your network computers, users, and resources. And this model worked just fine; according to Microsoft, a single domain could handle over 10,000 users.

However, the domain model did prove to be unwieldy on very large networks (from a management perspective) since the network had to be divided up into different domains or separate containers that shared resources using trusts. A **trust** (which is still used in the Windows networking environment) is a relationship between two domains that enable the domains to share resources.

With each domain having its own domain controller (and backup domain controllers) and also trusts with other domains, network administrators had a lot of issues to deal with in managing a network using this domain structure. Think of a number of containers connected by garden hoses. You need to keep the water level equal in all the containers. Got it? Now you understand what it was like (and still is like on NT networks) to try and balance bandwidth, user access, and resource availability on a domain-based network.

The Master Domain Model Deploys a User Domain and Resource Domains

In very large Windows NT implementations, Microsoft urged network administrators to use the Master domain model. This consisted of a domain that contained the users and groups, which then had trust relationships with domains that contained network resources; these domains were referred to as resource domains.

By the Way

With the release of Microsoft Windows 2000 Server, the flat domain model was abandoned by Microsoft and the Active Directory became the new logical hierarchy for Microsoft networks. Active Directory provides a tree structure that allows you to create a branching logical structure for your network that can contain multiple domains. The domain still serves as the basic unit of the Microsoft network structure, and each domain is still managed by a domain controller. (With Active Directory, multiple domain controllers can be deployed in a domain.)

The next largest unit in the Active Directory structure is a tree. A **tree** consists of a root domain, which is the first domain that you bring online. Trees can contain multiple domains (including the root domain). Domains that are added to the tree are considered child domains (see Figure 15.1). All domains in the tree have implicit transitive trusts with the other domains in the tree. Transitive trusts create a two-way street between domains, meaning that they share each other's resources equally.

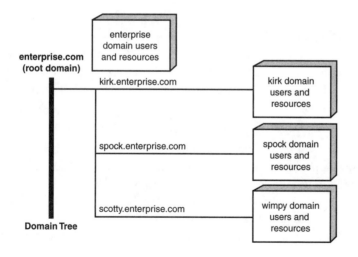

FIGURE 15.1
The Active Directory structure provides for a tree that contains a root domain and child domains.

To create a Microsoft network, you need to bring a domain controller online and create the root domain for the Active Directory tree. Very large networks can actually deploy multiple trees. And of course multiple trees can exist, which constitutes a forest. (I'm not kidding; it's called a forest.) Let's take a look at issues related to installing and configuring a Microsoft server running Windows Server 2003, which is the latest version of Microsoft's powerful NOS.

Installing and Configuring a Microsoft Server

Microsoft Windows Server 2003 requires a minimum hardware configuration to run (as does any software). The minimum hardware requirements and recommendations from Microsoft are listed here for the standard version of Windows Server 2003:

▶ CPU speed: 133MHz (550MHz recommended)

▶ RAM: 128MB (256MB recommended; 4GB maximum on Standard Server)

▶ Disk space for setup: 1.5GB

▶ CD-ROM drive: 12X

▶ Monitor: Super VGA capable of providing 800×600 resolution

The minimum hardware probably won't get you very far particularly in situations in which you are going to add a lot of users and services to the network. You probably should go with a processor in excess of 2GHz and have at least 512MB of RAM. You also want to have SCSI drives on your server so that you can take advantage of different RAID implementations that help protect server data and the system files.

Not only must you meet the minimum hardware requirements to successfully install and run Windows Server 2003, but you also must have a server that provides hardware proven to be compatible with the network operating system. If you are going to use the server in a true production environment in which you must supply mission-critical services to network users, your server hardware must come right off the Microsoft Windows Server 2003 Hardware Compatibility List. A copy of the list is available at http://www.microsoft.com/windowsserver2003/default.mspx.

Did you Know?

Windows Server 2003 Is Available in Different Versions

Windows Server 2003 is available in different editions: Standard Edition, Enterprise Edition, Datacenter Edition, and Web Edition. Standard is considered the entry-level edition of the NOS. The Enterprise Edition supports more processors and server clustering and is considered the workhorse for very large networks. The Datacenter Edition provides advanced clustering features and is only available through Microsoft's Datacenter program. Both Enterprise and Datacenter will be available for the 64-bit environment. The Web Edition is actually a scaled-down version of the NOS and is designed to serve as a Web server only. Another edition of Server 2003, Windows Small Business Server 2003 Standard Edition, includes Windows Server 2003 and a number of Exchange Server 2003 services.

When you have a server with the appropriate hardware in place, you are ready to install the Windows Server 2003 software. The server software provides you with the ability to perform a clean install or upgrade earlier versions of the operating system. It is really best to start with a clean system if possible. Although time-consuming, this allows you to configure all server settings from scratch, particularly security settings as they relate to this particular version of the OS.

Existing domains and forests (in the case of Windows 2000 Server upgrades) must be prepared for upgrade using a utility called addprep that is contained on the Windows Server 2003 CD-ROM. If you are going to upgrade, you need to spend some time researching the upgrade process. The subject is really beyond the scope of this book. You can get a start at http://www.microsoft.com.

Let's take a quick look at the installation process. We can then take a look at configuring a server as a domain controller and other roles such as a file server.

Watch Out!

Create a Network Diagram Before Creating the First Domain

The installation and configuration process for Microsoft Windows Server 2003 is very straightforward and can probably be categorized as "easy." But this doesn't mean that you should bring your server online before you plan your network. Create a network diagram and think about how you want to grow the network and the domains over time. For more about writing network specifications, see Hour 9, "Designing a Network."

The Installation Process

A clean installation of Windows Server 2003 on a server-class computer is very straightforward. You can actually boot from the CD-ROM drive. (You might have to go into your BIOS setup and change the boot sequence for the server.) Once the server has booted to the Windows Server CD-ROM, you are walked through a text phase that allows you to specify (and create if necessary) the drive partition that will contain the operating system. You are also provided with an opportunity to format the partition.

Windows Server 2003 supports three different file systems—FAT, FAT32, and NTFS. FAT is a legacy from DOS, and FAT32 was first available with the Windows 95 OS. NTFS 5 is the newest version of the NT file system and provides greater security for files with support for file system recovery. You really need to go with NTFS as the file system for your server because it is required by the Active Directory.

After you've taken care of the target partition for the NOS, the server will boot into a Windows-like environment that walks you through the remainder of the installation. You can set additional networking settings during the process such as adding network protocols; the default is TCP/IP. By default, the server is also assigned to a workgroup named WORKGROUP.

It is a good idea to go with all the defaults during the installation process. It is actually easier to change settings once the NOS is fully installed on the server. After the installation is complete, the system will reboot and you will be allowed to log in to the server using the administrative password that you set during the installation process. When you have the server up and running, you can configure it for particular roles and services. Let's take a look at some of the configuration options.

Configuring a Windows 2003 Server

Configuring a Windows 2003 server as a domain controller, file server, or to provide other services such as Remote Access, DNS, or DHCP is very straightforward. In fact, Windows Server 2003 provides the Manage Your Server window (it opens the first time you run the NOS), which can help you add, remove, and manage all the server's different roles. Figure 15.2 shows the Manage Your Server window. The Manage Your Server window lists the current roles filled by the server. It also makes it very easy to add new roles.

For example, if you want to make the server a domain controller (which would be necessary to create a new root domain for the network), you can select the Add or Remove a Role link in the Manage Your Server window. This starts the Configure Your Server Wizard, which lists all the possible roles for a server, such as file server, print server, domain controller, DNS server, and so on.

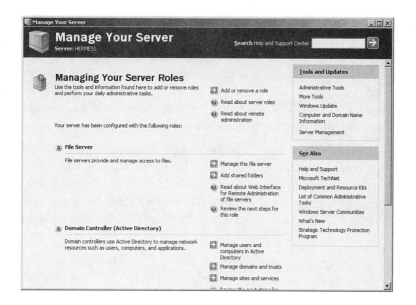

FIGURE 15.2
The Manage Your
Server window
makes it easy to
configure your
Windows 2003
server.

To add a role, all you have to do is select the role in the configure Your Server Wizard window and click next. In the case of making a server a domain controller, the Configure Your Server Wizard walks you through the steps of making the server a domain controller in a new forest and tree. During the process, you will have to supply a full DNS domain name for the root domain you are creating. Figure 15.3 shows the wizard screen that asks for the Active Directory Domain Name.

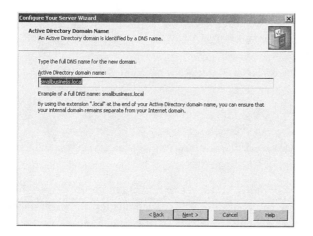

FIGURE 15.3
The Configure Your
Server Wizard
makes it easy to
add roles to the
server.

If services such as DNS or DHCP are not currently available on the network, the wizard can also configure the server to provide these services. After the process is complete, the new role (in this case, domain controller) is added to the Manage Your Server window, making it easy to manage a particular role. For example, after you add the domain controller role, you can quickly start the different Active Directory tools, such as the Active Directory Users and Computers snap-in, directly from the Manage Your Server window.

The Active Directory Users and Computer snap-in is used to manage Active Directory objects such as users, groups, and computers. Figure 15.4 shows the Active Directory Users and Computers snap-in. You will find that all the Windows server utilities have the same look and feel as this particular snap-in because all the tools run in the Microsoft Management Console. This provides a common interface for managing the server.

Obviously, you must create a user account for each user who will access resources on the network. Clients are added using the Active Directory Users and Computers snap-in.

FIGURE 15.4
The Active Directory Users and Computer snap-in is used to manage users, groups, and computers in the domain.

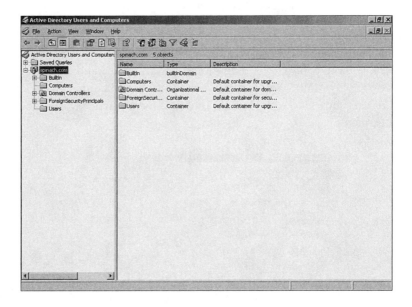

After you set up a domain, you have to add client computers to the domain. Let's take a look at how you configure Window clients for domain membership and also configure their network protocols so that they can talk to the domain controller.

By the Way

Microsoft Windows Server 2003 Is a Rich and Complex Network Operating System

Windows Server 2003 can be configured for many network services such as DNS and DHCP, and it can provide terminal and remote services to client computers both on the network and over remote connection. All the details related to configuring and managing a Windows server are beyond the scope of this book. For more information see *Sams Teach Yourself Microsoft Windows Server 2003 in 24 Hours* by Joe Habraken.

Configuring Windows Clients for Domain Membership

Configuring Windows clients to participate in a domain requires that you make them a domain member. You also have to make sure that the client is configured with at least one of the network protocols that is configured on the server. This typically is not an issue because Windows Server 2003 is configured with TCP/IP by default, as is Microsoft Windows XP Professional. However, we will still take a look at how you work with network protocols on a Windows client (because the information is also applicable in situations in which you are configuring a Windows peer-to-peer workgroup).

Adding Client Computers to the Domain

A domain client can be running any of the different versions of Windows from the current Windows XP Professional to Windows 98 and all the way back to Windows for Workgroups 3.11 (even MS-DOS). However, let's focus on adding a Windows XP Professional computer to the network because in terms of new implementations, this would be the operating system of choice for your clients.

By the Way

Microsoft Windows Server Can Supply Services to Non-Windows Operating Systems

A Microsoft Windows server can also supply services to Macintosh and UNIX/Linux computers. In both cases, special services are added to the server so that it can interact with these "special" clients.

For users (who already have a valid user account in the Active Directory) to log on to the network using one of your network client computers (those that are running Windows NT 4, Windows 2000, or Windows XP Professional), the computer itself must also be added to the domain. There are two ways to add the computer to the Active Directory. You can add it on the server using the Active Directory Users and Computers snap-in. Or, you can add the client by changing the computer's current membership on the Computer Name tab on the System Properties dialog box. The second method requires that you run around to each of the client computers or provide users with the administrative rights to add their computers to the domain (which probably isn't that great of an idea in terms of network security).

Try it Yourself   Adding a Computer to the Domain

▼

In this section, we will look at how you add a computer to a Windows domain using the Active Directory Users and Computers snap-in.

1. Click the Start menu, point at Administrative Tools, and then select Active Directory Users and Computers.

2. In the snap-in tree, click the Computer node.

3. Right-click in the snap-in Details pane (on the right side of the snap-in), and on the shortcut menu that appears, point at New and then select Computer. This opens the New Object-Computer dialog box as shown in Figure 15.5.

FIGURE 15.5
Enter the name of the computer that is being added to the domain.

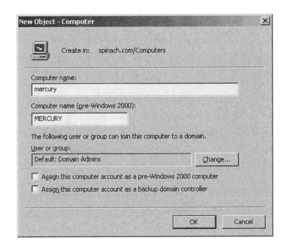

4. Enter the computer's name in the Computer name box.

5. Click OK to add the computer to the domain.

The computer is now part of the domain. Users can log on to the domain via the computer.

Adding a Client to the Domain from the Client Computer

To add a client to the domain from the client computer, log in as the administrator
and then right-click on the My Computer icon on the Start menu or the Desktop.
Select Properties from the shortcut menu that appears. On the Computer Name tab
of the Properties dialog box, click the Network ID button. The Network Identification
Wizard will open. It walks you through the steps of adding the computer to the Active
Directory. If you aren't logged in as a domain administrator, you will have to provide
the name and password for an account that has the rights to add a computer to the
domain to complete the process.

Configuring Network Protocols in Windows

You already know from earlier discussions in this book (such as Hour 5, "Network
Concepts") that if two computers are required to communicate over your network,
they must be configured with the same network protocol. TCP/IP is certainly the
de facto standard in terms of networking protocols. And the latest versions of the
Microsoft NOS (Windows Server 2003) and the Microsoft client (Windows XP
Professional) are both configured for TCP/IP by default. They are, however, configured to receive their IP addresses and subnet masks (as well as the primary DNS
server IP address and other IP-related settings) from a DHCP server. (DHCP is discussed in more detail in Hour 14, "TCP/IP.")

You can access your network connection in both Windows XP and Windows
Server 2003 via the Network Connections icon in the Control Panel. Right-clicking
on any local area connection (typically clients will only have one NIC; servers
can have multiple NICs, particularly if they are acting as routers, firewalls, or
supplying the Internet connection to a small network) allows you to open the
Properties dialog box for that connection. Figure 15.6 shows the local area connection Properties dialog box for a Windows XP network client.

You can add protocols to the connection's properties by clicking the Insert button
and then selecting a new protocol. Since NetBEUI is no longer supported by
Windows XP, your only real alternative to TCP/IP is NWlink, which is the
Microsoft implementation of Novell's IPX/SPX.

Configuring a network protocol such as the Internet Protocol (TCP/IP) is just a
matter of selecting the protocol in the Properties dialog box and then clicking the
Properties button. Figure 15.7 shows the default settings for TCP/IP on a Windows
XP network client.

FIGURE 15.6
The Local Area
Connection
Properties dialog
box shows the
installed protocols
and allows you to
configure protocols
such as TCP/IP.

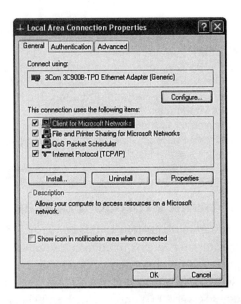

FIGURE 15.7
By default,
Windows XP clients
are configured to
get their IP address
dynamically from a
DHCP server.

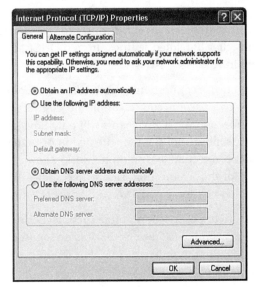

Note that the client is configured to get its IP address and subnet mask (as well as some other IP related settings) dynamically, meaning from a DHCP server (DHCP is discussed in more detail in Hours 14 and 17). To assign the client a static IP address, select the Use the Following IP address option button. You must then supply the IP address, subnet mask, and the default gateway (which is a router interface). You also need to provide other information such as the primary DNS server.

The Advanced button in the TCP/IP Properties dialog box allows you to set other settings related to the IP addressing. We discuss these settings in Hour 14.

Windows Servers Should Be Configured with Static IP Addresses

When you configure a network server for TCP/IP, you should assign the server a static IP address. This is essential for servers that act as domain controllers or provide services such as DNS or DHCP; even file servers should typically be assigned a static IP address. We discuss TCP/IP and IP addressing in more detail in Hour 14.

After you have set the static IP address for the client (or set up the client to receive its IP information dynamically from a DHCP server), you can click OK to return to the Local Area Connection Properties dialog box and then click OK to close it.

Sharing Folders and Printers on the Network

After you have configured your server, created user accounts, and connected clients to the domain, the next step is to share files and other resources such as printers. On a small network, a domain controller can also be configured as a file server, print server, and to offer services such as DNS or DHCP. On larger networks, you will deploy specialized servers to take care of one or more services.

On a Microsoft network, file or printer servers certainly do not have to be configured as domain controllers. They are merely member servers and are configured much the same as a network client. They must be added to the domain using the Active Directory Users and Computers snap-in and also configured for the appropriate network protocol (which, again, in most cases will be TCP/IP).

Adding a role to a member server running Windows Server 2003 has already been discussed earlier in this hour. You can use the Configure Your Server Wizard to configure a member server as a file server or a print server. In both cases, the wizard actually allows you to specify the files or the printer that will be shared on the network.

You can also manually share folders and drives on a server using Windows Explorer on the server. A shared resource such as a particular folder or a drive partition is referred to as a **share**. You can secure a share using share permissions. On a Microsoft network, you can also secure shares (right down to the file level) using NTFS permissions. NTFS permissions are available on drives that have been formatted with the NTFS file format. NTFS permissions allow you to secure a resource down to the file level.

To add a share to a file server using Windows Explorer, locate the folder (or create a new one). Right-click on the folder in the Windows Explorer window and select Sharing and Security on the shortcut menu that appears. This opens the folder's Properties dialog box with the Sharing tab selected, as shown in Figure 15.8.

FIGURE 15.8
Share a folder via the folder's Properties dialog box.

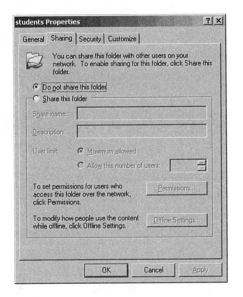

All you have to do is select the Share This Folder option button and then supply a share name for the folder. In cases in which you have pre-Windows 2000 Professional clients on the network, make sure that the share name is 15 characters or fewer, or these legacy clients will not be capable of seeing the share when they browse the network. The Sharing tab also allows you to set permissions related to the folder such as read/write permissions.

After you have set the share properties, you can close the dialog box (just click OK). The share will now be on the network.

You Can Create Hidden Shares

Administrators can set up hidden shares that network users cannot view using My Computer or Windows Explorer. When you create the share, follow the share name with a $ sign. Only administrators can see these "hidden" shares on the network.

Did you Know?

Sharing a printer on a Windows network is as simple as creating a share. After the printer has been installed on the server (both directly attached printers and network printers can be managed by a Windows print server), the printer can be shared by adding the print server role to the server using the Configure Your Server Wizard.

Although you can also share a printer via the printer's Properties dialog box, the Configure Your Server Wizard helps you locate the printer, such as a remote printer, and also runs an Add Printer Driver Wizard that makes sure that the print drivers (for the printer) needed by network clients can be downloaded from the print server when the client attaches to the printer. Figure 15.9 shows the Add Printer Driver Wizard screen where you select the operating systems running on the network that will need a driver for the printer.

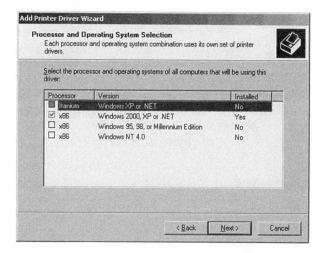

FIGURE 15.9
When you share a printer, you can also specify the print drivers that should be available for network clients.

A particular print server can actually be used to manage a number of printers directly connected to the network. (Most laser printers now have their own NICs for directly connecting to the network infrastructure.) Keep in mind that the print server must spool the print jobs, so the server will need to have a good amount of RAM and hard drive space. You don't want a print server to be a potential bottleneck on your network.

Managing a Microsoft Server

You've already seen the Active Directory Users and Computers snap-in, which is a good example of one of the Microsoft management utilities that runs in the Microsoft Management Module window. There are snap-ins for managing domain trusts, subnets, and specific services such as DNS, DHCP, and Routing and Remote Access.

Because we've already discussed creating shares and deploying a file server, let's take a look at the File Server Management snap-in. This tool allows you to see a list of users attached to the file server and also lists which files are being accessed. You can also use the snap-in to quickly create new shares and even back up the file server. Figure 15.10 shows the File Server Management snap-in.

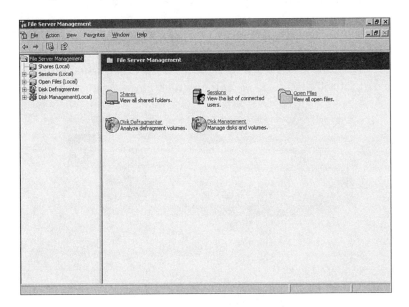

Obviously, there are a lot of other tools and utilities that are required to manage a Windows server. For example, you can monitor server and system performance using the System Monitor. The System Monitor allows you to add various objects to its window that supply you with counters related to specific hardware performance on the server.

For instance, you could monitor such things as virtual memory or paging use on the computer (when this graph spikes, it's time to add more RAM to the server) or monitor the processor by looking at the % Processor Time. Figure 15.11 shows the System Monitor snap-in window. It can provide statistics in a graph, histogram (similar to a bar chart), or a report view. Figure 15.11 shows the graph view.

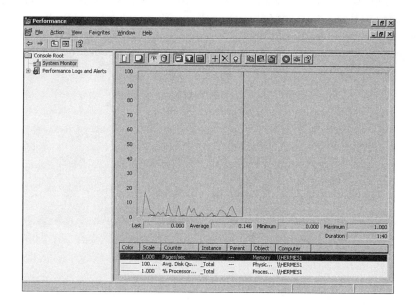

FIGURE 15.11
The System Monitor allows you to monitor server hardware usage.

You will find that managing a server not only requires that you keep a tab on the various services you are running on the network, but you really need to keep an eye on how servers are performing as well.

Baselining New Servers

Whenever you bring new servers online (any type of server: file server, domain controller, and so on), you should use a performance and monitoring tool to record baseline performance settings for the server's hard drive, memory usage, and processor. Baselining and performance monitoring is discussed in Hour 21, "Network Troubleshooting Tips and Tricks."

Summary

Although you might not think that setting up and configuring a Windows server is quite easy, don't be deceived by the fact that the tools are easy to use. The overall level of understanding and experience to appropriately configure a Microsoft network and keep it up and running is quite high. We have barely even scratched the surface in terms of server management and Microsoft networking in this hour. Many information resources are available at www.microsoft.com and check out www.samspublishing.com for both hands-on and reference books related to Windows Server 2003.

Q&A

Q *In a domain that has multiple domain controllers, is it possible to "decommission" a domain controller and use it for another purpose without reinstalling the Windows NOS?*

A Windows Server 2003 makes it easy to promote and demote servers as far as the domain controller role is concerned. If you have more than one domain controller and want to repurpose a server, you can remove the Active Directory from the computer without reinstalling the server NOS.

Q *How should I approach protecting network shares in terms of assigning permission levels?*

A Although you can assign permissions for a share to each individual user, the best way to assign permissions is to create groups in the Active Directory (such as accountants or sales) where the members of the group will need the same type of permission level for the share. You can then assign the permission level to the group, saving you a lot of time and keeping your assigned permissions better organized.

Q *As far as a quick look at how a server has been configured, where is the best place to get this information?*

A The Manage Your Server window provides a quick view of the roles that have been assigned to a server such as domain controller, file server, DNS server, and so on. The Manage Your Server window also provides quick access to the Configure Your Server Wizard, which allows you to modify the server's configuration.

HOUR 16

UNIX and Linux Networking

In this hour, you will learn about the following topics:

▶ A short history of UNIX

▶ Basic UNIX concepts

▶ UNIX and networking

▶ Working with Linux

Even if you are relatively new to the world of computer networking, you know that a number of software vendors vigorously compete for market share in the network operating system business. (An incredible amount of money is spent by these software companies just for advertising on television.) One of the first "networked" operating systems was UNIX. In this hour, we take a look at a short history of UNIX, and we will also look at the basics of how UNIX works.

We will also spend some time exploring Linux, an open-source UNIX derivative. Linux is open source and offers some interesting alternatives to other NOS platforms.

How UNIX Got Its Start

In the late 1960s, AT&T Bell Laboratories started work on a multiuser operating system, an operating system that could support more than one user session at a time, called Multics. Programmers made fun of it; it was large, slow, and unwieldy, built by rules generated by management committees. Multics wasn't extensible, either; the resources that came with the system represented the total sum of resources available to the system.

In an attempt to show up the Multics programming team, several ardent AT&T Bell Labs programmers set out to build a small, fast multiuser operating system that would be easily extensible and would encourage users to modify the system to suit their needs. When the dust settled, they had created exactly what they set out to create, and in a poke at the Multics crew, they named their operating system **UNIX**. (UNIX, implying one, versus Multics, implying many—get it?)

Initially, UNIX was considered an OS for the computer geek and wasn't taken seriously as an enterprise network operating system platform. After all, it wasn't your typical OS monolith of code and was also highly modular, allowing for the addition of operating system modules on-the-fly—and it hadn't been written in the typical plan-it-to-death corporate fashion. Obviously, you are looking at the reasons why UNIX wasn't taken seriously, such as its small modular design, and wondering why these were negatives. Well, it was the mindset of the times in the corporate world. However, a number of people found the small and modular design of UNIX (coupled with the fact that it was very inexpensive) a very compelling reason to use UNIX. Educational institutions and engineering businesses got on the bandwagon simply because UNIX could run on computers with less power than the high-end systems that ran operating systems such as IBM's VM or Digital's VMS. It made sense for people without deep pockets; they could get mainframe power for microcomputer prices. Although it was an inexpensive NOS, the original AT&T version of UNIX ran on very few hardware platforms.

In the mid-1970s, UNIX was rewritten from the ground up in the C programming language. Code written in C can be modified and recompiled to run on different types of computer hardware. The ultimate result of this was that UNIX became available for multiple machine types; every distribution of UNIX included the source code or the C language code; that source code could be recompiled or translated into computer code that could run on almost any platform.

In 1978 Billy Joy, a graduate student at the University of California at Berkeley (he was mentored by Ken Thompson, one of the original UNIX programmers who was on sabbatical at Berkeley), developed an alternative to the AT&T version of UNIX named the Berkeley Software Distribution or BSD. All the recent versions of UNIX originate from either the AT&T version or the Berkeley Software Distribution (including Linux, see the note that follows).

SCO Versus Linux

AT&T actually sold the UNIX trademark and licensing rights to Novell in the early 1990s. Then Novell turned around a few years later and sold the rights to the Santa Cruz Operation, or SCO, a company that creates SCO OpenServer and OpenDesktop, some of the most popular Intel-compatible UNIX products. In 2003, SCO made claims that programs within Linux were stolen from its UNIX intellectual property. Linux programmers including Linus Torvald, the "father" of Linux, denied these claims. But SCO has gone on to take IBM to court and has set the Linux community on edge. SCO also attempted to block Novell's acquisition of SUSE Linux, a popular version of Linux. SCO has also announced that it is actually considering suing individual Linux users over copyright infringements. Interestingly, SCO company servers were hit by two denial of service attacks late in 2003.

Many different types of UNIX installations are being used today. On the low end, Linux—an open source, primarily Intel-compatible version of UNIX—is used as a powerful, capable, and relatively inexpensive Web and mail server by many organizations. Network operating systems such as Novell are integrating Linux code and compatibility into their server platforms. At the next level, UNIX is used to run workstation computers—typically, Sun Microsystem's SunOS or Solaris running on a Sun-compatible SPARC box, Silicon Graphics' INDY machines, IBM's AIX running on RS/6000s, or Hewlett-Packard's HP-UX running on PA-RISC. Some of these machines aren't used as servers; instead, they're used as programming or engineering workstations running very complex and high-end graphic intensive software.

Now that you have a little bit of the UNIX history under your belt, let's take a look at UNIX concepts. We can then take a look at Linux, the UNIX clone.

Basic UNIX Concepts

An extremely important concept when working on a UNIX platform is that everything is really considered a file. This means that hard drives and other hardware devices, as well as program and data files, are all seen in UNIX as a file, meaning that you can read and write to them. For example, in the case of writing to the computer hard drive, UNIX sees it as writing to a special kind of file called a block device.

Second, UNIX has standard input and output, which is also called **redirection**. Standard input and output, from a UNIX perspective, means that you can chain programs together and stream the output from one file into the input of the next program in the chain. For instance, there's a command in UNIX to list all of the programs (in UNIX, they're called processes) called ps. If you type ps at a UNIX command-line terminal, it will tell you which processes are running. But if you're at a command-line screen, you're often limited to the 25 lines that the screen has, so the output of the ps command will scroll across your screen way too fast for you to read.

But you can redirect the output of the ps command to a command called more, which displays only one screen of data at a time, by typing ps ¦ more. This would give you the output of the ps command, but only display it one screen at a time, while you used the spacebar to scroll through all the pages of output. The ¦ symbol is called a pipe because, in this case, it "pipes" data from the output of one command into the input of the next.

In most operating systems, you have to do a significant amount of programming to be able to filter or modify the contents of a file. In UNIX, however, this isn't the case. UNIX is basically a kernel, the very center of the operating system; a series of small, modular programs with very focused purposes can be run on-the-fly. Using standard input (the keyboard or a file), standard output (the screen), and pipes (represented by the ¦ character), it is possible to pass data between programs and accomplish a variety of complex tasks right from the command line.

Pipes are neat, but they don't do everything that you need for redirection. Let's say that you want to take the output of a particular ps command and put it into a file so that you can read it in a text editor and print it. You could, at that point, type ps > /tmp/ps-output. What this would do is take the output of the ps command and redirect it into a file in the /tmp directory called ps-output. (This filename is ad-hoc; you can name a file whatever you want to.) Literally, this command would be read as, "run a ps command and redirect the output of it to the file /tmp/ps-output."

Pretty simple, no? What happens if you want to create a log file that just keeps having new information tacked onto the end of the file? Simple. Instead of using >, you use >> to make the command ps >> /tmp/ps-output. If you read *this* command literally, you'd get the following: "run a ps command and put the output into the /tmp/ps-output file. If there is an existing /tmp/ps-output file, don't overwrite it; instead, append the new output to the end of the existing /tmp/ps-output file."

The third UNIX concept is that every file on a UNIX system is mounted in a hierarchical file system. The file system starts with a slash / and is called the root file system. This logically includes the whole world (of the system). Disk drives are resources mounted within subdirectories of the root file system; consequently, all the disk space available within a system is theoretically available to any file system. Figure 16.1 shows the root of the file system on a computer running Sun Solaris UNIX and the subdirectories contained. (Linux uses a similar hierarchy.) The ls or list command was used to view the contents of the root directory.

```
# ls
TT_DB       dev         home        mnt         platform    usr
bin         devices     kernel      net         proc        var
boot        etc         lib         nsmail      sbin        vol
cdrom       export      lost+found  opt         tmp         xfn
#
```

FIGURE 16.1
The file hierarchy of UNIX/Linux.

UNIX enables file systems to use available disk space, whether there's 1 disk or 50 in the system. This makes UNIX file systems greatly extensible. Because more than one file system can span more than one disk, the concept of file system becomes independent of the concept of physical disk. In this way, UNIX makes efficient and extraordinarily flexible use of disk space.

It's difficult to cite a particular directory hierarchy as definitive for UNIX/Linux, but there are some fairly common standards. Table 16.1 shows a list of standard UNIX file systems and their uses.

TABLE 16.1 The Organization of a Typical UNIX File System

/	The root of the file system. This is the logical base for every other file system on the computer. The root file system usually contains the /dev directory, where devices such as hard drives and serial port (also called **ttys**, short for **teletypes**) are stored; the /etc directory, where password and group files are stored; and /bin, where system binaries are stored.
/usr	/usr is used for a variety of software available to users. Often, files in /usr/bin won't be "real" files, but will be special links to files stored in the /bin directory in the root file system. IBM installs a great deal of system software, such as compilers, under the /usr directory.
/var	/var is used for accounting and other *variable* items such as log files. /var/adm/logs or /var/logs is where many system log files are stored by default.
/opt	/opt is not used by every UNIX system. It's used for *optional* software. HP-UX uses /opt to store things such as compilers and programming languages such as C.

TABLE 16.1   Continued

/home	/home is where users get to put their stuff. If you're a user on a UNIX system, you'll have a **home directory** that matches your logon name—for instance, Joe Smith might log on as *jsmith*, and his home directory would be /home/jsmith. In every user's home directory is a file called .*profile*, which runs when the user logs on. The .*profile* file sets environments, starts menus, and does a variety of other things because the user can modify it to do whatever he wants on log on.
/tmp	The /tmp file system is where stuff that doesn't have a place to go gets stored. On many systems, it's flushed when the system boots up, so it's not necessarily a good idea to store anything of real value there.

Finally, before closing out this section of the hour, we should visit one more concept related to UNIX. This is actually something discussed previously in this book related to best practices for networking—interoperability and adherence to Open Systems standards.

Because UNIX systems adhere to the open standards published by the Internet Engineering Task Force (IETF), they can interact with one another without significant problems. A UNIX from one vendor can interoperate with a UNIX from another vendor at the standards level without fear that one vendor's interface won't work with another vendor's interface. This is why things such as Web services and Internet email are so often entrusted to UNIX or Linux systems; they adhere to the standards that have been agreed upon by committee and therefore can work together easily. This reduces cost and makes UNIX a much more predictable system than highly proprietary operating systems.

UNIX/LINUX as a Network Platform

UNIX/LINUX servers can offer file and print services as well as more complex services, such as DNS and Web hosting. Deploying UNIX servers for the first time required a network administrator to deal with a fairly steep learning curve since the environment was really administered from the command line. With the advent of Windows and the Mac GUI, even UNIX aficionados could see the usefulness of a GUI interface. UNIX and Linux distributions now provide GUI interfaces, which makes it easy to become familiar with the services and features that the UNIX and Linux platforms provide. Figure 16.2 shows the KDE graphical interface (KDE or K Desktop Environment is an open source product) on a server running Red Hat Linux.

FIGURE 16.2
GUIs such as KDE Desktop make it easy to navigate a Linux-based computer.

When a UNIX or Linux installation is made on a server (or on a workstation, in the case of Solaris and many Linux distributions, you can do a workstation or server installation with the same installation media), a root account must be established. This root account is equivalent to the administrator or admin account found on other platforms such as Microsoft Windows or NetWare, respectively.

The root account is used to administer the system, meaning setting configurations, managing the system, and monitoring the system. Network administrators who deploy UNIX and Linux servers do not run the servers as root because leaving the system up and running with root logged in can cause some security holes. When the system administrator wants to configure or manage the server, all he has to do is quickly log in as the root, which can be done from the command line using the su command. Once the su command is invoked, the network administrator need only provide the root password as shown in Figure 16.3 (which shows a server running Red Hat Linux).

Notice that the command-line prompt in Figure 16.3 changed to # when the administrator logged in as root. After the administrator has finished working as root, he can log off of root (and back to the other user account that was entered during the system boot up). It's just a matter of typing exit and then pressing Enter.

FIGURE 16.3
The administrator
can quickly log in
as the root at the
command line.

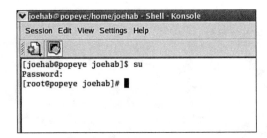

A great way to explore the possibilities of UNIX is to take a look at the open-source Linux platform. A number of different distributions of Linux are available. Many distributions can be downloaded free. In cases in which you would like support and easier access to system upgrades, you might want to purchase a particular Linux distribution.

By the Way

> ### Who Created Linux?
>
> Linux was created by Linus Torvalds when he was a student at the University of Helsinki. Linux is an open-system OS/NOS, and because the source code is freely available, a number of Linux distributions have popped up in the marketplace. Linux is similar to UNIX in many respects and uses a similar command set.

Red Hat Linux, SUSE Linux, and Mandrake Linux are some of the more popular distributions. Because the Linux kernel software operates under a free software licensing called the GNU General Public License, companies such as Red Hat are able to take the Linux kernel and add their own proprietary software code to create their own particular flavor of Linux. In the following sections, we will take a look at Red Hat Linux 8 in terms of network services and sharing resources on a network. You might want to download Red Hat Linux 8 ISOs from www.linux-iso.org and burn them to CDs. (An ISO is a software image of all the tracks on a CD-ROM. The ISO image can be burned to an actual CD, which in essence duplicates the original CD, such as an OS installation CD.) You can then install Red Hat (by booting from CD 1). The installation GUI walks you through the process of installing Red Hat. After you have a Red Hat system up and running, you can take a look at some of the features of tools that we discuss in this balance of this hour.

UNIX/Linux Hardware Requirements

UNIX/Linux distributions require slightly less muscle in terms of memory and processor speed than do some of the other platforms such as Windows and NetWare. However, as with any product, minimum hardware installations won't necessarily meet the needs of the network. For example, the base configuration for Sun Solaris version 9 running on a X86 32-bit server requires 64MB of RAM and 1GB of hard drive space. Linux Red Hat 8 actually requires a little more muscle; on a server with a 200 MHz or better processor, the base RAM required is 128MB with 2GB or more for a server installation.

By the Way

Network Services and Settings on a Linux Server

Servers running Linux distributions such as Red Hat can offer network services such as DNS, DHCP, and Web server. As far as server installations world wide, Linux actually comes in second to the Microsoft server platform (which is making Microsoft increasingly nervous). Configuring (and adding) network services to a Linux server requires that the administrator be logged in as root.

Providing Network Services

An overview of common network services and methods of providing them are covered in Hour 17, "Common Network Services and How to Provide Them."

By the Way

Network services can be configured from the command line or by using various GUI utilities. A common service deployed on Linux servers is that of Web server. Apache Web Server, which runs on Linux (and has been adapted to the latest version of Novell NetWare), is a very popular Web server platform and provides a very reliable and secure Web environment. Figure 16.4 shows the Apache Configuration utility, which can be used to set the server name and other settings related to the Web service.

Network settings for the server can also be configured via a GUI utility. The network configuration tool (or "neat" as it is referred to) allows you to view and configure network hardware devices (see Figure 16.5). It also provides you with the ability to configure TCP/IP protocol settings for a network interface. You can also create hostname to IP address mappings using the tool and enter information related to the DNS settings for your computer such as the hostname and DNS server settings.

FIGURE 16.4
GUI utilities make it easy to configure network services provided by a Linux server such as the Apache Web server.

FIGURE 16.5
The Network Configuration utility allows you to set parameters related to network connectivity.

Obviously, it is beyond the scope of this hour (and this book) to cover all the various command-line utilities and the GUIs that are provided to manage a Linux server. Interestingly (and unfortunately), you will find that unless you are using a proprietary customized distribution of Linux you purchased (such as some of the enterprise networking versions provided by Red Hat or SUSE), the "free" open source versions of Linux change like the wind. Very useful utilities come and go with each version of a particular distribution. This is mainly because of the open source nature of Linux; programmers build new utilities and then lose interest over time so that some very useful utilities never get upgraded and become unavailable.

The fact that the various GUI tools seem to come and go in the Linux environment is probably a fairly compelling reason to learn how to use the command line in Linux if you are seriously considering deploying Linux as a network server platform. Although any command line has somewhat of a steep learning curve, you will find that Linux commands (and the UNIX commands that they are based on) are fairly intuitive. For example, to add a user in Linux, you use the adduser command. Figure 16.6 shows the adding of a user kimrich with a password of password.

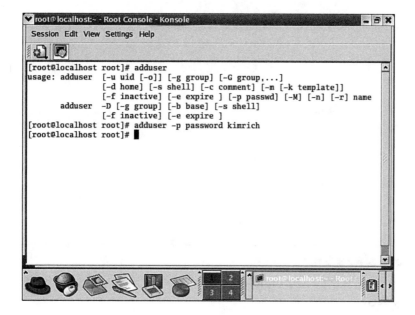

FIGURE 16.6
The adduser command and its various switches can be used to add users to a Linux system.

Options for Sharing Files

There is actually more than one option for sharing files on a Linux network. The **Network File System** (NFS was developed by Sun Microsystems for UNIX and has long been a mainstay of the UNIX world) is also available in the Linux environment, enabling Linux computers to share files using a Virtual File System interface that runs on top of the TCP/IP protocol. Shared files on a remote server can be manipulated by users as if the resources were stored locally on their computers.

NFS is a good example of a client/server environment in which a Linux computer can be configured as both a NFS client and server. To configure the NFS server, you can use the NFS Server Configuration tool in a GUI environment such as KDE or configure the NFS settings via the command line. Directories that you share using NFS are referred to as shares.

To open the utility from the KDE desktop, select the KDE menu, point at System Settings, and then select NFS Server. Figure 16.7 shows the NFS Server Configuration tool.

FIGURE 16.7
The NFS Server Configuration tool allows you to con-figure a NFS server.

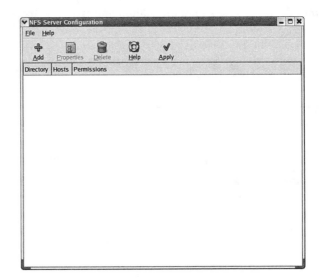

Try it Yourself   **Create a NFS Share**

In this section, we will look at how you add a NFS share to a Red Hat server using the NFS Server Configuration tool.

1. Click the Add button in the NFS Server Configuration tool. The new share dialog box opens.

2. Supply the directory name that you want to share. (You can use the Browse button to locate it.)

3. Specify the hosts that you will allow to access the share. You can specify hosts by hostnames (FQDN names) or IP addresses. To allow access from a number of hosts, you can use the asterisk (*) as a wildcard. For example, the entry of 192.168.186.* (as shown in Figure 16.8) allows all hosts in the 192.168.186 subnet to access the share. (IP subnets are discussed in Hour 14.)

4. You can also set the permissions to Read-Only or Read/Write by selecting the appropriate option button.

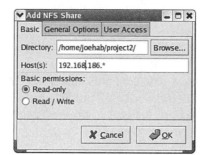

FIGURE 16.8
Specify the directory for the share and the hosts that can access the share.

5. You can also allow anonymous access to the share and set other access parameters, such as allowing remote root users to share local root privileges. Select the User Access tab on the Add NFS Share dialog box. Select the appropriate check boxes. You can also specify that anonymous users be assigned the privileges of a local user or assign the anonymous users to a particular group on the Linux computer.

6. When you have completed entering the information for the new share, click the OK button. The share will be listed in the NFS Server utility window.

After the share is configured, you must start the NFS service to make the share available. Click the Apply button in the NFS Server utility window. A message box will appear asking you if you want to start the NFS service. Click Yes. You now have a NFS share that can be accessed by users on the network.

Although NFS has also been ported over to the PC platform by Sun, an alternative way to integrate computers running Microsoft Windows and Linux and enable them to share resources, such as directories and printers, is called Samba. Samba derives its name from SMB, or Server Message Block. SMB is an important part of the NetBIOS protocol and supplies the data blocks that make requests between client and server or between peers on a Microsoft network.

Samba is able to simulate the operation of SMB and also provides NetBIOS over IP (TCP/IP being the protocol stack for Linux), which means that a Linux computer can actually pretend to be a Windows client. This means that the Linux machine can share folders and printers or access folders and printers in the workgroup. A Linux computer configured for Samba can be part of a Windows workgroup or actually serve as the equivalent of a Windows NT file server.

Many distributions of LINUX provide Samba on the installation CDs. In some cases, you will have to make sure that Samba is installed as an option when you install the LINUX OS.

Samba can be configured by editing the various Samba configuration files using a text editor or taking advantage of GUI utilities provided by your distribution of Linux. Probably the easiest way to configure Samba for the first time, however, is to take advantage of a Web browser-based utility called **SWAT (Samba Web Administration Tool)**. SWAT is included with some LINUX distributions, or you can download from one of the LINUX software repositories on the Web such as www.linux.org.

After SWAT is installed on the LINUX computer, you can access the Samba configuration file by invoking SWAT in any Web browser. Make sure that you know the root password; then in the Web browser address window, type http://local-host:901/ and press Enter. The number 901 is actually a port number that enables a TCP connection between SWAT and your Web browser. (The port number and the IP address provide the socket used as the communication avenue between TCP and HTTP on the Web browser.) Figure 16.9 shows the Samba SWAT program running in the Mozilla Web browser.

FIGURE 16.9
SWAT makes it easy to configure Samba on a Linux computer.

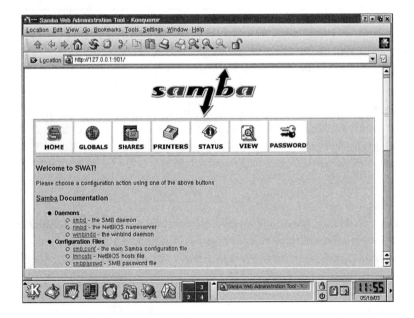

When SWAT is up and running, you need to configure Samba so that it enables the Linux computer to communicate in the Windows workgroup. This is accomplished using the Samba Globals settings, which is reached by clicking Globals in the browser window.

Shares are also created using SWAT. Directories on the Linux computer are mapped to a share name. This is done using the Shares screen (accessed by clicking Shares in the Web browser window). The Shares screen also allows you to set security options related to a particular share by specifying that the share is read or write. Access to specific hosts in the workgroup can also be allowed or denied using this screen.

When Samba is completely configured using the SWAT interface (SWAT provides easy access to help files for configuring Samba) and the smbd and nmbd services are started using the Status screen of the SWAT utility (these two services make Samba work), the Linux computer is ready to participate in the Windows workgroup. This means that files on the Linux box can be accessed by Windows computers, and the Linux box can access files on the Windows machines. For more about Samba, check out www.samba.org.

Upgrading a Linux Server

Upgrading a Linux server can be a little more complicated than a Windows or Netware server—particularly in cases in which you are using a freeware version of a Linux distribution and have not purchased any type of support for your version of Linux. Individual Linux software packages (such as a management utility, word processor, email package, or desktop utility) can be found in different file formats.

For Red Hat, you can easily install new software using RPM (Red Hat Package Manager) files. These files have .rpm as their extension. These files have been specially prepared so that they can be installed quickly on your system using the Red Hat Package Manager utility. All you have to do is download the file (typically from www.redhat.com) and then locate it on your system using the Conqueror browser (a combination file and Web browser used on Linux systems where KDE has been installed). Selecting the file in Conqueror starts the Red Hat Package Manager and allows you to install the software.

You might also run into software packages that exist as compressed tarballs. A **tarball** is a file archive created with the UNIX tar utility. It holds the source files for the software you want to install. Tarballs will typically be compressed with the Linux utility Gzip to make them easier to download. A typical Gzip compressed tarball will have the extension .tar.gz. In most cases, installing tarballs requires some annoying input at the command line in a terminal window. For example, let's say that we have a file named joe.tar.gz. To unzip the package, you would open a terminal console on your desktop.

In the terminal window, you would first switch to the directory that holds the file using the cd command (such as cd /directory name) and then type the following:

```
tar zxf joe.tar.gz /tmp
```

The zxf switches are used to unzip the archive (z), extract the file (x), and specify that this is the archive to work with (f). The /tmp at the end of the command places the unzipped and extracted files into the tmp directory on your system. (You can specify a directory other than tmp if you prefer.)

You can then go to the tmp directory (cd /tmp) or other directory that holds the extracted files. Now you have to type the following:

```
./configure
make
make install
```

This creates the installation file for the software and installs it. You should now be able to launch the application—typically from the terminal window or, in some cases, an icon will be created on the GUI menu system. Linux distributions will vary slightly on command sets, so for more about working with installation files, check out the Case Western Reserve University Linux Users Group's newbie pages at http://sigunix.cwru.edu/docs/newbie/. You will also want to become familiar with the documentation for the particular Linux distribution you use on your network.

Summary

In this hour, we took a look at UNIX and Linux. UNIX is one of the oldest and most reliable of the network platforms. Linux, a clone of UNIX, provides an inexpensive way to explore a UNIX-like server environment. Linux provides all the typical tools that you would expect from a network operating system. You can configure and manage a Linux server or client from a GUI or work with commands at the command line.

Q&A

Q *What distribution of Linux is best to implement?*

A The distribution of Linux that you select for your network will depend on your actual implementation. If you are using older (legacy) hardware and want to use Linux as a client OS, you will want to pick the distribution that requires the least amount of hard drive space and the most basic hardware configuration. For example, the DragonLinux distribution only requires 25MB of hard drive space for installation. A number of Linux distributions also support computers running x386 processors. In term of server implementations, you will want to go with distributions that provide both support and updates. Two popular Linux powerhouses are Red Hat Linux and SUSE Linux.

Q *What type of network services can be offered by UNIX/Linux servers?*

A UNIX/Linux servers can offer network services such as DNS, DHCP, and Web services (and pretty much any service you expect from a network server platform). UNIX/Linux servers are particularly popular for Web server implementations.

Q *I want to keep my Windows clients but add a file server to the network. Can I use Linux??*

A Yes, a Linux server running Samba can act as a file server on a Windows network. It is basically equivalent to a Windows NT Server. So, if you are running a Windows 2003 Server domain, you will have to run the domain in mixed mode to accommodate the Linux/Samba server.

Common Network Services and How to Provide Them

In this hour, you will learn about the following topics:

▶ Common network services

▶ Providing file and print servers

▶ Deploying DHCP

▶ Configuring a DNS server

We've already had an opportunity to discuss best practices for designing a network, and we have also looked at networking using the Microsoft and Linux network operating system platforms. In this hour, we will take a look at common network services and the different possibilities for deploying them on the network. Some network services, such as providing file and print servers, are essential for any network, even small networks that do not use the TCP/IP network protocol. We will also look at services directly related to TCP/IP networks, including DHCP and DNS.

Deploying Common Network Services

Creating a network really revolves around supplying different services to your network users. These servers can range from basic services, such as file servers and print servers, to more complex servers such as a DNS server, Web server, or communication/email server. Each service is provided by a particular type of server. However, this doesn't mean that every service must be provided by a separate server.

It is quite common for a server on a network to supply multiple services, particularly on smaller networks. The amount of server specialization (meaning the number of servers on the network that only supply one or two services) depends on the size of your network. A large network with heavy network traffic requires more servers (running specific services) than a small network that might be capable of deriving all of its services from one or two server boxes. The following list provides the different types of servers and the services that they provide:

▶ **File Server**—A file server's job is to serve as a home for the files that are needed by users on the network. This can include files that a number of users share. These files are typically held in what is called a public folder, which can include private folders that are specific for a particular user. The great thing about using a file server is that important files reside in one place, making it very easy to back up the data periodically.

▶ **Print Server**—A print server is used to host a network printer. It is basically the control conduit for the printer. Because print jobs need to be spooled (placed on the computer before they are sent to the printer) before they are printed, the print server supplies the hard drive space needed. The print server also queues up all the print jobs being directed to the printer.

▶ **Communication Server**—A communication server runs specialized software that allows users on the network to communicate. It provides services such as electronic mail and discussion groups to allow users to share information. We discuss communication servers such as Microsoft Exchange and Lotus Notes in Hour 12, "Network Applications."

▶ **Application Server**—Application servers host various applications, such as specialized databases. Even typical desktop applications, such as word processors and spreadsheet software, can also be stored on an application server. This makes updating software applications much easier because the software doesn't actually reside on every client workstation. Application servers, such as Microsoft SQL, are discussed in Hour 12.

▶ **Web Server**—Web servers provide you with the ability to create a Web site that can be accessed internally by your employees (this is called an *intranet*) or by folks surfing the Internet. Web servers aren't for everyone, and many companies still use Web hosting companies to get their Web sites up and running on the Internet.

▶ **DHCP Server**—A DHCP server uses the Dynamic Host Configuration Protocol to provide DHCP clients with IP addresses, subnet masks, and other TCP/IP configuration information such as a default gateway and preferred DNS server. Because TCP/IP is deployed on most networks, it makes sense to deploy a DHCP server, which can provide IP addresses to network clients dynamically from a pool of addresses specified by the network administrator. How DHCP works is discussed in Hour 14, "TCP/IP."

▶ **DNS Server**—Because connecting networks to the Internet has become an imperative, it is often necessary to deploy DNS servers on the network. The DNS server takes care of the IP address to FQDN (Fully Qualified Domain Name) resolution (and vice versa) on the local network (or local zone of authority as it is referred to). Some network operating system platforms require that a DNS server be available on the network even if the network is not connected to the Internet. For example, Windows Server 2003 requires that DNS be on the network for the Active Directory to function correctly. How DNS works is discussed in Hour 14.

All the network operating systems that we have discussed in the book—such as Microsoft Windows Server 2003, Red Hat Linux, and Novell NetWare (and UNIX platforms such as Sun Solaris)—provide these network services as either part of the "basic" NOS or as an add-on service. Although planning and configuring a network homogenously—meaning using just one network operating system for all services—makes the learning curve a little more reasonable for the network administrator, many networks are in fact heterogeneous.

These networks deploy different NOS platforms for different services. For example, a network might be running the Microsoft NOS to authenticate users and provide a number of other services, yet still take advantage of legacy NetWare file and print servers. The network might even be more heterogeneous in that the Web server might run a version of Linux or UNIX to take advantage of the Apache Web server platform.

Whether you have the luxury of deploying one NOS or work on a network that deploys more than one NOS, it is the network administrator's job to supply the appropriate services to the network clients. Let's take a look at some of the possibilities (in terms of NOS platforms) for providing file and print servers, and then we can look at some of the more specialized servers such as DHCP and DNS.

User Authentication and the Network Logical Hierarchy

One type of server that we did not discuss in our list of common network servers is the authentication server that also provides the logical hierarchy for tracking objects such as users on the network. Typically, the first server that you bring online will handle user authentication and store the object database for the network. In the Windows server environment, this is called the domain controller. On a NetWare network, this is the server that hosts the eDirectory directory services. Remember that before you bring other services online, you must configure the server that will authenticate your users to the network and set up the logical hierarchy for the network.

By the Way

Providing File and Print Services

File and print services are essential to even the smallest of networks. Providing a way to share files and printers were both important reasons that led to the development of the hardware and software that allows us to connect computers into a network.

Both file and printer sharing is such a basic need for all computer users that file and print sharing capabilities are built in to desktop operating systems such as Windows, Mac OS, Linux, UNIX, and so on for SOHO (Small Office/Home Office) peer-to-peer networking.

Let's take a look at deploying a file server. Then we can take a look at print server possibilities.

Deploying a File Server

File services can be provided from any number of different network operating systems. Although running a homogenous network is great in terms of network operating systems, providing files to your network clients does provide a fair amount of flexibility (again in terms of mixing different network operating systems on the network).

For example, even a network that has most of its servers running the Windows Server NOS can take advantage of file servers that are running on other NOS platforms such as NetWare and UNIX/Linux. Linux actually provides a very inexpensive alternative for adding a file server to a network (because the NOS is almost free and no additional client licenses are needed) and can provide file services to Windows clients using Samba (which is discussed in Hour 16, "UNIX and Linux Networking."

Now, I am not necessarily advocating that you go out of our way to run multiple NOS platforms on your network; it is possible to make them coexist, particularly in terms of files sharing. However, if you have the luxury of working with a single NOS (because of no legacy servers), you should deploy your file server using that NOS.

So, bottom line, all the NOS platforms that we have discussed in this book make deploying a file server a fairly simple process. On a Windows network, you create a share on a server (any server running one of the Windows network operating systems such as Windows Server 2003), and permissions related to that share (which is a shared folder on the server) can be assigned to users, giving different levels of access. For more about sharing folders and files on a Windows network, see Hour 15, "Microsoft Networking."

UNIX/Linux systems provide multiple ways to share files such as Samba and the Network File System. Both of these different file server strategies are discussed in Hour 16.

In the NetWare environment, which was really the first NOS to provide file and print services in the early days of the PC revolution, you first create a pool on the server, which is the amount of disk space that you want to make available for a new volume. Figure 17.1 shows the NetWare Remote Manager's pool creation screen. All the available free space on the disk can be used to create the pool or a portion of the free disk space.

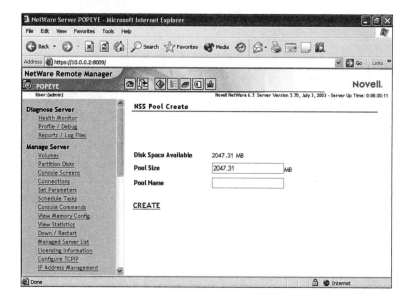

FIGURE 17.1
A pool must be created to configure a volume on a NetWare server's hard drive.

After the pool has been created, it can be populated with a volume or volumes (a volume being a portion of a server hard disk that can then function as a discrete logical drive). You then "mount" the volume, which makes it available to network users. Mounting the volume also enables it to be populated with directories and files that can then be accessed.

NetWare 6 and the Novell Storage Services

With NetWare 6.0, Novell made a number of fundamental changes to its NOS. First of all, the NOS uses a new directory service called eDirectory that provides a hierarchical database for storing network objécts. A new file system, Novell Storage Services NSS, was also launched. NSS allows the administrator to create and expand larger volumes than were provided for by earlier versions of NetWare.

By the Way

Creating directories on the new volume is also accomplished using the NetWare Remote Manager. (The remote manager is a Web-based tool.) As with any NOS, different levels of access can be assigned to users on the network in reference to the volume.

Because the administrator typically creates the directories on a file server volume (or Admin as the administrator account is called in the NetWare environment), the administrator has ownership of that directory (and also full access to that directory). If the administrator wants to create trustees (a trustee being a power user in relation to that directory) to help maintain the volume (and populate it with files), he can add trustees after the directory has been created. Figure 17.2 shows the NetWare Remote Manager screen that is used to add trustees to a volume directory.

FIGURE 17.2
Trustees can be added for the directory to help maintain it using the Remote Manager.

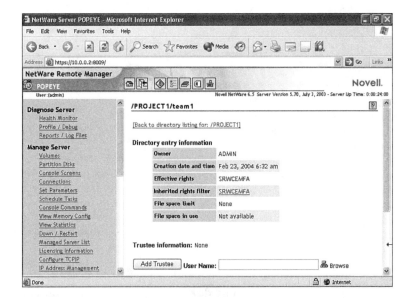

Having the ability to assign different levels of permissions and assigning trustee rights (or power user rights) to a particular shared directory is not solely found in the NetWare environment. Microsoft networks and UNIX/Linux networks also provide this ability. It will be up to you the administrator (as part of your overall network security plan) to determine the level of access that you give to users on the network in relation to the different file stores on your file servers.

On networks of any appreciable size, the file server should be configured for this single role because it will need to deal with a fair amount of client requests as your users work with their files. The files on a file server will change over time, and this is one of the network servers that should definitely be on the backup schedule. Because file servers can experience data corruption, virus infection, and even accidental erasure, it is important to back up the files regularly. For more about backing up network servers, see Hour 20, "Managing an Existing Network."

Providing Print Services

Giving your users the ability to print to network printers is another basic service. All the NOS platforms that we have discussed provide an administrator the ability to configure a network server to act as a print server. As already mentioned earlier in this hour, the server that acts as the print server is used to monitor and manage print jobs on the printer.

Network printing can be a little confusing in that different terms are used to refer to a printer depending on its location on the network in relation to its print server. These printer definitions based on network location are

- ▶ **Local printer**—A printer that is directly attached to a server. The printer is only local, however, in relation to the server that it is attached to. This server will, obviously, serve as the print server for the printer.

- ▶ **Remote printer**—A printer attached to a computer other than your server, which can be pretty confusing because the computer that the printer is attached to would consider the printer local. Whether a printer is local or remote depends on which computer on the network you use as your reference point.

- ▶ **Direct connect printer**—A printer that contains its own network interface, processor, and memory for print serving. These printers are typically attached directly to a network hub or switch using twisted-pair cable, just like any computer on the network.

Now that we have defined the different types of printers that we can have on the network, let's discuss how network printing actually works. When a user prints a document from a network client using application software to a network printer, the redirector on the client machine sends the data out onto the network to the print server computer that controls the particular network printer.

The print server uses software called a print spooler to accept the print job and place this job in its print queue, which is just some of the computer's memory used to hold print jobs until they can be sent to the printer. When the printer is free to accept the print job, it is released from the print queue.

On a Windows Network, printer shares are created much like folder shares. Printing on a Windows network is discussed in Hour 15. In the UNIX/Linux environment, printers can be shared using Samba (discussed in Hour 16) and can be quickly shared by crating a new print queue. In the Linux Red Hat networking environment, print queues can be created for local printers, UNIX printers on the network, Windows printers, Novell printers, and printers connected directly to the network. Figure 17.3 shows the Red Hat Print Printer utility.

FIGURE 17.3
Red Hat provides a GUI utility for configuring network printers.

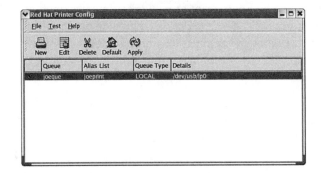

Printer servers don't necessarily have to be the newest or fastest servers on your network since most new laser printers have a substantial amount of memory allowing them to hold a number of print jobs. The hardware configuration for a print server will, as with all servers, depend on the volume of printing that is taking place and the type of print jobs. Documents or reports with a large number of graphics and other objects will require more printing power. Assuming that you can use that "old server" as your print server doesn't necessarily work for every situation.

Providing DHCP on the Network

The most practical (and time-effective) way to assign IP addresses, subnet masks, and other TCP/IP configuration information to network clients is via the Dynamic Host Configuration Protocol. This means that you will have to configure a DHCP server on your network. Networks of any size—particularly those that are divided into subnets—might require multiple DHCP servers. Because DHCP works using broadcast messages (as was discussed in Hour 14) and routers do not forward broadcast messages, you must generally place a DHCP server on each subnet.

DHCP Relay Agent

On routed networks, you can configure a server as a DHCP Relay Agent, which relays DHCP broadcasts to DHCP clients on other subnets. This allows you to forgo placing a DHCP server on every subnet. You may also have to configure the routers to pass the DHCP requests from the relay agents.

Did you Know?

Most network platforms, including Windows Server 2003, UNIX/Linux, and Novell NetWare, provide the DHCP service as part of their network operating system. So, you can configure DHCP in any network operating system environment.

DHCP servers provide the IP address range (and the subnet mask to be used) to their clients based on the scope that the administrator configures on the DHCP server. The scope is the range of addresses to be assigned to the DHCP clients on the network. Figure 17.4 shows the New Scope Wizard on a server running Windows Server 2003. Notice that this screen allows you to enter the start and end IP address of the scope and the subnet mask to be used.

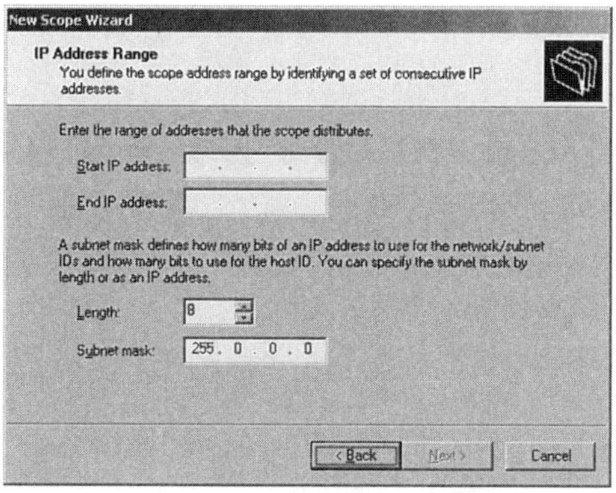

FIGURE 17.4
You must configure a scope on the DHCP server.

You can also configure exclusions from the scope. This allows you to configure a scope that contains your entire IP address pool. You can then exclude the addresses that you have assigned statically to the DHCP server and other servers or devices on the network (such as a router). Not only can you configure exclusions, but you can also configure reservations—a reservation meaning that a particular device on the network, such as a print server, will always be assigned the same IP address. This is particularly useful in cases in which users are using the IP address of the printer to print to the printer. (The IP address is dynamically assigned but it doesn't change.)

When an IP address, subnet mask, and other TCP/IP configuration information is given to a DHCP client by the server, it is referred to as a **lease**. When you configure the DHCP server's scope, you must also determine how long the IP addresses will be leased to the clients.

Lease time is really up to you. Extremely long leases can actually be a security liability because the IP addresses are pretty static and might be discerned by a hacker monitoring network traffic. Short leases will cause a great deal of network traffic (because of the broadcast messages) and eat up network bandwidth. You will have to balance the use of your bandwidth with security considerations when setting the lease time.

Another consideration is related to the number of DHCP servers you deploy on the network. As already mentioned, routed networks require DHCP servers on each subnet or the use of DCHP relay agents. Larger networks might also require that you use multiple DHCP servers to break up the total pool of addresses available. This also builds some redundancy into your network in case a DHCP server goes down. The other DHCP server on the network can pick up the slack and make sure that all the network DHCP clients have IP addresses.

Deploying DNS on the Network

The Domain Name System (DNS) supplies the domain namespace that we use on TCP/IP networks such as the Internet. DNS and the namespace are discussed in Hour 14.

If you are running TCP/IP on your network, you need a DNS server (or servers) to handle the name resolution on the network. (Small networks can use the DNS services provided by their Internet service provider.) If you are hosting your own domain, you are, in fact, required to provide the IP addresses of two DNS servers to the domain registration service that you use to obtain your domain name.

NetWare, Windows Server 2003, and UNIX/Linux all provide support for DNS. You can add the DNS service to an existing network server (if it can handle the additional workload), or you can deploy a new server and add the DNS service as you initially load the NOS (again, on any of the NOS platforms that we have discussed in this book).

For a DNS server to work, it must be configured with at least one zone. The zone is the area of the network that the DNS server will have authority for. The zone that you must create is actually called a **forward lookup zone**. A forward lookup zone allows for forward lookup queries, which allows a host to find the IP address using the hostname of a particular computer or device. (It finds the address because the DNS answers the host computers query.) Again, for DNS to work, at least one forward lookup zone must be configured on the DNS server.

When you create the forward lookup zone, you have to name it. The name of the zone will be the same as the DNS domain name for the portion of your network that this DNS server is authoritative. For example, if your DNS domain name for your portion of the network was `marketing.mydomain.com`, the zone name would be `marketing.mydomain.com`. If you have a network that operates at a higher level in the domain name space (no subdomain as in the `marketing.mydomain.com` example where marketing is a subdomain), the forward lookup zone would be your domain name such as `mydomain.com`.

When you deploy your DNS servers, you can set up a server that will provide the DNS server and maintain the master copy of the DNS database. The forward lookup zone on that server is called the **primary zone**.

You can also deploy DNS servers that use a read-only replica of the primary zone database and are set up on the network to help out the authoritative server for the zone. The replica zone used by these "helper" DNS servers is called the **secondary zone**.

The authoritative DNS server can also be configured with what is called a **reverse lookup zone**. This type of zone is used to resolve IP addresses to FQDNs (meaning that it does the reverse of a forward lookup zone). Reverse lookup zones are configured by entering the network ID of the network (which would be the network IP address provided by your ISP or other provider that you acquired your IP addresses from).

After the zones have been created on the DNS server, they must be populated with records. There are a number of different record types. One of the most important record types is the host record, which provides the FQDN and IP address of hosts on the network. Figure 17.5 shows a GUI utility on a Linux DNS server that is used to create a new record such as a host record.

A number of other record types also exist. The list that follows provides a description of some of the other record types you will work with on a DNS server:

▶ **SOA (Start of Authority)**—Identifies the name of the server that is authoritative for data within the domain and is the first record in the zone database file. It is created automatically when you bring your primary name server online.

▶ **NS (Name Server)**—A record is created for each name server assigned to the domain.

▶ **A Host**—Provides the hostname to the IP address mapping in a forward lookup zone.

▶ **PTR Pointer**—This type of record is the reverse of an A record and points to a host record. Found in the reverse lookup zone, the PTR record provides for the IP address to host name mappings.

▶ **SRV**—This type of record shows which services are running on a particular host computer. For example, SRV records could identify the domain controllers on the network.

▶ **MX (Mail Exchanger)**—This record type identifies the mail servers on the network and details in what order the mail servers should be contacted.

▶ **CNAME (Canonical Name or Alias)**—This type of record is used to create an alias for an existing record. This allows you to point to several different names at the same IP address. This would be particularly useful for pointing at your Web server on the network.

▶ **HINFO (Host information)**—This record type can be used as a sort of low-rent resource tracking tool for your DNS server. This record can provide information on the CPU, operating system, and other software/hardware information.

FIGURE 17.5
Host records must be added to the DNS database.

Depending on the type of DNS you are working with (which depends on the NOS platform that you are using on the network), you will have to create a number of the records in the DNS database. Some versions of DNS, such as Microsoft's DDNS (Dynamic DNS), actually populate the DNS database automatically and enter host and other record types.

The DNS server must also be configured with the IP addresses of its nearest neighboring DNS servers. This allows it to query these DNS servers when it can't resolve a request from a host. If these neighbor servers can't answer the query, they can query their neighboring DNS servers; so, in effect, all the DNS servers in the world actually provide DNS information to each other through this indirect method of forwarding queries to the nearest neighbor.

As with any other server on the network, you need to make sure that your primary DNS server (and any secondary servers that you deploy) has the hardware configuration that will provide the DNS service effectively on the network. When working with DNS, you should also keep an eye on your various server logs and watch for any potential problems. On a Windows 2003 server, a special DNS log is created on a server that is configured for DNS. You need to make sure that network clients are not experiencing problems with DNS resolution. This will not only eat up network bandwidth (because of the large number of requests), but it can also cause connectivity problems between clients and servers and those attempting to communicate with your network over the Internet.

Summary

In this hour, we discussed some of the common network services and how you provide them on your network. We took a look at the basics of file and print servers. We also discussed other important network services on a TCP/IP network, specifically, DHCP and DNS.

Q&A

Q *How can a network administrator control access to shared directories on a file server?*

A NOS platforms such as NetWare, UNIX/Linux, and Windows Server 2003 all provide different levels of access or permissions for network resources such as directories on file servers. The files can then be secured by providing different levels of permissions to network users.

Q *How can certain IP addresses be excluded from a scope so that they can be used on devices that require static IP addresses?*

A Rather than precluding certain IP addresses from a scope, it makes more sense to create a range of excluded addresses or exclusions when the scope is created. This allows you to use the excluded addresses for static IP addressing.

Q *What is a good way to take some of the workload off the primary DNS server?*

A Deploying "helper" DNS servers that operate via a secondary zone (which is a duplicate of the primary zone) allows you to handle a large number of DNS requests on the network without overtaxing the primary DNS server.

PART V

Introduction to Network Administration

What Is a Network Administrator?

A network administrator is the person responsible for ensuring the health and well-being of a network. I have discussed a great deal of the information that a network administrator must make second nature, such as computer hardware, network protocols, and network operating systems. Knowledge, experience, and plain old common sense enable a network administrator to keep the network up and running.

Depending on the size of the company, a network administrator might not actually be called a network administrator. For example, a network engineer at a large company would, in practice, also be a network administrator, although the scope and responsibilities related to a network engineer's job would probably be greater than those of a network administrator at a small company. A very small company that only employs a network support specialist to handle day-to-day problems and support (and uses consultants for major network installations or rollouts) has in effect made the network support specialist the de facto network administrator—at least in relation to basic network and client computer issues.

In this hour, we will take a look at some of the different jobs that relate to network administration. We will also look at issues related to different paths of education and certification for the network administrator. I will discuss planning and installing a network and look at some of the nontechnical issues related to network administration, such as budgeting and network project management.

Information Technology Jobs

Although we have concentrated on network administration in this book, there are actually a number of jobs and career paths that relate to network administration either directly or peripherally. In the mid and late 1990s, there was a huge boom in the information technology field, and job possibilities were numerous and plenty. Although hi-tech has cooled down somewhat, IT is still a good career choice.

Computer networking professionals operate at many different levels in a corporate structure; there is the chief information officer (CIO) operating at the very top of the corporate ladder, IT managers and administrators operating somewhere in the middle, and technicians and support personnel operating near the bottom rungs. IT itself definitely has a "pecking order." Let's look at a range of IT positions and their relative standing in the Information Technology field (from bottom to top):

- ▶ **Help Desk Analyst**—Help Desk personnel serve as the first line support for many companies and institutions. They help users diagnose computer or networking problems and provide necessary remedies either over the phone or online in real time. Working the Help Desk requires a broad knowledge of the company systems and network, potential end user problems, and an ability to provide quick fixes that get users up and running. The Help Desk analyst is an entry level position.

- ▶ **User Support Specialist**—User support personnel are responsible for setting up new computers, connecting them to the network, and making sure that the appropriate software is installed on the systems. Support specialists are also involved in diagnosing system problems and repairing them (similar to the Help Desk folks), typically onsite. Support folks are typically more hands-on than the Help Desk personnel. Support specialist positions are often entry level or one step up from the Help Desk.

- ▶ **LAN Support Specialist**—LAN support personnel are often responsible for a particular aspect of the network infrastructure, such as server maintenance, network expansion and setup (including pulling wires), or the maintenance of a particular set of services such as DNS or DHCP servers. Support specialists might also be responsible for network backups. In terms of the IT job ladder, a LAN support specialist would be someone who reports to a network administrator or systems manager.

▶ **LAN/Network Administrator**—LAN/network administrators are responsible for planning, implementing, and maintaining the network infrastructure for a company or institution. This position would require an excellent knowledge of network operating systems and networking hardware. He must manage the strategies for making network resources available to users and anticipate potential bottlenecks and security flaws in the network. The network administrator position can exist at the middle of the company's IT pecking order or at the senior level.

▶ **IT Director**—The director will be responsible for the overall planning and implementation of the network infrastructure. This often takes the form of managing personnel who are specialists in different areas such as LAN, databases, WAN, and Web services. The IT director is also the conduit to upper management and is responsible for the budgets, inventories, licensing, and reporting (to upper management).

This is a fairly generic set of descriptions for some of the computer networking job possibilities. Although not all of these positions would be at the network administrator level, they can serve as stepping stones and learning experiences as you work toward becoming a network administrator.

You will find that the actual job title for a particular position will vary from company to company. One company might call the LAN administrator a network administrator, whereas another might define the position as a systems manager. The salary potential of these generic positions will, of course, depend on the size of the business and the actual responsibilities listed for the position. The responsibilities of the job will dictate the level of knowledge and experience required of the person.

Computer Networking Education and Certification

It is safe to say that in many cases the first wave of computer gurus, programmers, and networking professionals were self taught or worked their way through the ranks by moving up the corporate pecking order through hands-on experience. It is not that uncommon to find network administrators who have business degrees or Web designers who majored in political science. It is also not uncommon to run in to computer professionals who have had very productive careers and either did not finish or did not attend college. (Remember, Bill Gates was a dropout.)

As the first wave ages and retires, a new wave of computer professionals is certainly required. Many technical schools, community colleges, and universities offer information science and information technology degrees.

Another way that IT professionals legitimize their knowledge base, gain new knowledge, and meet job requirements is acquiring professional IT certifications. These certifications can be vendor specific or generic.

For example, Microsoft offers a number of different certifications and designations related to its products as do Novell, Cisco Systems, and Sun Microsystems. In terms of generic (meaning nonvendor specific) certifications, the Computing Technology Industry Association (COMPTIA) offers a number of certifications related to different skill sets. For example, the COMPTIA Network+ certification is designed for professionals with nine months experience (or more) in network administration and support.

To attain a particular certification, you have to take an exam or set of exams. Some certifications only require one exam; others require a number of exams. Table 18.1 provides a short list of some of the vendor specific and generic certifications that you can work toward. Be advised that vendors update their certification exams regularly. You should check out the Web site for the specific certification to view the current exams and requirements.

TABLE 18.1 Some Networking Professional Certifications

Certification Name	Requirements	Additional Information
Microsoft Certified Professional	Requires the passing of one current Microsoft certification exam.	For more information on this certification and a list of exams, see http://www.microsoft.com/ traincert/mcp/mcp/default.asp.
Microsoft Certified System Administrator	Requires the passing of three core exams and one elective. This certification is designed for a professional with at least one year of experience.	For more information on this certification and a list of exams, see http://www.microsoft.com/ traincert/mcp/mcsa/default.asp.

TABLE 18.1 Continued

Certification Name	Requirements	Additional Information
Microsoft Certified System Engineer	Requires the passing of five core exams and two elective exams. This is an advanced certification intended for experienced network administrators.	For more information on this certification and a list of exams, see `http://www.microsoft.com/traincert/mcp/mcse/default.asp.`
Cisco Certified Network Associate	Requires the passing of one exam. This is the Cisco entry level certification. There are actually three different exams that can be taken to achieve this certification.	For more about this certification and its requirements, see `http://www.cisco.com.`
Cisco Certified Network Professional	Requires a valid CCNA certification and the passing of three or four additional exams related to building, troubleshooting, and securing Cisco Internetworks.	For more about this certification, see `http://www.cisco.com.`
Certified Novell Administrator	Requires the passing of one exam. Considered the entry level certification for NetWare server platforms.	For more about this certification, see `http://www.novell.com/training/certinfo/cna/index.html.`
Certified Novell Engineer	Requires the passing of four core exams and one elective exam. This is an advanced NOS certification.	For more about this certification, see `http://www.novell.com/training/certinfo/cne/index.`
Sun Certified System Administrator	Requires the passing of three exams for a specific Sun NOS such as Solaris 8 or 9.	For more about this certification and other Sun Microsystem certifications, see `http://suned.sun.com/US/certification/index.html.`

TABLE 18.1   Continued

Certification Name	Requirements	Additional Information
COMPTIA Network+	Requires the passing of one exam, the COMPTIA Network+ Exam, which tests a knowledge of topologies, protocols, network implementation, and network support.	For more about this certification, see `http://www.comptia.com/certification/Network/general_info.asp`.
COMPTIA Server+	Requires the passing of the COMPTIA Server+ exam. Designed for those responsible for server hardware functionality.	For more about this certification, see `http://www.comptia.com/certification/server/default.asp`.

This list really doesn't scratch the surface as far as the number of networking (and programming and software development) certifications that exist. Use the Web as a resource for determining whether the products you work with provide certification possibilities.

A large number of educational institutions and IT training centers across the United States. (and worldwide) offer courses that allow you to prepare for specific exams. There are even boot camps that allow you to prepare for an entire certification track, such as a Microsoft Certified Systems Engineer (MCSE) or a Cisco Certified Network Professional (CCNP) in a protracted period of time (in some cases, a week).

There are also a large number of self-paced training kits and books designed to help you prepare for the various exams and certifications. Check out `www.quepublishing.com`, and do a search for certification to view a variety of titles. You can also search for certification books at `www.informit.com`.

By the Way

The Cost of Certification

The cost of taking certification exams varies by the provider of the exam (and varies by specific exam). For example, the COMPTIA Network+ and Server+ exams cost $155.00. Most of the Microsoft exams for the various networking tracks are $125.00.

You can take these exams at testing centers in your area. Pearson Vue offers a large number of IT certification exams. For information on locations and exams offered, see Pearson Vue's Web site at www.vue.com. You can also take exams at Thomson Prometric testing centers. Check out its Web site at www.2test.com.

Planning and Installing a Network

Now that I have discussed some of the educational venues for acquiring network administration skills (the best way to gain network skills is hands-on experience), I will discuss broader issues related to planning and installing a network. We can then take a look at budgeting issues and managing projects related to your network.

As you have seen throughout the course of this book, two important tasks that a network administrator must face are the planning of a network and its subsequent installation. Hours 9, "Designing a Network," 10, "Selecting Network Hardware and Software," and 11, "Assembling a Network," discuss a number of issues related to planning and installing a network. However, it doesn't hurt to summarize the network administrator's tasks related to planning and implementation. The main tasks involved in any network planning are plan, design, implement, and tune. The specific things you typically have to do during network design and installation are the same things you've learned about in this book so far:

▶ **Know the design of your network.** If you designed your network, you'll understand how the pieces fit together logically and physically. This is very useful when solving network administration problems because the designer can rapidly identify potential points of failure.

▶ **Understand how the pieces fit together.** This knowledge comes from knowing the design of the network: understanding how data is supposed to flow inside the network. This understanding eases network software troubleshooting.

▶ **Make the pieces work together.** This is where the preceding two items come together in one concrete—and occasionally terrifying—ordeal.

When viewed in this light, network planning and building looks pretty simple, and in some ways it is. During network planning, the network administrator's job is to create an internally consistent plan for the network so that, in theory, the network will work. During the time the network is being built and thereafter, the network administrator's job is to ensure that the network does work. To do the former, it's necessary to understand networking in the abstract; to do the latter, you need knowledge of abstract concepts plus the ability to work with concrete reality.

A Few Thoughts on Budgets

Once you have worked through the issues related to planning a network (and running a network on a daily basis), another aspect of a network administrator's job, especially when you have climbed your career ladder into the realm of middle management, is dealing with budgets. I think most people have had a basic accounting or personal finance class at some time in their educational experience. Therefore, the math involved and the structuring of a budget is really no mystery. Most companies will also have some sort of form or template that is used to create a department's yearly budget. Getting the budget down on paper is relatively straightforward. The difficult aspect of working with IT budgets relates more to justifying the expenses rather than listing them accurately.

Learning About Budgets

There are many books on budgeting and other financial issues related to businesses. One book you may want to check out is *Business Analysis with Microsoft Excel, Second Edition* from Que Publishing.

In most companies, the network infrastructure serves as a communication and productivity tool for the employees. The problem with justifying a network budget is quantifying how the computers and the network make the employees more productive and therefore generate more income for the company. Now, I'm not talking about companies with Web sites that generate measurable sales or software companies in which programmers need computing tools to generate product. For the run-of-the-mill business that uses computer technology as just another tool, it is often very difficult to measure the cost effectiveness of the network infrastructure. IT doesn't directly generate direct income.

This means that when you create your network budget, you also need to accumulate any information that will help you justify the budget when you meet with upper-level managers. Here are a few ideas for providing the cost effectiveness of your IT implementation.

> ▶ Do some research on other companies that use a particular technology. Most hardware and software vendors provide white papers and case studies that allow you to see how a particular aspect of the network infrastructure

improved a particular company's capability to do business. Having some facts available, especially those related to a competitor, can help justify proposed expenses.

▶ Talk to sales people in the field and find out how certain aspects of your network infrastructure (such as dial-in or VPN connections for remote users) has made them more effective.

▶ Look at the average employee's workload and try to figure out the time savings and increased productivity that new hardware tools and software will provide.

▶ Compute the travel costs required for employees involved in a company project that includes branches of the company at different locations. Providing a groupware product that provides an environment for communication and collaboration, such as Microsoft Exchange or Lotus Notes, to employees might negate the need for much of the travel. You must prove that the cost of servers, software, and training to roll out the groupware environment will be less over time than the cost of travel, lodging, and so on.

▶ Determine whether older equipment such as PCs can be donated to a nonprofit organization and create a tax savings for your company that helps sweeten a proposal for upgrading workstations and servers.

There are, I'm sure, many other ideas that can be explored to help you justify your IT budget; look at your company or institution's core business and use that as a starting point. The bottom line is that you need to not only create a budget that provides accurate funding for your network plan, but you must also be able to sell the budget to the people at your company who control the purse strings.

Managing Network Projects

As a network administrator, you will become involved in various network-related projects. For example, you might need to roll out a new operating system or be part of the development of a new software product or device (depending on the type of business you are involved in). On the simplest level, managing a project requires that you exercise control over two things: resources, including technical tools and personnel, and time. Managing people and equipment makes sense, but how does one control time? Well, it relates to creating and then sticking to a schedule for the project.

Although any schedule is just a best guess, accurately assessing the human and technical resources for a project will go a long way to helping you meet the schedule. Identifying milestones in the schedule also will help you assess where you are at a particular point in time in relation to the completion of the project. If you are off schedule at a particular milestone, you can assess whether you need to increase the number of resources (such as technical staff) that are needed to complete the project on time. Remember that your project will also have a budget: Throwing a lot of overtime and other technical costs at the schedule might allow you to complete the project in time, but it might also run you way over budget.

Although project management is certainly a subject that can fill an entire book (and has) here are some general pointers related to network project management:

► Define the project in a short abstract (also known as an Executive Summary). An abstract is a quick overview. Supply the purpose and perhaps even the level of difficulty of the project so that you can then determine the staff and resources that will be required to complete the project.

► Organize the project around goals and outcomes rather than tasks. Each interim goal or outcome can then be quantified in terms of individual tasks. This makes it easier to create a schedule. Identifying the interim outcomes for the project allows you to break the overall project down into various phases (creating milestone dates for the completion of each phase). Breaking down the project into a series of interim goals makes it easier to schedule personnel and resources and take stock of the project as it is in process.

► After the project has been given the go-ahead, assign specific dates to your different interim outcomes or milestones. I have seen far too many badly planned projects in which the schedule is broken down into week one, week two, and so on with no specific dates other than a best guess completion date. You need to have a specific schedule and a plan to meet each milestone date. (This comment will probably get a laugh from my editors because authors like me have been known to miss a milestone date or two when working on a book.)

► Provide local authority to keep the process moving. If you are working on an implementation project at a number of sites, you need to designate a site manager (yes, sometimes you must empower your staff) who can make critical decisions related to keeping the project moving on a day-to-day basis. If every decision related to the project requires your authorization, and you are unavailable, you are going to have a lot of team members sitting on their hands waiting for you to make a decision as to their next step.

Delegating authority requires that you keep in constant contact with those who you have empowered.

▶ You need to monitor the progress of the project (in terms of interim goals) closely. This allows you to track the differences between your plan and what is actually happening. Monitoring will require regular meetings with project personnel. You should also build some type of reporting instrument (a weekly report, for example) that allows you to keep your finger on the pulse of the project.

▶ You have to build some sort of testing into the process. This allows you to test whether each interim goal or outcome has been met appropriately. For example, software development cycles products are tested at particular points typically referred to as alpha, beta, release to manufacturing, and so on.

By the Way

Project Management Skills Are as Important as Technical Skills

No matter how much you know about computer networking, managing projects is a whole different ball game. You definitely need to develop project management skills. Many books are written on the subject of project management. To see some IT related titles, check out www.informit.com and do a search for IT project management.

Although it is impossible to see into the future, you really need to keep up with the latest and greatest technologies and their relative expense (including rollout costs in terms of staff and other resources) so that your yearly proposed budget can reflect the possibility of special projects that might pop up in the coming year. I'm not saying that you have to pad your budget (budgeting is discussed in the previous section), but you do have to communicate effectively with upper management so that you have a clear understanding of where they expect computer technology (specifically the network infrastructure) to take them in the near (and far) future. If there is a chance that management wants a new tool made available, it should somehow be reflected in the budget even if it is only in some dollars that are earmarked for exploring a particular technology on a limited, test basis. The actual rollout of the technology can then be incorporated into the budget for the subsequent year.

You can keep track of your projects—including the resources and personnel required and the timeline for the project milestones—in a number of different ways. You can keep a hard copy notebook or calendar that tracks the project. Microsoft Excel can also be used to track resources, personnel, and timelines in a worksheet.

When you are managing a large, complex project, you probably should consider taking advantage of project management software. A number of project management software packages are available including Primavera SureTrak, Journyx Timesheet, Niku Projects, Vertabase Pro, and Microsoft Project (just to name a few).

Dedicated project management software makes it easier to track tasks, resources, and personnel. Most project management software also provides different views of your project data including a Gannt Chart, which provides a graphical view of the project's timeline. Figure 18.1 shows Microsoft Project 2003. Note that a task list and a Gannt Chart of the project are both displayed in the Project window.

FIGURE 18.1
Microsoft Project
2003 provides you
with the tools to
manage large IT
projects.

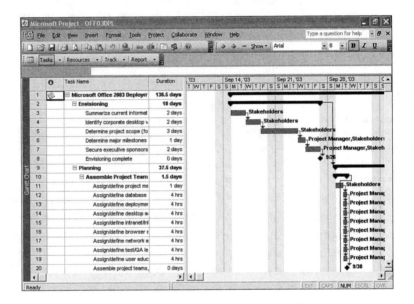

A real benefit of using project management software, such as Microsoft Project, is that you can configure each task in the project so that it is dependant on tasks that must be completed before the particular task can be started. This type of project tracking also keeps you honest in that you really have to stay on track and approach each task in the proper order as you move from the start of the project toward completion. Figure 18.2 shows the Task Information dialog box.

Being able to assign resources and predecessors (tasks that must be completed before the current task) and log notes related to a particular task really will help you keep a project organized. Project management software also makes it easy to generate reports related to a project.

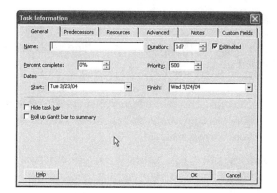

FIGURE 18.2
Information related
to each task can
be saved with the
task itself.

Using project management software allows you to centralize the information
related to a project. It really negates the mess of separate sheets of paper, Post-It
notes and other unorganized errata that become the downfall of many ill-fated
projects. Staying organized and using a timeline to accurately track the project is
a necessity of managing even the smallest of IT projects.

Open Source Project Management Tools

There are also open source project management tools, which allow you to explore
the concepts of working with project management software before you purchase a
particular package. There are Web-based open source tools such as Achievo, which
runs on both the Windows and UNIX platforms. There are also tools such as
Planner, which is an open source planning tool that runs as part of the GNOME
desktop on a computer running Linux.

By the Way

Summary

In this hour, I discussed some of the different information technology jobs related
to network administration and network support. I also discussed the certifications
that can be pursued by computer networking professionals. We also had an
opportunity to take a look at the big picture of planning and implementing a
network. The discussion also included information related to budgeting and network administration and tips related to managing network projects.

Q&A

Q *What are some of the ways to learn networking skills and upgrade your network administration skill set?*

A Many colleges, universities, and private training schools provide courses in network administration and related topics. There are also many vendor specific and non-vendor certifications such as those offered by COMPTIA, Microsoft, and Sun Microsystems.

Q *What are some ways that you can help explain a network implementation's return on investment to your corporate officers when you work with your budgets?*

A Research how other companies have improved their business by implementing the network technologies you plan to implement. Also talk to company employees, particularly sales people, and learn how new network tools will improve their ability to do their job. Also compare the costs of network communication tools in relation to the travel that would be required if the network infrastructure did not provide various communication possibilities.

Q *What are some good practices related to managing your various network-related projects?*

A Try to organize your projects around goals and outcomes. You can then determine the individual tasks that are required to meet a particular goal. This will make it easier for you to create the project schedule. Try to create a definitive schedule for the project using real dates, and also try and empower people who work for you so that you don't have to make every decision related to the project; this will keep the process rolling.

HOUR 19

Security

In this hour, you will learn about the following topics:

▶ Working with user accounts and resource permissions
▶ Understanding viruses
▶ Common network attacks
▶ Using IPSec
▶ Network security strategies
▶ What is wardriving?

Network security issues have changed a great deal over the last decade or so. Network security once related to protecting network resources from accidental erasure or unauthorized access to resources internally either by actual network users or individuals who have somehow gained internal access to the network. While remote access schemes related to dial-in network access posed a potential risk for the network (and still do), the administrator was required to secure what was essentially a closed system. This meant that issues related to user passwords and the rights assigned to various resources were the largest security holes.

Once a company's internal network was attached to the Internet, everything changed. Most security issues now relate to outside attacks. These attacks can take the form of a direct attack, such as a hacker accessing an internal network using IP spoofing (which is discussed later in this hour) or an indirect attack by attaching some sort of virus or other payload to an email message that is sent out as spam.

Is It Hacker or Cracker?

Most computer professionals and computer aficionados (who like to call themselves hackers) refer to individuals who attempt to break into networks or spread viruses as crackers. In the popular press, a cracker is actually most often called a hacker (which drives the "nice" hackers crazy). For continuity's sake, we will refer to cyber-criminals as hackers, meaning that we are actually referring to crackers.

Although computer security is inherently something of an oxymoron, particularly when networks enter the picture, it is essential to have a network security plan in place. This plan requires that you secure the network internally and also secure its external borders. In this hour, we look at some of the issues related to securing the internal network (from the internal "legal" users). We also discuss protecting a network from outside attack and take a look at TCP/IP related attacks and malware such as viruses.

Securing the Internal Network

In terms of network security, the first line of defense revolves around user logon issues and the different levels of access provided to network resources. It really goes without saying that users must have a valid username and password to log on to the network. But this simple statement is important to network security in that the network administrator controls the assignment of usernames and passwords to all the network users. This means that a set of rules should be devised to assign usernames and passwords so that they cannot be easily guessed by someone who would attempt to access the network by hijacking a particular user account.

Resources on the network can also be secured by assigning the appropriate level of access to the resource for each and every user on the network. For example, most users might only need to be able to read a particular database file on the network. So, it would make sense to only give those users the "read" permission or right for that file.

Resource Permissions and Rights

Depending on the network operating system you are using, you will either be dealing with permissions or rights, which are basically the same thing. On a Microsoft network, users are assigned permissions to resources. On a Novell network, users are assigned rights. Both are the level of access the user is allowed for that particular resource.

So, user authentication and resource permissions are both important to basic network security. Let's take a closer look at how a network administrator can use authentication and permissions to secure the internal network.

User Access

The network administrator is responsible for creating user accounts. Every network operating system provides a built-in administrator's account that is used to create and modify network user accounts and manage the resources on the network. This administrator's account is given various names in different operating systems, such as root, admin, and administrator (UNIX/Linux, NetWare, and Windows, respectively).

Not only does the network administrator determine the naming conventions for user accounts, but he also controls the rules for user passwords and the actual logon hours, as well as days that a particular user can log on to the network.

Assigning extremely complex usernames to your users won't really enhance network security. It will only enhance the possibility of users forgetting their usernames. Let's face it, most network administrators typically assign usernames based on the first initial and last name of the user. This is a fairly consistent and convenient way to assign usernames.

By the Way

Creating Usernames

Although the number of characters that can be used to create a username will vary from NOS to NOS, every operating system has naming conventions that you should be aware of before you create your user accounts. For example, Windows provides you with 20 characters for a username. NetWare eDirectory usernames can be up to 64 characters. Certain characters cannot be used in usernames. Typically, characters such as the slash (/), backslash (\), and other special characters cannot be used in usernames. Some operating systems allow spaces to be used in the usernames, and others do not. Again, you need to know your network operating system's naming conventions before you create usernames.

Password Protection

So, the password provides the security for the network authentication process. This means that you must develop a set of rules for the type of passwords that you will allow on the network. Although you have the option of assigning passwords to your users, it is definitely a better use of your time to create the rules for passwords on the network and allow your users to create (and update) their own passwords based on your rules. Network operating systems allow you to set the conditions that must be met for a legal password, such as the number of characters, the inclusion of both alphanumeric and numeric characters, and whether the password can contain the user's name.

The best practice for user passwords is to use what are called strong passwords. What constitutes a **strong password** varies slightly from NOS to NOS, but in general terms a strong password would be a password that would not be easy to guess by someone who has hijacked a user's account and is attempting to access the network. Microsoft defines a strong password as follows:

▶ A strong password must contain at least seven characters.

▶ A strong password does not contain user, real, or company names.

▶ A strong password does not contain complete dictionary words.

▶ A strong password is a combination of numeric, alphanumeric, and nonalphanumeric characters.

On Microsoft Server 2003, network password rules and other policies related to passwords (such as enforcing a password history) are handled using Group Policy, which provides a framework for controlling the user and computer environment in a Windows domain. Figure 19.1 shows the password policy settings. Note the policies have not been enabled for strong password protection.

FIGURE 19.1
Microsoft Windows Server 2003 provides Group Policy to control settings related to user password requirements.

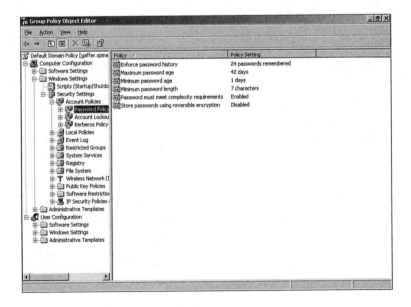

By the
Way

Microsoft Group Policy

Group Policy sets rules in a Windows network environment using Group Policy objects. These objects can contain settings for both computers and users. A Windows server will be configured with a number of default Group Policy objects; a network administrator can also create additional objects as needed. For a primer on Group Policy see *Sams Teach Yourself Microsoft Windows Server 2003 in 24 Hours.*

Another element related to keeping user passwords secure is to require your network users to change their passwords after a specific interval. Again, the various network operating systems provide you with the administrative tools to create password rules and also control the interval for password expiration. Be advised that forcing users to change their passwords on occasion is a good way to protect user accounts, but it can also lead to a lot of headaches in that users will either forget their new passwords or start writing passwords down to remember them. Choose an interval that balances security issues with the short term memory of your users.

Did you
Know?

Other Ways to Control User Logons

Some of the other ways you can protect the network from a hacker using a hijacked user account is to limit the actual logon hours for your users (if they don't work on the weekend, don't allow weekend logons), and you can also specify the computers that a user can actually log on to—again limiting the chance of someone co-opting a username and using it maliciously.

Auditing Logons

Once you have done your best to make sure that strong password protection is used on the network, you can use auditing to keep an eye on user logons. Auditing not only allows you to log successful logons, but also unsuccessful logons. This means that if you see a number of unsuccessful logon attempts for a particular user, the user account might have been hijacked and is being used by a hacker attempting to gain access to the network.

Most network operating systems have some form of audit mechanism. For example, Windows Server 2003 has its Security log, and UNIX has /var/adm/wtmp, /var/adm/syslog, and other logs. None of the tools provided by network operating systems for auditing will do you any good if you don't actually use them.

Each NOS will approach the enabling of auditing in a different way. So, because we have already briefly discussed Windows Group Policy, let's look at the enabling of the Auditing Policy on a Windows Server 2003 computer. Group

Policies for a domain can be accessed using the Group Policy Management snap-in as shown in Figure 19.2 (see Hour 15, "Microsoft Networking," for more about snap-ins).

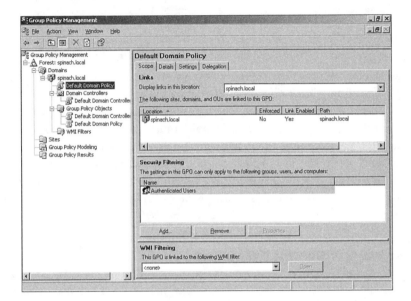

After the particular Group Policy has been located in the management snap-in, that policy can be edited. It's just a matter of right-clicking on a particular policy, and then selecting Edit on the Shortcut menu that appears. In terms of auditing, the Audit Policy allows you to audit logon events and a number of other events, such as object access and system events.

Figure 19.3 shows the Group Policy Object Editor and the Audit Policy objects available on a server running Microsoft Windows Server 2003. After these various audit objects are enabled, the actual events are tracked using the Windows Security log. (We will talk about logs and network monitoring in more detail in Hour 20, "Managing an Existing Network.")

As you can see from our Microsoft example, you can audit logon events and other events that allow you to keep tabs on your network. For example, attempts to access certain items on the network can also be audited, allowing you to not only track potential hackers by logon attempts but also attempts to access certain data files or other resources on the network.

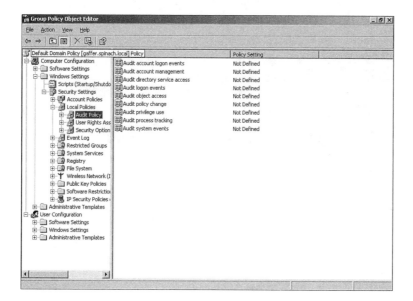

FIGURE 19.3
Auditing is enabled
using the Windows
Group Policy Object
Editor.

Disabling Accounts After Unsuccessful Logon Attempts

When you are setting the different configuration parameters for user accounts, you can set the number of unsuccessful logons that you will allow before an account is disabled. The actual settings will vary from NOS to NOS, but you should use this feature as another way to secure user accounts. If someone has obtained a username, you don't want to give him the opportunity to guess passwords and then access the network.

Did you
Know?

Resource Permissions

Securing the network using strategies related to user accounts and passwords is just one way of securing the internal network. Another method of securing important data and resources on the network relates to user rights or permissions to those resources. After a user has logged on to the network, he will typically need to access resources on a file or print server. The level of access that each user will have to a share or the volume on a file server is up to the network administrator.

Each network operating system provides a method of assigning permission (or rights) to folders or directories on network servers. Figure 19.4 shows the different rights that can be assigned to a volume on a NetWare file server using the NetWare Remote Manager utility. Rights such as read, write, and modify in the NetWare environment are also seen as permissions in the Windows and UNIX environments.

FIGURE 19.4
Each NOS, such as
NetWare, allows
you to assign per-
mission levels to
shared resources.

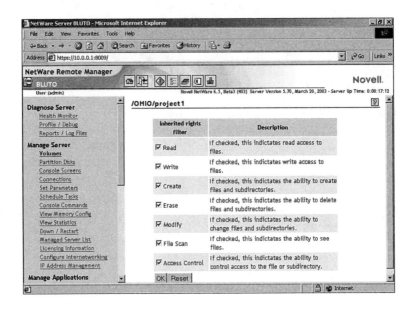

FIGURE 19.4
Each NOS, such as NetWare, allows you to assign permission levels to shared resources.

Although it is certainly convenient to give all your users the same access to a resource, you really need to take into account the fact that each user will require a different level of access to a particular resource—not everyone on the network needs the write and modify rights or permissions. For example, an accountant will need to be able to edit spreadsheets on a server, whereas an administrative assistant will only need to be able to view or read the data contained in the file. However, I think you can see that assigning individual permissions for each user to each resource would be extremely time-consuming and a nightmare to keep organized (in terms of documentation).

The great thing about network operating systems is that you can create groups and then assign access permissions or rights to the group. Then group membership will determine the level of access that a user has to particular resources.

Although access rights don't necessarily keep hackers off your internal network, they do allow you to minimize the damage that a careless user can make to important data files or the level of access that a hacker would have to a particular resource when they commandeer a particular user account.

Dealing with Viruses

Another threat to your network's security is the virus. A **virus** is a self-replicating piece of software code. Because a virus can copy itself, it can easily (and unfortunately) be spread from computer to computer.

Viruses come in several varieties. A number of different virus types have evolved over the years. These different types of viruses have been classified based on how they infect a computer:

▶ Boot sector viruses—Some of the first viruses were boot sector viruses. A boot sector virus typically spreads through infected floppy disks or other removable storage media. Boot sector virus infections are helped along by user forgetfulness. If I place a boot sector virus–infected disk in my computer, nothing will happen unless I reboot the system (meaning turning it off for the day and then turning it on the next morning) and have forgotten to remove the infected disk from the floppy drive. On boot up, the boot sector virus is loaded in to the computer's memory (because the computer will try to boot from the floppy). The virus can then infect the hard drive or any disks you place in the floppy drive once the computer is up and running. The Exebug virus is an example of a boot sector virus.

▶ File viruses—Although fairly uncommon now, file viruses actually infect an executable file such as an EXE or COM file. When the infected file is run, the file virus is loaded into the computer's RAM. It can then infect other executable files as they are run on the computer. A form of the file virus is the overwriting virus, which actually overwrites the executable file that it infects. Examples of file viruses are the Dark Avenger virus and the KMIT virus.

▶ Macro viruses—The macro virus is a fairly recent virus type. Macro viruses are typically written in Visual Basic code and can infect documents and spreadsheet data files rather than executables. When an infected document is loaded into an application such as Microsoft Word, the virus code runs as any other macro would in that particular application. Another scary thing about macro viruses is that they are not operating system specific. Because Microsoft Excel can run on a Macintosh and a Windows-based PC, the macro virus can actually be spread between the two platforms if the infected Excel worksheet is shared. Macro viruses are also not confined to Microsoft applications and have popped up in other office suites, such as Lotus SmartSuite. An example of a macro virus is the famous Melissa virus, a Word macro virus that automatically spread itself via email.

▶ Multipartite viruses—A multipartite virus has the characteristics of both a boot sector virus and a file virus. It can spread from the boot sector of a drive to another drive, and it can also attack executable files on the computer. Some multipartite viruses can even infect device drivers (such as the drivers for your network interface card). An example of a multipartite virus is Pastika. This virus is only activated on certain days of the month (typically the 21st and 22nd of the month) and can actually overwrite your hard drive.

The actual number of viruses in the "wild" (meaning those found on business computers and networks) at any one time varies, but in general the number is increasing. The number of macro viruses is definitely on the rise.

Staying Ahead of Viruses

To keep up with viruses currently found in the wild, check out `http://www.f-secure.com/`. F-Secure, who hosts this site, provides a range of network security products. Symantec also provides a great site related to current virus threats; check out `http://www.sarc.com`. Another good place to look for information related to viruses is the SANS institute. SANS, at `http://www.sans.org/`, provides information on viruses and other network security issues.

The only way to keep network computers free of viruses is to invest in antivirus software. Antivirus software is available in a variety of configurations ranging from desktop file scanning to server-based file scanning to firewall-based file scanning. It's wise to have as many file scanners as possible between the user and his files (whether the files come from the Internet or the local network). Although a slight performance degradation is involved with virus scanning, time spent cleaning out virus-infected systems is time well spent. Typically, virus software vendors have a method in which the software install on each computer can be automated and maintained successfully with minimal input from the user.

Trojan Horses and Worms

Viruses are not the only malware (meaning bad software) that can attack a network. You will also have to deal with Trojan horses and worms. A Trojan horse (or just Trojan, as it is often referred to) is a program that appears to be perfectly benign, such as a screensaver or a game. When executed, the Trojan executes and can do such things as using mail addresses found on the computer to mail copies of itself to others. A worm is a program that spreads itself from computer to computer on a network. It doesn't need to be activated like a virus. It just spreads all by itself. A worm can be potentially devastating on a worldwide network such as the Internet because it can quickly spread itself throughout the entire network. Most antivirus programs can detect Trojans and worms, but you must keep your antivirus software up-to-date.

Understanding External Attacks

With Internet connectivity a necessity, TCP/IP has become the standard network protocol stack. However, TCP/IP was designed to provide reasonable connectivity.

It wasn't designed with security in mind. Each protocol in the TCP/IP stack communicates on a particular channel, called a well-known port number. (Port numbers are discussed in more detail in Hour 14, "TCP/IP.") For example, HTTP operates on port 80, and FTP operates on port 21/20. There are, in fact, over 1,000 well-known port numbers: Each of these ports is a potential path for an attack on your network. Fortunately, firewalls provide a strategy for blocking these ports. (Firewalls are discussed in Hour 13, "Connecting to the Internet.")

So, because of the way the TCP/IP protocol stack works and the fact that a number of network monitoring tools and protocol sniffers are available (network monitoring is discussed in Hour 20), hackers have found a host of technical tricks for getting around network security strategies. The TCP/IP protocol stack and both client and network operating systems provide holes that can be exploited by hackers who monitor unsecured network communication via the Internet.

A number of different external attacks exist that network administrators must deal with:

▶ IP Spoofing—In an IP spoofing attack, a hacker monitors the data flow in and out of a network until he discovers the IP address of a system inside the firewall. Once the hacker has that address, he can begin to pass data in and out of the network as if it were being sent to the internal IP address.

▶ Brute-Force Password Hacking—Brute-force password hacking is pretty simple. Essentially, the hacker uses an electronic dictionary to keep trying different passwords for a known login name. It's a tedious process. If any auditing is being done on the network, the stealth attack is usually picked up in no time, which makes cracking the password all the more difficult. Password hacking, however, is a common occurrence and an effective way for a hacker to gain access to an internal network.

▶ Denial of Service—A denial of service attack isn't used to gain access to the internal network but is used to disable a target server. Denial of service attacks can take different forms. A SYN flood is named after the SYN message that is used on a IP network to request a connection to a server. Under the TCP transport, the SYN flood is a huge number of connection requests made by the hacker (usually via hijacked computers), which brings down the server. A number of corporate Web sites, including Microsoft sites, have been brought down by denial of service attacks in the last few years. Another type of denial of service attack sends a large number of emails to a mail server, which can cripple the server.

The Ping of Death

The ping command is very useful to check the connection between two computers on a network (see more about ping in Hour 21, "Network Troubleshooting Tips and Tricks"). It also has been used on the Internet to check lag time between two computers, particularly by computer aficionados who frequent Internet Relay Chat sessions. However, you can send a ping command and specify that the ping packet size is greater than 65,536 bytes. This illegal ping packet size can freeze a computer up and knock it off the network. Since newer network operating systems and the various client platforms have had their TCP/IP stack modified to negate this kind of attack, the ping of death does not pose a particularly real threat today to network servers.

▶ Email Relaying—A hacker is able to compromise a mail server (which can be done with a simple coding script, worm, or virus) so that the mail server actually relays spam that the hacker originates. This makes the spam look as if it originates at the compromised server. This type of attack can completely slow down any connections between the internal network and the Internet because of the high volume of mail relayed through the compromised mail server.

Although these different types of attacks are certainly a concern for a network administrator, strategies exist for negating these types of attacks—firewalls and proxy servers. Another method of protecting data from hackers trying to snoop on the network using protocol analyzers revolves around IP security and encryption. Let's take a look at IPSec, and then we can end this hour with a checklist of some general ideas on overall security for the network.

Using IP Security

In the preceding section, we discussed that hackers can gain a great deal of information by using network snoopers and protocol analyzers to capture unsecured network communications. Each IP data packet contains a great deal of information, and after a hacker captures a packet, he can read IP address headers that supply source and destination addresses.

IP Security or **IPSec** was developed by the Internet Engineering Task Force (IETF) to supply TCP/IP networks with a security mechanism that keeps data safe during transport. This means that the data cannot be read, replayed, or modified by someone intercepting the data on either the internal network or via external network connections such as those used by Virtual Private Networking.

IPSec protects against a number of different hacker behaviors. For example, IPSec encrypts data at the sending computer, which means that intercepted data (intercepted using a snooper program) cannot be read.

Cryptography is also used by IPSec to protect against data being captured and then modified by the hacker. A cryptographic key is required to read the encrypted data, and a cryptographic checksum is attached to each data packet that will enable the receiving computer to detect if the data has been modified during transport. Essentially, IPSec is using cryptography to establish a relationship between the sending and receiving computer that is very difficult for a hacker to breach.

IPSec is supported by network operating systems such as Windows Server 2003 and Sun Solaris. It makes sense to deploy IPSec on your network, particularly in cases in which you use Virtual Private Networking as a means for telecommuters or employees on the road to access internal network resources.

Thoughts on Securing a Network

We have already discussed the fact that you need to require strong passwords on user accounts and also make sure that your users change their passwords periodically. This is a good first step for securing user access to the network. Controlling other user behaviors—such as the hours they can log on and the number of concurrent connections that a particular user account can have on the network—are also good ways to build an overall security plan. You also need to secure individual resources such as shared folders and volumes using access rights and permissions.

Microsoft NTFS Permissions

As already discussed in this hour, the various network operating system platforms use rights or permissions to secure shared resources. Microsoft goes one step further on server drives that have been formatted with the NTFS file system. NTFS permissions can be used to protect down to the file level. The problem with NTFS permissions is that they will affect how your share permissions work on a Windows network. For more about the interaction of share and NTFS permissions on a network using Windows Server 2003, check out *Sams Teach Yourself Windows Server 2003 in 24 Hours*.

Did you Know?

Here is a general checklist of best practices related to network security:

- ▶ Make passwords secret. Enforce this policy strictly.

- ▶ Ensure that users log out of the network at the end of their workday.

- ▶ Keep and monitor security audit logs on your systems. Look for odd patterns of access: Should the junior accounting clerk be logged in to the network at 2:00 a.m.? Question the entries in this log just as you would question phone calls on your business long-distance service. And keep records of questionable access that apparently checks out; it's possible that someone is working from within the organization to compromise security.

- ▶ Add virus-checking software to your system. Ideally, you'll have one kind of antivirus software on your firewall, another on your server, and yet another on your workstations. Although this might sound like overkill, you definitely do not want to have to deal with a network-wide virus infection. It is an excellent way to lose your job.

- ▶ Build your network model in such a way as to foster security. This means adding a proxy and a firewall to secure the network's connection to the Internet.

- ▶ Make certain that your systems are patched against TCP/IP denial-of-service attacks and different types of email related attacks. The most recent updates provided by your software vendors should be installed on both your server and client computers. A recent series of viruses that plagued many networks running Windows XP and Windows Server 2003 was easily negated by applying a patch provided by Microsoft. However, I know of a number of colleagues who did not act quickly in applying the patch to network computers, which resulted in many infected systems.

- ▶ Instruct your users and system administrators that they are not to give out passwords, user IDs, or other computer-security–related material over the phone unless they are absolutely certain who they are talking to. Ideally, they should demand to call back any caller who wants password, user, or network information.

- ▶ Physically secure your server computers. Allow only password access to server's consoles, and log all attempts to gain entry to those systems.

- ▶ Secure backup media in a locked area. (Backup strategies are discussed in Hour 20.)

So, bottom line—every network needs a security plan that catalogs the possible threats to the network and the measures you plan to take to negate these threats. This means that you have to keep up-to-date on the latest virus threats and other new exploits that are being targeted by hackers—meaning that you have to do a lot of reading and stay abreast of the latest security threats.

Create a network security plan that leans toward user education, which can go a long way to securing the internal network in terms of user behaviors. Also keep in mind that no matter how small your company, you always run the risk of external attack, which can come in the form of email attacks or direct attacks from hackers.

Wardriving and Wireless Networks

In Hour 23, "Wireless Networking," we discuss the basics of wireless networking and some of the strategies you can use to secure a wireless network. However, since we are discussing network security issues in this hour, I think it is best to close out the hour with a discussion of security issues related to wireless networking, particularly because wireless implementations are growing rapidly in both the home and business markets.

In terms of security, wireless networking provides a number of challenges; these have been made extremely obvious by a new hacker exploit termed wardriving. **Wardriving** is basically driving around with a wireless enabled laptop computer, which is used to find and connect to unsecured wireless networks. This can often provide free access to the Internet and also allow hackers with the inclination to try and crack the wireless network. Wardrivers often outfit their vehicles with an external wireless antennae, which makes it easier to find wireless "hotspots." A handheld Global Positioning System device (GPS) is also often used to help map the actual borders of the hotspot, making future use of the hotspot for Internet access extremely easy.

Wardriving has become such a geek fad that many people are involved in trying to locate unsecured wireless hotspots. These hobbyists are really just looking for free Internet access and readily share information about mapped hotspots with other wardrivers via a number of sites on the Web. However, the fact that the wireless hotspots are easily and readily identified means that hackers are basically given a roadmap to unsecured wireless networks.

More About Wardriving

Wardriving has become extremely popular, and a large number of tools for snooping for wireless connections are available on a number of Web sites. (Just do a search with your favorite Web search engine for "wardriving.") There are even wardriving tools for PDAs and other handheld computing devices that allow you to capture packets from a unsecured wireless network. With the current 802.11 wireless standards, securing a wireless network against snooping and packet capture can be problematic. For a complete discussion of wireless network security, check out *Maximum Wireless Security* from Sams Publishing.

So, how do you protect your network against wardriving? First of all, you need to understand how wireless networking works and how wireless access points are configured. (An access point is the device that provides wireless clients to connect to a wired network, which is discussed in more detail in Hour 23.) No matter the vendor of your access point, the access point will have a default configuration, and this includes settings such as the administrative password, the default subnet (the range of IP addresses for the device), and security settings related to the 802.11 security protocols WEP (Wired Equivalent Privacy)and WPA (WiFi Protected Access).

Wardrivers know that the default configuration for an access point makes it extremely easy to promiscuously connect to a wireless network. Network administrators should also know this. You can't run a wireless network out-of-the-box; you must custom configure access points with the highest security possible.

However, even changing default settings for access points won't necessarily protect the network. For example, wireless networks use a network name or SSID (service set identifier) that identifies the wireless network. The SSID is used by mobile devices to connect to access points on the wireless network. Each access point vendor configures its access points with a default SSID. For example, access points from Linksys (a company providing a lot of different wireless access points and NICs) uses the default SSID "linksys."

The Scary Truth About Wireless Networking

There are tons of Web sites that provide you with all the information you need to wardrive. I'm not condoning wardriving (unless it's done diagnostically to secure your own wireless network); I'm just reporting the facts. For example, check out www.cirt.net. This site provides default SSIDs for access point hardware and default passwords using a search engine that allows you to search by vendor.

So, it immediately makes sense to change the default SSID for added protection because wardrivers will know what the default SSIDs are for most network access points. However, even changing the SSID doesn't protect the wireless network all that much. SSIDs can be determined using a packet sniffer because the SSID will appear in packets as plain text.

So, bottom line, even being very conscientious in terms of configuring wireless access points and other wireless devices isn't going to protect a wireless network from wardrivers with too much time on their hands. Hour 23 discusses the security protocols currently used by the 802.11 wireless devices and how security will be improved in upcoming versions of the 802.11 standards. You need to configure the currently available security protocols (WEP and WPA) on access points and take advantage of the security that these protocols provide.

Beyond access point configuration (including security protocols), you can take advantage of other strategies such as virtual private networking (also discussed in Hour 23). For a higher level of security, you will currently have to go beyond what is currently provided by the 802.11 standards and take advantage of third-party products. For example, Air Defense provides such products as RogueWatch, a hardware monitoring device, which allows you to monitor your wireless environment for rogue access points and neighboring wireless networks protecting your network from any unauthorized connections.

Although the wireless networking provides possibilities, security issues still might preclude its use in situations in which highly sensitive data is exchanged by network devices. If you do deploy wireless strategies on your network, remember that the wardrivers are probably driving around right outside your building.

Summary

In this hour, we took a look at issues related to securing your network. We discussed how you can use password policies and resource rights to help secure the network. We also discussed some of the external attacks that can be visited upon your network by hackers. Solutions such as firewalls and IPSec were discussed in relation to different hacker attacks. We also took a look at a basic checklist of things that you can do to keep your network secure. We ended our discussion of security with a look at wardriving and wireless networking.

Q&A

Q *Can using password expiration as a security measure on the network be a bad thing?*

A You really need to balance the use of password expiration with the fact that too many password changes over time are eventually going to confuse your user base, and they are going to forget their passwords. Use common sense to configure password expiration intervals. If you are also using strong password protection on the network, you can probably lower the frequency that you make your users change passwords because strong passwords are more difficult for hackers to guess.

Q *How can external attacks such as IP spoofing be negated?*

A You can use firewalls, proxy servers, and IPSec to help safeguard against hackers attempting to snoop network traffic from the internal network.

Q *How often should I update my security plan?*

A As often as it is required. Basically any time the network grows or implements new technologies, the security plan should address both the growth and the new implementations. Deploying technologies such as wireless networking will no doubt require a major addendum to any security plan.

HOUR 20

Managing an Existing Network

In this hour, you will learn about the following topics:

- ▶ Upgrading and growing a network
- ▶ Backing up data
- ▶ Server and client licensing
- ▶ Disaster recovery planning

Network administration requires people skills, hardware and software knowledge, and the ability to see in to the future. (Network operating systems do not typically include a crystal ball.) In this hour, we take a look at some of the issues that a network administrator will face as he manages a network. We discuss upgrading network hardware and also take a look at configuring RAID arrays and establishing a backup schedule. We also look at some of the issues related to client and NOS licensing and discuss some of the basics of establishing a disaster recovery plan for your network.

Upgrading the Network

Once your network is built, the immediate temptation is to sit back and relax. If the network is operating properly and is stable, it's certainly tempting to put your feet up on the desk and kick back. However, given that hardware and software change at such an exponential rate, it's pretty much a given that you're going to get caught in upgrade cycles. It's in your best interests to try to design the network so that it can be upgraded minimally when it requires upgrades. It's also in your best interests to try and temper management's enthusiasm for every upgrade; by advising moderation and testing, you can actually maintain network functionality while also negating unnecessary upgrades that aren't really cost-effective.

Although it is difficult to serve in the role of "naysayer," an important aspect of your job is to maintain and upgrade the network so that your company is getting the most bang for its buck and using the appropriate technology for its business. Return on Investment (ROI) is difficult to calculate for computer equipment, for a variety of reasons. For one, the use of computer equipment, either hardware or software, cannot be calculated in any sort of linear fashion; it's pointless to try to calculate the value of a memo done on a user's PC. But it is your job to keep the network in the best shape possible and substantiate any budgetary needs in as logical a fashion as possible.

Network upgrades should really be based on the need of the company in terms of the business tools that employees need to get their jobs done effectively (both in terms of cost and the user's time). So, it is obvious that as computer hardware and software evolves, you will need to replace servers, client machines, network operating systems, and client applications.

Let's take a look at some basic strategies for managing hardware growth and upgrades. We can then take a look at issues related to software upgrades and growth.

By the Way

> **Monitoring Network Health**
>
> I don't think any network administrator actually feels that he can sit back and relax after a network is up and running. Maintaining the network and developing strategies for detecting network problems is a set of tasks that will keep any network team busy. For more about monitoring and logging server performance and events, see Hour 21, "Network Troubleshooting Tips and Tricks."

Managing Hardware Upgrades and Growth

Not only will network hardware (including client PCs) need to be upgraded over time, but you will also add systems and other supporting hardware because of network growth. Any successful company will grow. This means that you will not only have to keep existing employees up and running effectively on the network, but you will also need to plan for and act on network growth. Some strategies for managing upgrades and growth follow:

- ▶ **Set floating standards for hardware.** In other words, every year or so, create a standard computer configuration based on the current most powerful computers and try to stick to it for as long as possible. The benefits of this approach are twofold. First, the computers are a known quantity. (If you spec a computer and discover a hardware bug, quirk, or incompatibility, you know that the remainder of the computers of that type will likely share that trait.) The second benefit is cost; over one year, the cost of most computers will decline significantly, making your bottom-line staff very happy.

- ▶ **Determine whether a complete computer upgrade is required or whether an incremental upgrade is acceptable.** Given the ridiculous pace with which computers get faster, many OEM computer manufacturers and a host of third-party companies are building upgrades that range from faster processors that plug in to the original processor socket to memory upgrades. It's possible that a processor upgrade and an extra shot of memory can extend the life of many an old PC by providing adequate performance at a bargain price (at least in comparison to the cost of a new computer).

- ▶ **Have a complete inventory of what's in your computers, not just the CPU serial number.** If you know what is inside the computer, you can more readily make a call about whether it's wiser to upgrade or replace it. This inventory list also helps when a part fails; rather than taking the case apart, you can simply look up the failed part in your database and order another.

- ▶ **Regularly do hardware audits with network management software that can handle the process.** If you have to do your inventory by going from computer to computer, it will never get done. However, most network management software has a hardware audit feature; used properly, this feature can help you diagnose a system on-the-fly.

The bottom line is that no matter how big your network and client base, you have to know the different hardware configurations that are running on the network. New employees will obviously receive newer equipment when they come on board (if they are addition to the staff rather than replacing a staff member). But you must make sure that veteran employees are not left in the lurch with older systems that make them less effective (than a newer employee).

Managing Software Upgrades and Growth

In many ways, software is easier to manage than hardware. The simple reason is that companies tend to standardize on certain software; not using that software puts a user outside the loop. The larger reason is that use of software has legal ramifications that force a company to treat software more rigorously than hardware. After all, hardware is a capital asset and can be depreciated out of existence; software, even expensive software, is often expensed. It's simply written off as a cost of doing business.

With software, unlike hardware, you can do a tremendous amount of management, ranging from the setting of corporate standards to auditing the versions used. The strategies you should follow for managing software are as follows:

▶ **Use site licensing or volume licensing on your network.** Most software vendors sell volume licenses. Even if only a few workers are using the application, you might still qualify for some kind of volume or site licensing. If you can't use volume or site licensing, it is imperative that you have enough individual licenses to cover all your products. I talk about another aspect of licensing, server and client licensing, in the next section.

▶ **Work with senior management to come up with company standards for software.** This sounds silly, but it's worth discussing. Suppose that your company has standardized on Microsoft Word for word processing, but you have a user that insists on using WordPerfect. It is much easier to support and license a single word processing product. So having a mandate from senior management that all users will use a particular product will provide you with better control of client behavior and software use.

▶ **Unauthorized software is unsupported software.** On any network, no matter how few users, you must lay down a particular law related to software installation: The rule is that no user-installed software is allowed on the network. If a user installs his own software in defiance of such an edict, and the installation creates a problem, the only support you will provide is to reset the user's PC back to the original, approved configuration. Allowing unauthorized software is problematic, not just because it's wrong (users do have a proclivity for installing unlicensed copies of software in a work environment), but because it raises the bar on the management hurdle to an unacceptable level.

▶ **Create a standard installation and stick to it if possible.** If you can install a fixed set of applications on each hard disk so that all disks match, that's good. Most network operating systems provide you with the ability to install standard installations on network clients. (For example, Microsoft Server 2003 provides the Remote Installation Service.) Also, products such as Norton Ghost and Symantec Drive Image exist that allow you to create a standard client configuration (including applications) that can be quickly installed on any client using the same standard hardware.

► **Use a license management utility.** License management utilities ensure that you're never in violation of the terms of your software agreements. License management utilities can be a pain for users who can't get an application because it's at its license limits, but they ensure that you're in compliance. Thanks to the efforts of the Business Software Alliance (BSA) and the Software Publishers Association (PSA), noncompliance is becoming increasingly expensive. It's not uncommon to see extremely large fines for gross and willful license violators.

As already mentioned, I discuss software licensing in the next section. My discussion centers around the requirements of network operating systems with regard to client licensing on the network.

In terms of managing software upgrades, it is important that you make new software tools and more up-to-date versions of software products available to as many users as possible. So in most cases, your software upgrade cycle must be linked to your hardware upgrade cycle. This is because most new software typically requires a more robust hardware configuration to operate.

Using Network Management Software

If you have a medium to large network, you might want to invest in network management software. These enterprise tools allow you to keep track of software installations, hardware configurations, and even supply software distribution and client behavior tracking mechanisms. A number of different network management software packages are available, such as HP's OpenView, Sun's SunNet Manager, and Microsoft's Systems Management Server.

By the Way

Dealing with NOS and Client Licensing

It is not only essential that you make sure that all applications running on the network and individual client computers are properly licensed, but you must also make sure that you have the appropriate number of client licenses to access the various servers and their NOS. Application licensing is fairly straightforward; you need a license for every occurrence of that application running on the network clients, including any remote users. This can take the form of individual licenses or some sort of volume or site licensing (or a combination of these licensing strategies). Client licensing in relation to network operating systems, however, can be a little more complicated because more than one licensing scenario can be available for a particular NOS.

A NOS will require that you have a server license for your server (a separate license for each server) and client licenses for your network clients. This just doesn't mean that you have a license for the client operating system but a license that makes it legal for you to connect to the server as a client.

For example, you can buy a Novell NetWare 6.5 base package that licenses the server and five client connections. To license more clients, you buy what is called a connection additive license. These additive client licenses range from the addition of 5 to 500 users.

Each NOS platform has its own licensing scheme. When you work with open source Linux products, you might not have to deal with licensing, but no matter what platform you are using, you should take the time to research the type of licensing required for each client on the network.

Microsoft Windows servers put an interesting spin on client licensing. Windows Server 2003 actually provides you with three different possibilities for licensing network clients: Per User, Per Device, or Per Server.

Per User means that you will purchase a license for each network user on the network. Each of these users can connect to any and all the servers on the network. Per Device means that you license each computer or device such as a Windows-based PDA. Because of the device license, the device can then legally connect to any and all servers on the network. Per Server means that you are licensed for a certain number of concurrent connections to the server. If you have 50 licenses, 50 clients can connect to the server.

Per Server licenses can actually save you money if you have a network situation in which your employees actually work in shifts. Because only a subset of the employees are connected to the network servers, you can go with the Per Server connection model. In cases in which employees put in the same hours, you are probably better off going with the Per User or Per Device models.

All network operating systems supply you with some type of utility that you use to add server or client licenses to the network. Microsoft Windows Server 2003, for example, provides the Licensing snap-in, which allows you to add licenses to the network. Figure 20.1 shows the Windows Server 2003 Licensing snap-in.

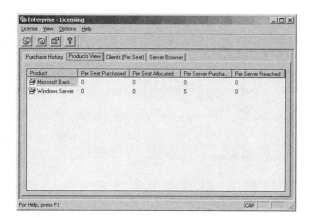

FIGURE 20.1
Network operating
systems such as
Windows Server
2003 provide a util-
ity for recording
server and client
licenses.

It is extremely important that you keep track of all your server and client licenses. The same goes for application licenses. You should have a well organized filing system that allows you to access any hard copy licenses that you have and also make sure that you use software utilities that allow you to keep track of your licenses. Being caught without the appropriate number of licenses is a very good way to lose your job because it could result in fines and extremely bad publicity for your company.

Backing Up Network Data

In Hour 5, "Network Concepts," RAID (redundant array of inexpensive disks) implementations are discussed. RAID provides a method of creating redundancy on network servers, which can help protect valuable network data. The best way, however, to protect network data is backing up that data. Creating a backup plan and implementing that plan is an important aspect of managing an existing network.

When your network is operating smoothly and you aren't detecting any potential problems in your server logs and performance monitoring tables, it's kind of hard to believe that you might have a sudden meltdown that could result in the loss of data. But it does happen. It's much wiser to assume that you will have a crash at some point and to prepare adequately for it.

The Basics of Back Up

On first inspection, it might seem a little confusing when you are trying to put together a backup plan for your network. You want to back up all the important data, but you want to do it as effectively (in terms of time and effort) as possible. Although you might throw up your hands and determine that you will just do a time-consuming and arduous complete backup periodically, there are ways to plan a backup strategy that will protect all the network data (with minimal loss) yet not require you to spend every evening backing up your servers.

Creating an effective backup strategy really begins with a consideration of the following:

- ▶ How much data you have to back up

- ▶ How often you want to back up

- ▶ Whether or not backing up your data requires dealing with open files and ensuring consistent data sets

- ▶ What kind of media you want to store your backed up data on and where to store it

- ▶ What kind of backup scheme you want to use

For what it's worth, the first three items determine the choice of the fourth. I discuss backup schemes in more detail later in the hour.

A number of different types of backup media can be used. Some of the popular tape backup types are as follows:

- ▶ **Digital Audio Tape (DAT)**—Developed for sound recording, this small high-density tape format can store around 12GB of data per cartridge. DAT has a moderate transfer speed but isn't as fast as some of the others (such as DLT and 8mm).

- ▶ **DLTtape** (or just **DLT**)—A half-inch tape format that holds up to 70GB of data and has transfer speeds of 5MB per second.

By the Way

Getting More Info on DLTtape

A great Web site that provides all sorts of information on DLTtape can be found at www.dlttape.com.

- ▶ **8mm**—Similar to the 8mm video format, these 8mm cartridges can hold around 30GB of data and can transfer data at speeds up to 3MB per second.

You can also back up data to removable media drives, such as the Zip and Jaz drives made by Iomega. You can also copy files to CD-ROM or DVD if you have access to an appropriate burner. Again, the media type that you choose will be dictated by the amount of data you need to back up. The media type, obviously, dictates the tape backup drives that you use.

A number of different hardware manufacturers make tape backup drives, including Seagate, Hewlett-Packard, and Iomega (the list goes on and on). Some of these products come with decent backup software, and some don't. (You might have to buy the backup software separately.) Most network operating systems also supply some type of backup utility. Some are better than others, and you will have to assess whether you can get by with the NOS backup software or you need something more sophisticated.

After you have chosen and deployed the backup hardware that you will use, you need to establish a backup scheme (as mentioned in our list), which needs to include a backup schedule. Let's take a look at the different types of backups that you can make, and then look at a simple scheme called the "Grandfather-Father-Son scheme."

Types of Backups

There are three different backup methods: full, differential, and incremental. These different types of backups are possible because of file markers. A **marker** is an attribute placed on a file. (In other words, the file is tagged.) Typically, any operating system you work with will mark or tag a file after that file has been backed up. A file that has changed since its last backup will also be tagged. The use of these tags or markers to denote which files have been backed up and which files have not enables backup software to perform different types of backups. Here's a breakdown of how these backup methods work:

- ▶ **Full backup**—This type of backup is also called a normal backup or a daily backup (depending on the backup software you're using). A full backup takes all the files that you select for backup and backs them up (no matter how the files are currently marked). The files' attributes are then changed to mark the fact that they have been backed up. (If you change the file after the backup, the marker will change and indicate that the file has not been backed up since the last changes were made.)

- ▶ **Differential backup**—This type of backup only backs up the files that have changed since their last backup. The differential backup does not, however, change the marker attribute indicating that the file has been backed up. It leaves the marker alone, meaning the file will still read that it has not been backed up since it was last changed.

▶ **Incremental backup**—This type of backup backs up only the files that have been changed since the last backup (just as a differential backup does). An incremental backup changes the archive marker on the files that are backed up to identify those files as having been backed up (which differs from the differential backup method).

The type of backup you use will depend on the backup scheme that you devise. You should determine a particular time of week when you do a full backup (perhaps on the weekend). You can then use differential and incremental backups (which don't take as long as a full backup) to make sure that you have the most recent copies of files that have changed since the full backup. A simple use of a single full backup and then sequential differential backups are discussed in the next section.

The Grandfather-Father-Son Scheme

An extremely simple backup scheme is the Grandfather-Father-Son scheme. Basically, the Grandfather-Father-Son scheme sets up a sequence of tapes ensuring proper tape rotation, so you won't lose data.

How do you do it? First, label four tapes (or tape sets, if you're using a tape changer that uses more than one tape per day) *Monday*, *Tuesday*, *Wednesday*, and *Thursday*. Then take four more tapes or tape sets and label them *Friday 1*, *Friday 2*, *Friday 3*, and *Friday 4*. After you've done this, you've created all your repeating tapes. The remainder of the tapes are labeled *Friday 5*. The Friday 5 tapes are your archive tapes; you use each one only once (at the very end of the cycle) and then archive it. This approach ensures that every five weeks, you have an archive tape.

Next, you have to configure your backup software. Typically, the easiest way to back up is a differential backup. In differential backups, the Friday tape is a full backup, and each successive tape (Monday through Thursday) captures all the changes since the last Friday full backup tape. With differential backups, you only need two tapes to restore a crashed server: the last Friday full backup and the most recent weekday tape. Most commercial backup software can be configured to do differential backups, and often have a Grandfather-Father-Son backup scheme or wizard to set it up.

Once your software is configured for differential backup (it's seldom hard to configure), you have to start rotating the tapes. Table 20.1 shows how that works.

TABLE 20.1 The Grandfather-Father-Son Backup Scheme

	MONDAY	TUESDAY	WEDNESDAY	THURSDAY	FRIDAY
First Week:					
Tape name	*Monday*	*Tuesday*	*Wednesday*	*Thursday*	*Friday 1*
Second Week:					
Tape name	*Monday*	*Tuesday*	*Wednesday*	*Thursday*	*Friday 2*
Third Week:					
Tape name	*Monday*	*Tuesday*	*Wednesday*	*Thursday*	*Friday 3*
Fourth Week:					
Tape name	*Monday*	*Tuesday*	*Wednesday*	*Thursday*	*Friday 4*
Fifth Week:					
Tape name	*Monday*	*Tuesday*	*Wednesday*	*Thursday*	*Friday 5*

Each fifth Friday tape is the Grandfather; Friday tapes 1 through 4 are the Father tapes; and the Monday through Thursday tapes are the Sons. Every Friday tape except the Friday 5 tape is reused in each five-week period; Monday through Thursday tapes are reused each week.

See? It is pretty simple. It just requires some time to set it up and understand it. Then it usually runs pretty simply. One caveat: Make sure that you change tapes according to the schedule. If you don't, you'll have incomplete backups and be asking for trouble. Also, store all your Friday 5 (archive) tapes offsite as part of disaster recovery. I discuss disaster recovery issues in the next section.

One more thing: Make sure that you periodically inspect your tapes. Magnetic media have a life span and will become more likely to fail over time. Just think about how scratched up a home videotape gets when you constantly reuse it to tape shows on your VCR. It makes sense to periodically work new tapes into the process so that you are not working with very old and possibly unreliable media.

Your Network and Disaster Recovery Planning

Having a backup strategy for your network is only one part of what should be a complete disaster recovery plan. No one can predict when disaster will strike. Unfortunately, it often takes a disaster to make people consider disaster recovery planning. In the wake of the September 11, 2001 World Trade Center disaster,

disaster recovery has become a hot corporate topic. Companies and institutions have spent more time and resources related to planning what they would do in the event of a disaster.

As the network administrator, your responsibilities related to disaster recovery are making plans that allow you to get important data back into the hands of people who need it. This means that your disaster recovery plan needs to be multi-faceted and anticipate different levels of disaster. Your plan should not center around one type of disaster, such as an earthquake or fire.

For example, in the case of a major snowstorm, employees might not be able to get to the physical location of the company offices. Yet your business needs them to be online and working. In this case, your disaster recovery plan might dictate that you activate VPN or dial-in access that allows employees to work from home. On the other hand, in the case of a disaster such as a fire that destroys the corporate offices, you will need to use your backup information to rebuild the network data servers at a new location and provide network access to that data.

You can see from the previous paragraph that different disruptions of business continuity (a fancy way of saying recovering from a disaster) will require different solutions. Any recovery plan that you implement needs to address different disaster scenarios. Let's take a look at some of the basics of fashioning a disaster recovery plan.

Creating a disaster recovery plan requires several stages. Those creating the plan will need to know a number of things, such as the current computing infrastructure, the business impact when the infrastructure is damaged, and suspected vulnerabilities in the infrastructure. Let's take a look at some of the stages required to assemble the information needed to create the disaster recovery plan.

Defining the Computing Infrastructure

Before any planning can take place, an inventory and definition of the company's computing environment must be made. This means that you need to know how many workstations, servers, and other devices are present on the network.

An inventory of network devices can be created in any spreadsheet program such as Excel. This information vital to the recovery plan should be kept in a safe but easily accessible place (such as offsite) in case it is needed. (Inventories are also very important when dealing with insurance companies—enough said about that.)

A detailed network map also needs to be created (although one should have been created when the network was first planned), and other documentation that provides an understanding of what's on the network and how it works must be assembled. Before you can create a recovery plan for the IT infrastructure, the project team creating the plan must understand the IT infrastructure.

Network maps can be created in a variety of software programs. Microsoft Visio, which comes in a number of versions, is an easy-to-use tool for creating network diagrams (and was used to create many of the network diagrams in this book). Another aspect of defining the network infrastructure is a listing of network support positions. It is important that management be aware of the personnel required to keep the network functioning on a daily basis. This means that a listing of positions and functions should be created to use in the disaster recovery planning process.

Not only do you need to assess the current state of the network infrastructure, including personnel, but you should also assess future needs of the computing environment. This provides information on how the disaster recovery plan will need to be amended over time to remain effective.

Assessing Business Impact

The next phase of the disaster recovery planning process requires that you do a business impact assessment. This means that you need to identify critical functions and systems in the computing environment and how their disruption will affect the core business of the company.

For example, let's assume that you work at a university. If there were a lightning strike that destroyed switches providing Internet connectivity to dormitories, you would end up with disgruntled students who want to surf the Web. However, the impact on the overall business of the institution isn't affected as dramatically as the meltdown of a database system that holds student records and account receivables.

You can see that Internet access in the dorms isn't as critical as access to an important database. Part of the process of identifying critical functions and systems on the network is assessing how long the institution can function with the key system unavailable.

Assessing Computing Environment Vulnerabilities

Another aspect of pooling the information for the disaster recovery plan is assessing the various vulnerabilities in your computing environment. For example, to use the university example again, one vulnerability is the large amount of data traffic that can be caused by students downloading programs, MP3s, and other stuff that we don't even want to know about. Let's say that there is a snowstorm and students don't have classes. So everyone sits in his dorm room downloading stuff like crazy. This clogs the network, and employees working from home are thus affected.

You have identified a potential infrastructure problem. Obviously this scenario wouldn't constitute a major disaster, but a good thing about doing the network vulnerability assessment is that you can fix some of the things that could create problems before disaster actually strikes.

Another vulnerability that you might find is that your company connects to an important resource (such as a financial institution) through a single WAN connection. You can minimize this vulnerability by having a redundant connection made to the resource. Identifying vulnerabilities is really troubleshooting the network before trouble happens (which I discuss in Hour 21).

Other vulnerabilities that you will find during the assessment might lend themselves to being fixed immediately, removing the vulnerability, or can be detailed in the disaster recovery plan. Going through the assessment can be a very eye-opening experience in relation to how well your network infrastructure was initially planned and then laid out.

Developing the Plan

After the corporate computing environment, disaster business impact, and vulnerabilities have been assessed, the project team can begin to develop the actual disaster recovery plan. This means that vulnerabilities, contingency plans, and how the plan will be implemented in light of a certain type of disaster must all be documented (along with other information such as the inventory and other items previously discussed this hour).

Although a disaster recovery plan will be specific to each type of business or organization, there is information that is common to most disaster plans. These items are

- ▶ Employee contact information—The plan should include information on contacting key employees in case of a disaster.

- ▶ Vendor and customer contact information—Depending on your business, the plan should also include contact information for key vendors and contact information for key customers.

- ▶ Location of backup information—The location of offsite storage facilities for data backup tapes and other network information should be identified.

▶ A listing of security information such as user Ids and passwords. Particularly those for administrative tasks. If the disaster is the loss of the network administrators, this type of information must be available. However, because it is so important to the security of the system, the disaster recovery plan must be considered a highly sensitive document.

▶ Disaster regrouping location—The plan should also provide information on the location that employees should go to if a disaster strikes and the corporate facilities are no longer usable. This location can be a branch office or another designated space (such as conference space provided by a local hotel). It is definitely a good idea to have a place for all employees to meet; think about the World Trade Center disaster and the fact that it was very difficult to determine whether employees had made it out of the buildings.

▶ Declaring a disaster—Although this might seem to go without saying, it is important that the plan detail who is in charge of actually declaring a disaster. Detailed staff information should also be included in the plan so that employees offsite (or on vacation) can be notified that a disaster has occurred.

▶ Succession planning—This is another one of those grim subjects; there needs to be information in the plan designating who is in charge. If the CEO or president of the company is a victim of the disaster, who should lead the company in the aftermath of the disaster. Remember when President Ronald Reagan was shot by John Hinckley, Alexander Haig, then Secretary of State, declared in a press conference that he was in charge. However, the order of presidential succession places the secretary of state, below the vice president, the speaker of the House and the president pro tempore of the Senate. It's a good idea to specify who will be in charge. Why add more confusion to a bad situation?

It certainly goes without saying that this list is just some of the information that should be part of the recovery plan. Creating a disaster recovery plan is a major undertaking and will require a lot of research and input from people within and outside your organization. Because IT disaster recovery plans require the assessment of tangibles (computers, software, and data) and intangibles (user behavior), you should definitely do some research before you begin the planning process. Check out www.sans.org. It is the Web site of the SANS (SysAdmin, Audit, Network, Security) Institute. Do a search on its home page for "disaster recovery." You will find that a number of papers and articles are provided on different aspects of disaster planning in the IT environment.

Remember that the purpose of a disaster recovery plan is to allow your company to survive a disaster and then continue with its normal day-to-day business. Although your customers will certainly be sympathetic to your plight, they will quickly begin to look elsewhere for the services that you provide if it begins to affect their bottom line.

Summary

In this hour, we discussed issues related to managing a network, including upgrading and growing a network. We also took a look at data backup and data backup strategies and some issues related to server and client licensing. We also discussed some of the basics of creating a disaster recovery plan for your network.

Q&A

Q *Do even very small companies really need to worry about making sure that they have the appropriate software licensing?*

A No matter how small the company, even a company with one employee needs to adhere to the licensing agreements for software products that are used on their computers. It is illegal to run software without the appropriate licenses. Just because a company is small, it doesn't mean that organizations such as the Software Publisher's Association wouldn't consider action if a license violation was brought to their attention.

Q *What is the best way to sort through the confusion related to the different types of software licensing programs?*

A You need to talk to a knowledgeable software reseller or with the software vendor themselves. Don't be afraid to ask questions and get the facts. Selecting the best licensing scenario for your company can often result in substantial monetary savings.

Q *Is it really necessary to have a formal disaster recovery plan for a small company?*

A All businesses, even small businesses, should have some sort of disaster recovery plan for their network. There must be a set of steps that have been recorded (and tested) that allow you to get users back on to the network with a minimum amount of downtime.

Network Troubleshooting Tips and Tricks

In this hour, you will learn about the following topics:

- ▶ Monitoring server hardware
- ▶ Using event logs
- ▶ Tricks for diagnosing TCP/IP connectivity problems

Even the best designed and configured network can experience problems. There can be connectivity issues on the network because of such things as a bad network interface card or a malfunctioning switch. Problems accessing important network services can also crop up because of hardware issues on a critical server. In this hour, we will look at some of the tools and thought processes that go into troubleshooting a network. We will also look at strategies for staying on top of network hardware and connectivity issues that allow you to address problems before they reach systemic proportions.

Monitoring Server Hardware

There is an old sport adage that the best defense is a good offense. In terms of networking, it means that a network administrator must be proactive and attempt to anticipate potential problems on the network before they affect network services. Because network servers are by definition mission critical, it is important to monitor server performance.

Using tools that allow you to keep track of server hardware performance provides you with the ability to track a server's performance over time and actually determine the computer component, such as a hard drive or server memory, that might become a possible bottleneck under high network traffic (a **bottleneck** being an impedance to server performance, which can slow a service and user access to that service).

Before we take a look at some of the different tools that are provided by the various network operating systems discussed in this book, a few words should be said about baselines. When you first deploy your network or anytime you deploy a new server on the network, you should record a set of baseline readings for the server's hardware (using the performance monitoring tools provided by the NOS). This allows you to then monitor the server's performance over time as it relates to specific server hardware, such as the drive array, or allows you to tweak server software settings, such as the amount of virtual memory configured on a server (which can be an issue with a server running Windows Server 2003).

As already mentioned, the different network operating system platforms will offer different types of monitoring tools. However, no matter what the tools available, there are certain hardware components on a server that you should monitor over time (using your baseline as a starting point). Let's take a look at some of the important server hardware components that you should monitor periodically to avoid bottlenecks. We will also look at specific tools from some selected network operating systems that allow you to monitor server performance.

Processor Performance

Servers are typically outfitted with fast processors. For example, a number of server vendors provide high-end servers that take advantage of Intel's Xeon processor that runs in excess of 3GHz. Many servers also provide a motherboard that can take more than one processor.

By the Way

Network Servers Come in Many Different Configurations

When you put together the specifications for a new server, the processor you select is as important as the number and size of the disk drives and the amount of RAM. Intel-based servers are available with Celeron, Pentium III and IV, and Xeon processors. A small office situation might only require a very basic server running a Celeron processor. Larger companies might require Pentium III or better and might even require a server that allows for multiple processors.

In terms of processor performance, a bottleneck can arise when the processor (or processors) can no longer keep up with all the system calls it gets from the different software processes running on the server. You can monitor processor performance by taking a look at difference performance parameters such as the number of events that are waiting in line to be acted upon by the processor or the time spent on a particular thread (a **thread** being a particular part of a program that can execute independently).

Each network operating system typically provides you with the ability to view counters (often in a chart format) that relate to processor (CPU) performance. For example, Novell NetWare 6.5 provides Server Health table that can be accessed using the Web-based Netware Remote Manager (meaning that you can monitor server health from any client on the network). Figure 21.1 shows the Server Health table for a NetWare server. Not only does this table allow you a quick view of server status issues such as CPU utilization and failed logon, but also any problems (if they exist) will be flagged with a red icon in the Status column.

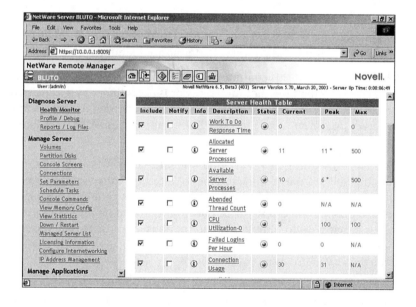

FIGURE 21.1
The NetWare Health table allows you to view CPU utilization and other server performance parameters.

In terms of CPU utilization, it is also nice to be able to see an actual graph of CPU utilization over time. By clicking the CPU utilization link on the Server Health table, you can view a chart as shown in Figure 21.2.

FIGURE 21.2
Server performance
can be viewed in a
chart format.

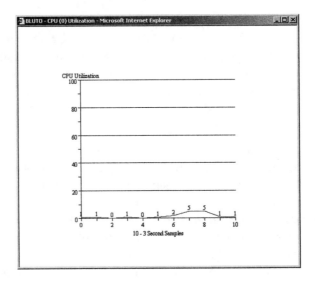

FIGURE 21.2
Server performance
can be viewed in a
chart format.

Windows Server 2003 also provides counters that can be viewed to monitor processor performance (and setup your initial baselines for the server). These counters are viewed using the Windows Performance Monitor:

▶ %Processor Time—If this counter (found under the Processor object), which is a measure of the time that the processor is executing a non-idle thread, is consistently around 75–80%, you might need to upgrade the processor on the server (or add another processor if the motherboard allows for dual processing).

▶ Interrupts/sec—If this counter (found under the Processor object) increases beyond 3,500 (it's the average number of interrupt calls that the processor is receiving from hardware devices, such as a network card or modem), and the %Processor Time counter does not, your problem might not be your processor, but a device that is sending spurious interrupts to the processor (such as a bad network or SCSI card). This can be caused by the device itself or the driver you are using for the device.

▶ Processor Queue Length—If this counter (which is found under the System object and measures the number of threads waiting to be processed) reaches a value of 10 or more, the processor might be a bottleneck. This means that you can go to a faster processor or upgrade to a multiprocessor motherboard on the server.

Figure 21.3 shows the Windows Performance Monitor in the graph view. Multiple counters can be configured in the monitor window, allowing you to track multiple hardware performance issues with one quick view.

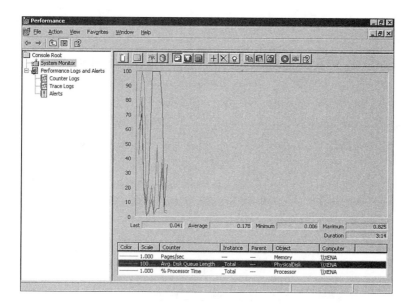

FIGURE 21.3
CPU and server
performance can
be viewed in a
chart format.

Out of Control Processes and Hardware

In some situations, a bad line of code or corrupted software can actually monopolize a server's processing, providing you with poor server performance. You could also have a bad hardware device such as a malfunctioning NIC that could be sending interrupts to the processor. Most of the tools used for monitoring CPU performance can also allow you to view the CPUs interaction with individual threads, which can help in diagnosing whether the problem is bad software (or hardware) rather than the CPU itself.

Did you Know?

If you determine that a server is slowing network services because of a processor issue, you are faced with the possibility of replacing the processor (or adding a processor if possible), adding an additional server, or upgrading the entire server. In cases in which one server is providing multiple services (such as a server that is providing DNS, DHCP, and perhaps even other services), you can always cut down on the number of services that the server is required to supply and deploy another server to pick up the service that was removed.

The bottom line related to server hardware always boils down to planning. If you planned well up front and determined potential growth on the network, you hopefully purchased servers that will provide services effectively even when you have growth spurts (in terms of users) on the network.

Hard Drive Performance and Space

Another area related to server performance that you will want to monitor is related to the server's hard drive (or drives). Not only is drive performance important, but the amount of available space is also an issue particularly on mail and file servers that host drives that allow users to store files that they create.

Server drives come in many different sizes and speeds. You want to outfit your servers with high performance drives. Servers that experience traffic of any consequence really need to be configured with multiple SCSI drives that can be configured in a RAID array. (RAID is discussed in Hour 5, "Network Concepts.")

The types of things that you will want to monitor related to a server's drives are the time that the drive is occupied with read/write functions, the size of the disk's queue, and the amount of free space on the drive.

A drive that is constantly busy with read/write functions is definitely experiencing some type of problem. In some cases, you can defragment the drive, and this might help. However, in most cases, you need to replace the drive with a faster drive or replace the drive with a RAID stripe set that supplies faster read/write capabilities.

Another drive performance parameter that can tip you off to a potential drive problem is the disk queue length for the drive. If the queue contains a large number of requests for access to the drive, your users are going to experience lag time in accessing and saving their files to the volume. Again, you might have to replace the drive or take advantage of a RAID array. Look back at Figure 21.3, which shows how disk queue length is monitored on a Windows Server using the Performance Monitor. (The Disk Queue Length counter is shown in the monitor window.)

It is really only common sense that you would keep track of the amount of free space on server drives. For example, if a file server's drive is filling up fast, you need to take action. You might add a drive to extend the size of a particular volume or set restrictions of the amount of drive space that you allocate to network users.

By the Way

Hot Swappable Drives

Many network servers are now available (many at reasonable prices) with hot swappable drives. The drives are actually accessed through the front of the server box, and you can add or replace drives while the server continues to run. These servers make an administrator's life much easier.

Figure 21.4 shows a simple Linux utility called Kdiskfree. This GUI tool provides statistics on disk usage and the percent of free disk space.

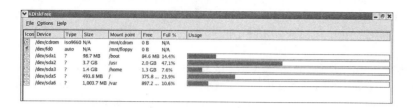

FIGURE 21.4
Utilities such as Kdiskfree allow you to keep track of drive utilization.

Memory Utilization

Another key resource on a network server is the server's memory. Although network operating system vendors supply you with specifications related to the amount of memory needed to run the operating system, you should always configure the server with enough memory to actually do its job. In most cases, this is going to be much more memory than the specifications require.

When a server uses its available memory, it will resort to a paging file that enables the server to temporarily dump some processes to the server hard drive. (In the Windows environment, the paging file is often referred to as **virtual memory**). If you have a server that too often relies on the paging file (because of low available memory), the server is going to slow down and become a potential bottleneck on the network. In most cases, you can remedy this problem by adding more RAM to the server.

Performance counters that you can use to track memory usage and health on a server are the number of bytes available to running processes and the number of times the computer must rely on the paging file. Each NOS will provide different methods of tracking memory usage statistics. For example, Windows Server 2003 provides the following memory counters:

▶ Available Bytes—If this counter (a measure of the physical memory available to running processes) consistently falls to less than 4MB, you need more memory on the server.

▶ Pages/Sec—This counter measures the number of times the computer must rely on the paging file (dumping items in RAM to the hard drive temporarily). This event is known as a **page fault**. If this counter consistently reads at 20 on the System Monitor, you should add more RAM. Excessive page faults can cause systemwide delays in terms of server access.

▶ Committed Bytes—This counter shows the amount of RAM being used and the amount of space that will be needed for the paging file if the data had to be moved to the disk. You should see a value on this counter that is less than the RAM installed on the server. If the value is more than the RAM, you are using the paging file too often; add more memory.

If you look back at Figure 21.3, you can see that the Performance Monitor has been configured to track the Pages/Sec counter. On a UNIX or a Linux system, you can use the command line tool vmstat. Vmstat can provide such information as the amount of free memory and statistics related to the swap file (page file).

The Linux environment also provides a system monitor that allows you to view memory and swap usage in a GUI format. Figure 21.5 shows the System Monitor and the counters that it provides.

FIGURE 21.5
Utilities such as the Linux System Monitor allow you to track memory usage.

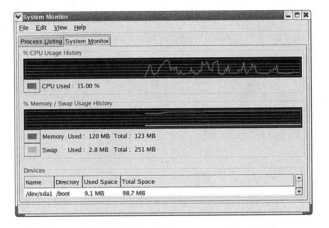

Taking Advantage of Event Alerts

Most network operating systems allow you to configure performance or event alerts. You set a particular threshold value for a particular parameter such as CPU utilization or hard drive free space. When the threshold that you have set is exceeded, the server's performance utility will alert you to the fact.

Using Event Logs to Track Problems

Another useful tool for tracking server problems is the system log. Each network operating system provides you with different ways to record logs on the server.

Periodically viewing these logs (even when a problem hasn't been reported or become obvious on the network) can help you nip a problem in the bud and keep important services running on the network.

These logs will also show when a particular process has failed, and, in most cases, you can configure the logs to accumulate specific information related to the server. Network operating systems typically provide a number of different types of event logs. System logs track events related to system services and resources. Application logs record events related to the applications running on a server. Security logs record events related to user behaviors such as failed logons or events that you configure such as the auditing of user access to a particular volume or resource on the server.

Event logs can be accessed via the command line or using a GUI utility (depending on the NOS). For example on a server running Red Hat Linux, system logs can be accessed using the System Logs GUI utility shown in Figure 21.6.

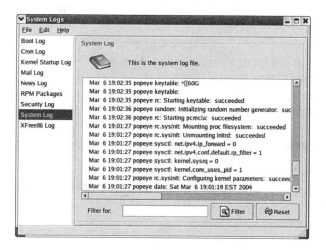

FIGURE 21.6
System logs can be viewed on a Red Hat server using the System Logs utility.

The System Logs utility allows you to view the system log, security log, and other logs configured on the system. Logs can be filtered and reset in the utility window.

When you view a system log, you are looking for red flags. You want to know if a particular process has failed or if a particular service on a server is having a problem. If you look back at Figure 21.6, you will notice that a kernel module failed when the server was booted.

By the Way

Understanding System Logs

For you to use system logs affectively as a diagnosis tool related to server perform-ance, you really need to be able to understand what you are looking at. Each NOS has a different way of recording and then specifying log events. You need to spend time with your NOS documentation to gain an understanding of what a particular event entails and how you might remedy it.

The Windows Server 2003 NOS provides the Event Viewer, which allows you to track events contained in an application log, a security log, and a system log. The Event Viewer uses a system of icons that helps you determine whether there has been a critical event on the server:

▶ The Information icon—Denotes the logging of successful system events and other processes.

▶ The Warning icon—Shows a noncritical error on the system.

▶ The Error icon—Indicates the failure of a major function (such as a driver failure).

Figure 21.7 shows the system log in the Windows Event Viewer. Note that there are error icons for NETBT. This means that there is a problem with the configura-tion of NetBIOS over TCP/IP on the server (which is also causing the Browser error shown in Figure 21.7).

FIGURE 21.7
The Windows Event Viewer uses a sys-tem of icons to cat-egorize events shown in the vari-ous system logs.

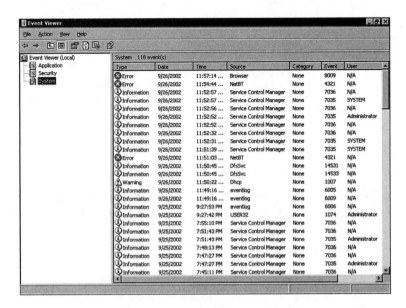

Event logs provide you with a method of tracking system issues and problems after they have happened. It is important to take the information that you find in system logs and use it to fine-tune your server's configuration before you face a major problem. Using event logs in conjunction with performance monitoring (as discussed in the previous section) should aid you in keeping up with server issues before you experience a major network meltdown.

TCP/IP Connectivity Command-Line Tools

So far, we have looked at tools that allow you to monitor server hardware and software performance and pinpoint real-time hardware and software errors using system logs. Another potential problem area that you will have to deal with is the realm of connectivity issues. Connectivity problems can be because of physical cabling or device malfunctions on the network, and they can also be because of incorrect software configurations. Because most networks now embrace TCP/IP, it makes sense to take a look at some of the command-line tools that you can use to help you diagnose connectivity problems on a TCP/IP network.

The great thing about these command-line tools, such as FTP, ping, and traceroute, is that they are available no matter what network operating system you are using. Each NOS platform also offers a number of other command-line diagnostic tools particular to that platform. Understanding the use of some of the basic TCP/IP related commands discussed here will certainly help you as you begin to develop your own strategy for diagnosing connectivity issues.

Ping

The ping command is extremely useful for checking the connection between a computer and a remote host or server. Ping uses Internet Control Message Protocol (ICMP), one of the foundations of TCP/IP, to determine whether another computer is on the network and whether you can reach it.

To use ping, simply type

```
ping the.remote.ip.address
```

such as

```
ping 172.16.0.12
```

This will return one of several types of values.

First, if your computer is capable of connecting to the computer it's pinging, it will look like the following:

```
C:\>ping 172.16.0.12
```

Pinging 172.16.0.12 with 32 bytes of data:

```
Reply from 172.16.0.12: bytes=32 time<10ms TTL=255
Reply from 172.16.0.12: bytes=32 time<10ms TTL=255
Reply from 172.16.0.12: bytes=32 time<10ms TTL=255
Reply from 172.16.0.12: bytes=32 time<10ms TTL=255
```

Ping statistics for 172.16.0.12:

```
    Packets: Sent = 4, Received = 4, Lost = 0 (0% loss),
```

Approximate round-trip times in milliseconds:

```
    Minimum = 0ms, Maximum =  0ms, Average =  0ms
```

This means that your computer is capable of sending 32-character packets to the remote computer. The time it takes to send and receive a packet is 255 milliseconds. The stats on the bottom tell you whether you had any errors or packet loss.

Now, if you can't connect to a particular computer, you'll get a different message:

```
C:\>ping 172.16.0.13
```

Pinging 172.16.0.13 with 32 bytes of data:

```
Request timed out.
Request timed out.
Request timed out.
Request timed out.
```

Ping statistics for 172.16.0.13:

```
    Packets: Sent = 4, Received = 0, Lost = 4 (100% loss),
```

Approximate round-trip times in milliseconds:

```
    Minimum = 0ms, Maximum =  0ms, Average =  0ms
```

In this case, you're sending packets, but no one's replying. Consequently, it tells you that all four packets it sent were lost. This means that the computer to which you want to connect isn't on the network—or else the computer you're using to ping isn't on the network.

ping can also be used to determine whether you can get to a particular network:

```
C:\>ping 156.234.84.95
```

Pinging 156.234.84.95 with 32 bytes of data:

```
Reply from 12.126.207.17: Destination host unreachable.
Reply from 12.126.207.17: Destination host unreachable.
Reply from 12.126.207.17: Destination host unreachable.
Reply from 12.126.207.17: Destination host unreachable.
```

Ping statistics for 156.234.84.95:
```
    Packets: Sent = 4, Received = 4, Lost = 0 (0% loss),
```

Approximate round-trip times in milliseconds:
```
    Minimum = 0ms, Maximum =  0ms, Average =  0ms
```

The Destination Host Unreachable message means that your computer's default gateway doesn't know how to get to the address at the other end. So this message might mean that your router needs some attention.

ping can also be used to see whether a particular computer has a functioning network interface card or TCP/IP configuration. This is done by pinging the loopback address 127.0.0.1. Figure 21.8 shows the results of pinging the loopback address on a Windows XP computer.

FIGURE 21.8
ping can also be used to check a NIC on a computer.

Using Ipconfig

On Windows-based servers and clients, the ipconfig command is extremely useful. It can be used to check the TCP/IP configuration of a computer and can also be used to release (ipconfig/release) and renew (ipconfig/renew) the TCP/IP configuration for the computer as supplied by the network DHCP server.

Did you Know?

FTP

FTP (or File Transfer Protocol) is the standard for moving files around on a TCP/IP network. That's what it's intended for, and it's what it's usually used for.

But FTP has an odd characteristic that makes it useful for system administrators. As it's transferring files across the network, it measures the throughput of the network, so you know how fast the network is running. If you can ping another computer but everything is running slowly, try to FTP a file to it.

Start with a file that's about 1 megabyte in size. That's big enough to accurately measure throughput, but small enough to not cause the network any problems. Then send or receive it from another machine. (You'll need to have an FTP server on at least one of the machines to do this.) If you remember in Hour 3, "Getting Data from Here to There: How Networking Works," we discussed TCP/IP. FTP is a member of the TCP/IP protocol suite, and an FTP server is a system containing files that other network users can download using FTP client software, which is built in to almost every operating system available.

To use FTP, you need to get to the FTP prompt. Type FTP at the command line of your OS, press Enter, and you will then have access to the FTP prompt as shown in the example that follows. You can then use the FTP command get to download a file.

```
ftp> get telnet
200 PORT command successful.
150 Opening data connection for telnet (512338 bytes).
226 Transfer complete.
ftp: 512338 bytes received in 0.57Seconds 897.26Kbytes/sec.
```

Note that this file shows that I received a 512KB file (half a megabyte) in about half a second, and then the system showed how fast the file transferred. There's a catch—the transfer speed is in bytes, which are equivalent to 8 bits each. So, you have to multiply the speed by eight to get the correct measure.

```
897.26 x 8 = a network speed of 7178.08 bits per second,
or about the best usage you'll see on a 10BASE-T network.
```

This is another use for FTP that isn't usually mentioned in teaching texts, but it's a great tool. If the network is slow, this can help quantify *how* slow.

Traceroute

Sometimes, networks get complicated without anyone realizing it. You'll find that sometimes packets seem to be taking 10 times as long as they should to get from point A to point B on your network.

Traceroute (or `tracert` on Microsoft systems) is a utility that enables you to see how your packets are being routed across the network. This is useful if you want to determine specifically which route your packets take. It's also useful if you want to see whether your packets are timing out on the network because they've gone through too many routers.

To use this utility, type

Tracert (or **traceroute**) *remote-ip-address or hostname*

```
Here's an example:C:\>tracert sams.com

Tracing route to mcp.com [63.69.110.193]
over a maximum of 30 hops:

  1    <10 ms    <10 ms    <10 ms    routerfrelan.anonymouscom [172.16.0.1]
  2    <10 ms    <10 ms     10 ms    12.126.207.17
  3    <10 ms    <10 ms     11 ms    gbr2-a31s1.sffca.ip.att.net [12.127.1.146]
  4    <10 ms    <10 ms     10 ms    gbr4-p70.sffca.ip.att.net [12.122.1.189]
  5     10 ms     11 ms     10 ms    gbr3-p20.la2ca.ip.att.net [12.122.2.70]
  6     10 ms     10 ms     10 ms    ggr1-p360.la2ca.ip.att.net [12.123.28.129]
  7     20 ms     20 ms     30 ms    att-gw.la.uu.net [192.205.32.126]
  8     20 ms     20 ms     30 ms    503.at-6-0-0.XR2.SAC1.ALTER.NET [152.63.53.6]
  9     20 ms     20 ms     30 ms    184.at-1-1-0.TR2.SAC1.ALTER.NET [152.63.50.142]

 10     71 ms     80 ms     80 ms    127.at-6-1-0.TR2.NYC8.ALTER.NET [152.63.6.13]
 11     70 ms     80 ms     81 ms    184.ATM7-0.XR2.EWR1.ALTER.NET [152.63.20.241]
 12     70 ms     80 ms     80 ms    192.ATM7-0.GW7.EWR1.ALTER.NET [152.63.24.209]
 13    290 ms    231 ms    230 ms    headland-media-gw.customer.ALTER.NET
➡[157.130.19.94]
 14     71 ms     80 ms     80 ms    63.69.110.193

Trace complete.
```

In this case, it completed the trace, and I can see all the routers (all 14 of them) between my network and `sams.com`. If you get timed out, or if you get starts in place of the times, that is generally where your problem is occurring. Consequently, `traceroute/tracert` is useful for settling disputes with ISPs and network providers over the quality of your service.

Nslookup

Sometimes, you need to use an IP address instead of a name (the DNS hostname). Other times, you don't know the IP address for the name. `Nslookup` (short for *name server lookup*) is a utility that can help you figure out what IP address is associated with a particular name. Here's an example:

```
/$ nslookup www.microsoft.com
Server:  rayban.tibinc.com
Address:  172.16.0.10
```

```
Non-authoritative answer:
Name:    microsoft.com
Addresses:  207.46.230.219, 207.46.130.45, 207.46.230.218
Aliases:  www.microsoft.com
```

Clearly, these four tools don't compose a whole suite of diagnostic tools, but they come with your operating system and can give you a place to start when you're having network problems. It is imperative that you not only know how to use ping, FTP, and these other commands effectively, but you should also become familiar with the other command-line tools that your NOS offers.

Summary

In this hour, we took a look at some of the tools that can be used to help you identify and possibly diagnose problems with server hardware, software, and general network connectivity problems. It is important that you use performance monitor data to establish a baseline and then monitor the server over time to identify potential bottlenecks. Using event logs allows you to pinpoint potential problems as they are occurring. "Universal" command-line tools such as ping and traceroute can be used to identify connectivity problems on a TCP/IP network.

Q&A

Q *What action should be taken when a server hardware bottleneck is identified?*

A A decision must be made. You must either address the bottleneck by upgrading the server's hardware configuration (such as more memory or an additional processor) or by replacing the server. In some situations, you might be able to deploy a "helper" server—as in the case of services such as DNS in which a second server can be used to take some of the workload off the server with the bottleneck problem.

Q *How should baseline information for servers be stored?*

A You can capture and then store baseline information for servers in a number of ways. For example, in the Windows environment, you can create log files using the Performance Monitor. You can also print hard copies of initial logs and make sure that you date the printouts. Arranging baseline data and subsequent readings can also be stored in a simple spreadsheet format in any spreadsheet software.

Q *If I am having problems with an Internet connection, how can I diagnose the problem?*

A The first thing you can do is use the `ping` command to check your default gateway. If there is a problem with the router, `ping` can help you quickly determine whether the computer can even communicate with the router. If the router is okay and the Internet problem relates to the World Wide Web, you might be dealing with a DNS server issue. Again, `ping` can be used to see whether the computer with the problem can communicate with the DNS server.

HOUR 22

A Day in the Life of a System Administrator

In this hour, you will learn about the following topics:

▶ A network administrator's typical day

▶ Tackling your daily tasks

▶ Providing help to network users

▶ Establishing policies for network use

The fact that two different types of computers—clients and servers—exist on the network means that people on the network will also play different roles. Users will make up most of the folks who you find on a PC network. They are there to access and use network resources.

The person who serves as the caretaker of the network is the network administrator. The administrator controls the network servers. This means that network access and the level of access is controlled by the administrator using the tools provided by the NOS.

It is up to the network administrator to create an environment that makes it easy for users to access the resources that they need while also protecting these resources. Often, it can be tough to strike the appropriate balance between access and control. In this hour, we take a look at some of the typical tasks required of the network administrator and provide some insight into an administrator's typical day.

A Day in the Life

Although on good days, a network administrator's morning won't deviate that much from a typical employee getting ready to show up at work, bad days can mean a quick roll out of bed because of a noisy pager or cell phone alerting you to the fact that there is a problem on the network. The fix might require breaking out a laptop and dialing in to the network to see whether the problem can be fixed remotely. In other cases, it might mean throwing on some clothes and speeding off to work as quickly as possible.

Whatever the case, because the network often is required for employees to do their jobs and execute the core business of the company, you have to resolve the problem as soon as possible.

In some cases, the problem might be very easy to handle; for example, you cruise into the user's office and discover that the correct printer wasn't selected on the client computer, and that's why the print job never showed up as a hard copy at the printer. In other cases, you might find that the print server had gone down, and you have to quickly replace a hard drive on the server and rebuild the server from backup media.

After you resolve the problem and get back to your desk, the chances are that you have a message or messages waiting for you on your phone. You listen to your messages and create a to-do list of users who need assistance right out of the gate, triaging them by order of seriousness, and then head out on your rounds. You're a computer doctor who makes office calls.

One user is complaining that his copy of the corporate database is locked up. You get to his desk and discover that he's caught in a transitional screen; there's a menu onscreen that he has to deal with before he can get control of the database again. You instruct him how to get through the screen and back into his application; he's happy but complains about the complexity. Oh, well. At least he's working again.

Another user is complaining that his operating system keeps locking up, and you find that he has downloaded a software program from the Web that is wreaking havoc with the OS. So, you uninstall the offending application and make sure that any file associations are back to their default settings. You also have to let the user know that downloading unauthorized software from the Web and changing major OS settings is not something that network users should be doing, and you have to impart this information in a professional, yet firm, manner so that the whole scenario doesn't happen again.

Starting to get the picture? The day often begins (and the start of the morning can be at the crack of dawn) with troubleshooting problems that have popped up with your user base. After you take care of user issues, you can then actually start your daily tasks. First, you head into the computer room (which is actually the server room; everyone has a computer on his desk, so computer room is sort of a misnomer) and change the media that you use for your server backups. (You make the change according to the backup scheme that you are employing; more about backups is covered in Hour 20, "Managing an Existing Network.")

You also need to take the time to check your various server logs. (Logging is also discussed in Hour 20.) For example, you might find that someone was trying to get through the firewall last evening, using an executive's user ID but the wrong password; you call the executive whose ID was being used and ask whether he was trying to get in. No, he answers, but his kid was on the computer all night; maybe he was trying to get in. You respectfully request that the executive ask his kid to quit trying to crack the firewall; having asked that, you move on to the next task. You might find that a log alert that you set for a file server has been tripped and the file server drive array needs more capacity, so you send out an email to all users that the file server will be going down at 5 p.m., and you adjust your personal calendar so that you can stay late and add a drive or swap out the array.

Your day will certainly be busy, and it will provide you with variety; other tasks that you might have to tackle are

- ▶ Get a senior executive's PDA synchronized with his desktop computer
- ▶ Install a switch to segment the network
- ▶ Call several vendors regarding products you're interested in
- ▶ Write a programming script to allow users to connect to a database over the corporate intranet
- ▶ Figure out which laptops offer the best value and submit a report to the CFO

Clearly, these different tasks have to be prioritized. Making the best use of your time and also keeping your users up and running (particularly executives) require some clever juggling of tasks.

Probably half way through the task list, you will take the time to look at your watch and find that the morning hours have passed; it's noon, and you're hungry. Often, you will find that you eat lunch on the run. And even before digestion sets in, chances are that more trouble reports will come in from users that force you to change the priorities on your task list and add additional tasks.

On a good day, you might make it through most of the list and even have a little time to take a look at trade journals; on a bad day, you will still be troubleshooting problems well after most of the other employees have called it a day. Obviously, you can't really end your day until you deal with "major" network problems and also take care of daily tasks related to the network, such as checking security logs and making sure that the backup media is ready to go when the daily backup automatically kicks in on the network.

I don't want to necessarily paint a picture that a network administrator's day is completely hectic and stressful, but it is a field that requires patience and high energy. If you work with a team of administrators, the team approach to problem solving provides a way to keep any one administrator's task list manageable. If you are the only computer guru at a small company, you will have to learn to deploy hardware and software that helps cut down on major snafus; good planning and implementation can save a lot of headaches in terms of the same problems cropping up day after day. Let's take a look at some of the common daily tasks that are necessary to keep a network up and running.

Daily Tasks

As you can see from the previous section, it is essential that you stay organized and keep your task list up-to-date. This also means integrating important daily tasks into the chaos of the moment as users report problems and you detect issues on the network. As you make your list and complete tasks, make sure that you keep old records of what you've done by date. The benefits of doing so are twofold: First, you have a record of what you did and when you did it (invaluable when you're trying to remember how to fix something you worked on six months before). Second, keeping dated records provides a list you can use during yearly evaluations. It also creates a linear timeline that can help identify patterns and avoid burnout.

A number of different calendar and scheduling programs exist that allow you to keep track of appointments, tasks, and project timelines. For example, groupware products such as Lotus Notes and Microsoft Outlook provide you with all the tools that you need to stay organized. Figure 22.1 shows just the beginnings of a network administrator's typical daily task list in Microsoft Outlook. Tasks can be arranged by due date, and Outlook also has the capability to assign tasks to other members of your network team.

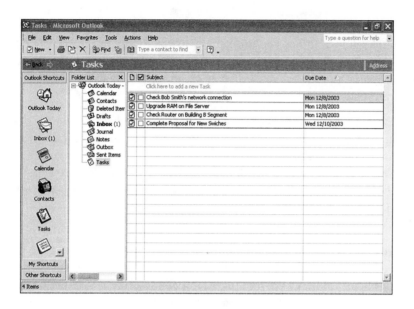

FIGURE 22.1
You can use group-
ware applications
such as Outlook to
stay organized.

Because you typically deploy these types of applications on the network, it makes
sense for you to use them. Believe it or not, I have seen cases in which the information technology staff had no problem deploying a particular groupware product but couldn't even answer basic end-user questions related to using the software. You have to be both expert and generalist. You need to know networking
inside and out, and you also need to know how to tell an end user how to create
a new task or send an email attachment in Outlook.

Groupware Products Are Covered in Hour 12

Some of the most popular groupware platforms are covered in Hour 12, "Network
Applications."

By the Way

Because you aren't always at your computer, it is important to make the case that
the company provide you with a PDA (discussed in Hour 23, "Wireless
Networking"). This provides you with a device that can be synched with the
groupware calendar that you are using. The PDA attached to your belt assures
you that you always have your schedule and task list readily available.

One of the most important things you can do, however, is to make time for yourself inasmuch as that is possible. Your effectiveness as a network or system
administrator is directly related to how much you know, so even if your company

doesn't pay for education, educate yourself. Read everything you can on networking and take note of things you think apply to you. If you have access to a more experienced networking professional, be shameless about learning as much as you can from him. Network professionals are usually quite willing to answer questions if you're polite.

If you can, take a half hour every day and dedicate it to learning a tiny bit of programming. Even if you don't intend to program, understanding the process of coding and being familiar with the data structures full-time programmers use is a definite advantage when you're talking to tech support. In addition, being able to put together a 10–15 line program to hotfix something in an emergency is a highly desirable skill—and one that will certainly be appreciated by your employer.

You have to keep your skills up-to-date, while juggling your duties. In the industry, it is a known fact that network administrators typically raise their salaries and their opportunities by moving from company to company. Many companies do not promote from within, so it is important that your skill set be up-to-date in case you find that ideal position on an Internet job site.

The various resources available for keeping your skills up-to-date and exploring new knowledge related to information technology are truly abundant. In terms of reference and hands-on books alone, there is a great deal of information related to networking and computer technology published every year.

You should definitely try and make room in your network budget for the purchase of resource books. Or, as a last resort, you need to spend some of your own hard earned cash and spend some time reading. Even if you have become the greatest Novell NetWare guru on the planet, that will do you little good if your company decides to migrate to the Microsoft networking platform.

By the Way

Keeping Your Skill Set Up-to-Date

There are many ways to keep your network skills and knowledge of networking up-to-date. Online courses, training courses in your city (from training companies and colleges and universities), and books that provide hands-on training all provide different learning environments. Yes, your job keeps you busy, but you have to ensure that your skill set will allow you to keep your job or move up the career ladder. Pursuing industry certifications such as those offered by Sun, Microsoft, and a number of other software vendors provides you with a context for learning a new body of technical information. Professional certifications also look very good on your resume in terms of promotions and seeking other employment opportunities.

Strategies for Supporting Users

Without network users, there wouldn't be any need for network administrators. So it's your job to keep your users happy—a job that most network administrators accept with alacrity.

Users, however, are not always reasonable. As a network administrator, you have certain charges laid on you, such as agreed on network standards and behaviors. If a user calls on you to violate those basic charges, you have to be able to either say no, escalate the user's request to someone who can grant an exception to the rules, or (in rare cases) escalate the issue because you see potential security breaches or behavior that exposes the organization to liability.

The bottom line is that your users are your customers. The following list provides some tips on how to work with and relate to your network users:

▶ Never get angry with a user, even if he is senselessly venting on you. The user's anger might come from a variety of sources, ranging from frustration at not getting his work done to a wholly unrelated argument with someone else.

▶ Stop and listen to the user when he complains. It's way too easy to interrupt a user in midsentence and announce that you've got a solution to the problem. If you take the time to actually listen to a user's complaint, you might discover that the problem extends beyond the computer per se; he might be upset that the software won't automate certain functions.

▶ After you've listened to the user, take a second and think about what your most appropriate response should be. It's all well and good for you to know that the user's TCP/IP configuration is incorrect and that changing the subnet mask will resolve the problem, but do you have to explain it? For most users, the answer is *no*; all they want is a functioning network, and they don't care what's behind it. So your response to the user should be based on a now or later fix: If it's a 5–10 minute fix, suggest that you can do it now; on the other hand, a long fix means that you have to defer the repair if the user needs the machine and can limp it along until you fix it properly.

When users experience problems on a network, the root cause of those problems will almost always boil down to three possibilities: user error, software problems, or physical connectivity problems. (I discuss troubleshooting network problems in Hour 21, "Network Administration Tips and Tricks.") Although network administrators have gotten the bad rap of always blaming the user for the problem, establishing policies that provide a set of rules for behavior on the network can alleviate a lot of problems. Let's take a look at some issues related to establishing policies for network use.

Establishing Network Policies

Providing end-user training and written policies related to network use can actually negate a lot of potential problems on the network. Some sort of educational opportunity for your users should be built in to your overall plan for your network implementation and management. Documentation that the users can actually read and refer to as they use the network can also greatly cut down on user error. A brief and concise manual that explains basic network logon and resource access can be a real help to your users.

This also gives you an opportunity to establish written policies for network use; for example, you might establish rules such as no software downloads from the Internet or no floppy disks from home. Both of these rules could actually help reduce the risk of virus infection, and no downloads mean that local hard drives remain pretty clean. (A user can fill up his own hard drive with junk pretty fast if he has a high-speed Internet connection and some free time on his hands.)

Establishing user policies for your company's network not only provides a set of rules for the network users, but it also allows you to assume (although users are not always going to follow all the rules) that network client machines will only be running software that is appropriately licensed and correctly configured and that important user files are stored in the appropriate place so that they can be periodically backed up.

Although everyone is aware of the often overused anecdote that accompanies the word "assume" when an assumption proves to be wrong, at least assuming that computers have been configured in a particular "standard" way allows you to concentrate on other issues when attempting to troubleshoot network problems.

Summary

In this hour, we took a look at the typical day of a network administrator. We also looked at keeping organized and issues related to end-user training and network use policies. And here's a final word related to this book. This is certainly not the only book you should read related to network administration and networking theory. There are many, many experts out there who share their insights and expertise through the printed page. Take advantage of the many printed resources available.

Q&A

Q *What is the one thing that you can count on as you tackle a network administrator's typical day?*

A You will have to work with your end users. Handling their requests and problems in a polite and efficient manager will actually make your job easier. Also be advised that your daily task list will constantly have to be reworked to accommodate "network crises" and lesser network problems.

Q *What are two important aspects of succeeding as a network administrator?*

A Staying organized and keeping your skill set up-to-date are both important aspects of succeeding as a network administrator. Use some sort of system, such as a calendar program, to keep your schedule manageable and take every opportunity you can to learn new things and upgrade your personal knowledgebase.

Q *What is a good approach to cutting down on user error on the network?*

A Provide your network users with a list of rules related to using the network. Also find different avenues of providing user training or end-user tips to your user base. It will help cut down the one-on-one training that you will have to provide to a user who doesn't understand how to use a particular network application.

PART VI

The Future of Networking

HOUR 23

Wireless Networking

In this hour, you will learn about the following topics:

- ▶ How wireless networking works
- ▶ Understanding the wireless standards
- ▶ Using and securing WiFi networking
- ▶ Implementing a wireless network
- ▶ Securing a wireless network

We've spent a lot of time in this book discussing planning, implementing, and maintaining local area networks. Our discussion has really centered on traditional wired networks, particularly those using the Ethernet architecture. In this hour, we look at wireless networking including wireless standards, implementing a wireless network, and wireless security issues.

Understanding Wireless Networking

The options for wireless networking have greatly increased over the last few years. Wireless network connections can take advantage of radio signals and infrared light. Longer distance wireless communications can take place through cellular telephone technology, which includes the use of microwave transmission and satellites.

Radio connectivity provides the easiest way to extend a wired LAN and can provide network access to roaming users at varying speeds. Wireless LAN equipment operates in part of the frequency range that the FCC has reserved for unregulated use; you will find that wireless LANs operate in the 2.4GHz and above ranges.

> **FCC Unregulated Frequency Ranges**
>
> The FCC is responsible for regulating the various ranges of frequencies that can be used for communication. The unregulated ranges are 902–928MHz, 2.4GHz, and 5.72–5.83GHz. These ranges can be used by consumer products such as telephones and wireless networking products.

In terms of how wireless networks work, the only real difference between a wired Ethernet network and a wireless Ethernet network is how computers or other devices, such as Personal Digital Assistants (PDAs), actually connect to the network. They use radio (or light in cases of infrared connections) waves to send and receive data. So, let's center our discussion on radio networks. A computer must be outfitted with a NIC that can send (and receive) data as a radio wave (rather than an electrical signal over a wire). To actually connect to the network, there must be some sort of central connection device.

In a wired network, the central connection device is a hub or a switch. In a wireless network, the central connecting device is called an **access point**. The access point is really a bridge between wireless and wired networks. Most access points not only provide for wireless connectivity, but also provide ports so that the access point can be tied into a wired network (by connecting it to a hub or switch).

A network that combines wired and wireless connectivity is often referred to as a **hybrid network**. Figure 23.1 shows what a basic hybrid network might look like schematically.

Ethernet 802.11 Wireless

The 802.11 standard for wireless Ethernet was developed by the IEEE (Institute of Electrical and Electronics Engineers). It provides the specifications for how wireless connectivity devices should work such as access point devices and wireless NICs.

Although the 802.11 standard provides for a number of different flavors or specifications for wireless networking, three specifications are currently in use:

- ▶ 802.11a—This 802.11 specification can provide up to 54Mbps and operates in the 5GHz band of the usable radio spectrum.

- ▶ 802.11b—This specification provides up to 11Mbps of throughput and operates in the 2.4GHz band, utilizing DSSS.

- ▶ 802.11g—This specification provides 20+Mbps in the 2.4GHz band. It is currently the fastest growing implementation of 802.11 wireless on home networks and small LANs.

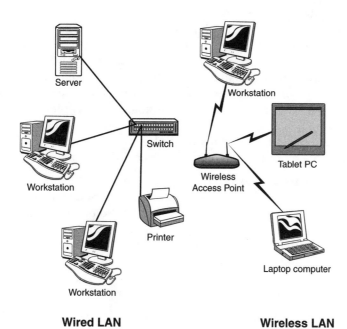

FIGURE 23.1
A basic hybrid network.

Wired LAN   **Wireless LAN**

The 2.4GHz and Below Bandwidth Crunch

The problem with operating in public bandwidth is that a number of different devices can use the same bandwidth and interfere with each other. The 802.11b specification suffers from competing with telephones and microwaves. Even the 802.11g specification, which is a fast implementation of WiFi, operates within a range (2.4GHz) that is also used by cordless phones.

Watch Out!

The 802.11 wireless specifications are collectively referred to as WiFi (Wireless Fidelity). To promote 802.11 as the standard for wireless (there is another possibility that is discussed in a moment), the Wi-Fi Alliance, a nonprofit organization, was formed by a number of the companies that provide 802.11 wireless technology and services.

WiFi uses a spread spectrum radio technology. **Spread spectrum** was developed for the military to guard against enemy radio frequency jamming and eavesdropping. Spread spectrum spreads the signal across a range of frequencies in the public bandwidths. There is actually more than one flavor of spread spectrum:

▶ **Frequency hopping spread spectrum (FHSS)**—The first implementation of the spread spectrum technology hops from frequency to frequency in a set pattern. The receiver can receive frequency hopping spread spectrum data only if the sender and the receiver use the same hopping pattern (which is controlled by what is called a hopping-sequence algorithm). According to FCC rules, no transmitter can stay on a single band for more than 0.4 seconds within a period of 20 seconds for the 902MHz band (30 seconds for the 2.4GHz band). Each transmitter must also cycle through 50 to 75 radio bands before restarting the hopping-sequence algorithm.

▶ **Direct sequence spread spectrum (DSSS)**—In DSSS, the transmitter modifies the data with "chips," or extra data bits (a minimum of 10) inserted in the data stream. Only a receiver that knows the algorithm for the insertion of chips can decipher the code. Because of the effect of the chips, the effective throughput of DSSS is currently limited to 2 megabits per second in the 902MHz band and 11 megabits per second—a usable speed—in the 2.4GHz band.

The WiFi implementations 802.11b and 802.11g use DSSS and DSSS/OFDM, respectively. Bluetooth (which is discussed in the next section) uses FHSS.

And what about 802.11a? Well this WiFi implementation does not use FHSS or DSS. It uses a multiplexing scheme called **Orthogonal Frequency Division Multiplexing (OFDM)**. OFDM splits the radio signal into a number of sub-signals that are transmitted simultaneously at different frequencies. This enables a large amount of digital data to be broken up in to chunks and then transmitted.

WiFi Ethernet networks work the same as wired Ethernet networks, meaning that you are dealing with a collision network in which computers sit on the network and wait until the network is clear before they transmit data. For more about Ethernet and how it works, see Hour 3, "Getting Data from Here to There: How Networking Works." Troubleshooting wireless networks is similar to a standard wired Ethernet network; however, the issues dealing with physical connections are supplanted by issues related to receiving a signal from network access points.

Did you Know?

New Flavors of 802.11

Additional specifications are being developed for 802.11. For example, the 802.11f task force is exploring ways to deal with compatibility issues between access points and other WiFi hardware from different vendors. There is also 802.11i, which is aimed at fixing security flaws in the 802.11a, 802.11b, and 802.11g standards.

Bluetooth

While not currently a competitor for wireless LAN implementations, another wireless specification shares the 2.4GHz bandwidth range with 802.11. It is called Bluetooth. Bluetooth was created in 1998 as a standard for connecting mobile devices such as PDAs, by a number of companies interested in mobile computing strategies such as IBM, Nokia, and Toshiba. Bluetooth was initially designed as a strategy for implementing a personal area network, or PAN—meaning that the Bluetooth specification would be used on devices that we work with on a daily basis, such as phones, printers, and even including personal convenience devices such as coffee makers. The wireless environment would surround us, allowing individuals to be freed up from devices that required wired connections.

Bluetooth is an open standard (as is 802.11). This means that Bluetooth specifications can be implemented with other technologies and new standards. Bluetooth provides a lot of possibilities for providing communication links between handheld computing devices, mobile phones, and other devices such as wireless headsets and even keyboards. There is also some talk of developing Bluetooth into a full-blown LAN infrastructure medium (which would make it a competitor of 802.11).

There is the possibility that Bluetooth devices could interfere with 802.11 devices because they share the same bandwidth. Both the IEEE and Bluetooth vendors are currently working on strategies for cutting down on the possibility of interference between these two standards.

Who Was Bluetooth?

Bluetooth is named after Harald Bluetooth, a Viking king. For more about Bluetooth technology check out www.bluetooth.com.

Did you Know?

Using WiFi Technology

WiFi wireless technology for the LAN continues to be developed, and its use is growing rapidly. But what are some of the reasons why you would want to use wireless? Several major benefits are outlined here:

▶ **Simplifies adds, moves, and changes**—Currently, the add/move/change process in wired networks is comparatively cumbersome. You have to run network wiring out to the area in which the user will be located; if that user is outside the geographical limits of the local LAN, expensive repeaters that extend the reach of the local network are often necessary. Wired LANs, for all the freedom they give their users, are not so different from the old telegraph line; you have to be on the wire to get the signals. If you have to move your network (or part of it) elsewhere, you have to bring all the cables, wiring, and so forth along, which makes transportable wired networks quite rare.

▶ **Quickly deployable**—Wireless networking offers quite a contrast to the cumbersome earthbound wires of wired LANs. Wireless networks work well in situations in which the requirements state that the network must be transportable, rapidly deployable, and very reliable.

▶ **Offers mobility for users who don't work in a single location**—In hospitals, for example, wireless networks enable nurses to monitor patients wherever they are; there's no need to be at a fixed network. Increasingly, doctors are using wireless PDAs, such as Palm devices or Windows CE devices, to connect to patient data; more than one metropolitan hospital now provides its physicians with such technology.

Although the benefits listed here are related to larger networks, there are also definite benefits related to using wireless networking on SOHO networks. First of all, no cabling is required, so cables do not have to be pulled through ceilings or placed under carpets (or run along floors, which provide a definite home hazard if you trip over one). Wireless networking is also fairly inexpensive. Both 802.11b and 802.11g access points that include switching and routing capabilities are available for less than $100. Wireless NICs and USB NICs are also inexpensive.

Considering that the whole process of setting up a small wireless network probably won't take even an hour or two, it means that you can get a usable network up and running fast. Because file and print sharing are built in to desktop operating systems such as Windows, users can immediately share files and printers. Wireless networking also offers an excellent way to share a single Internet connection with a number of users.

Did you Know?

WiFi Hot Spots

Although corporate and institutional networks have been a little slow to adopt WiFi strategies, small businesses—particularly restaurants, coffee shops, and pubs—have adopted WiFi as another service to their customers. Customers can stroll in with their laptop or tablet PC outfitted with a wireless NIC and attach to the Internet using the access point provided by the establishment.

Implementing a Wireless Network

Implementing a wireless network is really no different than implementing a wired network. You must first plan your network layout and then acquire the necessary hardware to get the network up and running. You should plan for growth, security, and all the other issues that you would plan for if you were implementing a wired network.

In terms of network size and growth, one thing that you should keep in mind is that WiFi implementations such as 802.11b are inexpensive and fairly easy to set up. However, they provide limited bandwidth right from the get go (no more than 11Mbps, which is about the speed of an old 10BASE-T network). Also, the more users you have on the network, the slower the throughput. The users are sharing the bandwidth. So, bottom line, although inexpensive (and I mean very inexpensive), 802.11b is best used on small SOHO networks of only a few computers.

So, a larger network will require a faster WiFi implementation. 802.11g provides more bandwidth, and it is backward compatible with wireless NICs and access points that use the 802.11b standard.

The number of access points you decide to deploy depends on the number of users. Each access point provides specifications for the number of users who can connect to the access point without suffering drops in performance and reliability.

As you plan your WiFi network, you also need to keep in mind the range of the medium. Indoors, you are looking at ranges of 150 to 300 feet (the maximum distance from a client to an access point). Building construction can affect the range, so you will probably want to set up some test equipment before you outfit all your users with WiFi hardware. You really need to determine the access point range boundaries in your building. This is going to help you determine the number of access points you will need to accommodate your users. It is also important to have some overlap between the access point range boundaries so that users can roam within the building.

Outdoors, you might be able to get a range of up to 1,000 feet, but the outdoor range doesn't necessarily translate to the type of range that you will get from a building to building connection. And, although users might take advantage of an outdoor WiFi connection on a nice day, it probably isn't as important as getting the most out of your indoor ranges.

As far as WiFi hardware goes, there are a incredible number of possibilities for both access points and WiFi NICs. For small SOHO networks, companies such as

Linksys and D-Link provide access points and wireless NICs. Many of the access points now available provide firewall capabilities, and some (designed for home use) also have parental control capabilities for home Internet connections.

> ### WiFi USB NICs
>
> Many home or small office users might want to implement a WiFi network but don't feel comfortable opening up PCs and installing internal wireless radio NICs. External radio NICs are available from a number of vendors and can be connected to a computer's USB port.

For larger networks, companies such as 3Com and Cisco provide high-end access points for enterprise networking. For example, Cisco provides the Cisco Aironet 1200 Series Access Point, which supports the WiFi standards 802.11a, 802.11b, and 802.11g simultaneously.

Make sure that you research and test your WiFi hardware as you would hardware for a wired network. A good starting point for more information about WiFi is the Wi-Fi Alliance at http://www.wi-fi.org. This organization provides information on WiFi standards and provides information on WiFi certified products, WiFi network implementation, and other WiFi related news.

Wireless Networks and Security

Wireless networking does make some networking professionals squeamish because of security issues. You are, after all, spraying your data out into the ether, making it a possible target for eavesdroppers. Data sensitivity has become increasingly important to those in the medical field because of HIPAA (The Health Insurance Portability and Accountability Act) regulations related to the protection of patient information. Even a dentist with a small practice might think twice about implementing a wireless network in the dental office because patient data could be at risk.

Wireless networking is not without its security strategies, however. The 802.11 wireless implementations use a couple of different, built-in strategies for securing data broadcast on radio waves: WEP and WPA.

WEP (or **Wired Equivalent Privacy**) is a protocol that runs in the MAC sub-layer of the Data-link layer of the OSI model. (For more about the OSI model, see Hour 3.) WEP encrypts the data sent from point to point on the wireless LAN using a shared secret key. This means that WEP is in force as data moves from a wireless client to an access point or to another wireless client. If the data enters a wired LAN, there is no encryption in force.

The problem with WEP is that it uses a short data stream, only 24 bits, for the shared keys. This means that as more and more data is sent, the key streams (the data stream containing the encryption/decryption shared key) will be somewhat similar. A hacker monitoring a radio network can eventually capture enough frames to determine the shared value in the key stream. This means that at some point the hacker will have enough information to determine the key and therefore decrypt data that was assumed secure.

WEP was actually rolled out as a security protocol for 802.11b. When WEP was determined to be less secure than hoped, **WPA (WiFi Protected Access)** was rolled out to improve the security features provided by WEP. WPA is backward compatible with existing wireless devices, which can be updated through software.

WPA uses the temporal key integrity protocol (TKIP) to scramble the keys provided by WEP. WPA also provides a key integrity checking capability to make sure that keys have not been tampered with. One of the biggest improvements that WPA provides is user authentication using EAP (Extensible Authentication Protocol)and 802.1x (port-based authentication).

EAP is actually an extension of the Point-to-Point Protocol and can take advantage of authentication strategies such as public key authentication, one-time passwords, and the use of certificates for authentication. In cases in which wireless users connect to wired LANs, EAP can be used to authenticate the wireless user to an authentication server on the wired network (negating the problem with WEP and transmission of data from the wireless network to the wired network).

The 802.11 task force is currently working on new strategies to secure wireless networks. But rather than waiting for improvements inherent in the wireless standards, there are other things that you can do to secure data on a wireless LAN. Two excellent strategies are IPSec and Virtual Private Networking (VPN).

VPN is discussed in Hour 7, "Remote Networking." IPSec or IP Security is a suite of cryptography-based protection services and security protocols that can be used to secure internal networks, networks that use WAN solutions for connectivity, and networks that take advantage of remote access solutions such as Virtual Private Networking.

IPSec embraces an end-to-end security model; this means that only the sending and the receiving computers are aware of the fact that the data has been secured. Each network operating system provides methods for enabling IPSec on a

network. For example, a network using the Windows Server 2003 platform implements IPSec using IPSec policies. Policies are enabled on a Windows domain controller (the authentication and directory database manager for the network) using
the Windows Group Policy Manager. Figure 23.2 shows the default IPSec policies
on a Windows server.

FIGURE 23.2
IPSec policies can
be enabled on a
Windows server.

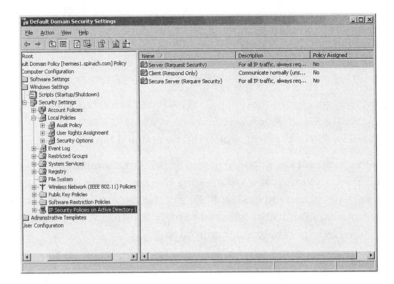

By the Way

> ## IPSec on Wireless Clients
>
> IPSec can also be configured locally on Windows XP clients using the Local Policy
> Manager, which is part of the Administrative Tools provided in the Control Panel.

In terms of securing your wireless LAN, you should definitely use WEP even
though it does have flaws. (It is well known that many wireless networks are out
there that don't even bother using WEP, making them pretty easy targets.) Also
implement WPA if your wireless hardware supports it (upgrade the hardware with
the appropriate software updates if available).

In cases in which you are dealing with sensitive data, it makes sense to create
VPNs between clients and access points and also consider using IPSec on the wireless network. As wireless networking matures, other security strategies will also
appear; so definitely make sure that you do your reading and keep up with new
security mechanisms for securing your wireless data.

More on WiFi Networking

There is much more to WiFi networking than can be covered in an hour. For more information, you might want to check out *Maximum Wireless LANS* (second edition) and *Maximum Wireless Security*, both from Sams Publishing.

Summary

In this hour, we discussed wireless networking. We took a look at wireless standards such as the IEEE 802.11 specifications. We discussed the different implementations of 802.11 and methods for securing a wireless network.

Q&A

Q *What type of device can be used to bridge a wireless network with a wired network?*

A Most network access points also provide hub/switch ports that allow you to connect the access point to a wired network. This provides communication between the wireless clients and the resources on the wired network.

Q *Where price is the major factor, which of the 802.11 standards would be best for home networking?*

A In terms of hardware costs, 802.11b provides a range of wireless NICs and access points at extremely reasonable prices. However, the more computers on a 802.11b WiFi network, the greater degradation of the available bandwidth. So, the slightly pricier and faster 802.11g standard might be best for a home or small office network with more than two or three computers.

Q *What are the best ways to secure a WiFi network, particularly a WiFi used in a business setting?*

A It makes sense to take advantage of both WEP (Wired Equivalent Privacy) and WPA (WiFi Protected Access), which are security protocols that are part of the current 802.11 specifications. It also makes sense to take advantage of Virtual Private Networking and the IPSec security protocols when using wireless networking in a business environment.

Where Are Networks Going from Here?

In this hour, you will learn about the following topics:

▶ The Linux explosion

▶ What will happen to the Internet?

▶ Coming soon: IPv6

▶ The continued evolution of wireless networking

You've reached the end of the book. You now know the standards and practices of implementing networks. We discussed both planning and building networks and also looked at different NOS platforms and how to connect your network to the Internet.

Now it's time to look at the future of networks. And although this requires some dusting off of the old crystal ball, one can only guess at what networks will look like in the next 5 to 10 years. We are currently seeing a rise in the use of wireless networking strategies and the increased use of Linux as both a client and NOS platform. Let's start our discussion with Linux and then look at some other factors that will affect networking in the future.

Linux: Lawsuits and Open Source

It certainly can be said that Linux has caught the imagination of many networking professionals. It provides a secure and highly flexible NOS and development environment (see Hour 16, "UNIX and Linux Networking"). In fact, Linux implementations are on the rise.

By the Way

Microsoft and Linux

Microsoft has spent a great deal of time and money making the case that its networks actually have a lower total cost of ownership than the Linux platform. Microsoft is also trying to make the case that the Microsoft .NET development environment is more cost-effective than the Java 2 Platform Enterprise Edition from Sun Microsystems, which can run on both the Sun and Linux platforms. Microsoft also seems to be backing SCO in the legal battle and has agreed to a deal in which it will license SCO's patents and source code. It will be interesting to see whether Linux can continue to evolve as an alternative platform to products from some of the major players in the industry such as Microsoft.

In 2003, the Linux community was rocked by allegations and by the SCO Group (Santa Cruz Operation) that Linux contained proprietary UNIX code. The allegations were followed by a SCO lawsuit naming IBM. The lawsuit claims that IBM is guilty of misappropriation of trade secrets, unfair practices, and other illegal actions. The suit is asking for at least one billion dollars in damages. SCO has also threatened to file lawsuits against some of its customers.

Red Hat fired back with a lawsuit against SCO, seeking the courts to affirm that Red Hat has not violated any of SCO's intellectual property as Red Hat has developed its own version of Linux. Red Hat also went one step further and has implemented an open source assurance program for its Linux enterprise customers, stating that Red Hat will replace any software affected by intellectual property issues.

Interestingly, the litigation and corporate posturing does not seem to have dampened the level of interest in Linux. IBM has launched an international marketing campaign for its Linux products, and Novell has acquired SUSE Linux (a popular distribution of the Linux platform).

By the Way

Attacks on SCO

Although Microsoft has typically born the brunt of many email-related hacker attacks, at the time of the writing this book, a new worm WORM_MYDOOM.A (and its variants) has been showing up via email to Windows-based machines. The catch: The worm might infect Windows systems, but it sets up a denial of service attack against www.sco.com. Yes, that's the SCO Group's Web site.

The question is where will Linux go from here? Novell (SUSE Linux), IBM (Blue Linux), Red Hat, and a number of other Linux vendors have spent a great deal of capital and development time in providing high-end, enterprise-ready versions of Linux for a number of hardware platforms including mainframes, Risc, and Intel-based hardware.

Both the private (large companies) and the government sectors have increasingly looked at Linux as an alternative to the more vendor-centric products that have been a mainstay of the industry. Linux provides an open standard for development and interoperability. The pluses of using open source software platforms have been mentioned several times throughout this book. This is the very real attraction of adopting Linux. It is an open, nonproprietary platform that does not require proprietary hardware (although some flavors of Linux only run on certain vendor hardware products).

The Linux revolution has created some odd bedfellows. You have old-time industry heavyweights such as IBM and Novell singing the praises of Linux open source origins along with open source developers who have never trusted the large companies that have driven the computer industry over the last 30 years.

It can be safely said that Linux is definitely making inroads in commercial and governmental installations. So, what is happening with smaller companies and the home market?

Smaller companies are often looking for platforms that are easy to install, configure, and then support. There is also often an attitude of "if it isn't broken, don't fix it." This means that companies often are still using the same network and service platforms that they have used since their businesses were first computerized. For example, there are an incredible number of NetWare installations around the world. Microsoft also has done a fantastic job of promoting the various versions of the Windows server platform and providing a series of certifications that actually attracted network professionals because they truly added dollars to their salaries. (Just check out any technical salary reports you see on the Web and see how much more a Microsoft Certified Network Engineer can make.)

Some large institutions haven't really made a move to the PC platform and still maintain cumbersome and costly legacy mainframe systems. Again, some institutions just haven't seen a compelling reason to turn their operations upside down to embrace a new technology.

No doubt, computer hardware has decreased in cost over the last 20 years. With the development energy and competition that we see in the Linux open source environment, I think it will become clear that moving to Linux for Web services, database services, and even client desktops will become more attractive and fairly hard to ignore in the coming years. This isn't to say that Microsoft will go by the wayside without a struggle. The competition between the open source community and proprietary software platform vendors will certainly heat up.

As far as the consumer market goes, probably the biggest factors driving the use of an OS is price, ease of use, and whether it was installed on the PC when it was purchased. Linux desktop distributions are less expensive than the alternatives. Also, a number of PCs are now available with Linux preinstalled. (Lycoris, which we discuss in a moment, is available on PCs sold by Wal-Mart.) So, the big question related to Linux and the home market is ease of use.

A variety of different GUIs are available for Linux such as KDE and GNOME. Linux distributions, such as Lycoris and the LindowsOS, are extremely easy to configure and look so much like Windows that many users probably would not immediately be able to tell the difference. Figure 24.1 shows the Lycoris XL desktop. Lycoris uses Samba and is configured by default to share files and printers with Microsoft Windows–based computers. Lycoris is also very good at identifying and configuring the hardware on a computer, as well as configuring an Internet connection for it.

FIGURE 24.1
Lycoris provides a very Windows-like desktop environment.

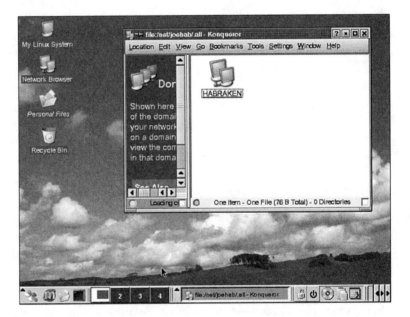

By the Way

Linux-Ready PCs

A number of PC hardware vendors now include Linux distributions as a choice for the installed operating system on a new PC. Even the fairly new tablet PC market has been affected. Lycoris LX Tablet Edition is now available on tablet PCs.

So, bottom line: Linux is not going away (neither is Microsoft, Sun, and a number of other NOS vendors). But I think it is safe to say that if the high interest in Linux and open source development for the platform isn't dampened by the SCO lawsuits, Linux installations will continue to grow and play some part in nearly every new network installation. And yes, that means Linux will have a growing installation base in the next 5 to 10 years.

The Internet and Regulation

I would be remiss in making predictions related to the networking world without mentioning regulation and the Internet. The increasing amount of spam email, Internet fraud, and easy access to Internet pornography not only raises the ire of many Internet users, but they also provide ammunition to those who want to regulate the information superhighway.

The United States, the member countries of the European Union, and a number of developing nations are all debating issues related to regulating the Internet. Not only are regulations discussed related to limiting spam, but there are also discussions related to content offerings.

Some countries already have laws on the books: For example, Saudi Arabia already has laws on the books that relate to both access and content. In China, laws are in place that control how service providers connect to the Internet backbone (providing state control of connections).

The Internet certainly did not develop without governmental regulations. The way the Internet was born and then built really relates to different government regulations and initiatives (see the following note).

Accessing the Internet Backbone in the United States

By the Way

Even the United States regulates connections to the Internet backbone. The MFS Communications Company manages the MAE backbone in the United States. This control was provided by the National Science Foundation to MFS through government regulation.

The fear of regulation for most Internet "purists" is free speech and content censorship. Many countries not only attempt to control content, but they also have laws on the books that allow them to prosecute individuals who provide content on Web sites that violate those laws. So, censorship of Internet content is already a reality. We see this in countries such as China, Vietnam, and Tunisia (among others). In most cases, the arrests are related to free speech issues and often revolve around a Web site that has criticized the government.

Although most of us (particularly in the United States, Canada, and Europe) think of the Internet as a fairly open and free environment, there has been attempts to regulate Internet content. For example, in the United States, the Federal Communications Decency Act of 1996 was signed into law by President Clinton. It was an attempt to ban obscene or indecent material from being communicating via the Internet to anyone under 18 years of age. The law was under immediate legal challenge by the American Civil Liberties Union and other organizations almost immediately after President Clinton signed the legislation into law.

In 1997, the U.S. Supreme Court ruled that the law was unconstitutional. So, in terms of our constitution and free speech protections, it will be interesting to see whether the U.S. Congress can really regulate the Internet to any degree in terms of content and access.

There has also been talk of a "no spam" list similar to the no call list that has been established in the United States to stop unsolicited sales calls. However, because email address spoofing and email header editing can make it almost impossible to track the origin of spam, it will be very difficult to actually enforce any laws related to a no spam list.

So, in the final analysis, I think attempts to regulate the Internet will periodically surface especially in terms of protecting children from offensive content. Whether these laws (in the United States) will pass any constitutional tests placed on them will depend on the courts. Companies and users really have to establish their own policies and formulate their own plans for blocking content and setting rules for how the Internet is used. All the tools for blocking unwanted spam, Web content, and protecting systems from hackers are out there and available. So, a proactive stance by Internet users and companies that relies heavily on the Internet is a much better solution than attempting to pass laws that might not be enforceable.

The Advent of IPv6

It has become a fact that the address space for the Internet is rapidly shrinking. This is true because the original designers of the Internet never envisioned a world in which personal computers would exist; they never imagined that the 4,294,967,296 (also described as 2 to the 32nd power) addresses their 32-bit address space provided for would even be close to fully used.

They also never imagined that ordinary mortals would one day come into acutely close contact with the protocols of the Internet and have the unenviable task of configuring IP addresses, subnet masks, DNS, and the like.

And they can't have imagined a world in which palm-based computers or cell phones were connected to the Internet. Clearly, it's time for a change.

Because the Internet designers' initial network was noncommercial, they never imagined that they would need a method to ensure secure transactions. They knew that networking was fast, but they didn't realize that bandwidth would become a constraint on a massive scale to the network's growth. And because they didn't envision the growth the Internet has seen, they didn't realize that the Internet protocol had to be capable of prioritizing the importance of traffic for Quality of Service reasons.

Because of the shortcomings of the existing Internet Protocol, the Internet Engineering Task Force (IETF), in late 1993, issued Request for Comments 1550 (RFC 1550) titled "IP: Next Generation (IPng) White Paper Solicitation." The purpose of this RFC was to draw together the disparate ideas about what specific features various constituencies wanted in the Next Generation Internet Protocol.

In a document titled RFC 1726, "Technical Criteria for Choosing IP: The Next Generation (IPng)," the initial specifications for an improved Internet Protocol were outlined. In January 1995, RFC 1752, "The Recommendation for the IP Next Generation Protocol," was issued. Table 24.1 specifies the improvements IPv6 offers over IPv4 (the current Internet Protocol). RFC 1883 later followed with an official specification for IPv6; these specs reflect the influence of both RFC 1883 and RFC 1752.

TABLE 24.1 The Differences Between IPv4 and IPv6

	IPv4	IPv6
Address space, bits	32	128
Number of possible addresses	2^{32} or 4,294,967,296	2^{128} or 3.402823669209^{38}
		It's difficult to explain here, but the number of addresses in IPv6 is enormous. The 128-bit address space is not four times larger than IPv4's 32-bit address space; instead, it's something like a billion billion times larger. With IPv6, we won't run out of addressees for a long, long time.

TABLE 24.1 Continued

	IPv4	IPv6
Header length, bytes (also called octets)	20 octets	40 octets Note that even though the address space is four times as long in IPv6, the header, which contains packet routing information, is only twice as large. This represents a very efficient use of bandwidth.
Extendable	No	Yes
		In this context, extendable means that options that don't have to be read each time the packet is routed are located in extension headers located after the core header information. This arrangement makes better use of bandwidth.
Encryption, Authentication, and Privacy	No	Yes. IPv6 has the built-in facility to authenticate the sender of a data packet and to encrypt the data in a packet.
Autoconfiguration	No	Yes. IPv6 has facilities to automatically configure an IP address for itself and can work with networks to receive appropriate unique network addresses.
Quality of Service capabilities	No	Yes

In addition to the differences listed in Table 24.1, IPv6 also prepares for a simple transition from IPv4 to IPv6. The requirements of RFC 1752 and RFC 1883 state that the transition from IPv4 to IPv6 must fit the following four requirements:

▶ It must be possible to upgrade an IPv4 network to an IPv6 network without having to do it in an all-or-nothing scenario. IPv6, therefore, must be backward compatible with IPv4.

▶ New IPv6-capable devices must be capable of being deployed on the network without changing any of the IPv4 computers on the network.

▶ When IPv4 computers are upgraded to IPv6, they must be capable of using their existing IPv4 addresses in an IPv6 context—no change should be needed.

▶ The cost of deploying IPv6 must not be excessive; very little preparation work should be required to do an IPv4-to-IPv6 upgrade.

IPv6 was intended to remedy the shortcomings of IPv4, and it has done so magnificently. Early implementations from IBM Corporation, Digital Equipment Corporation, and FTP Software provide proof of the concept. Over the next 5 to 10 years, IPv6 will hopefully begin to replace IPv4 implementations. Because IPv4 compatibility is included in the IPv6 specification, the upgrade can be done incrementally and should not cause any undue displacement. System administrators and network builders will be able to relax as well; IPv6 offers an autoconfiguration facility in which a network card's MAC address is built in to the IPv6 address. This arrangement guarantees unique addresses and prevents address conflicts. The autodiscovery and autoconfiguration features also have an additional benefit: Workstations with IPv6 software and hardware can automatically configure themselves for the network to which they're attached.

The net benefit of IPv6 is to simplify connection to a common protocol, thus simplifying networking and creating an open, interoperable standard that regular users can use. As IPv6 becomes more widely adopted, networking will be freed from many of the current technical hurdles and will grow exponentially. Building networks will no longer be a peril-filled process with a steep learning curve.

In addition, the authentication and encryption features built in to IPv6 will satisfy consumers who currently fear to do business on the Internet, and it will help enable secure electronic commerce, giving business the green light.

IPv6 isn't the fix for all ills, but it certainly offers a great deal of promise for fixing the problems of the Internet. New versions of both client and NOS platforms now offer support for IPv6.

By the Way

More IPv6 Information

If you would like to read more about IPv6, check out the IPv6 Forum at www.ipv6forum.com. You can also find IPv6 information as it relates to specific operating systems. For example, go to www.sun.com or www.microsoft.com and do a search for IPv6.

It will be interesting to see how smoothly the move from IPv4 to IPv6 will be. Although many network professionals embrace the possibilities of using an expanded addressing system, there are misgivings about the actual logistics of deployment and support for IPv6. The move to IPv6 certainly won't happen overnight, but it is an imperative that network professionals begin to get up to speed with IPv6 today so that they can plan for tomorrow.

Wireless Technology Gains Ground

Wireless networking is gaining ground as a serious alternative to wired networking. Although there are still issues related to throughput and security on wireless networks, new standards are rapidly being developed that negate many of the "cons" related to deploying a WiFi network.

In Hour 23, "Wireless Networking," we discuss the 802.11 standards now available for WiFi networking. Most WiFi implementations are using 802.11b and 802.11g, but I think it is safe to predict that 802.11a implementations will become the rule rather than the exception in the very near future. In terms of 802.11, faster and more secure standards are in the works.

A standard to watch for the future is the 802.11i standard. Currently being developed by the 802.11i IEEE working group, we have already seen some results of this new standard, which is the WPA securing enhancements that have been implemented in recent WiFi products to shore up WEP. (For more about WPA and WEP, see Hour 23.) 802.11i also will offer other security enhancements for WiFi that now fall under the collective term Robust Security Network. This collection of security standards will use authentication protocols and advanced encryption methods to better secure data and provide authentication over radio waves.

In terms of wireless devices that provide Internet and email access, there are a number of emerging alternatives. We discussed Bluetooth in Hour 23, and I want to mention another rapidly growing technology in the wireless personal digital assistant arena called BlackBerry.

BlackBerry certainly isn't new, but it has increasingly made inroads in the PDA and digital phone market. BlackBerry, developed by Research in Motion, Limited (or RIM, as it is often referred to) provides a wireless (and secure) environment that allows a BlackBerry device to access email, the Web, and other communication services. Not only do many cellular companies provide connectivity for BlackBerry devices, but also a company can actually deploy its own BlackBerry server, which provides wireless connectivity directly to the corporate network.

BlackBerry devices can access communication platforms such as Lotus Domino and Microsoft Exchange. This means that a BlackBerry user can directly connect to network messaging services such as email and scheduling. BlackBerry devices can also access Web data, and most of the newer BlackBerry devices provide cellular phone support.

Whether BlackBerry will become the standard for a PDA in the future is pretty much anyone's guess. Other devices, such as the HandSpring Treo PDA and cell phone, provide the same type of functions found on the BlackBerry. Whatever the case, the isolated PDA (meaning a PDA that only syncs up with your PC) will rapidly become a thing of the past as it becomes more cost-effective and easy to connect PDAs to wireless networks.

Summary

In this hour, we had an opportunity to discuss some issues related to the future of computer networking. We looked at Linux and its future potential and discussed some of the issues related to Internet regulations. We discussed IPv6 and looked at some of the new things that we will see in the wireless networking environment.

Over the course of this book, the emphasis has been on theory rather than practice. The reason for this focus is quite simple: It's easy to figure out how to plug a network in and get it physically connected. The difficult part of networking is figuring out why the network works (or alternatively, doesn't work) and the causes of various problems.

I hope you will take what you learned in this book and put it to good use. My charge to you is this: Go forth and build a network. You know what you need to know by now, and you know where to find the resources to help you figure out the rest. Good luck and good networking. I wish you success.

Glossary

As networking terminology changes, so do glossaries. This glossary does not claim to define everything; nothing can. However, there are Web glossaries (such as www.webopedia.com) that offer frequently updated definitions of current computer and networking terms.

10BASE-2   Ethernet networking running on coaxial cable. Also called thinnet or cheapernet, 10BASE-2 supports network segments up to 185 meters in length. It is a bus topology and cannot withstand any interruption in any cable between two computers.

10BASE-5   Also called yellow-cable Ethernet, 10BASE-5 is similar to 10BASE-2 but uses a thicker cable. Each computer attached to a 10BASE-5 segment has a device called a transceiver (also known as a Vampire Tap) that connects the computer to the network wire. 10BASE-5 is a bus topology and cannot withstand disconnections of any computers.

10BASE-T   Ethernet in a star topology. 10BASE-T uses unshielded twisted-pair wiring (UTP) with eight connectors terminated according to specific standards called TIAA 568B. Because it is a star topology, 10BASE-T is much more robust than 10BASE-2 or 10BASE-5 and makes it much easier to disconnect computers from the network without actually disrupting the network.

56K   A digital phone line that can carry data at speeds of up to 56 kilobits per second.

Access point   A device that provides a connection between a wireless client and the rest of the network. It acts as a layer 2 bridge providing connectivity between the wired and wireless network.

adapter card   This definition applies primarily to Intel-compatible computers. An adapter card is an electronic assembly that connects to a computer through a standard interface (see *card-slot interface*, later in this Glossary) called a card slot. Adapter cards can provide a variety of services to the computer, including video, network, modem, and other functions as required.

administration   An impossible task that involves figuring out how to keep a network running without problems all the time. Part V of this book, "Introduction to Network Administration," is dedicated to this topic.

agent   A piece of software installed on network clients that interacts with the administrative database used by network management software.

analog   Based on waveforms rather than on binary patterns of voltage.

analog phone line   A phone line that transmits the sound of your voice as a waveform (such as a radio wave). Analog phone lines are common; chances are that analog phone lines are what your home phone is plugged in to. To transmit data over an analog phone line, you must convert it from digital data to sound—that's why modems (devices that convert data to sound) make funny sounding squawks and hisses. That's digital data being converted to sound.

application   A software program intended to accomplish a single task. For example, Microsoft Word is intended to ease document preparation.

ARPA   Advanced Research Projects Agency, the government group responsible for starting the Internet.

ASCII   American Standard Code for Information Interchange, a way that computers format 1s and 0s (binary code, which computers can understand) into the alphabet, numerals, and other characters that humans can understand.

ATM   Asynchronous Transfer Mode, a new topology for transmitting data across a network. ATM is complex but has many advantages compared to older topologies such as Ethernet and Token Ring. ATM offers Quality of Service and a standard frame (or "cell") size. ATM is rarely used on small networks because of its cost; it is most commonly used in large WAN networks.

authentication   The process of ensuring, as much as possible, that logons and messages from a user (such as a password or email) originate from an authorized source.

backbone   A series of very high-speed phone lines (ranging from 155 to 622 megabits per second—really fast!) that phone companies use to transmit high volumes of traffic. Compare this speed to that of your

LAN, where data moves at 10 megabits per second, and you begin to see why it's called the backbone. New technologies are offering increased speed of over a gigabit per second, which will be useful as more people want to use the Internet.

backward compatibility The capability of a software or hardware product to work with earlier versions of itself.

bandwidth The measurement of the amount of data a particular medium can carry. For example, the bandwidth of the average phone line is only about 33.6 kilobits per second; the bandwidth for a T1 digital phone line is 1.544 megabits per second.

batch processing A situation common in early mainframe environments in which many tasks were scheduled to run at a specific time late in the evening. The user never directly interacted with the computer in batch processing.

Bayesian Filters A form of spam filter that actually learns from the spam and so provides greater spam protection than simple content filters.

binary Having only two states; used to describe the base 2 arithmetic that computers use. In binary notation, 1, 2, 3, 4, 5 is represented as 1, 10, 11, 100, 101. The place value of each place in binary notation doubles with each digit to the left of the decimal point, hence 16, 8, 4, 2, 1. Contrast this with decimal notation (base 10) in which each place value is equal to 10 times that of the column to its right.

bit One piece of information, represented as a 1 or a 0. To the computer, a bit is actually a difference in voltage: high voltage represents a 1; low voltage represents a 0.

bridge A device that links different networks together so that they form a single logical network. Bridges work at layer 2 of the OSI model.

browser A program that provides a way to view and read the documents available on the World Wide Web. Netscape Navigator and Microsoft Internet Explorer are browsers.

bus topology A network topology in which all computers are serially connected to a length of cable. Bus networks are not terribly reliable; if one cable segment goes bad, the whole network fails. 10BASE-2 and 10BASE-5 are examples of bus networks.

byte Eight bits (also called one octet when discussing TCP/IP). A byte is equal to one character; for example, the letter e is one byte. One byte (eight bits) can represent 256 numbers (0 to 255) in binary numerals.

C programming language Also known as "C," a high-level computer language developed by Brian Kernighan and Dennis Ritchie at Bell Labs. The C language enables programmers to write code that can be compiled to run on different types of computers. C programming is widely regarded as a cross between an art and a science.

cable modem   A device used by cable providers to provide high-speed data access using cable as the media.

card-slot interface   The place in which adapter cards are installed in Intel-compatible personal computers. Card-slot interfaces come in several varieties: ISA, EISA, VESA (now outdated), and PCI.

CDPD   Cellular Digital Packet Data, the most common way to send data over wireless links. Most commonly, CDPD uses the 2.4GHz radio spectrum.

cheapernet   A colloquial name for 10BASE-2, so called because it is just about the least expensive type of network one can build.

checksum   A part of a packet header that ensures that the packet has not been damaged during transmission across the network. A checksum is a number calculated on-the-fly based on the size of the packet; if the checksum is incorrect, the receiving computer discards the packet and asks the originating computer to resend it.

ciphertext   The text of an encoded message. Ciphertext is not readable unless it is decrypted into plaintext. In other words, up cf ps opu up cf is an example of a ciphertext message.

CIR   Committed Information Rate, a guarantee from the provider of a digital phone line service (usually your local telephone company) that ensures the slowest data transmission speed your network will ever have. CIR is usually calculated at a fraction of the rated line speed; for example, a 128K frame relay line often has a CIR of 64K, or 50 percent of the bandwidth.

client   A computer that uses the resources shared by server computers.

client/server model   A network in which the processing is distributed between a server and a client, each with specific roles. Also used to describe networks with dedicated servers. Opposite of peer-to-peer.

clustering   In networking, clustering is aggregating several servers so that if one of them fails, other servers seamlessly take over.

coaxial cable   A two-conductor cable with a solid center conductor and a braided outer conductor. Coaxial cable is used for 10BASE-2 networks and is similar to the cable used for cable TV.

collision   In terms of networking, what happens when two computers attempt to transmit data on the same network wire at the same time. Doing so creates a conflict; both computers sense the collision, stop transmitting, and wait a random amount of time before retransmitting.

collision domain The group of computers that communicate on a single network wire. Each computer in a collision domain listens to every other computer in the collision domain; each computer can transmit data only when no other computer is currently transmitting.

compiler A program that takes computer source code (which is just plain text, the same kind you see in Windows Notepad or the DOS Edit utility) and translates it into machine language, which is a string of instructions that the computer can execute. Compilers are synonymous with UNIX; almost every variety of UNIX is packaged with at least a C compiler. Many versions of UNIX now also come with C++ compilers. Compilers exist for many languages; C is simply the most common.

concentrator Also called a hub or MAU, a concentrator helps ensure the robustness of the network by making sure that the network can't be disconnected because of a single cable failure.

configuration management The art (or science) of ensuring (from a central console) that user workstations have the correct hardware and software installed and that the software and hardware is set up according to consensual and preset standards.

CPU Central Processing Unit, the microprocessor inside a computer that enables it to function. Examples of CPUs include Intel's Pentium and Pentium Pro, Motorola's PowerPC, and Digital Equipment Corporation's Alpha chips.

cracker Someone who makes unauthorized accesses into others' computer systems, usually maliciously. Not the same as hacker.

CSMA/CD Carrier Sense Multiple Access/Collision Detection, the means by which computers exchange data in Ethernet networks.

CSU/DSU Channel Service Unit/Data Service Unit, a device that changes local network packets into packets that can be transmitted over a WAN.

DARPA Defense Advanced Research Projects Agency, or ARPA after it was taken over by the military.

database A file or collection of data structured in logical relationships. For example, the phone book is a database on paper, with names in one column and phone numbers in another column.

datagram See *packet*.

decimal The way of writing numbers we use all the time; base 10. In base 10, you count from 1 to 9 like this: 1, 2, 3, 4, 5, 6, 7, 8, 9. Contrast this with binary and hexadecimal notation.

denial-of-service attack   An attack on an Internet-connected computer that forces it to cease performing its designated function (Web serving, file serving, and so on).

device driver   Software that controls specific hardware on your computer. For example, the software that controls your mouse and keyboard is a device driver.

DHCP   Dynamic Host Configuration Protocol, a piece of the TCP/IP protocol suite that handles the automatic assignment of IP addresses to clients.

dial-on-demand   Whenever a user needs a resource on another LAN (a file, database access, whatever), the local LAN catches the request and dials the remote LAN using either garden-variety Plain Old Telephone Service (POTS) or a switched digital phone line such as Integrated Services Digital Network (ISDN).

digital   A data transmission type based on data that has been binary encoded (that is, data that has been formatted into 1s and 0s).

digital phone line   A phone line that converts the sound of your voice into digital data. Digital phone lines work better for computers than analog phone lines because computers transmit information digitally. Digital phone lines are often used for WANs in which data has to be transmitted at high speeds over long distances.

directory services   A set of tools that enable network administrators to provide users with access to certain specific resources independent of where on the network the users log in. In other words, if Tom in Marketing has access to Server1 and Server2 but no access to Server3, he can access only Server1 and Server2 regardless of whether he logs in to the network on a computer in Marketing, Production, or Administration. As networks have grown more complex and required management of greater numbers of users, directory services have become a saving grace for network administrators trying to manage access across thousand-plus–user, multisite networks.

disk   A device that stores digital 1s and 0s (also called bits) on magnetic media such as a hard drive or floppy drive. CD-ROM drives use light rather than electrical impulses to retrieve data.

DNS   Domain Name System, the pieces of the TCP/IP protocol suite that resolve IP addresses to names. For example, DNS resolves 192.168.1.5 to alice.library.net.

domain   A group of computers whose logon across the network is authenticated through a Microsoft server such as a server running the Windows 2003 Server NOS. Essentially, a domain takes authentication out of the hands of the individual workstations and centralizes it on the server.

Domain controller   The server that provides user authentication and maintains the database of network objects for a Microsoft domain.

DSL   Digital Subscriber Line, a means by which the phone company provides high-speed digital data services over standard two-pair copper wire.

email   Electronic mail, a way of sending text and files across a network with postal-mail–like notification.

encapsulation   The process of taking a packet of one protocol and putting another protocol's information around it. Equivalent to taking a letter, sealing it in an envelope, addressing that envelope, and then placing the first, sealed envelope into a second envelope addressed in a different language. It's not really efficient, and it wastes materials and time. Unfortunately, that's often the only way to accomplish something.

encryption key   A series of letters and numbers used to make plaintext messages into ciphertexts. An encryption key's security depends on how long it is.

error correction   The process of ensuring that data transferred across the wire is done so correctly. Typically, error correction works by using a checksum to determine whether data has been corrupted in transfer. The process of error correction takes a certain amount of the bandwidth of any connection. The more failure-prone the connection is, the more robust (and hence, the larger in bits) the error correction should be in relation to the entire bandwidth. In other words, a dial-up line tends to be noisy and unreliable, so error correction takes up a lot of the connection's bandwidth. By contrast, a digital connection such as a T1 is much cleaner and hence has less error correction.

Ethernet   A local area network (LAN) topology based on a method called Carrier Sense Multiple Access/Collision Detection. Ethernet comes in many varieties—the specification is available in IEEE 802.3. Other versions of Ethernet include 802.2, SNAP, and II. Ethernet is, by all accounts, the most common network topology in the world today.

fail over   The logical extension of fault tolerance. In a fail-over system, there are two (or occasionally more) servers, each with identical copies of a master server's drives and resources. If the master server fails, the backup server takes over dynamically and users never see the difference (except for a small and brief slowdown).

fault tolerance or redundancy   The capability of a computer system to shrug off failure of a device and continue operating normally. Generally, fault-tolerant devices send a message to an administrative user when a particular device fails so that the device can be replaced. Fault tolerance is often implemented by simply adding a second device (a second hard drive, network card, or whatever). Of late, however, IBM-compatible computers are beginning to use clustering for fault tolerance; that's when a whole extra machine is on standby, waiting for the first one to fail. See also *clustering*.

FDDI   Fiber Distributed Data Interface, a method of transmitting data across a network using lasers and pulses of light sent over a glass fiber cable rather than sending electricity over a copper wire.

fiber   Optical fiber is used instead of copper wire in some networks. It looks like coaxial cable with flexible strands of glass in the center rather than copper wire.

firewall   A computer or other device that controls access to an Internet-connected network.

Forward lookup zone   The database zone on the DNS server that holds the records that provide for FQDN to IP address resolution.

frame relay   A method of reframing (or repacketizing) already packetized data to enable it to be transmitted over the phone company's frame relay network.

frame type   A type of packet. NetWare 2.x and 3.x used the Ethernet 802.3 packet scheme; NetWare 4.x uses more-standard Ethernet 802.2 frames. The only thing you have to know about frame types in a NetWare context is that you must run the same frame type on the client's network card as you're running on the server's network card so that they can communicate.

FTP   File Transfer Protocol, the piece of the TCP/IP protocol suite that enables users to copy files between computers.

Fully qualified domain name (FQDN)   The name assigned to a domain or host on the Internet. The Domain Name Service defines the hierarchy for how FQDNs are determined.

gateway   A catchall term to describe a system that essentially bridges two systems. Gateways can pass mail, translate protocols, forward packets, and perform other tasks. A gateway's primary purpose is communication.

gateway protocols   Members of the TCP/IP protocol suite that routers use to determine the best route for data packets.

groupware or **groupware application**   A software application that allows people to use networked computers to work together. Groupware often helps increase efficiency by automating the flow of work from person to person and reducing the overall amount of paper generated by a task.

GUI Graphical user interface, a shell on a computer's operating system that graphically represents data. Windows, the Mac OS interface, and UNIX's Motif are all GUIs.

hacker A much misused term. A hacker does not break in to computer systems (a cracker does that); instead, a hacker is a skilled programmer and problem solver. The sobriquet is seldom accurate if self-endowed.

hard drive A nonremovable magnetic media drive that stores data on a computer.

header The part of a packet that carries information about the source and destination of the packet, the checksum, and any other data about the packet.

hexadecimal notation Base-16 notation. In hexadecimal notation, you count from 0 to 15 like this: 0, 1, 2, 3, 4, 5, 6, 7, 8, 9, A, B, C, D, E, F.

HTML Hypertext Markup Language, a way of formatting plain text so that it can be displayed as graphical text in a browser window. HTML uses tags, or inline formatting commands, to define how things look. For example, <h1> This is a header </h1> is interpreted by a browser as a command to format the text This is a header in the header-1 style (whatever that has been defined as).

HTTP Hypertext Transfer Protocol, the piece of the TCP/IP protocol suite used to transmit World Wide Web documents across the Internet.

hub A device that provides a central connection for a wired network. Hubs do not enhance or route the signal; they merely provide a central connection point.

Hybrid network A network that uses both wired and wireless connectivity strategies.

I/O or throughput Generally, a loose measure of the speed at which a particular piece of hardware can move data. A fast processor, for example, is said to have better I/O than a slow one. I/O is most commonly applied to devices that have to actually move information: hard drives that have to read and write information to and from their drive platters and network cards that have to send and retrieve data from the network.

IDE Integrated Drive Electronics, a way of attaching hard drives to computers using logic built in to the hard drive rather than using a third-party device.

IMAP Interactive Mail Access Protocol, a new piece of the TCP/IP protocol suite that handles the transmission of mail between server and client. IMAP largely supplants POP; its current revision is IMAP4.

infrared   The light spectrum just shorter than red; invisible to human eyes. Infrared is often used for line-of-sight data transmission in wireless networks.

Internet   The global network of networks now used for everything from email to electronic commerce to research.

Internet Access Provider (IAP) Companies that provide direct connection to the Internet backbone. Internet service providers connect to the Internet via Internet Access Providers. See *ISP*.

Internet mail standards   A set of nonproprietary standards developed for email functionality on TCP/IP networks. The standards will developed by the Internet Engineering Task Force.

interoperability   The capability of two products to operate together, ideally according to open standards such as the TCP/IP protocol.

IP   Internet Protocol, the part of the TCP/IP protocol responsible for providing addressing and routing services to packets. IP ensures that packets are addressed properly.

IP address   A sequence of numbers associated with a network adapter's MAC address. It is 32 bits long and is divided into four 1-byte strings that have values ranging from 0 to 255 (for example: 209.61.64.1).

IPX   Internetworking Packet Exchange, the part of Novell NetWare's IPX/SPX protocol responsible for addressing and routing.

IRQ   Interrupt Request, a request to the processor that it give its attention to the requesting device. Each device on a computer is typically assigned a different IRQ.

ISDN   Integrated Services Digital Network, a switched digital phone service that in its Basic Rate Interface (BRI) can carry up to 128 kilobits per second of data; in its Primary Rate Interface (PRI), it can be as fast as 1.5 megabits per second. ISDN has actually fallen by the wayside and has been replaced by newer technologies such as DSL and broadband connections using cable modems.

ISP   Internet service provider, a company that provides connections to the Internet. The connections can range from dial-up to frame relay, depending on the ISP and the connection speed desired.

Java   A programming language invented by Sun Microsystems that enables programmers to write software that can run on any platform using a Java Virtual Machine developed for that platform.

jumper   A very small piece of plastic (less than $1/8$ inch on a side) with a conductive metal strip inside it. Jumpers are used (like switches) to make electrical connections on a card.

LAN Local area network, a group of computers in a local area tied together without any routers between them. All computers are connected to the same set of hubs or switches in a LAN, and all network resources are "local," running at the full speed of the network.

Linux A freeware UNIX-like operating system developed by Linus Torvalds and a host of Internet programmers. Linux is free, fast, and astonishingly stable. If you have to learn UNIX, Linux is a great place to start.

logical diagram A diagram that details the software and services that will be provided by a network. This type of diagram summarizes what the network will offer rather than what the network will actually look like in terms of wiring and device deployment.

logical segment A network configuration in which a single network segment is simulated through the use of devices called concentrators.

login script A text file stored on the server that has a list of commands. When a user logs in, the server reads the text file, executes the commands included in it, and often maps drives and connects network printers on-the-fly for each user. Typical login scripts can include lines that don't do anything except let the user know that he

is being logged in; the login script can also include commands such as net use, which establish network connections to other computers.

MAC address Media Access Control address, a 6-byte (48-bit) address unique to each and every network card, represented in hexadecimal notation.

MAN Metropolitan Area Network, a group of LANs in a relatively small geographical area joined by digital phone lines or by other technologies such as microwave radio.

Marker A file attribute placed on a file. Markers can denote whether a file has been backed up.

MAU Multistation Access Unit, IBM's name for a Token Ring concentrator.

memory The chips that provide a place for the computer to store the 1s and 0s it needs to do computations. Memory chips are fast—an order of magnitude faster than virtual memory.

modem Short for modulate-demodulate. A device used to convert digital signals into analog tones that can be transmitted over the telephone network.

multitasking In operating systems, the capability to divide computer time among two or more running programs simultaneously.

NDS   NetWare Directory Services, a set of standards for organizing enterprise networks. Proprietary to Novell, but available on many systems. Very powerful for organizing and logically segmenting networks.

NetBEUI   NetBIOS Extended User Interface, an extension of NetBIOS that includes the capability to frame packets (NetBEUI Frame, or NBF) among other extended features. NetBEUI is a common implementation of NetBIOS.

NetBIOS   Network Basic I/O System, a small, nonroutable protocol developed by IBM for small PC networks.

NetWare   Novell's network operating system. Powerful and extremely scalable. Quite complex to administer but very fast.

network   Any conglomeration of parts working together in a predictable order. In computer terms, a group of computers connected by a common topology that enables data to be transmitted.

network adapter   An adapter card installed in a computer that allows it to communicate on a network.

network access point   A connection point on the Internet backbone.

Network address translation (NAT) Enables a number of computers using private IP addresses to interact with the Internet via one public IP address. The computers basically hide behind a firewall or proxy server that is using NAT and is configured with the public IP address.

NFS   Network File System, Sun Microsystems' standard way of allowing a computer to access the files on another computer's hard drive as though the files were part of the local file system.

NIC   Network Interface Card, also called network adapters; an add-in card that plugs in to a computer and enables it to communicate on a network. NICs are usually ATM, Ethernet (of one variety or another), Token Ring, or FDDI.

NLM   NetWare Loadable Module, a program that can execute natively on a NetWare server. Most NLMs can be loaded and unloaded on-the-fly. They control a great many NetWare functions—from the protocols it uses (IPX.NLM and SPX.NLM) to backup and administration (MONITOR.NLM).

NOS   Network Operating System, software that enables a computer to perform certain network-centric tasks such as authenticating users, handling file security, and providing connections to network resources. Windows NT Server, UNIX, and NetWare are NOSes. Part IV of this book, "Network Operating Systems and Providing Network-Wide Services," is dedicated to this topic.

octet   The "official" name for a byte (eight bits, or eight digital 1s and 0s).

open standards Hardware and software standards that are not proprietary to any given manufacturer. TCP/IP and Ethernet are both open standards.

operating system The software on a computer that enables the user to communicate with the hardware and get tasks done. Windows 95, Windows NT Workstation, OS/2, and UNIX are all operating systems.

optical fiber The medium used by fiber-optic networks. Most networks use either coaxial cable or UTP.

Orthogonal Frequency Division Multiplexing (OFDM) This radio networking strategy splits the radio signal into a number of sub-signals that are transmitted simultaneously at different frequencies.

OSI model Open Systems Interconnect Model, a reference model that details seven layers of functionality for networks. The OSI model offers an ideal way to understand the theory of networking.

OSPF Open Shortest Path First, a routing protocol that uses what's called a link-state algorithm. Link-state algorithms look at the available routes a data packet can take to its destination and decide the best route. OSPF does not have a maximum hop count as RIP does.

packet Also called a datagram; information placed inside a "wrapper" called the header. Packets contain headers (which handle addressing), error correction, checksums, and (eventually) the data sent across the network.

packet header See *header*.

packet-switching A technology in which binary data is divided into small packages that handle error correction and address information to transmit data across a physical medium such as cable.

PC card A credit-card–sized electronic device that slides into a slot on the side of a laptop. PC cards can be almost anything, but they are usually network adapters and modems.

peer-to-peer A network built without a central server. In a peer network, all computers can be both servers and clients as required. Generally unmanageable, but useful for small networks.

Personal information manager (PIM) A software suite that provides email, scheduling, and task tracking on a client computer. A PIM can run stand-alone but is often the client side of a groupware product. See *groupware*.

plaintext The text of a message in human-readable format. In other words, to be or not to be is an example of a plaintext message.

Plug and Play Adapter card hardware for which I/O addresses and IRQs are set through software rather than through hardware jumpers of some sort.

POP Post Office Protocol, the TCP/IP standard for mail transmission between server and client. POP3 is the current version.

porting The process of recompiling C language source code into versions that can run on different computers.

POTS Plain Old Telephone Service, the regular old Ma Bell dial tone used for voice and modems.

PPP Point-to-Point Protocol, the part of the TCP/IP protocol suite used to connect computers across switched telephone lines—either regular phone service (POTS) or switched digital service (ISDN).

primary zone The forward lookup zone on the primary DNS server. See *DNS, forward lookup zone.*

programming languages
Standardized ways of creating instructions for computers. Common programming languages include C, Fortran, Java, Smalltalk, COBOL, APL, and others.

protocol An agreed-on standard. In networking terms, a protocol is used to address and ensure delivery of packets across a network.

protocol translator A device that can translate between two network protocols. Typically, protocol translators translate NetWare IPX to TCP/IP so that users on an IPX network can access the Internet or IP resources.

proxy server A server that hides internal network IP addresses from the Internet by making requests for the internal clients.

QoS Quality of Service; in packet data, QoS is very similar to QoS in regular mail. In regular mail, you have a choice of services—first class, second class, third class, bulk mail, overnight, and so forth. When you send an overnight letter, it receives priority over first-class mail, so it gets to its destination first. A few bits of data in a packet of data indicate the QoS required for that data. QoS is an evolving standard that will hopefully be common on all platforms and topologies within the next few years.

RAID Redundant array of inexpensive disks, a method of ensuring data security, ranging from simple disk mirroring with two disks (RAID 1) to striping all data across three or more disks (RAID 5).

redirection In terms of the UNIX OS, redirection is the basic input/output provided by the system software.

redundancy or fault tolerance The capability of a computer system to shrug off the failure of a device and continue operating normally.

Generally, redundant devices send a message to an administrative user when a particular device fails so that the device can be replaced. Redundancy is often implemented by simply adding a second device (a second hard drive, network card, or whatever). Of late, however, IBM-compatible computers are beginning to use clustering for redundancy (when a whole extra machine is on standby, waiting for the first one to fail).

Remote node   A computer that connects to the network via a remote access strategy such as dial-in or Virtual Private Networking.

repeater   A device that enables networks to communicate reasonably well. A repeater amplifies and cleans up digital signals and forward them on toward their destination.

reverse lookup zone   The zone on a DNS server that holds the records that provide for IP address to FQDN resolution. See *DNS*.

RIP   Routing Information Protocol, a protocol that works by counting the number of times a packet has been moved toward its destination. Each new routing is called a hop, and the maximum hop count is usually set to 16. In RIP, if a packet is routed more than 16 times, it's discarded.

RMON   Remote Monitoring, the part of the TCP/IP protocol suite that handles network management and network data collection. RMON is much more efficient than its older sibling, SNMP.

router   A device or (optionally) software that routes packets toward their destinations. Routers must be connected to at least two networks. They decide how to send data based on network conditions.

routing tables   A database of routes between networks that routers carry in their memory. In general, the smaller the routing table, the faster the router.

RPC   Remote Procedure Call, a method used on client/server networks for communicating between processes (applications) running on different computers. RPC is sometimes used to distribute work across a network according to appropriateness. For example, a server running a database might handle searches locally, whereas queries are generated at the client computer.

Samba   Samba derives its name from SMB or Server Message Block, which is an important part of the NetBIOS protocol. Samba is capable of simulating the operation of SMB and also provide NetBIOS over IP (TCP/IP being the protocol stack for Linux), which means that a Linux computer can actually pretend to be a Windows client.

scalable   The measure of a system's capability to grow. It is not quantifiable; unfortunately, there is no standard against which to compare a particular system. As a result, scalability is relative. For example, if a network has 10 users and grows to 100, will the current network architecture continue to work well? If the answer is yes, the system is scalable; if the answer is no, the system is not scalable.

scope creep   A process in which the scope of a job grows while the job is in process. Scope creep is the bane of project managers; it almost guarantees that a given project will be over budget and late.

scripting language   A limited programming language built in to many operating systems. Examples would be JavaScript and Visual Basic for Applications.

SCSI   Small computer system interface, pronounced "scuzzy;" a method for connecting a variety of peripherals to a computer. SCSI devices include hard drives, CD-ROM drives, scanners, and so on.

separate memory spaces   In Windows NT (versions 3.5x to 4.x), it is possible to run 16-bit applications (that is, older Windows applications) in their own memory space. This means that if and when these applications misbehave, they theoretically can't crash other applications.

server   A computer on a network that shares a specific resource (file, print, applications) with other computers.

share   Microsoft's method for enabling computers to access other computers' drives and printers as though those resources were local.

shell   The interactive user interface in an operating system or network operating system. The shell takes the user's commands either at the command line (the DOS C prompt, for example) or through a graphical user interface (the Windows interface, for example) and passes them to the operating system or network operating system.

shell script   In UNIX, a text file containing operating system commands. When the name of the shell script is typed at a command line, the series of commands in the file runs. DOS has a pale shadow of shell scripting called batch files. Batch files do much the same thing; but because DOS can do only one thing at a time, batch files are of limited use.

SLIP   Serial Line Internet Protocol, an older standard, part of the TCP/IP protocol suite used to connect computers over phone lines. Superseded by PPP.

slot interface   See *card-slot interface.*

SMTP   Simple Mail Transmission Protocol, the TCP/IP standard for Internet mail. SMTP exchanges mail between servers; contrast this with POP, which transmits mail between a server and a client.

Sneaker Net   How files got moved before networks—usually with floppy disks and a bit of shoe leather or sneaker rubber (hence the name).

SNMP   Simple Network Management Protocol, the piece of the TCP/IP protocol suite that deals with the transmission of network information for system administration and management. SNMP is not as efficient as its younger sibling, RMON.

soft-set   See *Plug and Play*.

SOHO   Small Office/Home Office, a term used to describe the increasingly decentralized office market. SOHO devices typically support from one to four users instead of many users.

source code   The text files written by programmers that are fed into compilers; the compilers output executable files that the computer can understand so that programs can run.

Spread spectrum   The strategy used by wireless 802.11 networking strategies. Spread spectrum spreads the signal across different frequencies in the public radio bandwidth.

stack   Or hub stack refers to a number of connected hubs, which increases port density. Stacks are usually deployed in some sort of hub rack.

star topology   A network topology in which all connections pass through a central device called a concentrator. 10BASE-T, Token Ring, FDDI, and ATM all use star topologies.

striping   The process by which a RAID drive controller card writes data to multiple disks.

subnet   A way of dividing TCP/IP networks into smaller pieces for management or security purposes. Subnets are bridged by routers.

subnet mask   The dotted decimal mask used to determine which portion of an IP address is network information and which portion is node information. For example, a computer with an IP address of 192.168.1.5 might have a subnet mask of 255.255.255.0. The portion of the address that reads 192.168.1 is the network address, and the .5 is the address of the specific machine on that network. The subnet mask explains that the first three numbers in a dotted-decimal address (for example, 192.168.1) are the network and that the last number denotes a specific computer on that network.

SWAT (Samba Web Administration Tool)   A Web-browser–based tool that can be used to configure Samba on a Linux computer. See *Samba*.

switching   A technology in which each connection between two computers has a dedicated channel available to only those two computers at any given time.

T1   A digital phone line that can carry data at speeds of up to 1.544 megabits per second.

tag   In HTML, a formatting device. A tag starts with a formatting command between two angle brackets (<HEADING 1>) and ends with the same command preceded by a slash (</HEADING 1>).

tape changers   Devices that act much like a jukebox in that they can hold and manage a large number of tapes for backup.

Tarball   A file archive created with the UNIX tar utility.

TCP   Transmission Control Protocol, the part of the TCP/IP protocol suite that ensures reliable delivery of packets to their destinations.

TCP/IP   Transmission Control Protocol/Internet Protocol, a catchall term to describe the multifaceted protocol suite on which the Internet runs. TCP/IP is also an open standard; it is not owned by or proprietary to any company. Anyone can create an implementation of the TCP/IP protocol if they want to do so.

thinnet   Yet another colloquial name for 10BASE-2 Ethernet.

Thread   A portion of a software program that can be processed separately by the computer processor.

throughput or I/O   Generally, a loose measure of the speed at which a particular piece of hardware can move data. A fast processor, for example, is said to have better throughput than a slow one. Throughput is most commonly used to describe devices that

have to actually move information: hard drives that have to read and write information to and from their drive platters and network cards that have to send and retrieve data from the network.

Token Ring   A topology that exchanges data between computers by token passing rather than CSMA/CD.

topology   In networking terms, a topology is nothing more than the arrangement of a network. The term can refer to the physical layout of the network (which is where 10BASE-2, 10BASE-T, and fiber come into the arrangement) or the logical layout of the network.

transceiver   The part of the network adapter card that manages sending and receiving data packets from the network wire.

tree   On a Microsoft network running the Active Directory, a tree consists of a root domain, which is the first domain that you bring online. Trees can contain multiple domains (including the root domain). Domains added to the tree are considered child domains.

trust   A mechanism used by Microsoft domains that enables the domains to share resources across the domain boundaries.

tunneling protocol   A protocol that ensures that data passing over a company's Virtual Private Network is secure. Tunneling is similar to putting a letter/envelope addressed to a non-local company mailstop in another, larger envelope that uses postal mail to send it to another company location. When the mail gets to the nonlocal company mailstop, the mail clerks take it out of the large envelope and send it on to the person to whom it's addressed.

UDP User Datagram Protocol, the part of the TCP/IP protocol suite that handles "unreliable" delivery of packets. In other words, UDP handles the delivery of packets over links that aren't always available.

UNIX An operating system developed by Bell Labs during the late 1960s and early 1970s. Arguably the best OS for mission-critical applications because of almost 30 years of refinement. Common UNIX vendors are Sun Microsystems and Santa Cruz Operation (SCO).

Usenet A network of news servers connected to the Internet. Users can read and reply to posts on Usenet servers using a newsreader client.

user group In Windows NT domains, a class of domain users grouped together for simplified administration. Groups are created and managed in the Windows NT User Manager for Domains application. Users can have specific privileges assigned and specific resources made available as the result of their membership in a user group. For example, user group Accounting might have access to the system's accounting files and applications. Users not in the Accounting user group do not have access to those resources.

UTP Unshielded twisted-pair wire, a cable with four pairs of wires (blue, orange, green, and brown) used for Ethernet and Token Ring network wiring.

VAR Value Added Reseller, a reseller who also handles integration and project management tasks.

virtual memory Space on a disk dedicated to providing memory space when the capacity of physical memory chips has been exceeded.

VLAN Virtual Local Area Network, a network that appears to be a small LAN to its users but which is actually a logical construct. Users can be local or distributed across several sites; connectivity is provided by various software packages.

VPN Virtual Private Network, a network established over a carrier's digital phone lines (such as AT&T or Sprint lines) and dedicated solely to connecting several specific client sites. Used to implement WANs by using the Internet to create a quasi-private network.

WAN Wide area network, a network composed of two or more LANs connected by phone lines (generally digital phone lines) and routed between segments.

winsock A set of files, usually centered around a file called `Winsock.dll`, that Windows uses to interact with TCP/IP.

workgroup The term used by Microsoft for a peer-to-peer network that provides file and print sharing. Workgroup capabilities are built in to the various versions of the Windows OS.

WWW World Wide Web, the resources that can be accessed on the Internet using HTTP, often published in HTML.

yellow-cable Ethernet Another term for 10BASE-5 ("thicknet") Ethernet.

Index

X-Y-Z